Hunting & Stalking Deer in Britain through the Ages

By the same author

Deer and Their Management in the Deer Parks of Great Britain and Ireland
(Country Life)

The Deer Stalking Grounds of Great Britain and Ireland
(Hollis & Carter)

The Deer of Great Britain and Ireland
(Routledge & Kegan Paul)

Deer Stalking in Scotland
(Percival Marshall & Co.)

Deer of the World
(Constable & Co.)

The Wild Goats of Great Britain and Ireland
(David & Charles)

The Ancient White Cattle of Britain and Their Descendants
(Faber & Faber)

Hunting & Stalking Deer in Britain through the Ages

G Kenneth Whitehead

B T Batsford Ltd London

First published 1980

ISBN 0 7134 2083 9

Phototypeset in 'Monophoto' Baskerville by
Servis Filmsetting Ltd, Manchester
Printed in Great Britain by
Redwood Burn Ltd, Trowbridge and Esher
for the publishers, B T Batsford Ltd,
4 Fitzhardinge Street, London W1H 0AH

Contents

List of Photographs

List of Line Illustrations

Acknowledgment

No writer can claim to be an authority in any subject except the one with which he is most conversant, and whilst some forty years or more of stalking deer in many parts of the world have taught me a little about that particular sport, the same, unfortunately, cannot be claimed for hunting deer with hounds. In the chapters, therefore, that describe the pursuit of deer with horse and hound, I have been fortunate in having received assistance from the following, who have been kind enough to read through the chapters relevant to their particular form of hunting, and offer invaluable advice: Mrs Anne Millar and Sir Dudley Forwood (fallow buck hunting); E R Lloyd (stag hunting) and to Raymond A Keogh and the late Frank M R Byers (hunting the carted deer).

A similar service has also been supplied by Messrs John Dean and David Buchanan Smith, M.A., LL.B., Advocate, Sheriff of North Strathclyde, for my two chapters on deer legislation in England and Scotland respectively, and of both I am extremely appreciate for their co-operation.

The sketches have been prepared by Miss Helen Backhouse.

Introduction

Man has ever been a hunter, and according to the fifth book of Moses (Deut. 12) it is God's will that it should be so. '. . . Thou mayest kill and eat flesh' it is written, '. . . according to the blessing of the Lord thy God . . . the unclean and the clean may eat thereof, as of the roebuck and as of the hart'. And 'These *are* the beasts which ye shall eat . . . the hart, and the roebuck, and the fallow deer. . . .'

During the past century, although there has been a number of books concerned solely with the hunting of deer with horse and hound, and an equally large number on stalking deer with rifle, only one worthwhile volume combining these two sports has appeared. In 1927 those two famous sportsmen/artists, Lionel Edwards and H Frank Wallace, joined forces to produce that quite admirable work *Hunting and Stalking the Deer* which is now becoming a collector's piece and hard to find. In the main, however, it only covered the sport of hunting and stalking the deer in the twentieth century.

One of the earliest known documents on hunting was written during the fourteenth century by William Twici who was huntsman to King Edward II (1307–27), whilst during the following century two other important works on the subject appeared – the Duke of York's translation of Gaston de Foix *Livre de Chasse* (*c.* 1410) which he called *The Master of Game*, and the *Boke of St Albans* by Dame Juliana Berners (*c.* 1486). Subsequently much of the information contained in the above named volumes was included in George Turberville's *Noble Arte of Venerie or Hunting* (1576).

Twici divides the animals that can be pursued with hounds into three categories, and in the first, which are those animals which may be properly called beasts for hunting, he includes the hart along with the hare, wolf and boar. The roe and the fallow deer, however, are considered beasts of the chase rather than hunting, and accordingly are designated second-class animals of pursuit. The fox appears also in the latter class.

In Britain, when anyone goes hunting, it is generally assumed that it entails the use of hounds for the pursuit of deer, fox, hare or otter. In North America the pursuit of all game, whether it be with hound, gun, rifle or even rod, is always referred to as 'hunting'.

In this book I have endeavoured to cover the pursuit of deer in Britain during the past thousand years or so, describing the various methods that have been practised by men of all walks of life, from the humble peasant or poacher to the lord of the manor, or the monarch of the realm himself. This has involved, quite naturally, considerable research, and the most important books of reference covering this subject are listed numerically in the Bibliography so that when any particular extract has been quoted in the text, the reference number has been inserted to indicate the source of reference.

In Saxon England, before the Norman Conquest, hunting was not so much a sport as a necessity or means of survival. Hunting in those days was probably all done on foot and great skill was required to kill or capture the wild forest creatures with the primitive weapons then available. Hounds were also much used, not only to drive the deer and other game to an ambushed hunter, but to move the game into traps or deadfall pits, or follow up wounded animals. It is recorded that in 1045 Athelstan Atheling, son of Ethelred II, had some hounds trained especially to hunt red deer – or the 'tall deer' as they were often then referred to.

One favourite method of hunting deer at this period was to drive them into a sort of ambuscade called a 'deer haye' which was sited in a suitable clearing or valley, surrounded by a fence behind which the ambushed hunters were waiting to deal with the animals when they came within range of their spears or arrows.

The same haye could not, of course, be used repeatedly for the deer would soon become wise of the ambush, so there would doubtless be a number of hayes located in a district. Eventually these hayes became something more permanent and the deer park came into being.

Throughout the ages the popularity of deer parks has fluctuated, depending much on the whims and fancies of the nobility. Their original popularity can be dated back to the years following the Norman Conquest, when many of the noblemen and clergy, fond of hunting, began to form parks in the various forests throughout Britain. By the time the Commonwealth was declared (1649) the number of parks had probably reached an optimum level for all time, but as soon as the Roundheads came into power, one by one the parks were destroyed and those deer that escaped butchering once more rejoined the wild forest herds. However, during the latter part of the reign of Charles II there was a renewed interest in deer parks, which continued until the end of the last century when the number in England alone stood at about 395. Today that number is between seventy and eighty.

The advantage of the deer park was that it was able to provide 'instant deer hunting' for its owner should he wish to entertain a guest without the worries of having to provide an array of beaters in order to move the wild deer from the open forest into the hayes. These park battues never, of course, provided sport of a very high order, yet were much practised by the nobility of the sixteenth and seventeenth centuries, who enjoyed potting at the unfortunate deer with an arbalist or crossbow at close range from a specially prepared butt.

The early formation of the deer park also coincided with the date when man's liberty for free hunting in the forests was being severely restricted by the harsh forest laws that were formulated during the eleventh century, and as a result the beasts of the forest, as well as ever-increasing tracts of land, were being reserved exclusively for the monarchy and their privileged friends; the penalty for poaching at one time being disfigurement, loss of sight or even death.

Man's liberty to hunt deer in Britain has, therefore, a close connection with the law of the land and in later chapters I have endeavoured to trace the history of legislation in England and Scotland so far as it affects deer, since King Canute's *Charta de Foresta* decreed that 'he that doth hunt a wild beast and doth make him pant, shall pay ten schilling'.

For many centuries, despite the interest taken by so many people in deer as an object of pursuit, it is surprising that only since 1959 (in Scotland) and 1963 (in England and Wales) has legislation provided these animals with definite close seasons during which period it is, with certain exceptions, illegal to hunt them. Unfortunately, existing legislation is far from satisfactory, for as the law stands at present, deer in Scotland come under the *Deer (Scotland) Act* 1959 with amending *Deer (Close Seasons) (Scotland) Order* 1966 and *Deer (Amendment) (Scotland) Act* 1967, whilst deer in England and Wales come under the *Deer Act* 1963 and the *Roe Deer (Close Seasons) Act* 1977. As a result an almost *completely different* set of dates operate, dependent on whether the deer live north or south of Hadrian's Wall. It would be far better that both Acts should be repealed and replaced by one that provides identical close season dates for all species and sexes of deer in Britain, with the exception of the red deer stag. For the last named deer, since their habitat in England and Wales is mainly woodland in contrast to the bare hillside which is the home of the Scottish red deer, it is only when the leaf is off the tree that proper deer control can be accomplished. Hence a longer open season is required. Moreover, it is the custom of the three packs that hunt red deer in England, to hunt young stags during March and April. Although I am suggesting the start of the open season for the males of red, fallow and sika deer should be 1 July, it is only to enable legal action to be taken against crop marauders. Normally one would not start to shoot these deer until the end of August or September. Similarly, I believe the open season for female deer should be extended to mid-March, for this extra fortnight would enable some estates to complete the doe cull which might have been held up by bad weather in January or February. The extension, however, should not be used as an excuse to kill beyond the number originally planned. In an attempt, therefore, to reduce the number of dates that exist under present legislation, I would like to see the following close season dates operate throughout Britain:

Proposed Close Season Dates

	Stags & Bucks		Hinds & Does	
RED DEER				
Scotland	21 Oct–30 June	(21 Oct–30 June)	16 Mar–31 Oct	(16 Feb–20 Oct)
England* } Wales	16 Mar–30 June	(1 May–31 July)	16 Mar–31 Oct	(1 Mar–31 Oct)
FALLOW DEER				
British Isles	16 Mar–30 June	(1 May–31 July)	16 Mar–31 Oct	(16 Feb–20 Oct) Scotland (1 Mar–31 Oct) England & Wales
SIKA DEER				
British Isles	16 Mar–30 June	(1 May–31 July)	16 Mar–31 Oct	(16 Feb–20 Oct) Scotland (1 Mar–31 Oct) England & Wales
ROE DEER				
British Isles	1 Nov–31 March	(21 Oct–30 April) Scotland (1 Nov–31 Mar) England & Wales	16 Mar–31 Oct	(1 Mar–20 Oct) Scotland (1 Mar–31 Oct) England & Wales

* For deer hunting only in Devon & Somerset, the start of the close seasons could be put back until 1 May as at present.

The dates in brackets are those that operate at present in England, Wales and Scotland under existing legislation.

It will be noticed that if the above suggested close seasons applied, not only would there be just one season operating throughout Britain for female deer of all species (16 March to 31 October), but it would also be illegal to shoot all species and sexes of deer (except roebuck) during the period 16 March to 30 June. At present there are no close seasons for muntjac and Chinese water-deer – the two Asiatic deer which now have an increasing feral distribution in England, and for *both* sexes of these two deer, the close season should be the same as for all female deer.

Before the advent of the firearm it was the practice in Scotland to drive deer into compounds where they could be slaughtered with the spear or other primitive weapons, and even in the early days of the firearm the hound had to be in attendance to follow up any wounded deer. It was not, however, until about the middle of the last century that deerstalking, such as we know it today, started to become popular. Prior to that date it was generally considered that for a gentleman or man of rank, it was much too undignified to crawl after deer on hands and knees!

Hunting deer on horseback with a pack of hounds has never been much practised in Scotland, but south of the border it has been carried on, without break, for close on one thousand years. At what period the horse was introduced as an auxiliary in the chase is not very certain, but it was probably during the eleventh century. When Julius Caesar invaded England in 55 BC he was confronted by the ancient Briton riding in a horse-drawn chariot, but at this date the horse seems never to have been used for hunting. The pursuit of the stag, boar and wolf, etc. was always followed on foot and even long afterwards when the Saxons became masters of the country, the same practice was followed. Indeed, it was not until those ardent hunters, the Normans, were in power that the horse gradually took its place in the hunting field.

For a number of centuries only the wild deer, both red and fallow, were hunted, but as agriculture improved and spread, and the land available for hunting gradually shrank, some substitute had to be found if the chase of the deer was to continue. Thus hunting the carted deer, in which a park-fed animal is taken by cart for release in the open country, was developed, and so popular did this form of hunting become that by the end of the eighteenth century over 130 such packs were in existence.

Hunting the carted deer continued in England until 1963 when the last pack, the Norwich Staghounds, had to give up. In the previous year the Mid-Kent Staghounds – the only other pack of carted-deer hounds in England that had survived the war – had also been abandoned. Hunting the carted deer, however, still survives in Ireland, where two packs – the Ward Union and the County Down – still hunt to big fields, and this is the only form of deer hunting at present being practised across the Irish Sea.

In England, however, four packs that hunt the wild deer still survive, and these include three in the south-west that hunt the red deer of Exmoor, and one in the New Forest which has the fallow buck as its quarry.

Of all the field sports currently in Britain, deer hunting as well as hare coursing, has long been the principal target for those people anxious to abolish all forms of 'blood sport', not only on the grounds of cruelty but also because, in their opinion, it is morally wrong for anyone to get pleasure from a sport that involves killing a wild creature, and as a result there have been several abortive attempts to get a bill through Parliament to ban both of these sports. How much longer deer hunting with hounds can continue in England is anybody's guess, for it was public opinion as much as anything else that resulted, during the early sixties, in the abandonment of the last two packs of carted deer hounds in England. One thing is certain, however, and that is that if the abolitionists have their way with deer hunting as well as hare coursing, they will turn their attention to other sports.

Even the abolitionists agree, however, that there *must* be some form of deer control, otherwise quite apart from over-stocking, damage to crops and forestry would soon become intolerable, and so instead of hunting, the alternative is shooting. It would seem apparent, therefore, that deer shooting – or stalking – must survive so long as there are deer to control, and provided a rifle is used, and those entrusted with the 'culling' go about their business without any flicker of enjoyment on their faces, it can cause no offence to anyone – except, of course, the deer!

Chapter I
Monarchy & the Chase

Monarchy and the Chase is the title of a book in which *Sabretache* (1948) describes how the sport of hunting, be it after fox or hart, has always held a strong fascination to the monarchs of Britain, and in the preparation of this chapter this book has been a constant source of reference.

Stag hunting such as we know it today dates back to the eleventh century – indeed it has often been said that William the Conqueror was the father of modern English hunting. William's love for the chase, however, was insatiable and in order to ensure that no one interfered with his sport, he not only extended the number of royal forests but also framed the harsh forest laws under which the penalty for poaching in the royal forests was death, and for killing one of the royal hounds, blindness at the hands of the red hot poker. Of a truth it was said that 'he loved the tall deer as if he were their father'.

Harsh though the forest laws were, they only applied to game within the royal forests, and it was therefore not an offence for anyone to hunt and kill wild beasts outside the forest limits with one important exception – namely a 'royal harte proclaimed'. Such a beast was a stag that had been hunted by the King, and after a good run, had managed to escape capture. On conclusion of the hunt the King would have a proclamation posted in all districts where it was thought the stag might take refuge, forbidding anyone to hunt or harm it in the hope that it might, if left undisturbed, make its own way back to its home forest. If anyone should kill such an animal his punishment was probably a heavy fine such as that suffered by one T de la Lynde, the proprietor of some lands near the Forest of Blackmore, Dorset, during the reign of Henry III, for killing a white hart that had previously given that royalty 'much amusement'. This fine became known as White-Hart silver, and continued to be paid annually until the latter part of the sixteenth century.[62] *

William I ruled for twenty-one years (1066–87), most of which was spent in England, hunting in the royal forests. It would have been appropriate if his death, which was the result of a riding accident, could have occurred whilst hunting the hart, but this was not so – it occurred during a visit to France when his horse reared up and fell on him inflicting serious injuries, from which he subsequently died in Rouen.

---

* **Note** – Superior figures in text refer to the Bibliography.

He was followed by his son, William II, 'Rufus', who was also a hunting fanatic. He too met his death in the saddle, but on this occasion it was whilst hunting in the New Forest, being killed by an arrow allegedly fired by Sir Walter Tyrrel who had already fled the country before the King's body was discovered by a charcoal burner on the following day.

Henry I (1100–35), who succeeded William II, had not the same interest in hunting as the two earlier Norman monarchs and one of his first actions was to grant a charter to the citizens of London which permitted them 'to hunt, to own hounds of their own and appoint their own master' It also allowed them to hunt deer as freely as their ancestors had done in 'the Chiltern Hundreds, Middlesex or Surrey and the wolf in Middlesex up to the northern gate of the city'. Henry I was also responsible for establishing the Common Hunt, with the Lord Mayor of London as the *ex-officio* Master.[166]

Although King Stephen, who followed Henry I, had neither time nor interest to indulge in much sport, when Henry II ascended the throne he immediately started to put hunting on a more organized footing and during his reign an establishment which in later years became known as the Royal Buckhounds, was formed.

Richard I (1189–99) was almost as great an enthusiast of the chase as William the Conqueror had been, but as much of his reign was spent abroad, he did not have the same opportunity. It is on record, however, that in 1194, on one of his hunting visits to the north, a stag was found in Sherwood Forest which took hounds as far as Barnesdale in Yorkshire – a point of over a hundred miles – before escaping, and so accorded the honour of being 'a royal harte proclaimed'.

Then followed four monarchs who had little time or inclination for the chase although Edward I (1272–1307) is supposed to have encouraged the Church to take a little interest in hunting. In fact, there already was a clause in the Forest Charter which granted any archbishop, bishop, earl or baron, when travelling through the royal forests, *at the king's command*, the privilege to kill one deer or two in the sight of the forester, if he was at hand; if not, then he was commanded to cause a horn to be sounded that it might not appear as if he had intended to steal the game. Edward III (1327–77) was a great sport-loving monarch and not only is he accredited with being the first monarch to hunt unharboured deer with hounds, but is also reputed to have taken 300 couple of hounds and over a hundred falcons with him to France at the time of the Battle of Crecy. His beautiful consort Philippa of Hainault shared his interest, and on one occasion dislocated her shoulder following a fall.

The last of the Plantagenet kings, Richard II was also fond of the chase, and a regular attender at meets of the Royal Buckhounds. He was, however, jealous of the amount of free hunting enjoyed by the clergy, and an edict was established which prohibited any priest or other clerk, not possessed of a benefice to the yearly amount of ten pounds, from keeping a greyhound, or any other dog for the purpose of hunting, or to use any hayes, nets or other engines to take or destroy the deer, hares or rabbits under the penalty of one year's imprisonment. However, the clergy of rank, at all times, had the privilege of hunting in their own parks and enclosures and most of them saw to it that they were well stocked. At the time of the Reformation the See of Norwich, for one, was in the possession of no fewer than thirteen parks well stocked with deer and other animals of the chase.

Between the years 1406 and 1413 Edward, the second Duke of York, who was the grandson of Edward III, wrote *The Master of Game*, which is one of the oldest and most important works on the chase in the English language. True, much of the contents of this work, which was dedicated to Henry, eldest son of his cousin Henry IV, had been extracted from a translation of Count Gaston de Foix's famous book on hunting, *Livre de Chasse* but this does not detract from its value. In it he details what preparation should be made by the Master of Game and the park keeper or forester, should the King decide to come and hunt the hart in the parks or forests under their care, with either bows or greyhounds. It was, it states, the duty of the sheriff of the county wherein the hunting was to be performed, to furnish suitable stabling for the King's horses and carts to carry away the dead game. The hunters and officers under the forester were to erect a sufficient number of temporary shelters for the royal party in the hunting area, and these were to be suitably covered with boughs and greenery to give both shade and shelter should the weather be wet.

Early in the morning of the day appointed for the hunt, the Master of Game, with the officers deputed to him, was to see that the greyhounds were properly placed, and the person nominated to blow the horn, which would indicate to the royal hunting party, the type of game that had been disturbed from cover. People had to be stationed to police the area, and so prevent the public interfering with the sport. The yeomen of the King's bow, and the grooms of his tutored greyhounds, had in charge to secure the King's standing and prevent any noise being made to disturb the game before the arrival of His Majesty. When the royal family and the nobility were conducted to their places, the Master of Game or his lieutenant, sounded three long notes or blasts on the horn which was the signal to uncouple the hart hounds. The game was then driven from the cover and turned by the huntsmen and the hounds so as to pass by the stands belonging to the King and Queen and their guests.

There are also certain instructions as to the disposal of the game. Any beast slain by the bows of the royal family could not normally be claimed by the huntsmen or their attendants who had, however, certain portions of all other game killed assigned to them by the Master of Game.[6]

It would appear that similar arrangements, on perhaps a less ambitious scale, were made for the sport of the great barons and clergy whose tenants sometimes held land in exchange for the service of finding men to enclose the grounds and drive the deer to the stands whenever required.

During the period of the Civil War few, if any, of the Lancastrian or Yorkist monarchs had any time for serious hunting. It is recorded, however, that Edward IV, during a visit to Warwickshire, killed a very fine white fallow buck in Arrow Park, belonging to one Thomas Burdetts. Now this particular buck was held in great esteem by Thomas Burdetts, and when he heard of its demise, 'wished the buck's head and horns in the belly of him that moved the king to kill it'. Unfortunately for him, these sentiments were misconstrued, and he was accused of treason and in due course lost his head. It was some wonder, therefore, that during this troublesome period the Royal Buckhounds were able to survive – but survive they did, and although one Master of Hounds, Sir Bernard Brocas, lost his head in 1400 for his part in a conspiracy against the monarch, there were other members of the Brocas family to carry on the mastership.

Of the six Tudor sovereigns who followed, only Henry VIII (1509–47) and his daughter Elizabeth had any real interest in the chase. Henry's VII's daughter, Margaret, however, seems to have had a taste for sport, for it is recorded that on her way to Scotland, a hunting party was arranged for her amusement in Alnwick Park, during which she killed a buck with an arrow.

For a time, Henry seems to have got on very well with the hereditary Masters of the Royal Buckhounds, until about 1528 when he decided that he would perhaps do better with a pack of his own. Thus the Household, or Privy Pack, was formed with George Boleyn, brother of Anne Boleyn, as Master – an office which he held for eight years before relinquishing it along with his head, when found guilty of treason.

In his early days Henry VIII seems to have been not only a first class horseman but also a tireless one, who was 'very fond of hunting and never takes his diversion without tiring eight or ten horses, which he causes to be stationed beforehand along the line of country he means to take, and when one is tired he mounts another, and before he gets home they are all exhausted'. One only hopes the deer ran true to prediction – the line of retreat, no doubt, influenced in places by the use of hayes or nets.

In later years, Henry VIII was not only too fat for active riding, but he was also a sick man. He therefore became interested in shooting deer in parks – the park battue. 'This system,' comments *Sabretache*, 'was the very prostitution of hunting and it is strange to find a man of Henry VIII's sporting instincts and upbringing sinking to such a level, and still more so, to find him using the arbalest, or crossbow, when he was so fine a shot with the sportsman's weapon, the long bow.'[166]

Little of interest – in the hunting world – seems to have occurred during the short reign of Edward VI (1547–53), who died at the tender age of sixteen.

Then followed two queens, and although Mary I (1553–8) had little interest in sport, Elizabeth I (1558–1603) was passionately fond of deer shooting at the battue – which generally consisted 'in driving a number of deer up and down inside a netted space in front of a well-screened butt, in which the Queen was stationed with her arblast [arbalest]'. Her companion on many of her hunting exploits was the Master of the Buckhounds, the Earl of Leicester, who is recorded as having given her many presents, including a richly enamelled crossbow.

In April 1557, the year before she became queen, it is recorded that during her stay at Hatfield House whenever she went out to hunt the hart or buck at Enfield Chace, she was attended by twelve ladies clad in white satin and riding sturdy palfreys, as well as twenty mounted yeomen in green. It was all very magnificent, and on 'entering the Chace she was met by fifty archers in scarlet coats, blue lapels and yellow caps and vests, and by way of closing the sport the Princess was gratified with the privilege of cutting the throat of the buck.'[166]

In her journeys around the English countryside, she seems, whenever possible, to have included some 'deer shooting', whether as an invited guest to some stately home or not. John Smyth in *The Lives of the Berkeleys* makes reference to an occasion when the Queen was staying at Berkeley Castle, the owner, Lord Henry Berkeley, apparently being away at the time at Callowden. Adjoining the castle was Worthy Park, wherein Lord Henry 'had a stately herd of red deere' which greatly took the fancy of the Queen. Accordingly, she ordered Henry Ligon, the keeper, to arrange some sport for her, with the result that '27 stagges were slaine in the toiles in one day, and many others on that and the next stollen and havoked'.

Needless to say, Lord Henry was far from pleased at hearing of the Queen's exploits amongst his deer, 'having much set his delight upon that game', so 'he sodainly and passionately in discontent disparked that ground'.

At Windsor there were said to be no fewer than sixty parks full of game, and many high-ranking visitors were entertained at these deer shoots. On one occasion the Duke of Württemberg was the Queen's guest, and it is recorded that he 'had a capital day's sport', even though he shot off the leg of a fallow deer with an arquebus which was, however, subsequently caught by a dog. Meantime, the Queen was having a great time knocking the deer over 'as they raced up and down great netted spaces'.

Although the Queen was said to be a good shot with a crossbow, being able to shoot a buck as it galloped past her ambush, she did not always conduct her sport on a very high sporting level. On one occasion in August 1591, during a visit to Cowdray Park in Sussex 'her Highness tooke horse, and rode into the park at eight o'clock in the morning where was a delicate bowre prepared, under which were her Highness musicians placed; a cross-bow, by a nymph, with a sweet song, was delivered into her hands, to shoote at the deere; about some thirty in number were put into a paddock, of which number she killed "three or four, and the Countess of Kildare one". On another occasion, at the same park, after dinner the Queen saw from a turret "sixteen bucks, all having fayre lawe, pulled downe with greyhounds in a laund or lawn"'

Five years later she travelled from Theobald's to Enfield House for dinner and after dining she had toils set up in the park to shoot at the buck.[166]

On one occasion, whilst the Queen was witnessing a hunt in Oatlands Park, Walton, Somerset, the keeper John Selwyn 'vaulted from his horse on to the back of the deer and steered him with his drawn sword to where the Queen was and then leaning forward, he stabbed him to the heart so that he fell dead at the Queen's feet'. This remarkable exploit is recorded on his brass monument in the church at Walton.[45]

North of the border, the Scottish kings were also having good sport with the deer. James II (1437–60) spent part of at least two seasons in Darnaway in Moray, hawking, trapping and spearing wolves, and hunting deer with hounds. At this period both red and roe deer abounded in the woods on both sides of the Findhorn, but by the middle of the nineteenth century had become almost extinct as they were continually being hunted by the Earl of Moray who 'kept hounds, for the sole purpose of extirpating these destructive animals', not only 'for the preservation of the young wood' but on account of their depredation on arable land.

When King James IV (1488–1513) was in Glenkinglas he had to pay for his sport, and in 1508 there is a record that he engaged and paid 306 beaters for a day's drive there.

One June day about the year 1528 in Ettrick Forest, James V accompanied by 'money of the nobillis and gentillmen of Scotland with him to the number of XIj^{M} men . . . slew in the boundis XViij^{xx} of harttis'. After this hunt, the historian (Lindsay of Pitscottie) then adds that the King 'hangit Johne Armestrong and his compleces to the number of XXXvj persouns' but what their misdemeanour had been is not recorded.[135]

During the following year (1529) a drive was organized on the Atholl Forest in Perthshire, for King James V of Scotland when the bag amounted to 'thirty score of harts and hynde, with other small beasts, as roe and roe buck, wolf and fox, and wild cats'. In 1563 Queen Mary witnessed another great deer drive which embraced both the Mar and Atholl forests. On this occasion, although the bulk of the deer broke back, trampling to death two or three of the drivers, no fewer than '360 deer, five wolves and some goats*' were accounted for.[135]

When James I (1603–25) acceded to the English throne he travelled south overland instead of going by sea in order that he could enjoy as

* In some accounts 'roes' replaces 'goats'.

much hunting as possible *en route*. It seems, however, that it was not until he reached Stamford Hill that he was able to enjoy any stag hunting after a carted deer had been especially brought there for him. Although hare, rather than deer hunting seems to have been the King's favourite sport, he did enclose with a brick wall ten miles in extent, Theobalds Park in which there was a herd of deer valued at £1,000. Theobald's had only come into his possession in 1606, for in that year, after being entertained there by Sir Robert Cecil, he was so impressed with the fine deer-hunting country surrounding the manor that he exchanged it for Hatfield Palace.

James I considered that the shooting of park deer as practised by the late queen was extremely unsporting, for 'it is a thievish form of hunting to shoot with guns or bows'. It was said of this monarch 'that he divided his time betwixt his standish, his bottle and his hunting' and he would not allow either age or illness to prevent him partaking of his favourite amusement. In 1619, when only able to be carried in a chair or litter, he came to Theobald's Park and would have the deer mustered before him, whilst five years later, contrary to the order of his physicians, he left Royston to see some hawks fly at Newmarket.

The chase of the deer, however, appealed strongly to the succeeding monarch Charles I (1625–49) and in order that he could have both red and fallow deer hunting close to London, he had Richmond Park enclosed and stocked with deer. Needless to say, he was a strong supporter of the Buckhounds.

In 1649 Charles I lost his head, and for a time the country was too disturbed for much sporting activity. 'Cromwell's Court was not renowned for seemliness' wrote *Sabretache*, 'it was in fact very rowdy. It was considered funny to spill posset over the ladies' dresses, and to drop live coals into an officer's boots, yet they pretended to consider hunting, and racing the works of the devil!'[166]

However, following the Commonwealth, once Charles II (1660–85) had gained full control, he showed his interest in deer hunting by building some new kennels for the Buckhounds at Cumberland Lodge, Windsor Park, and we are told that these new buildings were all that a royal hunting establishment should be.

By the middle of the seventeenth century the stock of deer in Britain had reached a low ebb, so Charles II set to work to replenish the royal forests and parks. In some cases parks already stocked with deer were requisitioned – in others deer were given to him freely by such men as Lord Warwick and Sir John Cutts, even though the cost of their removal involved considerable expense. Other deer were obtained from abroad, and for one consignment a sum of £148 1s. 0d. was paid for taking 'thirty-three Jermayne Deere out of a Shipp at Tower Hill and conveying them in five waggons to Waltham Fforest with several other charges insident thereto'.

Having replenished the royal forests with deer, the hunting and killing of either red or fallow deer in these forests was forbidden for a period of three to five years so that they might increase. However, it would seem that on special occasions the ban was lifted, for on 11 August 1661 it is recorded 'a great match the King had at hunting a Stagg; and how the King tired all their horses and came home with not above two or three able to keep pace with him'.

During this period Colonel James Graham (or Grahm) was both Master of the Royal Buckhounds and Lieutenant of Windsor Forest, and is reputed to have given the King some highly successful hunts. The best run on record under Colonel Graham's mastership was in 1684 after a 'wild' deer found at Swinley, but the King was not present on this occasion, when the deer was finally pulled down at Brentwood in Essex, after a run estimated to be about seventy-five miles. There was a very large field out at the start but only five saw the end, the Duke of York, the King's brother and subsequently James II, being one of them. During this reign Lady Mary Wortley Montagu often hunted her staghounds in Richmond Park, a practice which was considered most peculiar and undesirable in a female.

As proved by his showing in the great hunt from Swinley, James II (1685–8) was no mean horseman and passionately fond of all things connected with hunting and horse racing. However, once on the throne, affairs of State forced him to reduce some of his sporting activities and in particular, racing, but he still managed to make time to hunt. On one occasion the King was invited by the Duke of Albemarle to hunt an outlying red deer in Essex. On 4 May 1686 a stag was found in New Hall Park, and after circling the park once or twice, finally succeeded in leaping the fence, and after crossing the river, ran through Hatfield Regis after a twelve mile point.

James II, however, reigned only for three years before he had to abdicate in favour of William III (1689–1702) who was also a keen hunting man. In fact, it was following a hunting accident in Richmond Park that William died at the comparatively early age of fifty-one. During his life, William received a gift of 108 head of deer from Germany for use by the royal hunt which at that time was under the mastership of Baron de Hompesch.

Although it is doubtful if Mary II (1689–94) took any interest in sport, Anne (1702–14) who succeeded is said to have inherited all the love of sport of her forebears – she was the second daughter of James II – but gout forced her to give up riding at an early age and so precluded her taking an active part. She was, however, a keen follower of the hunt in her light two-wheel carriage with a black horse in the shafts. During her reign the kennels of the Royal Buckhounds were established at Ascot. She was also the inaugurator of Ascot Races, and generally seems to have been extremely popular with all classes of people. On one occasion it is recorded that when near Lippock as she was journeying to Portsmouth she reposed 'herself on a bank smoothed for that purpose [which still retains the name of Queen's Bank and is about half a mile from Wolmer Pond] there saw, with great complacency and satisfaction, the whole herd of red deer brought by the keepers along the vale before her, consisting of about five hundred head. These deer belonged to Wolmer Forest. . . .'

Anne was succeeded by George I, the first of the Hanoverians who were to rule England for close on two centuries. George was a German – and never appreciated why anyone should want to chase an animal with horse and hound when a gun would do the job equally well. It is possible that he had patronized the Common Hunt on some of its Easter Monday excursions to Epping Forest, and it is recorded that he went out hunting at least once in Windsor Great Park, but soon got bored with it, and finished the day shooting ducks. During this reign 'and the two which succeeded it, hounds were lawed and, if that did not take the pace off them, stopped so that the royal pursuers should not be hopelessly outdistanced'.[166]

George II (1727–60) was said to have been a better horseman than his father and took enough interest in the Buckhounds to publish in orders that Wednesdays and Saturdays were 'the King's hunting days' – but it is doubtful if he attended many meets outside Windsor Forest or Bushey.

At some of these meets such great crowds came out with the Royal Buckhounds that in 1735 hunting with the pack was by ticket only, and the ticket had to be signed by the Ranger of Windsor or his deputy. The Court at this point also seems to have been very keen, and some of its members were 'always coming to grief and having to be bled!'[70]

George II was succeeded by his grandson, George III (1760–1820) and once again England had a monarch who upheld the highest tradition of the chase, even though, according to *Sabretache*, hounds were still being lawed during this reign. Lord Ribblesdale in *The Sporting Magazine* gives an account of a fine hunt that George III had with the Buckhounds on 1 October 1797: 'Upon his Majesty's arrival at Ascot Heath . . . the deer *Compton* was liberated below the obelisk, and going off with the most determined courage and inexpressible speed, bid a seeming adieu to all competitors. The hounds were laid on with only five minutes law and the scent laying well they went away breast high in a style that beggars all description: eight of the fleetest horse only out of at least one hundred being enabled to lay anywhere by the side of them till headed in absolute racing by Johnson, the Huntsman, assisted by Nottage and Gosden, two of the yeoman prickers. They brought him to view at Black Nest; here he repeatedly endeavoured to leap the high paling of Windsor Great Park, but without success, and the deer, hounds and horsemen were all intermixed in one general sea of confusion, when by a most wonderful exertion the deer reached the Park by the haw-haw through the shrubbery and plunging into the immense sheet of Virginia Water passed entirely through it. Here, His Majesty entered most energetically into the spirit of the chase, absolutely assisted in getting the hounds forward, laying them on where the deer left the water and speaking to them in a sporting like style'.

George III hunted regularly with the Buckhounds and *Sabretache* records a number of runs attended by that monarch, the majority of which lasted over the hour, with the longest four hours. On at least two occasions the hunt ended with the deer being drowned, once at Bourne End, near Cookham and another at Sunning Hill, which went from water to water in Mr Crutchley's park before being finally drowned.

George III also did his best to popularize the hunt, and encouraged as many people as possible, either on horseback or in carriages, to attend the meet. Unfortunately, he allowed the pack to sink to a pretty low ebb and three years after George IV had acceded to the throne, they were sold in 1823 to a Colonel Thornton, who took them to France. The pack was then replaced by hounds from the Charlton Pack, which were presented to the King by the Duke of Richmond. George IV (1820–30), however, seems to have patronized the royal hunt but little, either as a prince or when king, although he kept the establishment going in great splendour.

He was succeeded by William IV (1830–37) who although keen on riding was really too old for any serious hunting, as he was already sixty-five when he came to the throne. In fact, 'the first and almost the only record of a hunting adventure was that when he was a midshipman and was on leave from his ship at Portsmouth he went poste haste to Windsor to have a day or two with the staghounds. The huntsman mounted him on a pony, and during the hunt rendered hideous by the large contingent of French émigrés and their noises on their horns, the Prince and his pony were engulfed in a deep ditch and did not see much of the battle. It is said that Sharpe tried to take all their funny curly horns away from the French visitors, but that they would not give them up, or refrain from blowing them whenever they felt like it'.[166]

When William IV died in 1837 England once more had a queen. Queen Victoria (1837–1901), however, was not a hunting lady and although the Royal Buckhounds soon became known as the Queen's Hounds, she never once hunted with them during her long reign. Nevertheless, the hunt still enjoyed considerable popularity during the earlier part of her reign and on one occasion in 1877 the Earl of Hardwick, who was then Master, took the Queen's Hounds together with a deer or two, to Barleythorpe, a hunting box in the Cottesmore country belonging to a brother of the famous 'Yellow Earl', Lord Lonsdale. The deer was uncarted at Knossington, and after a long and very muddy hunt over water-logged country, was finally taken near Wing. This was the first time for over 150 years that the Buckhounds had hunted in the Midlands.

However, towards the end of the last century the hunting of carted deer started to receive adverse criticism in the press, and so on his accession to the throne in 1901 King Edward VII decided to abolish the royal stag hunting establishment.

Even if Queen Victoria never went deer hunting in England, she often accompanied the deer stalking party on the hill at Balmoral. One such occasion was 18 September 1848 when she accompanied Arthur Farquharson, the old stalker at Invercauld and a deer was spotted on the Balloch Buie beat. After a detour on their ponies, they dismounted and according to the Queen's own journal, 'scrambled up an almost perpendicular place to where there was a little *box* made of hurdles and interwoven with branches of fir and heather, about five feet in height. There we seated ourselves with Bertie, Macdonald lying in the heather near us, watching and quite concealed; some had gone round to beat, and others again were at a little distance. We sat quite still, and sketched a little; I doing the landscape and some trees, Albert drawing Macdonald as he lay there. This lasted for nearly an hour, when Albert fancied he heard a distant sound, and in a few minutes, Macdonald whispered that he saw stags, and that Albert should wait and take a steady aim. We then heard them coming past. Albert did not look over the box, but through it, and fired through the branches, and then again over the box. The deer retreated; but Albert felt certain he had hit a stag. He ran up to the keepers, and at that moment they called from below that they "had got him", and Albert ran on to see. I waited for a bit but soon scrambled on with Bertie and Macdonald's help; and Albert joined me directly, and we all went down and saw a magnificent stag, "a royal" which had dropped, soon after Albert had hit him, at one of the men's feet. The sport was successful, and everyone was delighted – Macdonald and the keepers in particular; the former saying "that it was her Majesty's coming out that had brought the good luck"'.[192]

Prince Albert, however, seems to have been a distinctly erratic shot, and the Queen's journal is full of his misses and woundings. However, in the park at Blair Atholl the Prince took only one shot to shoot a fat stag from out of the dining room window – an incident that made the poor little Princess '. . . dreadfully distressed' and the Queen 'shake and be very uncomfortable'. Notwithstanding, Prince Albert repeated the performance the following day. On another occasion he killed a stag by leaning across the Queen and firing out of the carriage window as the couple drove home in a horse-carriage after a day on the hill.[96]

The Glasgow Exhibition of 1901 exhibited two fine royals shot by the Prince Consort, one of which had been shot in 1856 and the other in 1858.

During this period a pack of staghounds was kept at Balmoral and up to about 1860, was used to course deer. However, the head stalker of that day, Donald Stewart, was very much against their use, and is quoted as saying 'I would rather allow a man a week's shooting in the forest than let loose a hound on a single occasion'.

About the middle of the last century the Duke of Leeds was tenant of Mar Forest, Aberdeenshire, and on one occasion, 5 October 1850, he entertained Queen Victoria, the Prince of Wales and the Prince Consort for a massive deer drive, during which, it is recorded, 'a herd of 300 deer passed at full speed within a short distance of the Royal party. An hour before their arrival no fewer than 3000 deer, it was estimated, were in the glen. The wind, however, changed and twenty-five beaters were powerless to prevent the herd breaking up, 800 moving off by one pass'.[135]

Eight years later, when the Prince Consort, as a guest of Earl of Dalhousie, was attending a drive on Invermark Forest in Angus, a change of wind likewise spoilt a well-planned drive, and 'high on Skarroch as the uneasy herds were moving, some blunder, some shift of wind – and anon, with a dry clatter of light hooves on loose rock, every beast in the forest, hundreds of them, came crowding into the little pass within twenty-five yards of the guest of no importance'.[44]

However, if the Prince of Wales (later Edward VII) was disappointed with the results of the Mar drive, it would seem he was more fortunate at Achnashellach Forest in Ross-shire. Here, as a guest of the proprietor Mr Tennant a drive was arranged on 5 October 1870, in Corrie Vanie, and it is recorded that 'nineteen good beasts' were slain. In the following year it would appear that there was a repeat performance, and on this occasion 'twenty-five stags fell in response to one hundred shots'.[135] Thirty-four years later, the Prince, now Edward VII was the guest of Mr Arthur Bass (later Lord Burton) at Glenquoich Forest, Inverness-shire, and in 1904 during the course of one drive in Kingie Glen, three stags fell to the royal rifle.

Even after the death of the Prince Consort in 1861, the Queen continued to take a special interest in the management of the forest, and no one was allowed to stalk without her permission. She kept a *Stag Book* in which she entered up daily any events that happened, including weights of deer killed and antler measurements of good or unusual heads, many of which were illustrated by her own pen and ink sketches.

Although during his reign (1901–10) Edward VII was never able to take an active part in any deer hunting, as a young prince he frequently attended meets of the Queen's Hounds, and enjoyed some excellent runs. In 1868 the pack had a twenty-eight mile point which lasted almost three hours, the first forty-five minutes at almost racing pace during which the Prince kept well up with the leaders.

In 1873, shortly after a serious illness, the Prince had a day with the Buckhounds and a week later had an excellent run with an untried Scottish stag which was eventually named *The Prince* in honour of the occasion. The animal, after being uncarted near Wokingham Church, went away at a strong pace, and, running in a perfect ring, was taken an hour later at Binfield. The Prince was not satisfied, so a second deer *The Duchess* was enlarged, which after another cracking run was taken at Northtown after one hour twenty minutes. He had many more such runs before retiring from the hunting field about 1880. Shortly after this there was increased agitation against this form of hunting, and for a time it was debated whether the Royal Buckhounds should be turned over to a fox hunting establishment – a sport which the King had formerly enjoyed even more than hunting deer. However, these suggestions came to nought, and as already mentioned, when Edward VII acceded to the throne, the Royal Buckhound establishment was disbanded.

On one occasion the Prince had a day with the Devon and Somerset Staghounds. This was in 1879 and since during the previous season the entire pack had had to be destroyed because of rabies among hounds, it must have been with a pack of draft hounds which had been collected together by Mr Bissett, the then Master.

Edward VII as Prince, had also been an ardent deerstalker – a sport to which he was first introduced at the age of about seven when he watched his father shoot a stag at Balmoral on 18 September 1848. Ten years later he killed his first stag on Conachcraig in Glen Gelder; its weight was 14st. 12lb.

That was the first of many stags that fell to his rifle. On 30 August 1866 he killed seven stags in a day's stalking – one on Creag-nan-Gall and the remainder in Corrie Buailteach. By the time he had become king, stalking the high hills of Balmoral was too much for him, so deer drives in the lower glens and woods were arranged. On one occasion, 10 September 1902, he shot six stags, which included a royal weighing 16st. 6lb.

During the present century many of the royal family, during their annual trip to Balmoral, have enjoyed a certain amount of deerstalking, particularly our present Queen who is reputed to be a very good rifle shot. In 1909 King George V, then Prince of Wales, shot forty-three stags to his own rifle, one of which was an extremely heavy ten-pointer weighing no less than 21st. 11lb. whilst at an exhibition in London in 1913 a royal of his was displayed. His eldest son, Edward – later Edward VIII – killed his first stag at Balmoral on 23 August 1910 at the age of sixteen. It was a six-pointer weighing 13st. 11lb.

On 3 September 1945, as it was an indifferent grouse year, it was decided to change from grouse shooting, to fill the game card with everything from fur to fin and feather which the resources of Balmoral could provide. King George VI (1936–52) undertook, with John Elphinstone, to climb Lochnager in search of ptarmigan, whilst Princess Elizabeth, accompanied by Margaret Elphinstone, was to try for a stag. Included in the *Game Book* at the end of this novel day's sport in which nine guns accounted for fifty-seven head of game, was one ptarmigan shot by King George on Lochnager, and a stag for 'Lilebet' – as the Princess was generally known to her friends.

In 1958 Her Majesty Queen Elizabeth II, who first started stalking when she was sixteen, killed an 11-pointer which was one of the best heads killed in Scotland that year. The following year she shot a royal, but it wasn't nearly such a good trophy as the previous one. Her husband the

Duke of Edinburgh, who is regarded as much the best shot among the royal family, is also a keen deerstalker, and each season kills a number of stags. However, it would seem that he prefers to have a polo stick or shot gun in his hand to a rifle! Their son Charles, the Prince of Wales, is also a keen deerstalker, and according to the Balmoral *Game Book*, killed his first stag on 1 September 1962.

During the present century, none of the royal family has ever hunted deer with horse and hounds, and owing to public feeling in some quarters against stag hunting, it seems certain that no British monarch will ever again do so on English soil.

Chapter II
Deer Hunting in Southern England

Deer hunting – particularly after the carted deer – was formerly a favourite pastime in southern England, and during the last two centuries over twenty different packs have operated at one time or another. In this chapter I am excluding Devon and Somerset as well as the New Forest, for in both these areas active packs of stag or buck hounds still operate and these have been dealt with separately in later chapters. A separate chapter is also devoted to deer hunting in East Anglia.

One of the first records of a private pack of staghounds in Britain comes from Sussex, for in about 1738 the second Duke of Richmond and Gordon, who lived at Goodwood House, built what is believed to be the first private kennels in the village of Charlton and appears to have hunted both fox and stag, all at his own expense, for the sport of himself and friends. In hunting the stag he would travel great distances, even into distant counties, and this was in all probability necessary because of the too-thickly wooded nature of his home county.[48] The second Duke of Richmond and Gordon died in 1750 and there is no record of the pack of staghounds existing after that date.

During the early part of the last century there seems to have been a pack of deerhounds operating from Surrenden Dering Park in Kent, but just how long this pack existed or what type of deer it hunted is not known. It appears, however, that the pack was disbanded about the middle of the last century, and it is also stated that some of the descendants of the Dering Staghounds formed the nucleus of the Mid-Kent Staghounds which was founded in 1868 by Mr Tom Rigg of Wrotham.[27] Tom Rigg's hounds first started hunting hare, but within a year or so were hunting fallow deer. The followers of the hunt were so delighted with deer hunting that 'they subscribed among themselves to present Tom Rigg with some red deer, for they considered the large red deer would give the hunt better runs'. From about 1870 onwards, therefore, the Mid-Kent Staghounds, which latterly kept its deer at Boughton Monchelsea, near Maidstone, hunted the carted red deer, the majority of which since the Second World War, had been obtained from Warnham Park in Sussex.

During the early part of its existence, the Mid-Kent hunted any deer which were available in their paddocks – hinds, haviers and the occasional stag – but more recently prior to the disbandment of the hunt in 1962, the hind was the most usual type of animal to be uncarted. Moreover, during the post-war years there were also a number of outlying deer dotted around the countryside, and whenever possible an effort was made to bring these into account.

The oldest pack of deerhounds to operate in south-east England was the Royal Buckhounds – sometimes referred to as the Queen's Hounds – and the existence of this royal hunting establishment dates back to the twelfth century. Prior to the beginning of the eighteenth century there were two branches of the Buckhounds – the Hereditary or Manorial Pack being one, and the Household or Privy Pack being the other. About 1703 these two packs merged to form the United Pack – generally referred to as the Royal Buckhounds or Queen's Hounds during Queen Victoria's long reign. Unfortunately, during the latter years of her reign there were bickerings in the non-sporting press as to the cruelty of this form of sport, and so on his accession to the throne in 1901 King Edward VII decided to abolish the stag hunting establishment.

When this occurred the Berkshire and Buckinghamshire Farmers' Harriers were converted into staghounds and hunted approximately the same country as the royal establishment. This latter hunt survived until the outbreak of war in 1939, but did not restart when hostilities ceased.

The meet of the royal hunt seems to have been a most decorative and splendid affair, as one can gather from this description by William Chafin (1818) who attended a meet in 1741. 'In the month of June,' he wrote, 'it so happened that a stag had strayed away, or been driven from Windsor Forest, and had taken up its abode in Heckfield Woods, and on a certain fixed day the whole Royal Hunt from Windsor assembled on Heckfield Heath in pursuit of the deer which had been harboured and ready for them. A grander sight of the kind could not possibly be exhibited, and much beyond my power to describe. A considerable part of the Royal Family were present, his Royal Highness William Duke of Cumberland and his sister Amelia, one of the best and most amiable Princesses that ever lived. Prince Frederick was prevented from joining by an unfortunate accident which he met with in playing tennis, a game he was fond of, and a great proficient in it. A ball had struck him with great force in his side, and much injured his health at the time, and if I am not mistaken his premature death many years after was attributed to it. . . . The huntsmen, yeomen prickers, and other attendants, all in the same uniform dresses, were in waiting on the Common with two packs of hounds, one of them as a relay to intercept the stag in case he should take a different course towards the Forest, from what was expected. The Princess Amelia, attended by Lady Charlotte Finch and many others of her gentlewomen, were mounted on fine horses, and the ladies all dressed alike in scarlet habits, bespangled with red ribbons formed to resemble very small roses; their velvet caps were also adorned in the same manner. The nets also, with which the ladies' horses were covered, were plentifully spangled over with the same little roses as were the dresses of all the retinue, and all their accoutrements, even the reins and bits of the bridles were covered with red ribbons, in the form of roses; whether to celebrate any particular day I never heard, but it was long before the new style was introduced. As soon as His Royal Highness the Duke of Cumberland had joined the party, and given some orders, the stag was roused and came out in view of the hounds over Heckfield Common, to the delight of the numerous spectators who were there assembled; and took his course near Stratfield Say, the fine seat of Lord Rivers; from thence by Mr Dod's of Swallowfield; and was run into and taken alive, near the town of Reading: the illustrious Princess Amelia, with several of her maids of honour, were in at the end of the chase, and by her gracious intercession the deer's life was saved, and the next day he was conveyed to Windsor, his native place, and turned into one of the enclosed parks there, where I have no doubt but he lived and enjoyed himself many years in peace, plenty and quietness.'

It would seem also that it was not only the women-folk who were adorned with roses, for during the 'course of the Chase on that day, His Royal Highness, in taking a dangerous leap, had a fall, owing to his horse's slipping on a clay bank, but fortunately received no injury, but the soiling of the scarlet uniform dress, and the total destruction of the red roses'.[43]

Even the illustrious Amelia, however, had her tumbles, and it is recorded that following a meet at Richmond, she 'was thrown and due to her Petticoat hanging on the Pommel of the Saddle' she was dragged about a couple of hundred yards before being rescued by Mr Harry Pelham. On this occasion, 'His Majesty order'd the Stagg's life to be spared, to the end he might be hunted again'.

The old records show that during the early eighteenth century the Royal Buckhounds used to kill a great many deer. 'During the four years from 1727 to October 1730, they accounted for 131 stags, 22 hinds and 4 bucks, and between 5 November 1731 and 2 January 1733 for 100 stags and 64 hinds. In the season which finished in October 1734 they killed 60 stags and 17 hinds. . . . In the following season 54 stags, 36 hinds and 2 bucks were the record, and in 1737, 101 deer were killed and in 1739, 87 stags and 35 hinds.'[169] During this period the Royal Buckhounds often hunted in Essex, and in 1729 the Treasury records that 13 stags were accounted for in that county.[50] It would seem that although wild deer were often hunted, in many instances the hunted deer had been previously turned out. On one occasion, on 29 September 1737, a hind which had been turned out on Sudbury Common, gave hounds a 'delightful chace of about three hours' before being killed on Sutton Common between Kingston and Epsom. During the hunt 'it was remarkable that . . . the Huntsman mistook an Ass for the Hind in the Chase, and led on the Dogs, who followed the scent for about Ten Minutes, to the Great Diversion of the Company when it was discovered'.[169]

Appropos mistaken identity, William Scarth-Dixon records an incident with the Easingwold Staghounds, when during an extremely long run the Master asked an old woman he met on Huggate Wold if she had seen the stag: 'Ah knaw nowt aboot t'stag,' said the old woman, 'but ah see'd summat varry like a donkey wi' an airmchair on his head, an' he wur a lang way afore ye'.[169]

Not always was it considered wise to spare a stag that had given hounds a good hunt, as the following incident, which took place in 1734, shows. 'The first stag that was rous'd, not being capable of giving Diversion, the dogs were called off, and a second unharbour'd, which ran for three Hours, when His Royal Highness, declaring his pleasure to have his life sav'd, the Huntsman acquainted him that the Dogs would receive great Prejudice in being so often call'd off in full Scent, whereupon the Chase was continued some Hours longer, till most of the Field, being thrown out, and all the Hounds to two or three couple, His Royal Highness was Pleased to command the Stag to be spared.'

However, during the next few years, His Majesty, with increasing frequency, 'ordered the stag's life to be spared'. Whether this was because deer were becoming scarcer, or His Majesty becoming softer hearted is not recorded, but it seems more likely to have been the former. Be that as it may, by the middle of the century fewer and fewer deer were being killed, and the average soon fell to little more than half of what it had been. The day of the carted deer was fast approaching.

In 1799 the Duke of Cumberland tried his hand at hunting deer with cheetah, two of which had been received from India, and were being kept at Windsor. A large enclosure, surrounded by a strong netting fence fifteen feet high was erected in the park and into this a stag from nearby Windsor Forest was driven. A cheetah, accompanied by two Indian attendants, was then brought in and unhooded. The stag lowered its antlers and showed fight, whereupon the cheetah immediately took fright, and after bounding clean over the netting fence – much to the consternation of the terrified spectators who had gathered to watch the event – finally killed a fallow deer. Some seventy years previous an elk had been uncarted and was reported to have given a 'brilliant hunt'!

Both the royal kennels and deer paddocks were at Ascot in Berkshire, and from the latter, deer were taken to meets principally held in the counties of Berkshire and Buckinghamshire. On occasions, however, the royal hounds went further afield, and a press cutting dated 19 September 1824 stated that 'the King's hounds have left the New Forest for Windsor, quite out of order, from the hardness of the runs and the thickness of the cover. They are to return in October. The stags have shown their amazing speed and cunning by mixing with the herds and avoiding being taken by the lurchers which were posted in all points. A man at Lyndhurst has offered to drive them, only on horseback, into a toil or, as he says, through that town simply in the same manner as they take the forest ponies. As it is, not one stag has been taken alone; three stags and one hind have been killed'.

Moving and catching up deer in this manner seems to have been quite commonly practised in former times for during the last century it is recorded that a herd of fallow deer were brought to Reevesby Abbey park, near Boston in Lincolnshire by road from Syston Park, near Grantham, a distance of about thirty miles – the deer being driven by dogs and horses. A similar method was used to drive the whole herd of fallow deer from Watlington Park to Stonor Park, near Henley-on-Thames in Oxfordshire, a distance of about five miles, the deer being driven along the roads.

A herd of fallow deer was also taken by road a distance of about nine miles when being moved to a new park from Turville Park, near Henley. On this occasion the deer were got into a subdued frame of mind 'by incessantly keeping the Deer walking for three days and nights in the park from whence they were driven; this want of rest rendered them so tame, that they gave no trouble upon the road in their removal, but went quietly along like a flock of sheep, tho' the herd consisted of three hundred head'.[62]

On another occasion, 'a herd of about twenty stags' was persuaded to travel from Yorkshire to Hampton Court by following a bagpipe and violin, 'which while the Music played went forward, when it ceased, they all stood still'.[62]

An even more ambitious feat was achieved by Joseph Watson, the park keeper at Lyme Park, Disley in Cheshire. His employer, Squire Legh had a wager of 500 guineas with Sir Rodger Mason, that Joseph Watson would drive twelve brace of stags from Lyme Park to Windsor – a distance of some 170 miles – and in due course the feat was satisfactorily accomplished. Joseph Watson died in 1753 at the age of 104, having been park keeper at Lyme for sixty-four years. During Watson's lifetime the contents of a handbill dated about 1720 read:

To the Nobility, Gentry or Others

Who have Occasion to remove Red or Fallow Deer out of any Forest, Chace, Park or Paddock, they may be inform'd of a Person who has the safest Method of removing Deer, and is provided with Waggons, Toils &c. for that Purpose. He was brought up under his Father who was Yeoman of the Tents and Toils to their Majesties King Charles II, King James II, King William and Queen Anne.

The said Person takes them, not in the usual Manner with Curr Dogs and Buckstalls, to throw them, but so as to cause them to walk into the Waggons themselves, be their Number ever so great, or the Distance to be removed, even to the furthest part of England, any Time betwixt November and April.

If any Person has a Park of Deer to dispose of, or wants to stock one, he can assist them therein; likewise, if a Woodman or Keeper is wanted, he can recommend a Person of Probity and Judgment, who has been regularly bred to the Business.

N.B. Enquire of C.H. at Christopher Martin's, at the Star, by Fleet market, near Fleet-street, London.

But to return to the royal hunt, meets were generally held on Tuesdays and Fridays, and were attended by large crowds many of whom came from London. Indeed, support from this direction was so great that the Great Western Railway Company ran a special train on each hunting day to the nearest station to the place of meet, which was never very far away.

There is a record of a wonderful run in the time of Charles II, from Swinley near Ascot, when hounds were taken to Lord Petre's park at Thorndon Hall, near Brentwood in Essex, a distance of some seventy miles, the Duke of York, brother of James I being one of the few who saw the deer pulled down. The line lay through Amersham and Chesham in Buckinghamshire, Redbourn and Hatfield in Hertfordshire and thence to Brentwood. There was another fine run during the reign of George III when a deer took hounds from Aldermaston to Reading – a run of some eleven miles. On this occasion it is recorded that both His Majesty's horses were done 'to a turn', and their rider had to make his way back to Windsor in a butcher's cart, chatting affably to the driver.[14]

As mentioned earlier it is generally assumed that the practice of hunting the carted deer was carried out during the reign of this monarch, and to suit King George's sober pace the custom of stopping hounds to give the deer – and the field – a breather was inaugurated. According to Major E W Shackle, formerly Master of the Berks and Bucks Staghounds, 'In the days of the Royal Pack a stag used to be turned out in Windsor Forest once a week through October and hounds were allowed to hunt them to the death. This was to make the hounds keen. Also, after a hunt, when the official season had begun, they would put the stag or havier in a shed, and hold him with his head to the door, and they would then bay the hounds in front of him'.[173] Major Shackle, however, did not think this was necessary, as hounds were just as keen without having to resort to such practices. It was also the practice of the royal hunt to hunt poll haviers during November, as during and just after the rutting season the stags were sulky and disinclined to run.

Occasionally the hunted deer met its fate from 'other' canine influences, and on one occasion in 1825, a hind, after running before hounds for 26 miles, 'took to soil in a pond and before hounds came up was killed by the village bulldog!' (*The Sporting Magazine*, 1825).

Often stags kept for His Majesty's hunts obtained names and celebrity from particular events connected with the chase. *Marlow Tom* became famous by clearing a seven foot fence at Marlow, which had a fifteen-foot drop on the far side, and surviving without injury. This deer subsequently gave the hunt many fine runs. *High Flyer* was another 'leaper' – so called after jumping over the park wall near Datchet Bridge into Windsor Home Park, and then out again and thus extending the chase into the Great Park and Windsor Forest. *Moonshine* earned his title by prolonging the chase into the evening, and being taken by moonlight.

In 1813, when the Charlton Hunt (foxhounds) was broken up,

Charles Davis joined the Ascot kennels as first whipper-in and brought some of the Charlton foxhounds along with him. There seems little doubt that Davis's appointment was a big success, and during his term of office he wrote down in his well-kept diaries, events of each day's hunting and also some prudent observations on the preparation of deer for hunting.

'On the day before hunting' he wrote (1840), 'the Stag should be lightly fed in the morning, and about the middle of the day, put into a hovel, made nearly dark, with plenty of clean water, that he might not be thirsty in the chase; if this be not attended to, he will help himself so bountifully at the first river or pond he meets with, that pace becomes instantly out of the question; driving them about with a cur dog in their paddocks, by way of getting them into wind, is most objectionable, as it only irritates them, and spoils their temper; they quickly discover the impotence of their assailant, when they will turn round and show fight, and often become in turn the aggressors; after practising this a few times they are inclined to try a similar trick with the pack; this injudicious step has been the cause of many a bad day's sport, for they are by nature cunning animals, with retentive recollections. Deer, after a severe day, even if caught without any *visible* injury, should not be hunted for three weeks, their muscular powers being called into action after long rest, causes great soreness and disinclination to feed, consequently time must be given them to recover. These remarks are contingent on the constitution of the animal, for as well as horses, hounds, and etc. they are not all made of the same metal.'

Davis also suggested that the deer should be loaded into the deer cart the evening prior to the hunt, 'where he ought to be kept without food, and with but a *small* quantity of water'.

On the running of certain deer Davis said that he had 'known knobbers run surprisingly well, but for their tender age it is not advisable to hunt them, as they seldom survive the first chase; hounds too, as now bred, are much too fast for them, or in fact for stag hunting generally. Deer at three or four years should be taken into paddock, and fed on beans, or oats, with second-cut clover-hay, and plenty of water; carrots are not good for them when in health. They have been known to last twenty years hunting, but that is a rare occurrence: one was killed last year [1839], for instance, which had been hunted twelve seasons; latterly, however, he became cunning, and of course would not show sport. Stags above four years should not be hunted till near Christmas, as during the season of the rut, which continues through October and November, their temper is bad, they refuse food and become savage and weak. Dry Hinds and castrated Deer are now found of great use; the latter are called Haviers; this operation, which neither improves their temper nor their running, should be performed early in the spring. In April they shed their horns, others grow and remain as long as the animal lives; nor should they be cut off as they never become hard, but are covered with a kind of felt or velvet, and are full of blood, frequent hunting often bruises them, when they crumble away'.

As already mentioned, owing to adverse criticism in the press and increasing public opposition to hunting the carted deer, Edward VII, in 1901, decided to abolish the royal stag hunting establishment and although the Berkshire and Buckinghamshire Farmers' Harriers were converted into staghounds to hunt much of the country formerly occupied by the Royal Buckhounds, they did so with their own hounds rather than taking over a draft from the royal pack. The latter, consisting of eleven and a half couple were, it seems, handed over to Lord Chesham who was already in South Africa, in order to provide sport and recreation for his troops out there. Accordingly the pack, under the care of Colonel Cape, proceeded during the spring of 1901, to Durban and by July they were already hunting bush buck in the forests near that city.

Shortly afterwards they were transferred to more permanent kennels at Pietermaritzburg, from where they had their first meet after duiker – an antelope of the size of a small roe deer – but owing to lack of scent the day was not very successful. In subsequent outings, both duiker and oribi – another small antelope – were hunted indiscriminately, but their survival in South Africa did not last long for the pack was decimated by disease – a virulent form of 'yellows' – and had to be disbanded. Such was the end of the royal pack which had been in existence during the reigns of over thirty monarchs.[140]

During the early part of the last century, the Earl of Derby formed a pack of staghounds to hunt much of the country contained in the counties of Kent, Surrey and Sussex, his hounds being kennelled at The Oaks, his estate near Epsom from which the famous flat race takes its name. The deer, which came from his Lancashire park at Knowsley, were noted for their speed and the hounds were said to be a good match. One of the best runs took place on 2 April 1822 – the last day of the season – when a deer which was uncarted at Wickham Cross near Hayes Common, was taken only after a thirty mile point, lasting some three and three-quarters of an hour, the animal having taken refuge in some farm buildings near Speldhurst. The actual distance covered was probably nearer fifty-five miles.

In 1851 Lord Derby gave up his hounds, and they were taken over by a committee and thereafter, until their disbandment in 1915, assumed the title of Surrey Staghounds.

Owing to Lord Derby's close association with the pack, it was not surprising that the source of many of the deer was Knowsley Park in Lancashire, and although many of the transfers of deer went unrecorded, it is known that in the spring of 1869 Lord Derby offered Le Duc de Chartres, who was a member of the Committee of Management of the Surrey Staghounds, 'four deer from Knowsley Park for the use of the pack, but that not being the proper time to take them up, their presentation was deferred' until January 1870[3]. The same authority mentions that deer had also been received from France.

One of Lord Derby's best deer was *Ben the Sailor* who would always take a line for the Thames about Gravesend or Woolwich. Another good animal was the *Lancashire Havier* which would generally finish up in the neighbourhood of Kingston and Hampton Court, although turned out more than twenty miles away. He was, apparently, finally shot by a gardener at Moulsey after a run of three hours. *Ploughboy* and *Alexander* were also good deer, generally making, after being uncarted, for the Kentish hills to Penshurst, Westerham and Limpsfield, the former once having been taken within two miles of Tunbridge Wells, and *Alexander* even two miles beyond, both animals having been turned out at Hayes Common near Croydon. These runs, apparently, killed many horses and when *Ploughboy* was taken near Tunbridge Wells no fewer than nine died, either in the field or during the next day.[3] Horses were not the only ones to suffer from a hard run, for occasionally a stag would run itself to death. Such a one was the little *Herring* which died near Horsley. A hind by the name of *Piccolomine* jumped on to some spiked railings in Ashurst Park and killed herself.

One of the best hinds was *Keston*, who more than once beat the pack and had to be left out. On one occasion she ran to Chobham, but hounds lost her. She was next heard of at Leatherhead, and once again the hounds ran her to Chobham without taking her. As it was late in the season and as she was thought to be in calf, a house of thatched hurdles was constructed as a trap, with a door operated by long string release. After several days out she was eventually enticed into the trap with food, and caught. During one of her outlying runs, *Keston* had taken hounds into three counties – Surrey, Sussex and Kent.[3]

Empress was another hind to give a run lasting two hours or more whilst *Ashurst*, uncarted on Epsom Downs, ran with hounds for three hours before hounds had to be whipped off near Godstone owing to darkness. She was subsequently taken the same evening by some foot followers. Of the haviers, *Sweep* was one of the best, though on occasions was decidedly moody and would not run at all. On one of *Sweep's* off-days the second deer *Empress* had to be uncarted before the followers got any sport at all. *Sweep*, incidentally, got his name by jumping on to a heap of soot and covering himself. Another good havier was *Valentine*, whose longest point about 1907 was from New Plumpton to Netherfield. One of the best deer during the mastership of Mosse Robinson was *Apology*, who covered some extraordinarily long distances and was frequently left out.

Lady Effingham was another very fine hind and she gave the hunt a number of twenty mile points. On 23 March 1889 *Lady Effingham* made a straight point of twenty-three miles from Lympne above Romney Marsh to Herne Bay where Mr Gregory – the honorary secretary of the hunt – was rowed out to sea by the Coast Guard for one and a half miles before she was taken and brought safely back to the shore. The distance of that run, as hounds went, was estimated at over thirty miles.

Another pack of staghounds which hunted in West Surrey during the latter part of the last century was the Surrey Farmers' – which was formed in about 1885 and subsequently became known as the West Surrey Staghounds. One of the hunt's best deer was a havier called *Master Walter* which had been obtained from the Queen's after a joint meet of that pack with the West Surrey, and which, after a long run, had been left out. This deer was eventually taken by the West Surrey and presented to the hunt by Lord Ribblesdale. Subsequently, this havier, no matter where uncarted, always made a point straight back to the paddocks and on all but three occasions arrived back before the hounds.

One of the best runs on record was from a meet at Cheam Court. The deer was enlarged at Cheam Warren, and running via North Looe to North House and Burgh Heath, made his way to Headly Park and Mickleham Downs, on through Norbury Park to Polesdon, Horsley Towers, Clandon and Newark Abbey to Woking, and from there to Knaphill, Pirbright, on to Worplesdon where, darkness setting in, they left him out; out of a field of one hundred and twenty, only eight were left in![24]

Other packs to hunt the carted deer in Surrey and Sussex during the last century were Lee Steere's Staghounds (*c.*1840–65); Farnell Watson's Staghounds (1867–82) and the Warnham Staghounds (1882–1917). Mr Lee Steere seems to have kept about twelve deer for hunting in his paddocks, one of the best of which was the *Horned Deer* which gave the hunt five good runs in one season, all with long distance points. In 1853 one of his deer *No. 12* whilst being hunted, jumped into a chalk pit and was killed.

When Mr Lee Steere gave up stag hunting some of his hounds passed to Mr Farnell Watson who already had a pack of harriers, and in 1867 this gentleman started to hunt the carted deer. The pack continued to hunt under the Farnell Watson family name until 1882 when it assumed the title of Warnham Staghounds.

In 1869 the Farnell Watson Staghounds had a wonderful run lasting some four hours, after a stag named *Borealis*. Some thirty-nine years later a deer named *Miss Eileen* was uncarted by the Warnham Staghounds at the same place and took the same line of country, being finally taken at the same spot as *Borealis*. Driving the deer cart on both occasions was Walter Botting.

One of the most famous deer belonging to the Warnham Staghounds was a havier called *Jim Crow*, which always, apparently, made an easterly point, generally of about four hours' duration, over a good country – skirting the woods, roadways and railway lines, and keeping well to the open. *Jim Crow* was hunted for ten seasons without a scratch, and one of the best runs he gave was when uncarted from East Grinstead, being subsequently taken near Lewes after a very fast run. Other deer which generally gave the Warnham Staghounds good runs were *Marquis*, who made a habit of lying down until hounds were almost on him before making his point, and *Actress*, a hind which evaded capture on five occasions before being taken at sea off Pevensey on the last day of the season.

The Warnham Staghounds suspended hunting during the First World War and never re-started – in fact the only stag hunting (carted deer) in south-east England after 1918 was with the Mid-Kent Staghounds and during the brief existence of the Sussex Staghounds (*c.* 1930–31). About the turn of the century the South Coast Staghounds, which had their deer paddock near Emsworth, Sussex, for about five years, were hunting deer and hare on alternate days, before disbandment about 1902.

The First World War also saw the end of Lord Rothschild's Staghounds which had been established in 1839 to hunt the Vale of Aylesbury in Buckinghamshire, and throughout its long existence of over seventy-five years it was maintained by a member of the Rothschild family.

Baron Meyer de Rothschild was the first Master, and from a chronicler of the time it seems that in its early days 'the county did not take kindly' at first, and accused the members of the hunt of trespassing. However, Baron Meyer, with his genial and unassuming manner, soon won the affection of the local country folk, and the 'threats for Trespass soon died out, and with no class did he become more popular than with the farmers'.[28]

Coaten (1909) had a very high opinion of Lord Rothschild's pack 'which crosses the Vale of Aylesbury as a flock of pigeons cross a parish. . . . Admirably mounted, as I have personally seen, from the days of Tom Balls, a steeplechase huntsman of the fifties, to Fred Cox, Jack Boore, and Will Gaskin, all these huntsmen have gone like flashes of lightening through a gooseberry bush. The men have usually been mounted on blood hunters of steeplechase type, and they were expected to be *on the premises* when the hounds ran up to the stag; then they could safely take him'. 'Fields ran into the hundreds, and on one occasion after a thirty-mile point, only eleven of the three hundred horses that attended the meet were in at the take and, even then, according to Coaten 'some of these never hunted again'. On another occasion about 1840, five horsemen 'raced side by side for first cut at Rowsham Brook, a yawning watercourse that likes to be called a rivulet. Though their horses made magnificent bounds, they all landed mid-stream, and swam like a gaggle of geese in a field'.[50]

Mention has already been made of the Berkshire and Buckinghamshire Farmers' Staghounds, which in 1901 converted from harriers to staghounds when the Royal Buckhounds were abolished. The change seems to have been a happy one for they soon received 'the important and highly valuable support of farmers, and others, to such an extent that those very few gentlemen who were not exactly in accord are now diplomatically induced to acquiesce in the excellent arrangements' made by the Master.[50] This pack survived the First World War, but was disbanded in 1939. Probably its best deer was a stag by the name of *Highway* which for six seasons just prior to the 1914 war frequently ran a point of 10 to 13 miles – or more than 20 miles as hounds ran – and earned the title of *King of the Paddocks*.

Another pack to hunt deer in Buckinghamshire was the Berkhamsted Staghounds which had been formed in 1870 to hunt fallow buck in both that county and Hertfordshire. Initially the deer were obtained from Ashridge Park, and were taken to the meet in crates on a trolley – a rather primitive form of transport. Subsequently the hunt acquired a proper deer cart and from then onwards red deer became the normal quarry.

The hunt enjoyed some remarkable runs, including one in 1876 of four hours ten minutes' duration after a deer which was finally taken in Berkhamsted Hall garden. That season seems to have been a 'vintage one' for sport, for in addition to another run of over four hours, there were several others resulting in the deer being left out at dark. Normally, however, the outlying deer seems to have been taken the following day. In 1880, a run of twenty-two miles from Harpenden Common, which took the field through the Puckridge Hounds in Bennington High Wood, was generally considered one of the best runs this pack ever had. The following season there was another run lasting four hours fifteen minutes from Harpenden Common before the deer was finally taken at Cherry Tree Farm, near Hemel Hempstead after dark. On another occasion the Berkhamsted covered eighteen miles of country in ninety minutes without a check of any sort, going straight from Sandridge Village to Barnet Gate, and on to Mill Hill before taking their deer at Edgware.

In September 1896, a great gale blew down one side of the deer paddock and six deer got out. Some rare sport was had after these outlying deer but within a fortnight, after ten good runs, all the deer were taken without mishap.

Nearer London the Enfield Chase Staghounds had been established in 1885 by Colonel Somerset. Prior to that year the Enfield country had not been hunted with staghounds since the time of Queen Elizabeth I.[7] This pack of hounds hunted by invitation in Middlesex, Hertfordshire and Bedfordshire. In 1912 Major (subsequently Colonel) R P Croft took over the mastership, and thereafter the pack was generally referred to as Colonel Croft's Staghounds. After the First World War, Colonel Croft took his staghounds to Essex, and subsequently anyone living in the Metropolis and wishing to join in any carted deer hunting would have to go either to Kent or Berkshire and hunt with the Mid-Kent or Berkshire and Buckinghamshire Staghounds respectively.

Chapter III
Deer Hunting in East Anglia

Stag hunting in East Anglia, and Norfolk in particular, dates from a very early period. We read that during the twelfth century a certain Bishop of Norwich (Bishop Herbert de Losinga) kept a pack there, while a few centuries later King James I used Thetford as a hunting lodge until about 1610. James I had a great attachment for the country round Thetford until, it is recorded, he was warned off by a farmer who, quite naturally, did not appreciate the hunt, albeit it contained royalty, riding over his wheat fields. Charles II hunted the stag in Norfolk and during the eighteenth century members of the Suckling family, well known in the county, hunted both fox and fallow deer. About 1750 a pack of staghounds, stated to be the first pure staghound pack in the county, was being maintained by Lord Orford and shortly afterwards there was another – the Dunston Staghounds – being hunted by John Gurney and Mr Long, which seems to have lasted until about 1779. During the last century there are frequent references to hunting the carted deer – in fact, this form of hunting appears to have been practised in Norfolk, probably without a break for close on 170 years since 1793, when Mr Sturt hunted a pack.

Prior to this date a pack called the Carrow Abbey Hunt seems to have operated in Norfolk, and hunted anything from hare to deer. One can assume that the latter were either red or fallow deer, being escapees out of one of the numerous parks in the county which, at that period, included North Elmham, Holkham and Houghton. On 18 January 1783 an advertisement (*see page 42*) appeared in the *Mercury*, and although the name of the hunt is not mentioned, one must assume that it refers to the Carrow Abbey Hunt.

In 1809 a Captain John Darell was running a pack of staghounds, but nothing is known of the activities of this hunt. Captain Darell had the Wymondham Troop of the Norfolk Yeomanry.

The deer for hunting have not always been kept in the same locality. It is of interest to read that when the Westacre Staghounds were at Swaffham (*c.* 1825) they 'were kept like horses, tied by the head in stalls, and fed on oats, beans and hay, and tremendous runs twice in the week did they give . . .' (*My Life*, Charles Loftus). At other times the deer did quite the opposite, and we read from another source that on one occasion the stag 'kept trotting up and down among the horses and more than once had a good stare at the master . . . so was put back in the

Holt Jubilee.
Will be on MONDAY, the 27th. instant

Deer Hunting
On Monday, the 27th. and Thursday the 30th.

Fox Hunting
On Tuesday, the 28th. and Friday the 31st.

Hare Hunting
On Wednesday, the 29th. and Saturday, the 1st. February.
An ordinary everyday at 3 o'clock at the Feathers.
On Thursday Evening there will be a BALL
On Friday Morning, on the Course, will be various Amusements, such as Ass Racing, Sack Races, Grinning Matches, etc. etc. etc.

Edward Pratt
Jacob Astley Stewards.

cart'! In the year 1818 a pack of staghounds seems to have been kept by Mr Edward Dewing of Guist, which ran deer, hare or fox. Mr Dewing died in 1827.

About the same time as Mr Dewing was running his pack of staghounds another pack, which was kennelled at Burgh Hall, near Melton Constable, was being hunted by Sir Jacob Astley. This latter pack, which was founded in 1815, subsequently changed about 1823 to hunting fox.

A further pack which, about this time, hunted the occasional deer, was the Union Harriers, for on 17 March 1827, the following announcement occurred in the local press: 'The Union Harriers will meet on Monday next, at Fritton Green Man, near Hempnall, to run a deer, presented by Alexander Adair, Esq., to the gentlemen of the Union Hunt.'[98] These hounds hunted in south Norfolk and north Suffolk and are the forebears of what later became known as the Henham Harriers. Still another pack – the Westacre Staghounds – was operating in Norfolk during the 1820s under the mastership of the Reverend Robert Hamond (*see page 251*). It seems to have existed for about nine years before being sold at Newmarket in 1829. The first mention of this hunt appears in 1821, for the *Norfolk Annals* states: 'that on December 7th Mr R Hamond turned off a deer at Swaffham, which led the field a chase of nearly 30 miles. It crossed the river twice, and what is most extraordinary, Mr A Hamond, who was in his 81st year, took part in the run, and was at the take of the deer near Lynn.'

On 8 February 1828, the *Norfolk Annals* records a trial of speed between the Westacre and Melton Constable Hounds. 'A stag was selected, as the animal best suited to ascertain the respective merits of the two packs. This deer stood up before the hounds an hour and ten minutes, but the enormous field, amounting to at least 400, the greater part of whom rode the roads and headed the stag at every point, prevented any brilliant sport from being shown. The Westacre hounds are said to have taken the lead through the greater part of the day. They carried the best head and did all the work. At the same time, they appear to have ben been out-manoeuvred by the huntsman of Sir Jacob Astley, who kept lifting on his hounds. The Westacre hounds . . . did not like being over-ridden by the crowd as they are more timid by nature than the foxhound, and the field appear to have pressed on them in a most shameful manner. In consequence, most of Mr Hammond's were thrown out, and never recovered their lost ground again. The match took place in the neighbourhood of East Dereham'.[98]

One of the best meets of the Westacre took place at Watton on 5 March 1829, and a better run could not have been had. Describing this remarkable run, the *Norfolk Annals* stated: 'The meet was at Watton, where the stag was turned off, and led a field of between 60 and 70 to Ovington, Shipdham, Whinberg, over Reymerston Common, touching Southbergh, to Carbrooke, crossing Griston Common to Thompson Heath. Here there was a short check, but they were soon away again for Tottington, on the Wretham, leaving the decoy on the left; thence to Kilverstone and Brettenham Heaths; then to the left of Croxton, and to the River Ouse, which was forded between Santon Downham and Thetford. Only nine horsemen forded the river, who made away in the direction of Barton Mills, where another check occurred. They then passed over Wangford Warren to Lakenheath Common, straight for Bramber Hall, and the stag was killed in the plantation of Mr Edward Bliss, after a run of three hours and three quarters.'[98]

It would seem that in 1822 two Corsican red deer stags were presented to Rev. Robert Hamond for hunting. Recording this event, Lt.-Col. Harvey, quoting from the *Norfolk Annals* states: 'An innovation was introduced by Mr Robert Hamond, in his endeavour to show sport in the western part of Norfolk, as we notice, that in 1822 two Corsican stags were presented to this pack by Lord Maynard. The first of these animals was turned off at Rougham, on 28 January, and gave the followers of the Westacre Hunt a severe chase of nearly three hours, from the effects of which two horses died. It does not state whether these stags were persevered with. . . . They were described, however, as being very superior to the red deer of this country, for their capability to endure extreme fatigue and to take the most extraordinary leaps.'[98]

Five years after the sale of the Westacre Staghounds, a new pack was formed by Sir James Flower in 1834 which, during its three years' existence seems to have been run on a lavish scale before being abandoned in 1837. Sir James Flower resided at Eccles Hall, and in consequence the pack was sometimes referred to as the Eccles Hunt (*page 218*). Whenever meets took place at Eccles Hall they were marked with great hospitality and splendour, with brass bands and champagne breakfasts. The pack hunted carted red deer. One of the best runs seems to have taken place on 28 November 1836. The meet was held at Stow, where the stag was enlarged, and he was taken some five hours later at Garboldisham

Lings. Although the distance from point to point was only eleven miles, it was estimated that the stag ran at least forty miles. Only the huntsman and first whip were up at the finish.[98] Another run of upwards of thirty miles took place in 1837 when the meet was held at Wymondham, the stag finally being taken some three and a quarter hours later at South Lopham, having taken a circular run round Diss.

At about the same time that Sir James Flower was hunting the Eccles Staghounds in south-eastern Norfolk, Mr Harry Villebois was keeping a pack of staghounds in west Norfolk. Mr Villebois' pack started as harriers in 1827, but about 1837 changed to stag. How long he continued to hunt the deer is not recorded but it is probable that this form of hunting was abandoned about 1841–2 when he disposed of his deer.

J R Harvey gives the following account of a good run after a stag by the Villebois Staghounds on 16 February 1837. 'The Staghounds of H Villebois, Esq, had a most superior run on Thursday. The place of meeting was Lynn Scoote. The Reffly stag was uncarted on the left of the Swaffham Splashes, and after twenty-five minutes' law, the hounds were laid on, the stag going gallantly away through the parishes of Sporle, Necton, over Mr Farrar's farm to Pickenham Heath, leaving the town of Swaffham on the left, back over the stiff enclosures to Sporle, from thence through Little and Great Dunham, Fransham, Beeston, Kempstone, to Longham, and was taken, after two hours and twenty minutes, in a pond belonging to the Rev. Dennis Hill, of Gressenhall. The distance run over is computed at thirty miles, and, from the deep state of the country and great pace was most distressing to the horses, not more than seven out of a field of thirty being in at the take.'[98]

A month later the Villebois Staghounds had another memorable run, after a stag which had been uncarted on Bradenham Green on 20 March, and after taking a line via Ovington, Watton, Scoulton, Ellingham, Caston, Rockingham, Attleborough, Besthorpe, Snetterton, Eccles and Larlingford, was finally taken at Roundham, the total distance covered being estimated at thirty-five miles, not more than 200 yards of which was run on roads.[98]

Stag hunting seems to have been extremely popular in Norfolk in the late 1830s for still another pack, belonging to the fourth Lord Suffield, was hunting the carted deer. Little is known, however, of these staghounds, but Lt.-Col. Harvey did 'not think that this pack could have had a very long existence, as Lord Suffield assumed the Mastership of the Quorn in the autumn' of 1838.[98]

On 12 March 1838 there is mention in the *Norfolk Annals* of an eighteen mile run with this pack. The meet was on Crostwight Common. The stag, after being uncarted, crossed the road to Beeston Hall and then ran by way of Rackheath to Wroxham, Salhouse, Woodbastwick, Ranworth, Burlingham, Upton and Acle. Here he crossed the Bure and made for Stokesby, Thrigby and Caister, going within a mile of

Yarmouth. He then took to Breydon Water, where he was secured.

About this time a cavalry regiment was quartered in East Anglia, half the regiment being stationed at Norwich and the remainder at Ipswich. Many of the officers were undoubtedly very interested in stag hunting and following a meeting at Ipswich in October 1841* the 13th Light Dragoon Staghounds, under the mastership of Captain J Anstruther Thomson, was formed – probably the first regimental pack of hounds to hunt in East Anglia. Hounds and deer were obtained from various sources, including some of the latter from Mr H Villebois. This regimental pack seems to have hunted both fallow deer and red deer (*see page 217*).

To begin with, a hind was bought in London from Herring, which was christened *Salt Fish* and another hind was presented by Lord Rosslyn, who was then Master of the Royal Buckhounds. With these two red deer hinds, and a fallow buck called *Bob*, belonging to a farmer called Morgan on whose farm at Bramford the deer were kept, the pack commenced hunting the carted deer. Later in the season Harry Villebois gave the hunt a stag called *Sir Walter Scott*, but he proved very temperamental, sometimes running and sometimes not. 'He was very savage,' wrote Harvey, 'and could defend himself from the hounds. When turned out of the cart, if he saw two or three horsemen together, he went straight at them; and it was very ridiculous seeing them gallop in all directions to avoid him.'[98]

A second stag was also obtained from Villebois for £15. Unfortunately, one day after a long run *The Sheriff*, by which name this stag was known, ran into a farmyard. A farm man tried to capture it by throwing a rope round its neck, but before the unfortunate animal could be released, it had suffocated. With another of Mr Villebois' deer the hunt was more fortunate, and on one occasion its members had a capital run lasting one hour and twenty minutes, which included a non-stop run by hounds of forty minutes, before the deer was taken in the pond at Akenham. From point to point the distance was twelve miles, but the line the deer took must have made it over fifteen miles.

Captain Thomson of the 13th Light Dragoons had the staghounds for only one season, for in the following year they were taken over by Lord William Hill of the 2nd Dragoons. Once again, a regimental unit control of the pack lasted only but a season, and Lt.-Col. Harvey suggests[98] that the regiment was posted elsewhere, for he was unable to discover if at that date the hounds were passed on to any succeeding cavalry regiment at Norwich. In 1844, however, a pack of staghounds was being hunted in Norfolk by Charles Kett Tompson of Witchingham.

Charles Kett Tompson (for one season only) and his brother Henry,

---

* Lt.-Col. J R Harvey in *Deer Hunting in Norfolk,*[98] p. 34 gives the year 1842, yet on p. 83 he mentions that the 13th Light Dragoon Staghounds were running the pack in 1841, and that in 1842 the pack was taken over by the 2nd Dragoons (The Royal Scots Greys), so 1841 is probably the correct date.

then hunted staghounds in Norfolk until 1851 and during their regime, when it appears that the pack was, for the first time, referred to as the Norfolk Staghounds, some excellent hunts were enjoyed. One in particular was after a stag named *Sailor Boy* which, after being uncarted at Drayton, led the field a run calculated at nearly twenty-five miles, before being taken at Swanton Mills. On 13 December 1845 another stag gave hounds an excellent run 'of at least from twenty to twenty-five miles, without a single check' after being uncarted at Woodrow, being finally 'pulled down' by hounds. Fortunately the huntsman, John Turner, and Mr J Abel were at hand so the hounds were whipped off and the deer secured subsequently to be led off to the Rising Sun, where a number of the hunting party also took refreshment.[98]

It also appears that the hunt did not confine itself to hunting the red deer stag, but also, on occasions, hunted fallow buck. The latter, however, did not give such long runs, being generally short but fast. One such hunt took place in December 1845 and it is recorded that after a meet at Lenwade Bridge a buck was enlarged. The deer was, as usual, headed off after a mile and a quarter, and ran through Witchingham and Alderford to Attlebridge, a short but fast run, before he was secured.[98]

Whether there was any stag hunting in Norfolk between 1851, when the Tompsons gave up, and 1854 when Charles Harbord, the fifth Baron Suffield founded the Gunton Staghounds, is uncertain. Lt.-Col. Harvey, however, was informed by Mrs C Waters that a certain Stephen Abbott of Castleacre was keeping a pack of staghounds, and that he himself had attended a meet at Castleacre in 1853. Subsequently, Lt.-Col. Harvey was informed that Mr Stephen Abbott's pack was a harrier pack that hunted deer as well.

The next pack of staghounds in Norfolk was the Gunton Staghounds which was formed to hunt anywhere in the county, by the Fifth Baron Suffield in about 1854. In a letter to Lt.-Col. Harvey (19 December 1909) Lord Suffield wrote, 'I went with hounds wherever I was asked throughout the whole county, and used to leave generally one of the two stags which I sent out to the various meets to take care of itself, and later on used to draw for the outlying stag when I heard of his whereabouts.... One of these had been about East Norfolk a long time and had a grand head of horns, which, of course, are sawn off during the hunting season. I found him one day in the woods of Westwick, where old Mr Petre never allowed him to be disturbed. He was off before we had begun to draw for him, and went away for the sea, on reaching which he jumped down a cliff into the sea. The hounds, which were close to him then, followed him. I myself was the only one who rode down this cliff side (by no path) to save the hounds. There I luckily obtained a boat and brought them back to the shore with him. The stag swam on the tide, and was eventually taken, and towed by a line over his horns into Yarmouth by some fishermen who caught him. He was then sent back to the park at Gunton, whence he came, and where he lived afterwards for many years.'

As Staghounds, this pack does not seem to have survived very long, for in 1856 in response to local request, Lord Suffield relinquished hunting stag in Norfolk and converted the Gunton Staghounds into the Norfolk Foxhounds.

For the next sixteen years or so, there does not appear to have been any organized stag hunting in Norfolk, though from reports in the local press, it does seem that the various packs of harriers operating in the county did occasionally turn their attention to hunting the stag or fallow buck – the latter, presumably, outliers from the numerous parks in the district, although at times a deer seems to have been provided for the occasion. Such an occasion was when the North Walsham Harriers received a stag from Lord Suffield of Gunton Park as a fitting quarry for the last meet of the 1858 season. The stag was uncarted in a field near North Walsham and after giving the hunt a fast and excellent run lasting two and a quarter hours, was finally taken near Dilham. During the run a check of some minutes occurred, 'owing to the number of hares'.[98]

During the 1870s stag hunting seems to have gained popularity and at one time at least two packs were operating in Norfolk. One of these packs – the Norfolk and Suffolk Staghounds – was started by Mr Charles Chaston in 1873, at which time he was also apparently Master of a harrier pack which he called the Waveney Harriers. This pack, which operated in south-east Norfolk and the northern part of Suffolk does not seem to have survived for more than about a season under Mr Chaston (*see page 249*). At the same time Mr William Angerstein was hunting a pack of staghounds in Norfolk.

Charles Chaston '. . . used to drive up to the meet with a large van, containing both packs of hounds and the deer; all in separate compartments. He arrived wearing his green coat, and his red one used to be carried on the top of the van. The hour of the meet used to be ten o'clock, and the opening hunt was with the harriers, and then towards midday, he would change into his scarlet coat, and treat his followers to a stag hunt, the same hunt horses being used for both purposes. These hounds were styled at various periods, the "Waveney Staghounds" and the "Norfolk and Suffolk"'.[98] This confusion of names probably arose from the fact that Chaston's Harriers were generally referred to as the Waveney Harriers.

Occasionally, Mr Chaston's hounds would hunt an outlier. One such occasion was 22 January 1874 when an outlying deer was located about mid-day in a wood near Chedgrave. After taking some refreshment with Mr Gilbert, on whose land the deer was found, the wood was drawn and in due course the deer broke away, giving the hunt an excellent run, mostly over plough, before being finally taken at Starston Hall shortly after 5 pm.

Just when Charles Chaston gave up the Norfolk and Suffolk Staghounds has not been recorded, but it does not seem to have survived for long. There is a reference in an old directory to the effect that he was Master of Suffolk Staghounds in 1883 but it may have referred to the Norfolk and Suffolk Staghounds, or perhaps indicated that his pack no longer hunted in Norfolk.

As already mentioned, about the same time as Charles Chaston was hunting his Norfolk and Suffolk Staghounds, Mr William Angerstein was operating a pack of staghounds in the western half of Norfolk. This pack was brought from Rugby in 1872, and kenelled at Mr Angerstein's residence at Weeting. For four seasons Angerstein hunted this pack and then resigned in 1876 in favour of Captain Haughton of Fundenhall Grange, who himself resigned, after one season, the pack being taken over by C T Hoare.

Once again, however, within a year a fresh Master had to be found, and from being a private pack it once more became a subscription one under R A Barkley of Palgrave Priory, Diss, Mr Hoare's successor. The selection of Mr Barkley was very popular and for five years the pack, which was then known as the Norfolk and Suffolk Staghounds, hunted practically the same country as the Norwich Staghounds did in the following century.

Towards the end of Barkley's regime, subscriptions began to fall off, so he decided to relinquish the mastership at the end of the 1882–3 season. At that time the 4th Hussars were quartered at Norwich, and they immediately offered to take over the pack from Mr Barkley and run it at their own expense. So started a new era in the history of this pack, and for the next seventeen years, with only one short break from 1885–6, when Mr R A Barkley temporarily slipped into the breach, each cavalry regiment stationed at Norwich took over the hounds as follows, the pack taking its name from the unit in command at the time:

1883–5	4th Hussars Staghounds
1886–8	19th Hussars Staghounds
1888–90	20th Hussars Staghounds
1890–93	8th Hussars Staghounds
1893–5	1st King's Dragoon Guards Staghounds
1895–8	7th Dragoon Guards Staghounds
1898–1900	7th Hussars Staghounds

Sport in Norfolk, therefore, at the close of the last century, owed much to the cavalry regiments stationed at Norwich.

After the 7th Hussars had been posted to South Africa an order was issued by the War Office forbidding further units to indulge in such luxuries as running a pack of hounds. The pack once again became a subscription pack and from 1900 was known as the Norwich Staghounds.

For over sixty years the Norwich Staghounds continued to hunt the carted deer in any part of Norfolk to which the hunt was invited.

During the first thirty years of the present century, the red deer were kept at Brooke Lodge, Norwich, and the number of deer in the enclosure was generally about twenty-five. During the early thirties the deer were moved to Rackheath Park, near Norwich, the home of Sir Edward Stracey, Bart. Subsequently they were kept at Winfarthing (The Lodge) Park, near Diss. This small park of about fourteen acres was enclosed in 1947 and was supplied with deer from Woburn. In 1948 two four-year-old hinds and two two-year-old hinds were obtained from Warnham Court, Sussex, while the following year two more two-year-old hinds were received from the same source. At this date the park contained one stag and seventeen hinds.

Prior to the Second World War, stags for stocking the hunt's enclosure were obtained from a number of parks, which included Richmond Park, Surrey, and Ashridge Park, Hertfordshire. Hinds had also been obtained from Blickling Park, Norfolk and Warnham Park, Sussex. In fact, for over sixty years there have been traces of Warnham blood in the deer hunted by the Norwich Staghounds, for as far back as 1896 the hunt received three hinds from this park, to be followed in 1897 with another one. It would appear, however, that the hunt never purchased any stags from Warnham, these having been obtained from such parks as Woburn and Richmond.

On occasions the Norwich Staghounds – who in later years only hunted hinds – failed to take their deer and this has resulted in feral deer being established in East Anglia and in particular, in Thetford Forest belonging to the Forestry Commission, and some of the stags killed there in recent years by sportsmen with the rifle have had magnificent antlers as the following measurements of three stags killed in Thetford, shows:

Date	*No. of points*	*Length cm Left*	*Length cm Right*	*Beam cm Left*	*Beam cm Right*	*Inside span cm*	*Shot by*
1958	9 × 12 = 21	96.4	93.6	15.2	14.7	92.0	L I Biggs
1956	9 × 12 = 21	86.2	86.9	14.4	15.8	78.0	E Czarnowski
1959	9 × 11 = 20	91.0	88.5	14.5	14.1	69.0	Dr E Heitz

At times the roads which intersected this part of Norfolk were found to be something of a handicap as the deer sometimes used to prefer to run down them rather than taking to the country. Nevertheless, some grand hunts were had, and among the more memorable was a fifteen mile point in the spring of 1878 from Attleborough to Shipdham, past Scoulton Mere, with only one check of one and a half hours.[27] The same authority records an even longer run in March 1880 after a meet at Eye. On this occasion the deer, after being uncarted near the town, crossed the brook and ran towards Occold. At first the pace was tremendous and there were many falls. Bearing south, the deer ran through Kenton, Brandeston and Hoo, and then on to Easton where, for a time, it was able to lose hounds and so gain a bit of ground. Eventually, when hounds had reached Marlesford, it was decided to call hounds off, as the scent was bad and the deer had gained too great a lead. The distance covered was nineteen miles from Eye to Marlesford.

One hind about 1894 seems to have given the pack a remarkable run. After being uncarted on the Reedham Marshes she ran, by way of Fritton Common, Herringfleet Hall, Somerleyton Park, Blundeston to Corton where she took to the sea. After a chase by some Corton beachmen in a boat, she was eventually captured – about a mile from the shore – and with some difficulty, got into the boat and taken back to Lowestoft, where she was temporarily housed in the Suffolk Hotel stables.

Another hind called *Melton* also gave a good run, and eventually, after a chase covering, on the map, at least twenty-five miles, had to be left out near Riddlesworth Hall. At one time followers were so exhausted due to the pace of the hunt that the hounds were whipped off the trail for a welcome five minutes' breather.

On another occasion about this time a havier gave the hunt an extremely good run, for after being uncarted near Yaxham at about 12.30 it was past three o'clock before the animal was eventually taken near Drayton after making a fourteen-mile point.

During the three seasons the pack was being hunted by the 7th Dragoon Guards, some excellent sport was enjoyed, the best run lasting no less than two hours thirty minutes after an outlying hind which had been located in a copse near Pulham St Mary, before hounds had to be whipped off with the deer still at liberty.

On a different occasion another outlying hind was run for some thirty-five miles following a meet at Hardwick, before being finally taken in a pond near Pulham.

There seem to have been a number of outlying deer about, for on several other occasions the 7th Dragoon Guards Staghounds went after such quarry. A stag near Hempnall, after a run lasting four and a half hours, had to be left out again on the marshes near Mettingham, whilst on the last meet of the 1898 season a young stag which had been left out the previous week near Thorpe Woods, had again to be left out after a two and a half hour run.

Hounds, apparently, were going to try on the following day to take this stag, but meantime the animal had wandered home on its own accord and had been safely housed. With the capture of this animal only one outlier had been left for the 7th Hussars (the regiment which relieved them) to capture the following season.

During the present century some great runs have been given by both stags and hinds. One of the longest runs given by a stag was that by *Sir Paignton* in 1909, which after being enlarged proceeded to treat his followers to an eighteen-mile point before being taken near Southolt. The run lasted two hours forty minutes, and the actual distance covered was estimated at over thirty miles. During the run *Sir Paignton* had time to soil in the river at Syleham, which seemed to revive his strength for he carried on for another hour and a half. Another good stag was *Peter*, who, on 28 February 1907, after being uncarted at Tibenham, gave the pack a fifteen mile point before being taken near Kirkstead church. *Hannibal*, however, who was a most promising stag, came to a sticky end, destroying himself in a conservatory at Diss.

One of the finest deer to evade capture by the Norwich Staghounds was a hind called *Visitor* which, on 10 December 1900 after a long run, managed to get lost in the marshes near Harford. On 11 February 1901 an attempt seems to have been made to catch this deer, but once again, after a really good run – a point of twenty-five miles – hounds had to be whipped off as there was 'danger of killing her by over-running'.[98]

Lady Ethel also seems to have given the hunt several very good runs about this time, including one lasting four hours and ten minutes, the run passing through sixteen parishes. On another occasion in 1904 *Lady Ethel* gave a twenty-mile point before being taken at Hargham.

One of the best hunts since the war took place in 1949 following a meet at Gissing Crown. A deer had been harboured in the grounds of Burston Hall, and after being roused by hounds, she took a line via Heywood and the Manor Farm almost to the Long Row. Here the deer turned right-handed, and after crossing the main Norwich to Ipswich railway by way of the cattle arch, she took hounds to Wacton Common, then on to French's Farm and Pulham North Green, and almost to Gawdy Hall where she doubled back in the direction of Pulham North Green. By this time hounds had been following for two hours forty minutes so it was decided to leave her out. The going had been very heavy owing to recent frosts and rain.

During the early part of 1963 the Norwich Staghounds gave up hunting the carted deer in favour of drag and fox, with the intention of eventually converting the pack into foxhounds.

Thus ended a chapter in Norfolk's sporting history which is never likely to be re-opened, for there is growing public opinion against any form of deer hunting. During the past 180 years, over twenty-five different named packs of staghounds – some private, some subscription – have operated in the county, though on several occasions, such as when the cavalry regiments looked after the hounds, the pack has been the same but with a different title.

Long before the first record of any organized deer hunting in East Anglia, it was the practice to hunt deer in some of the many parks in the district. Thus on 29 August 1677, some hunting took place in Euston Park, Suffolk, during which 'a very fat buck' was killed. At that time there were almost a thousand red and fallow deer in the park, but they have long disappeared.[174]

As already mentioned, as early as the eighteenth century a pack of staghounds was being maintained by Lord Orford for hunting in East Anglia. The third Earl of Orford (George Walpole) was quite a character for he used to drive around Newmarket in a phaeton or curricle drawn by four red deer stags instead of horses. One day, in about 1750, when he was out he met a pack of hounds which forthwith hunted him from Bury Hill, outside Newmarket, to the doors of the Ram Inn – now the Rutland Arms – where the stags were usually stabled. Luckily an ostler had the presence of mind to slam the doors on the noses of the pack. It appears that Lord Orford's grooms and outriders were unable to stop the stags and the huntsman could not check his hounds. Lord Orford no doubt obtained his red deer from his park at Houghton in Norfolk.

This same Lord Orford – the 'mad Earl' – once made a match with Lord Rockingham to race five turkeys against five geese from Norwich to London in 1756. The geese won because the turkeys would fly up to roost! Lord Orford died at Houghton on 5 December 1791.

Some seventy years later Mr (later Sir) E Walter Greene's Staghounds were hunting the carted deer in west Suffolk, but when in 1870 Mr Greene took over the county pack of foxhounds, the staghound pack was temporarily suspended. However, in 1889 Sir Walter reinstated the staghounds and hunted hounds two days a week, until handing over the pack and deer to Mr F Riley-Smith in 1900. In 1904 Mr Riley-Smith was succeeded by Mr Eugene Wells, who was already hunting a pack of foxhounds, so was only able to hunt the staghound pack one day per week. In 1906 Mr Wells gave up both packs and was succeeded in the mastership of the staghounds by WP Burton, under whose mastership the pack later became known as the West Suffolk Staghounds. In 1910 Sir William Burton (formerly W Burton) made many unsuccessful attempts to take an outlier near Thetford, a beast which had always succeeded in beating hounds by swimming the river into Norfolk. A joint day was therefore arranged with the Norwich Staghounds which resulted in the elusive deer finally being captured. On this occasion the Norwich pack waited on the Norfolk side of the Little Ouse whilst the West Suffolk, after an early start, found the stag which made its customary point to cross the river following which the Norwich pack took over. This manoeuvre resulted in the deer recrossing the river when the chase was again taken up by the West Suffolk, who proceeded to push him along at a good pace until being finally taken about 12.30 pm after a hunt that had lasted close on six and a half hours. In 1911 Sir William was joined in the mastership by Mr P Middleditch, the pack continuing to be a private one until its disbandment during the First World War.

Deer hunting also figured prominently in the past sporting history of Essex, most of which took place in the Epping Forest district.

In the *Forest of Essex* by Fisher, we read that the kings of England had hunted in Epping Forest since Edward the Confessor's time and perhaps earlier. Queen Elizabeth had a hunting lodge there, and the story goes that she had her horse led up the shallow staircase so that she could mount it outside her door.[74]

James I was very indignant at the lax way in which the forest laws were enforced in this area, and spoke his mind about the matter. During the Civil Wars and the Commonwealth, the deer were so badly treated and poaching carried on so extensively, that in 1660 a sum of £1000 was voted to be expended on re-stocking the forest. James was an enthusiast of the sport, and Sir John Bramston of Skreens, tells of the King's hunting in his *Autobiography*. The Royal Buckhounds (*page 238*) hunted here early in the eighteenth century; in 1729 they killed thirteen stags in Epping Forest, and in 1730, nine.

As long ago as 1740 regular hunting was taking place in Epping Forest when it was the practice to catch up some of the red deer in the forest for hunting. The red deer, however, unless by accident, were never killed. Nevertheless it was the custom to hunt the fallow deer at times, and when buck hunting took place the deer was often killed. The red deer, when caught up, were kept at Loughton Bridge where the Epping Hunt kennels were also located. To take the deer a net (kept at Loughton Bridge for the purpose, and about a mile long) was fixed from the milestone in the forest down to Monk Wood and the deer driven up from Monk Wood into the net. Two or three were then selected and the rest, with the young ones, set at liberty. A cart for the purpose was in readiness, and the deer caught were placed in it to be taken to Loughton Bridge where they were kept in the paddock until required.

Before this pack became known as the Epping Hunt, the deer were hunted by a pack which is supposed to have been kept at Tilney House by Earl Tilney, and to have been known as the Tilney Hounds. The Earl died in 1784, but some time before that event occurred the pack had been taken over by some of the sport-loving enthusiasts from London.[27]

The Epping Hunt probably reached its height under the mastership of the two Mellish's – Joseph, who was killed by a highwayman in 1798 and William who, as MP for Essex, hunted both red and fallow deer. William Mellish, a nephew of Joseph, continued to hunt the pack until about 1806 or 1807, when Lord Middleton bought them and sent them up to Yorkshire, with their huntsman William Cranston. The pack at this time had consisted of about thirty-two couple.[27] This, however, was not the total end of deer hunting in Epping Forest.

Long before the Epping Hunt came into being it had been the practice for the citizens of London to accompany the monarch on an annual hunt in the forest – a hunt which is best remembered by the comic verses of Tom D'Urfey and Thomas Hood, and the caricatures of George Cruickshank. When this festive occasion was first promulgated is not very certain, but PJ Perceval thought that the story which credits the founding of the hunt to Richard I 'is more picturesque than accurate'. 'The statement which declares that the Easter hunt in Essex "commenced in the year 1226" by favour of Henry the Third has more to recommend it, but cannot at present be substantiated.'[155]

Among the monarchs who patronized the Common Hunt was quite possibly George I, for one Humphrey Parsons, twice Lord Mayor of

FOREST OF ESSEX.

Otherwise called,

Foreſt of Waltham.

Names of Perſons licenſed to HUNT, SHOOT, and FISH, within the Foreſt.

NAMES	RESIDENCE	DATE OF LICENCE
WILLIAM LEVERTON, Eſq.	*Lincoln's-Inn Fields.*	—
THOMAS COPE, Eſq.	*Bond-Lane, London.*	—
P. TEMPLEMAN, Eſq.	*Walthamstow*	20th January - 1800.
WESTGARTH SNAITH, Eſq.	*Woodford, Essex*	19th November 1800.
JAMES GASCOIGN, Eſq.	*Loughton*	10th September 1800.
WILLIAM WILSON, Eſq.	*Mile-End*	10th September 1800.
RICHARD WILSON, Eſq.	*Lincoln's-Inn Fields*	10th September 1800.
JOHN WILKINS, Eſq.	*Chigwell-Row*	18th November 1800.
FRANCIS HENRY TAYLOR, Eſq.	*Great Marlbro'-Street,*	10th September 1800.
JAMES STEERS, Eſq.	*Tottenham*	14th November 1801.
JOHN MAITLAND, Eſq.	*Woodford Hall,* {(now CHIEF FORESTER of West Heynault Walk.)}	—
The DUKE of BOURBON		21st April - - - 1808.
LOUIS JOS. DE BOURBON, Prince De Condé		21st April - - - 1808.
SOLOMON PEELE, Eſq.		10th September 1800.
HENRY BURCHALL, Eſq.	*Walthamstow*	29th August - 1807.
WILLIAM BANBURY, Eſq.	*Copthall-Green*	12th March - - 1810.
THOMAS FELLOWS, Eſq.	*Aldersgate-Street*	December - - 1811.

THE above Licences do not allow the Parties the liberty of hunting or ſhooting *Deer or Fares.*—The Licences allow SPORTING from 1st September to 12th February in each Year.

The Party licenſed is, before Hunting, Shooting, or Fiſhing, to *acquaint the Keeper of the Walk,* where he intends to Hunt, Shoot, or Fiſh; and he is to uſe the liberty given *with fitting moderation:*—Only *one Perſon* is allowed to be *in company* with each Perſon licenſed.

All the foregoing Licences have been *enrolled* at Courts of Attachment holden for the Forest; and no other Licences are to be conſidered as valid, until they ſhall be ſo enrolled.

The Underkeepers are to take care that the above Regulations are duly attended to, and to report every Treſpaſs by any unlicenſed or unauthorized Perſon, in Hunting, Shooting, or Fiſhing, to the Steward of the Forest Courts, at his Office, in East Heynault Lodge.

By Order of the Lord Warden of the Forest.

Steward's Office,
East Heynault Lodge,
August 1812.

T. E. TOMLINS,
Steward.

Printed by Luke Hansard & Sons, near Lincoln's-Inn-Fields, London.

Notice posted in the forest of Waltham in 1812, giving a list of persons licensed to hunt, shoot and fish within the forest

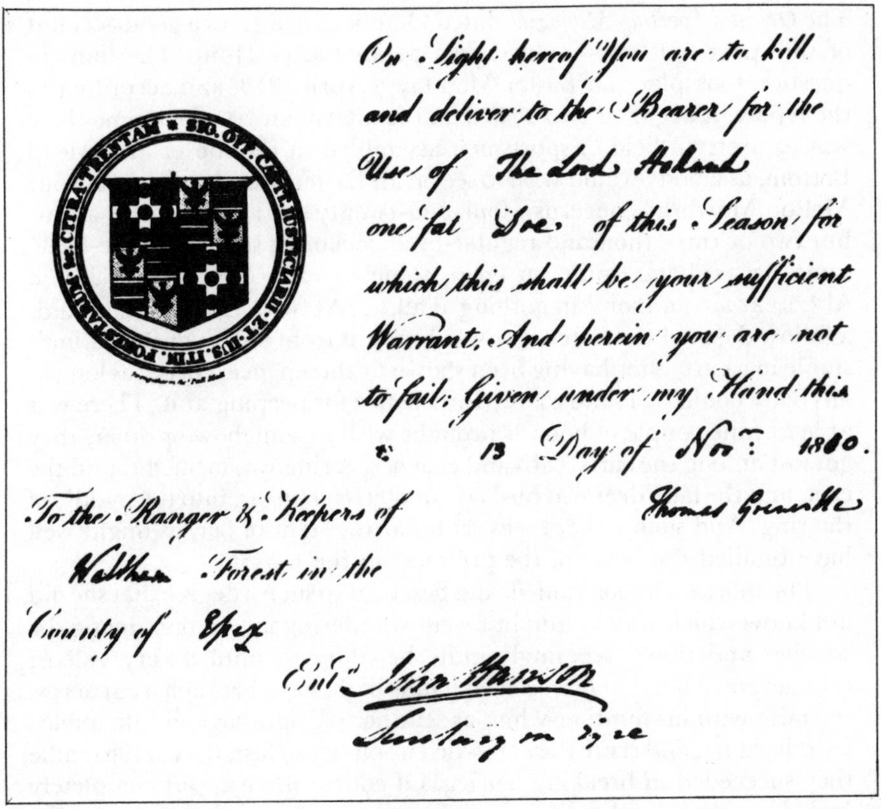

On Sight hereof You are to kill and deliver to the Bearer for the Use of The Lord Holland one fat Doe of this Season for which this shall be your sufficient Warrant. And herein you are not to fail; Given under my Hand this 13 Day of Novr 1810.

Thomas Grenville

To the Ranger & Keepers of Waltham Forest in the County of Essex

Entd John Hanson
Secretary in Eyre

Licence issued to the Ranger of Waltham Forest in 1810 ordering him to kill a doe and deliver same to the Lord Holland

London, and thus an *ex officio* Master of this picturesque hunt, was wont to present himself at Windsor for an occasional day with the royal pack and, unless things were very different from what they subsequently became, he cannot have failed to suggest to the monarch that, if he wanted to see how the thing should really be done, he should come down Epping Way.[166]

An old number of *The Sporting Times*, however, bearing a date in the early part of the last century, suggested that in Lord Tilney's time his hounds used to be spoken of as 'The Ladies' Hunt' because of the numbers of the fair sex of the neighbourhood who followed it, and that a meet took place annually on Easter Monday, generally at Fencepiece, near Hainault Forest, with a dinner and ball to follow.

On 27 March 1807 the following notice appeared in *The Times* proclaiming the continuance of this ancient hunt.

Epping Forest – Stag Hunting
The public are informed that there will be a Deer turned out, at the usual place on Easter Monday next, March the 30th. by the Authority of the Ranger of the Forest.

The *Oriental Sporting Magazine* dated October 1828 gives a good account of the sport that one could expect at an Easter Hunt. The hunt in question took place on Easter Monday 7 April 1828, and according to the report, it began at two o'clock in the afternoon 'at which time there was as pretty a field of sportsmen assembled at the top of Fair Mead Bottom, as a body would wish to see on an Easter Monday. None of your Melton Mowbray concerns – four-and-twenty scarlet coats all in a row; but two or three thousand regular-bred cockneys; some on horse-back, some on ass-back, some on *drags*, some in *rattlers*, some in Captain Abbott's *cabs*, and some in nothing at all. . . . At two o'clock, as aforesaid, a fallow deer (of the softer sex) was brought from old Tom Rounding's stable in a cart, after having been shown at threepence a peep, as long as anybody could be found to pay threepence for peeping at it. There was at least nine couple of hounds brought with it; somehow or other, they got lost among the carts, cabs and coaches. A ring was formed round the cart, and the lady deer was pushed out of it, *vis et armis*, into the middle of the ring. And such a shout was set up at the sight of her, as might well have quailed the heart of the proudest in the Forest.

'The sportsmen soon rallied, and beset her to such a degree that she did not know which way to run; but went wandering in and out among the coaches and things seemingly quite bewildered, until a very valiant cockney, on a horse at least eleven hands high, gave her such a cut across the nose with his hunting-whip, as sent her off right an end into a fold-yard hard by, and there they crowded upon her so fast, that in the scuffle they succeeded in breaking her leg. Of course she was put completely *hors de combat*, as the French say, and no doubt she was speedily converted into venison, for they took her away in the cart more dead than alive.

'It was now after three o'clock, and as the sportsmen had not had sport enough, the managers gave notice that they would bring them another deer. Accordingly they went back to old Tom Rounding's, and about four o'clock they brought down another – a more sprightly one than the first; and one that seemed to have been "trained up in the way he should go"; for he was no sooner out of the cart than away he went with a bit of a circumbendibus towards old Tom Rounding's stable again. Everybody – except the hounds – followed him at the top of their speed; but he would have got safe into the stable nevertheless, if some two or three hundred of them had not faced him, by a short cut; which he perceiving, he very unfairly ran upto his knees in a horse-pond. Though some two or three of the foremost tumbled in after him, he did not take the least notice of them. A consultation was then held as to what should be done with him; and at last, by general agreement, it was settled that he should have another start. So the managers got him out of the horse-pond at last, and he ran about in the wood a good deal, until everybody was very hot, and then he was lost.'

The Easter Hunt was probably wound up about 1865 when,

according to Perceval 'but one "pink" put in an appearance in keeping with the woebegone condition of the field, the deer was feeble with age'.[155]

This, however, did not entirely see the end of stag hunting in Essex for the Essex Staghounds continued to hunt the carted deer until about 1926 (*see page 220*).

A few years after William Mellish had sold his hounds (*c.* 1806) a pack of staghounds was again in residence at the old kennels at Wanstead House, their Master being Mr Tilney Long Wellesley, a nephew of the 'Iron Duke' who had become their owner by his marriage with the heiress of the last Lord Tilney. But the extravagance of Mr Wellesley's *menage* was too great to last. He kept forty or fifty horses, arrayed his hunt servants in Lincoln green, scattered *largesse* of golden sovereigns right and left, and generally spent his money so freely that, although his rent-roll in Essex alone was upwards of £70,000 a year, and despite the fact that he shortly became Earl of Mornington and head of the family, before ten years had passed he had to fly secretly and by night, in an open boat down the Thames, to escape his creditors. His wife died from the effects of worry and anxiety.[27]

When Mr Wellesley's hounds were sold, Tom Rounding, who is supposed to have been his huntsman, bought a few couple and continued to hunt deer with them. However, by the beginning of the nineteenth century the number of wild red deer in the forest was steadily diminishing, until in 1820 orders were given for the remaining deer to be caught up and transferred to Windsor Park. This was carried out as far as practicable and the few that escaped the toils soon fell victims to poachers until only one stag remained. This unfortunate animal was subsequently hunted by Tom Rounding and his hounds, and after a great run was finally killed at West Ham. Just exactly when this took place is not recorded, but it was probably the beast which was roused at Hainault Forest and taken at Plaistow on 20 October 1827. So passed away the last of the indigenous red deer of Essex – animals which Camden had praised as being the largest and fattest in the kingdom.

Before the transfer of the deer to Windsor took place, it appears that an attempt was made to revive the Epping Forest Staghounds under the mastership of John Conyers, who was also Master of the Essex Foxhounds. At Wallsgrove House, Lt.-Col. Buxton once told me that he had a print by Wolstenholme dated 1816 which was inscribed Epping Forest Staghounds and depicted a good red deer stag being bayed in what appears to be Cuckoo Pits pond, near Fairmead. There is, however, considerable confusion over the various packs of staghounds that have operated in the forest, and it seems probable that at various dates two packs overlapped – one a 'snob pack' such as would be under the mastership of John Conyers, and the other a Common Hunt, under the control of such men as Tom Rounding.[214]

This should have been the end of the red deer in Epping Forest but about 1883 an effort was made to re-establish the species by enlarging a stag and two hinds in the forest. It was an unhappy venture for the deer proved so mischievous that within a very short time they all had to be destroyed. Prior to their reintroduction taking place, however, Perceval records that a six-year-old red deer was hunted in the forest in 1858, and says that its head 'was afterwards presented to the Corporation of London by Colonel Palmer, the oldest of the verderers of the forest at that time.' The head was afterwards 'placed in the Guildhall on a tablet which bears an explanatory inscription'. Perceval believed that this stag had been kept in a paddock and enlarged for the occasion, which seems to have been a very special one, for Lord Brougham and some of the city aldermen were in attendance.[155]

Shortly after Tom Rounding had killed the last red deer at West Ham, Mr Sheffield Neave, assisted by Messrs Tufnell and Drummond, began to hunt the carted deer. This pack, which was kennelled at Myles's, was formed in 1831 and subsequently became known as the Essex Staghounds (*see page 220*). Apart from two short breaks between 1844–5 and 1847–50, this pack continued to hunt the carted deer in Essex until it was finally disbanded in 1926. During the period 1911 to 1914 the pack was frequently referred to as the Essex Farmers, the kennels and deer paddocks being at Writtle. Whether any deer hunting took place in Essex during the years 1844–5 is not recorded, but for part of the time between 1847 and 1850 it seems that two private scratch packs were kept for stag hunting in Essex – one owned by James Parker and the other by Tommy Crooks, who was a butcher by trade, in Chelmsford.

The country of the Essex Staghounds was, for the most part, duplicated by the Essex Foxhounds, and was nearly all plough. The deer, during the mastership of Theodore Christy (1911–14), were obtained mainly from Lord Brownlow of Ashridge Park, but eight also came from Lord Petre's park at Thorndon in Essex. Describing the capture of the latter, Christy stated: 'This was a Field day, with 25 of us mounted and 70 men off the Estate with long nets about 10ft high into which we galloped the deer.

'The three other Masters of Staghounds amongst whom the catch was divided were Sir John Thursby (New Forest), Colonel McTaggart (Surrey) and Major Shackle (Berks and Bucks).

'This was great fun for the majority of those taking part as it lasted two days. I say this because personally I had had bad luck at the very first round-up. Having vaulted off my horse at the end of a gallop, and whilst holding down one deer, another sprang at the nets and fell on top of me, cracking a rib. I viewed the rest of the sport from the floor, not being able to attend the second day.'[48]

The usual complement in the deer paddocks at Writtle was about sixteen head of deer and, as each animal was only hunted twice in a whole season, they had a fairly easy time of it. The deer were treated exactly like cattle and sheep, being given hay, corn, and chaff and, when available, chestnuts and acorns.

In Essex, Christy wrote that, 'the relations between hunting men and farmers were of the friendliest character, and some of the best men who followed the fox and stag were local farmers'. Christy thought that the farmers 'preferred stag hunting to fox hunting so far as their crops and fences were concerned, even those not keen on the sport regarded stag hunting as the lesser of two evils, and for these reasons. In the first place there were fewer riders in a staghunt, and in the second, we did not go all in a line but each took his own line, thus being able to avoid any jump which might cause damage to the farmer'.[48]

Apart from local members, the Essex Staghounds always held a great attraction for sportsmen living in London, and many business men thought nothing of catching an early morning train in order to have a day's sport with this pack.

All the fun of hunting the stag did not, however, end with the chase, and many a gay evening was spent with wine and song to round off the day's sport. At such functions, no doubt, W Blyth the 'Deermaster' took a leading part, for he was a great character and local wit. He was famous for his anecdotes – which he always referred to as 'nannygoats' – and Christy mentions a number of them. On one occasion Blyth was seen at a meet wearing a set of false teeth which had cost him no small sum of money to buy. The next day it was observed that he was not wearing them, and on being asked why, replied 'I left them in the drawer, because they fitted the drawer better than my mouth'.

On another occasion Blyth, a staunch churchman, was asked for a subscription by a local parson who was renowned for his long and dreary sermons. When told that the money was being collected to combat dry rot in the roof of the church, Blyth replied 'Oh, that's news to me. But I always knew there was dry rot in the pulpit'.[48]

One of the best runs enjoyed by the Essex Staghounds was after a deer enlarged near Chelmsford, which took the pack thirty miles before being taken in the front room of a cottage at Widford, in Hertfordshire. Another good run was after a deer uncarted in the Roothings, and after several detours, the hind took the pack through Epping and across to Copt Hall before being finally taken at Beech Hill near Loughton.

One of the most elusive hinds the hunt owned was named *De Wet* after the celebrated Boer General. Many exciting runs did this remarkable deer give, invariably taking the same line of country. For a period of twelve months she was found many times only to be lost again. Indeed she was as tantalizing as De Wet was to the British troops in South Africa.[48]

Hinds – at any rate during the closing years of the pack's existence – were the usual quarry. When the pack was disbanded the deer, to the number of fifteen, were shipped to Ireland for use by the Ward Union Hunt.[214]

East Anglia has always been rich in deer parks, and these, no doubt, provided a convenient source of replacement for any hunt requiring a deer. Escapes, also, provided outliers so there was never any shortage of deer, be it red deer or fallow deer, though the former has been the principal quarry of the hunts. According to Evelyn Shirley in 1867 there were nine deer parks in Norfolk, fourteen in Suffolk and eleven in Essex – a total of thirty-four parks.[174] By the close of the century the number was about three less, for Whitaker, in his survey for these three counties gave Norfolk ten parks, Suffolk eleven and Essex ten.[203] Fallow deer were present in all these thirty-one parks but only nine (Blickling, Melton Constable and Sandringham in Norfolk; Helmingham and Somerleyton in Suffolk, and Easton, Hatfield, Thorndon and Weald in Essex) had red deer as well. By 1950 the number of parks in these three counties had been reduced to ten, of which three held red deer – Melton Constable and Winfarthing in Norfolk, and Helmingham in Suffolk. At that date only the Norwich Staghounds were still hunting the carted deer, but thirteen years later this pack had also discontinued the practice.

Chapter IV
Deer Hunting in the North of England

Although the north of England is one of the few areas in England where the indigenous red and roe deer have survived, comparatively few packs of staghounds have been kept, the majority of which have operated in Lancashire.

During the sixteenth and seventeenth centuries Lancashire was described as being one of the finest hunting centres extant. The chase of the deer at this period was, however, carried out by one or two hounds which were used to drive the quarry up to a given point where the hunter with his gun or bow was waiting in concealment so as to shoot it when it passed.

During this time there was a number of forests in Lancashire and in the adjacent parts of the West Riding of Yorkshire, and these included the forests of Wyresdale and Quernmore, which lay near Lancaster; West Derby or Derbyshire Forest, which lay near Liverpool; the forests of Accrington and Rossendale and the extensive forest of Blackburnshire, which covered much of central Lancashire. By the nineteenth century, apart from the deer which still remained in the Furness district and a few park escapees elsewhere, all the deer in Lancashire's more central forests had been exterminated. One of the areas where a few feral deer in the form of fallow still remained was south-west Lancashire, in the area lying south of the Ribble and north of the Mersey. It was in this district that the Gerard Staghounds hunted the feral fallow buck throughout most of the last century and early years of the present one until the First World War caused the pack to be disbanded (*see page 221*). These fallow, which were of the black variety, undoubtedly escaped originally from one or more of the numerous parks that then existed in south Lancashire, which during the early part of the last century included Latham and Knowsley, the former being stocked, in 1867, with about 120 fallow deer and the latter with some 300 fallow and as many red deer.[174]

One of the best runs of the Gerard Staghounds took place on 23 February 1900. A buck was found in Shevington and after taking a line through Wrightington, Parbold and Euxton, he was finally killed in front of Worden Hall, the run lasting two hours and twenty minutes.

At the beginning of the present century, whilst the Gerard Staghounds were hunting both fallow deer and fox south of the Ribble, both fallow deer and Japanese sika deer were being hunted by the

Ribblesdale Buckhounds a few miles away in the Gisburn/Bolton-by-Bowland district.

The idea of starting the Ribblesdale Buckhounds seems to have stemmed from some very good sport which the Pendle Forest Harriers had, about the turn of the century, after some carted stags which had been supplied by a Mr Peebles who was then resident in the district, and which were hunted on byedays as an alternative to the hare. After a few years, however, Mr Peebles left the district and with his departure hunting the carted deer ceased. However, having once tasted the deer hunt, there seemed to be such a demand for this form of hunting that Lord Ribblesdale, in October 1906 invited all landowners, tenant farmers and Masters of packs in the district, and indeed anyone who might be interested, to attend a meeting at Gisburn so that the matter could be thoroughly discussed.

As a result of this meeting, the Ribblesdale Buckhounds were formed with Lord Ribblesdale and Peter Ormrod as Joint Masters, the latter carrying the horn. The country over which the Buckhounds operated extended to some 375 square miles, most of which was open grassland and a little moorland, the whole area being bounded by such towns as Preston, Clitheroe and Garstang in Lancashire, and Settle and Skipton in Yorkshire. Hounds were principally a cross between a foxhound and a Kerry bitch which produced a black and tan dog hound of about 24in. to 25in. high at the shoulder, the bitches being an inch or two smaller.

Within a year of the formation of the Ribblesdale Buckhounds, considerable friction developed between that hunt and the Pendle Forest Harriers on whose country the former pack primarily operated. The main trouble arose over clashing of hunt fixtures and as a result a letter was received by the Secretary of the Pendle Forest from Lord Ribblesdale in September 1907 requesting that since deer hunting took place only on three days per month between 20 November and 28 February, two of these meets should be held at fortnightly intervals on Saturdays and the other on one Wednesday in each month. This request did not receive a favourable reception from the Pendle Forest who considered that the loss of two Saturday meets each month would seriously interfere with their own hunting activity, and could not be agreed to.

Correspondence and meetings between officials of the two hunts continued for over two years without any agreement or compromise being reached. Eventually, on 18 October 1909, at a meeting of members of the Pendle Forest Harriers held at the Old Bull Hotel, Blackburn, the secretary read a letter from Lord Ribblesdale dated 11 October, closing the Gisburn estate entirely to the hunt, and as this included the country around Paythorne and Newsholme, which was their best hunting country, its loss to the Pendle Forest Harriers was extremely serious. Moreover, it was suggested that Lord Ribblesdale might allow another pack, prepared to fall in with his wishes, to hunt this particular country.

Eventually reason prevailed, and by the time the 1910 hunting season commenced, the two hunts were able to hunt amicably together. While discussions were in progress it was suggested at a meeting held in Blackburn on 9 January 1910 that in that part of the country where hares were in short supply, the Pendle Forest might hunt the occasional carted deer, or perhaps have a drag. The former resolution was accepted, but in view of subsequent reconcilliation between the hunt and Lord Ribblesdale, was never implemented. For the next nine years, until the hunt was disbanded in 1919, the Ribblesdale Buckhounds had good sport after both sika and black fallow deer, the majority of which had been liberated from Peter Ormrod's estate at Wyresdale Park, near Garstang. At first black fallow deer were liberated for the purpose of stocking the country, but these were shortly replaced with Japanese sika deer which gave the hunt better runs. Initially the sika deer were placed in a small deer park at Bolton-by-Bowland and although the park deer were never hunted their calves were turned out each year, and by this means feral deer were established in the surrounding country. At Bolton-by-Bowland the deer were in the charge of John Draper, who also acted as harbourer on hunting days.

At the outset, from his past experience in hunting the carted fallow deer at Wyresdale, Mr Ormrod warned his field that they must not expect the highest class of sport until about the third year, by which time there would be sufficient warrantable deer in the district that had been bred in the wild, and any animals that had previously been used for carted deer hunting, killed off. During the first season (1906–7) the Ribblesdale Buckhounds killed twelve fallow (7 bucks and 5 does) and five sika deer (4 stags and 1 hind, and although in the following season the number killed had dropped to eleven, consisting of seven fallow (4 bucks and 3 does) and four sika (3 stags and 1 hind) the 1908–9 season saw no fewer than thirty-one deer brought back to the larder. These consisted of twenty fallow deer (17 bucks and 3 does) and eleven sika stags, no hinds being killed that season. By 1910 there were sufficient wild deer in the district for the pack, now numbering forty couple, to hunt twice a week during the season. As is the practice when hunting red deer on Exmoor, Mr Ormrod found it necessary in many instances to use tufters first to get his stag away from the covert, the tufters being handled by Charles Taylor who was first whipper-in.

Prior to the formation of the Ribblesdale Buckhounds, Peter Ormrod had hunted the carted deer from his home at Wyresdale Park, some deer having been obtained in May 1899 from Barningham Park, near Barnard Castle, following the death of its owner Sir Frederick A. Millbank. At one time Barningham Park held a fair stock of red deer but by 1892 only five stags and two hinds remained.

Shortly after the formation of the Barnstaple Staghounds in 1901 Peter Ormrod moved his pack for a short time, to Barnstaple, so as to gain some experience in hunting the wild red deer in north Devon – an experience that stood him in good stead when, five years later, he took over the mastership of the Ribblesdale Buckhounds.

In the extreme north of Lancashire, but mostly in southern Westmorland, now Cumbria – the Oxenholme Staghounds – subsequently to be called the Lunesdale and Oxenholme Staghounds – hunted both carted deer and the wild deer for just over fifty years before being disbanded during the Second World War (*see page 225*).

The Oxenholme pack, which started as harriers, changed in 1888 to hunt stag as well, the first red deer being enlarged at Low Bleaze on 9 February of that year. For the next seven years deer and hare were hunted on alternate days, but in November 1894, the latter were abandoned and the career of the Oxenholme Staghounds really commenced.

The deer for hunting were kept in some paddocks at Oxenholme, and according to the Oxenholme *Deer Account* of 1889, the first animals were obtained from Gowbarrow Park near Ullswater (two), and from the Surrey Staghounds (two), for which £5 each was paid. During the next twelve years there were a number of further purchases of both stags and hinds and by 1902 the number of deer in the paddock was just over twenty. In the majority of cases no record has been kept as to the source of these deer, but two hinds, supplied in 1894, came from Lord Henry Bentinck – a brother of the Duke of Portland – so they probably came from Welbeck Park in Nottinghamshire. At first both stags and hinds were hunted, but within a year or two the running deer consisted almost entirely of haviers, as it was found that the hinds were more apt to hurt themselves, and the stags, at times, were sulky and would not run.

During the inter-war years the hunt, which was now known as the Lunesdale and Oxenholme Staghounds, obtained further deer, to the number of forty-one hinds, from Raby Castle Park (Durham). By this time, 'there were,' wrote the late Major J W Cropper, 'enough deer scattered over the area to enable the Staghounds to hunt two days a week after wild deer – but in order to increase the numbers, about twelve hinds were let out'. There is no doubt, therefore, that by 1939 the deer of south Westmorland had a fair percentage of park blood in them.[214]

During the Second World War years hunting ceased and the wild deer in the district were, in consequence, much reduced by shooting and even snaring. Thus, when hostilities ceased, there were insufficient deer in south Westmorland to make it worthwhile to recommence deer hunting, so the last pack of hounds to hunt the deer in the north of England faded from the scene.

During its existence, however, some great runs after both the carted animal and the wild deer were enjoyed by the hunt followers. *Mabel* was the first great deer, and according to Major Cropper 'she ran for seven seasons with never a scratch, and at last the Master felt she had earned her rest, and sent her back to Gowbarrow Fell, whence she came'.

Berks and Bucks Farmers' Staghounds.

POINT-TO-POINT RACES

"Highway."

Chairman:—LORD DESBOROUGH, K.C.V.O.

WINE:

Roper Freres.

1904.

—

Whiskey

—

Ale

—

Minerals, Etc.

—

Cigars

Menu.

Mayonnaise of Salmon
Roast Beef. Pressed Beef.
Ham. Ox Tongue.
Galantine of Veal.
Roast Lamb. Mint Sauce.
Veal and Ham Pies.
Pigeon Pies.
Hot New Potatoes. Salad.
Sweets.
Rhubarb Tart. Custards. Jellies.
Blancmanges.
Fancy Pastry.
Rolls. Butter. Cheese.

HEYWOOD FARM,
April 11th, 1911.

SPINDLER & SONS,
Caterers.

7 Dinner Menu of the Berks and Bucks Farmers' Staghounds, 1911

8 *Above opposite* The Norwich Staghounds baying a hind. From the original painting by Lionel Edwards

9 *Below opposite* A wounded stag is pulled down by a couple of deerhounds. From the original painting by Richard Ansdell

5 *Left* Meet of the Berks and Bucks Staghounds at Taplow Court, 1910

6 *Above* Hunting with the Berks and Bucks Staghounds, 1910

4 Joint Masters of the Berks and Bucks Staghounds 1907–14: F.W. Headington and A.H. Headington

2 Taking the deer in water – as illustrated by an old picture of carted deer hunting

3 *Jim Crow* in the deer cart of the Warnham Staghounds

1 Queen Elizabeth I was a keen hunter; in this woodcut she is being offered the hunting knife by her huntsman, with which to make the ceremonial incision at the kill

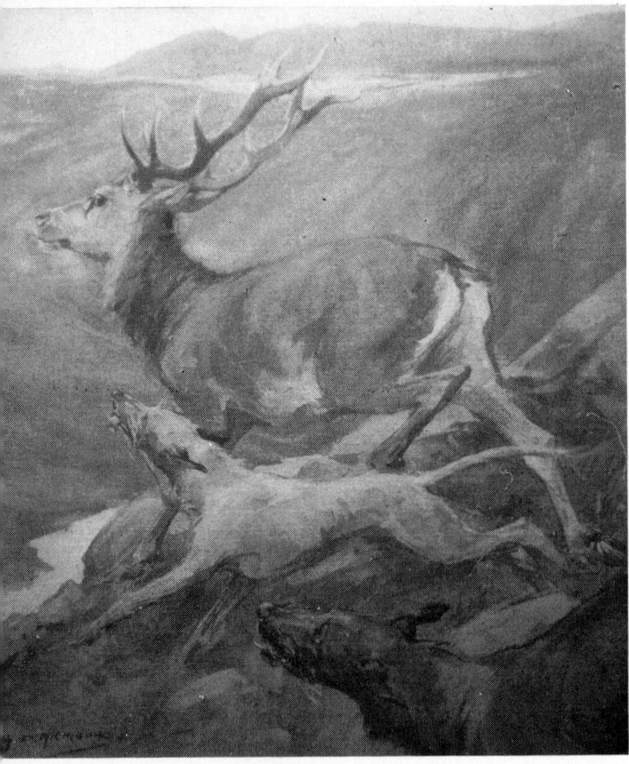

10 *Above* A deerstalker of the nineteenth century taking a downhill shot

11 In former times the deerhound was used extensively to either course a 'cold' stag or to bring down a wounded beast. From the original painting by G.D. Armour

Lion was another great deer: 'In the spring of 1897 he discovered a brilliant line between Dallam Tower Park and the Covers at Endmoor, and ran back and forward several times, and never was caught till, on the last day of the season, he jumped into Levens Park, where he was left to spend the summer'. On a number of subsequent occasions *Lion* was caught, and although turned out in different parts of the country, as often as not he would take a line for the Lune and finish in Levens Park. Incidentally, Levens Park, which extends to about 175 acres, has never held red deer but only some black fallow deer a few of which have, from time to time, managed to escape.

One of the best hunts took place on 29 December 1896. The meet was at Hundhow, near to where an outlying deer had been harboured in the Side House Woods. Describing this epic hunt, Major CJ Cropper (1902) stated: 'He crossed the Kent at once, and, leaving Staveley on the right, crossed the hills to Windermere. He swam the lake above Bowness, while the hounds were taken round by ferry. They hit off the line on the far side, and continued the hunt through the hanging woods above the lake, and over the brow to Esthwaite. There he was seen, and a boat was procured and the deer captured as he was coming out on the Grizedale side.'[59]

On 16 March 1901 a meet was arranged at Middleton Hall for a hind which was known to be frequenting Barbon Fell. In due course she was found, and after crossing the Lune near Rigmaden, finally took the pack to Levens Park where she was left.

During the 1936–7 season, following a meet at Barbon, a stag was found in the Manor Wood which took hounds on a ten-mile point before standing at bay near Burton, during which it killed one hound. During the same season following a meet at Hutton Bridge, hounds hunted a hind and calf which after a short while divided, the calf running up to Lilly Mere tarn where it got stuck in some ice, resulting in a broken leg.

When the pack was first formed both stags and hinds were hunted, but by 1900 the quarry was almost exclusively haviers. However, during the inter-war years in addition to hunting wild deer of both sexes, the carted hind was also used.

Any account of the deer of south Westmorland would not be complete without reference to an exceptional stag that was hunted by hounds from Witherslack on 27 January 1927. Describing the hunt, Major J W Cropper wrote: 'He ran by Fell End, past the Derby Arms and into the Foulshaw Moss. We hurried round by Ulpha Farm, hearing hounds in the Moss on our way and we caught them just south of High Foulshaw Farm. They ran to the sands and we were able to get their heads and stop them, for we could see by slot marks that the stag had crossed over. The sands are impossible for horses, and it is many miles round the head of the bay, so we collected the pack and went back to Witherslack to try for a fresh animal.

'Next day I was rung up on the telephone and told that a big stag had been found drowned at the Sedgwick Gun Powder Works and was being sent to the kennels for the hounds to eat. The evening before a hound had been heard howling in the Mill Race, which had deep perpendicular concrete sides, and had been rescued only just in time to save him from drowning. The stag had not been found until the next morning.

'I was able to find the stag's slots,' Major Cropper continued, 'and to trace his course for some distance prior to where he met his death, as he had enormous feet and the ground was pretty soft. He had run right through Levens Park, evidently knowing where he could get over the park wall. Then he ran out at a place where there was a tree stump close against the wall. Then he ran north to a big copse wood that lies east of Sizergh Castle. Here his tracks became very involved, evidently he had been hunted round and round the wood by the one hound that had followed him, and had evidently been driven to the water in the head race of the mill. He got out of sight under a bridge, but when the mills were stopped the water rose and he could not get out up the concrete walls of the race and so was drowned.'[214]

The measurements of this outstanding head, which carried 16 points were as follows:

No. of points	*Length longest antler*	*Beam thickest antler*	*Inside span*
9 + 7 = 16	$39\frac{3}{4}$in. (101cm)	$5\frac{3}{4}$in. (14.6cm)	$32\frac{1}{4}$in. (81.9cm)

During the present century roe deer increased tremendously in the area hunted over by the Lunesdale and Oxenholme Staghounds, and during the 1930s many a run was spoilt by hounds being split. There were also a few wild sika deer in the Barbon/Middleton Fell area, the original deer having escaped from Rigmaden Park. On a number of occasions sika deer were hunted and during their last season in 1939, following a meet at Rigmaden Bridge the hunt enjoyed two runs after sika, one being accounted for.

Other packs of staghounds that operated in the north of England during the past century and a half were the Cheshire Staghounds which were being hunted by Mr Shakerley in the late 1830s, and two packs in Yorkshire, one Sir Clifford Constable's Staghounds which operated in the East Riding of Yorkshire from about 1839, and the Easingwold Staghounds. Little information is available about either of these Yorkshire packs except that after being in existence just over thirty years, Sir Clifford gave up his hounds in about 1870, the pack subsequently being bought by Messrs Rawle and Bovingdon and taken south to form the Berkhamsted Staghounds (*page 208*). In 1839 the pack was said to be bloodhounds.

Sir Clifford Constable, however, kept a deer park at his residence at Burton-Constable, which extended to about 290 acres and contained both red and fallow deer, there being, in 1867, about 160 of the former and 350 fallow deer of all colours.[174] Presumably, therefore, the quarry of Sir Clifford's pack was the carted deer, and probably red deer.

One of the longest recorded hunts took place about the beginning of the last century when a stag was turned out of Whinfield Park and hunted by the hounds of the Earl of Thanet, till, by fatigue, the whole pack was thrown out except two staunch hounds through the greater part of the day. The stag returned to the park from whence he had been turned out, but on leaping the wall, the final effort was too great, and he fell dead on landing.

One of the hounds followed the scent up to the wall, but he too died of exhaustion as did the other hound, some distance behind. The length of the chase could not be exactly ascertained, but as they had been seen at Red Kirks, near Annan in Scotland during the chase – a distance of about forty-six miles by road from Whinfield Park – it was estimated that the run could not have been less than seventy or eighty miles.[118]

In addition to hunting the red, fallow and sika deer, roe deer hunting with hounds was also practised for a short period during the last century in Durham. Describing this pack Mr G A Cowen informed me (*in litt*) that 'for a period of about eight to ten years in the late 1840s and early 1850s, Mr Richardson of Woodlands Hall, Consett, had a pack of hounds originally formed to hunt the roe deer in the large woodlands south of Castleside, known as Lord Bute's plantation. These were known as the Castleside Hounds but Mr Richardson soon found the roe was a poor quarry for his hounds and took to hunting local foxes.[214]

Chapter V
Deer Hunting in Ireland

So far as can be ascertained, hunting with hounds the *wild* deer – either fallow or red – has never been practised in Ireland, but there have, of course, been numerous occasions when some outlying deer have been hunted and taken by one or other of the packs that hunt the carted deer.

One of the earliest packs to hunt carted deer was the Garrison Staghounds whose country was in Co. Dublin. In 1840 Lord Howth, who lived at Howth Castle, Baily, near Dublin, brought over from Leamington in England, a pack of staghounds owned by Mr Broadley, and with the help of a subscription from the local military, hunted them himself until 1848, when the pack was acquired by the Dublin Garrison and became known as the Garrison Staghounds – a pack that soon gained the reputation of being one of the fastest in the country.

The Garrison Staghounds were not quite the earliest to hunt deer, for about four years earlier a Mr Alley was hunting fallow deer with hounds. Mr Alley was associated with the Ward Hounds, but whether the Ward or some other pack ever hunted fallow – and subsequently red deer – is not certain.

The Ward Union (*page 247*) is one of the two last surviving carted deer hunts in the British Isles – the other being the Co. Down Staghounds in Northern Ireland. Its country lies in counties Dublin and Meath which it shares with the Meath Foxhounds.

The origin of the Ward Union – which has been in existence for over a century – is interesting. In the 1820s there were two packs operating in the vicinity of Dublin – the Dubber and the Hollywood. In 1830 these two packs were amalgamated and after being renamed the Ward, for a time hunted bagged foxes. Shortly after their amalgamation, Mr Peter Alley of Newpark became Master, and from about 1836 it seems that the pack hunted deer, first fallow and then red deer with still an occasional day after fallow, the quarry being obtained, presumably, from one of the numerous private deer parks in the vicinity.

Shortly after the purchase of Lord Howth's hounds in 1848, the Dublin Garrison also acquired the Ward Hounds, and from about 1854 the combined pack became known as the Ward Union – the second part of the name being derived from the name of an inn – the Union – in the north of Co. Dublin.

Prior to the First World War, fields often numbered 250 riders or more, and to take the followers to the meets which were held twice weekly on Wednesday and Saturday, the Midland and Great Western Railway Company used to run special trains. During the last century (1879–81) the Empress of Austria used to come over to hunt in Ireland, for she always enjoyed hunting with the Ward Union. The soldier element has also been strongly represented in the past.

In the early days the deer were kept at Howth Castle – the home of J Gaisford St Lawrence – but after being transferred for a few years to Ratoath Park in Co. Meath, the deer were kept at Slane Castle – the home of Lord Conyngham – until about 1960 when they were removed to the kennels at Ashbourne. One of the disadvantages of the deer paddock at Howth was that it was far too small, and this resulted in the deer becoming too tame. The enclosure at Ashbourne is about ten acres and will accommodate about thirty deer.

During its early existence some good runs are on record, one of the best being on 23 February 1861, when the deer, uncarted near Ballymacartney, took hounds some thirty miles in about three hours before being taken in the courtyard of Gormanston Castle. During the following season the hunt had a tremendous run after a deer uncarted near Kilrue and in the end, the hounds outstripped the whole field and, running on their own, finally killed the deer. On 29 December 1876, another fine run ended tragically for the deer – an outlier named *London* – and on this occasion, although the deer was safely taken in the river near Sodstown, it died shortly afterwards.

When the deer were first moved to Slane Castle, the practice persisted for a few seasons of letting a number of them roam at large in the country at the beginning of the season. This proved a very successful innovation and, in consequence, they ran straighter and with more dash. Of course, sometimes the difficulty of taking them arose and one evaded capture throughout his hunting career with the one exception, when his very tall antlers got caught in a gate at Summerhill.[20] Another outlier was *Miss Dunsany*, and although she was several times hunted, she was never taken.

A stag which often got the better of the pack was named *Liberator*. However, as often as not after a few days of liberty this stag would return of his own accord to the vicinity of the kennels as though inviting another hunt. On two occasions the gate into the paddock was left open and he re-entered. Another stag which had been left out at the end of a season after a long hunt well into Co. Kildare, returned to the kennels very appropriately on the morning of the following opening meet.[20]

A stag named *Lord Holmpatrick's Deer* gained its name from the habit it had of, regardless where enlarged, always taking a line to Lord Holmpatrick's home near Castleknock, where it generally took refuge in the river. On one occasion this stag gave a fast point of fourteen miles, running from Culmullen to Abbotstown in just under one and a quarter hours without a check. Probably the most famous deer of all time was *Flathouse* – a stag that was bred at Howth and subsequently hunted for twenty seasons. Generally, *Flathouse*, wherever enlarged, took the pack towards Fieldstown Bridge, but on occasions he brought the hounds straight back to kennels.[20] Sometimes the hunt terminated on a more comical note, such as when a stag jumped through a mulled glass window into a kitchen, or had to be 'ridden' by a jockey out of a pond in which it had taken refuge (*see page 133*).

One of the longest hunts ever enjoyed by the Ward Union followed an end of season meet at Summerhill in 1952, when the stag took hounds twenty-five miles, which included a point of fourteen and a half miles – their longest for ninety-one years! The hunt was after an outlier named *Baldarra* which had, apparently, evaded capture for three seasons. After being found at Ballybotha, the stag took a route via Drumlarkin, Summerhill, Chaplecole, Ballon, Gallow, Garridice and Coolcor before taking a short swim in the Grand Canal at Fern's Lough. After crossing a railway line the chase continued via Timahoe Bog, which entailed a detour for the horses, on to Allenswood, near where the stag was finally taken in the centre of a bog which extended to some 4000 acres, by the turf workers who subsequently brought *Baldarra* to a nearby farm. This stag, which had a single antler, apparently had only once before been captured, and that was three years previously at Baldarra – hence the name.[20]

For a number of years now the usual quarry for the Ward Union has been red deer haviers. During its early existence, as already mentioned, fallow deer were also hunted, and this species was still being used in 1876, for M O'Connor Morris mentions a day when the Ward Union enlarged first an untried red deer hind which, after a very short run, met with an accident, and then a fallow doe which gave the field a very twisting gallop, lasting some fifty-five minutes before being taken. During the same season a stag enlarged near Dunshaughlin gave the pack a fifteen-mile run before being taken at Churchtown. During the hunt the deer was temporarily lost, but word eventually came to the effect that 'a cow had been seen swimming' in the turbid current of the Boyne, then in full spate after much rainfall. Hounds were immediately brought and as they crossed a bridge they suddenly winded the deer, which was found sheltering under one of the arches.[143]

During this period it seems that hunts were often 'marred by the customary intervention of curs or sheepdogs' and it was not uncommon for a collie dog to have a cut at the running deer.[143]

Other packs of staghounds which formerly operated in Eire were the Roscommon (1874–1903), the Templemore (1879–1908) and the South Westmeath (1889–*c.* 1907).

The Templemore Staghounds were established in 1879 by C D Webb, when Sir John Carden gave up his pack of harriers. Their country included the northern part of Co. Tipperary and the southern parts of Counties King's (Co. Offaly) and Queen's (Co. Leix). During the early part of its existence the Templemore Staghounds hunted fox and deer alternately, but in 1896, under Captain Lloyd's mastership, the pack hunted stag exclusively, the deer being kept at Brittas Castle, Thurles.

The South Westmeath Staghounds were established in 1889 to hunt the southern part of the Co. Westmeath, but it lasted only about eighteen years (*see page 241*). The Roscommon Staghounds were formed in 1874 by Major Balfe and as its title suggests, operated in the county of that name. It is not known what species of deer the pack hunted. The pack was disbanded in 1903.

At the end of the last century, two packs of staghounds then existed in Northern Ireland, the Co. Down and the East Antrim Staghounds – but only the former pack now remains.

The Co. Down Staghounds were really a development of Captain Ker's Harriers which, prior to 1881, had occasionally hunted fallow deer. In that year they became known as the Co. Down Staghounds and turned their attention solely to red deer.

Prior to the First World War hounds were out three days a week, and by all accounts sport often reached great heights. 'On St Stephen's Day, 1908, hounds met at Hillsborough and enjoyed a twelve-mile point. The 1909–10 season was one of the severest ever in Northern Ireland, with very cold weather and much snow throughout. Though sixteen days were missed because of bad weather, hounds were out on fifty-eight days. On 5 April 1910 a stag enlarged at Sentry Box ran to Ballywill, a twelve-mile point and twenty as hounds ran. On the 15th of the same month the followers enjoyed a run from Ballyerine to Ednigo, a distance of twelve miles over a fine line of country in one hour forty minutes. It was during this season that a stag was taken in the sea at Newcastle.'[20]

As was common practice elsewhere, the deer were given names and one of the most famous stags hunted by the Co. Down was an animal called *McRoberts*, so named after Johnny McRoberts who was a notable character among the hunting fraternity. *McRoberts*, which was bred in the deer park at Montalto, Ballynahinch, where the Co. Down Staghounds keep their deer, was hunted for eleven seasons, before dying in the park at the age of fifteen. Not all his life was *McRoberts* confined to the deer park, for from 1924 to 1933 he remained at large before being finally taken in March of the latter year at Lough Henny after a three hours' hunt. During his life of liberty, *McRoberts* had given two or three good hunts each session. Oddly enough, March 1933 also marked the capture of five other stags that had all been at large for long periods. One of *McRoberts'* hooves is now in the possession of Lt.-Col. J G Cunningham who was a Master of the hunt during the period 1950–62. One of the best hunts during Lt.-Col. Cunningham's mastership occurred in February 1951. Following a meet at Sentry Box hounds had an eight-mile point – fifteen as they ran – and the time was one hour and fifty minutes.[20]

In the Montalto enclosure, which extends to about thirty acres, about fifty red deer are generally maintained. Although at times the number of hinds in the paddock has slightly exceeded that of the stags, the hunt aims at keeping a larger proportion of stags – including haviers – than hinds. Under normal conditions the deer are fed on hay, corn and turnips.

The hunt prefers to hunt stag rather than hind, the advantage being that an outlying stag will generally return to the park so long as there are no hinds out as well. Also, if the stags are young and well 'done for', they generally give a better hunt than hinds, unless the weather be very heavy.

'We do not hunt,' writes the Secretary of the Hunt Club (*in litt.* 1959), 'a stag more than three or four times in the season, unless he is an outlier, when he may be hunted more often if marked. We usually find that an outlier, i.e. a stag roaming the country at large, thrives better than those in the park, although he is not as good to hunt as he carries too much condition. We also find that both stag and hind run very true to form, i.e. giving approximately the same time for a run and if enlarged anywhere near where they were previously enlarged, will endeavour to run the same line, unless headed or upset by outside conditions.'

Prior to 1939 haviers were never hunted, but owing to the war, the stock of deer got rather low, so a few stags were gelded, and some fresh beasts obtained.

Since 1949 fifteen stags and two hinds have been obtained from Warnham Court, Sussex, the last consignment consisting of a stag and two hinds being received in 1963.

The 1976–7 hunting season was marred by the tragic death of Lord Faulkner – who, as Brian Faulkner, was the last Prime Minister of Ulster, for at the end of the day, on 3 March, his horse hit an oncoming car, slipped and rolled on him, with fatal results.

Another pack which hunted the carted deer for about fouiteen years in Northern Ireland was the East Antrim Staghounds. Founded in 1895 to hunt hares and to run drag under the mastership of Richard Cecil (*page 218*) the pack changed from drag to deer in 1906. Mr Cecil had purchased a new pack of staghounds as well as a number of deer to hunt but he acted as Master for only one season. However, until about 1920 the pack, under Mr James Craig, continued to hunt deer at weekends, and hares on the mid-week meet.

Probably the best run of the East Antrim Staghounds took place on Saturday, 28 January 1911 when, following a meet on the Ballymore Road, the deer *Miss McCreary* was enlarged at Lisnalinchy. The hounds ran fast over good country by Covenknowes, Strandnabannagh and Loganstown; over the Three Brothers and Carn Hills (1000 feet high), then on through Dorisland to the golf course near Belfast, and back to Dorisland again, and after passing through Cloughley and Woodburn, was finally taken at Thompson's Point after a grand run of two and a half hours with one check at Dorisland.[29]

The East Antrim Staghounds were abandoned in about 1920.

Chapter VI
Hunting & Stalking the Red Deer in Scotland

Since the earliest times, deer have been the principal quarry of man in Scotland, and it was to such forests as Jed, Ettrick and Caledonia, which were forests in the true sense, that the hunter went in pursuit of the 'hart, hynde or buck'. With the destruction of the forests, however, it would seem that not only did the majority of those areas which were denuded of trees retain the title of forest, but the title of 'forest' was also applied to those barren wastes and mountain sides to which the homeless deer had been driven by virtue of the fact that they were being populated by a 'forest beast'.

The definition of a deer forest today is rather nebulous. Formerly a deer forest implied a tract of land that was populated by deer to the exclusion of all else, i.e. sheep and cattle. At present, however, a large number of deer forests do carry a stock of one or the other of these domestic animals on some part of the ground. It might, therefore, be logically agreed that with the intrusion of sheep or cattle the ground should no longer be considered as a 'deer forest'. Quite apart from the fact that deer forests are, for the most part, without trees, the term is an historical one, and it is nigh impossible to decide on a definition, for it is difficult to draw the line between, say, a deer forest in which sheep are grazed and a lightly stocked sheep farm on which it is possible to stalk and kill deer.

Deerstalking, such as we know it, has been practised in Scotland for only about two centuries, for it would appear to have come 'into general practice only after the deforestation of Scotland at the end of the eighteenth century'.[44] Cluny Macpherson, chief of the Clan Macpherson, has generally been credited as the first Highland gentleman to stalk in the year 1745, a stag on the open hill, and thereby initiated a sport which has been followed by an increasing number of sportsmen ever since. At one time, however, it was considered that stalking was 'no ploy for a gentleman'. To bring in venison for the larder was the work of a forester or ghillie, and it is recorded that the youthful Lord Lovat of the period was instructed by his guardian that it would be hoped that his lordship 'would not so far derogate from his position as to go into the forest to shoot deer for himself as such a practice was neither dignified in a nobleman nor customary'.[70] The practice was, at that period, for the nobility to shoot their deer at the *tainchell*, or drive, at which many hundreds of men and dogs took part so that a large number of animals

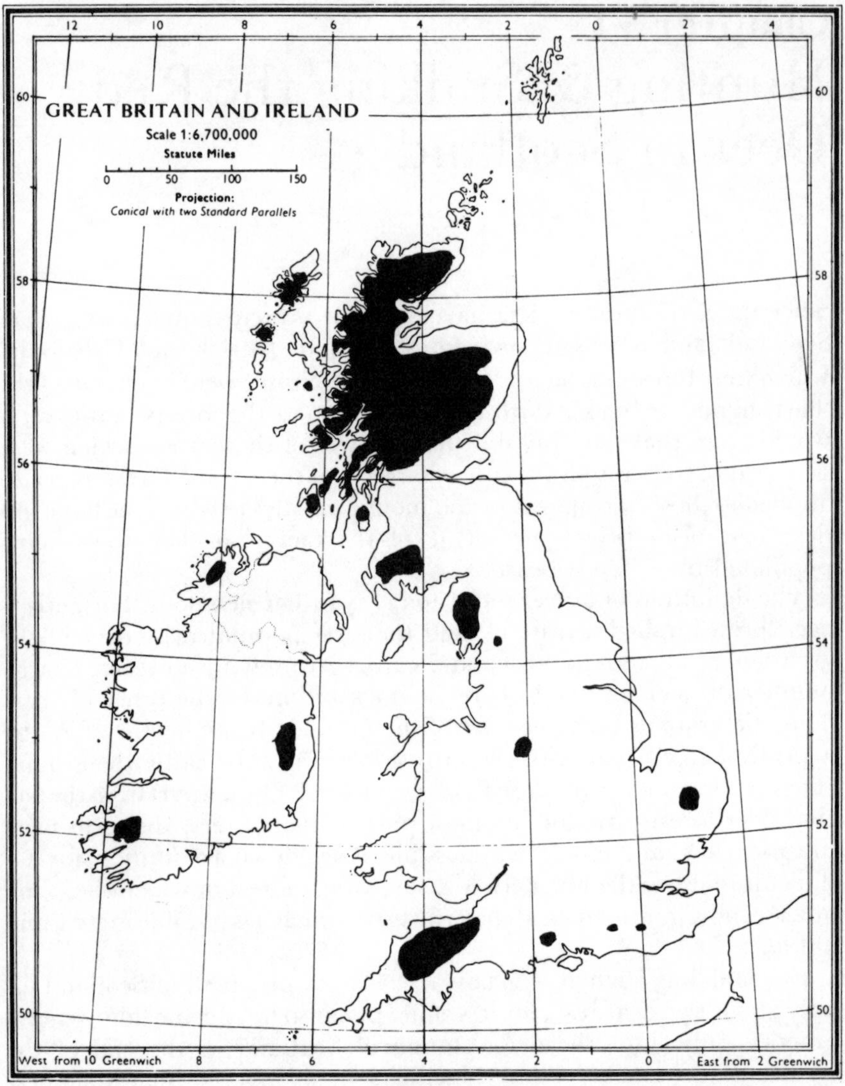

The approximate distribution of red deer in Great Britain and Ireland. Apart from south-west England, where three packs of staghounds hunt red deer, the wild animal elsewhere is shot either by stalking or from a high seat. In Northern Ireland and Eire two packs of hounds hunt the carted deer

would be driven to concealed marksmen who, with luck, were able to take a considerable toll of the deer.

As to the manner of hunting in very early times, sculptured stones in various parts of the country afford very definite information. A stone at Shandwick in Ross-shire shows three men on horseback with a hound after a stag; also a man kneeling and shooting with a bow at a stag. A stone at Cadboll depicts a woman on horseback, two men on horseback

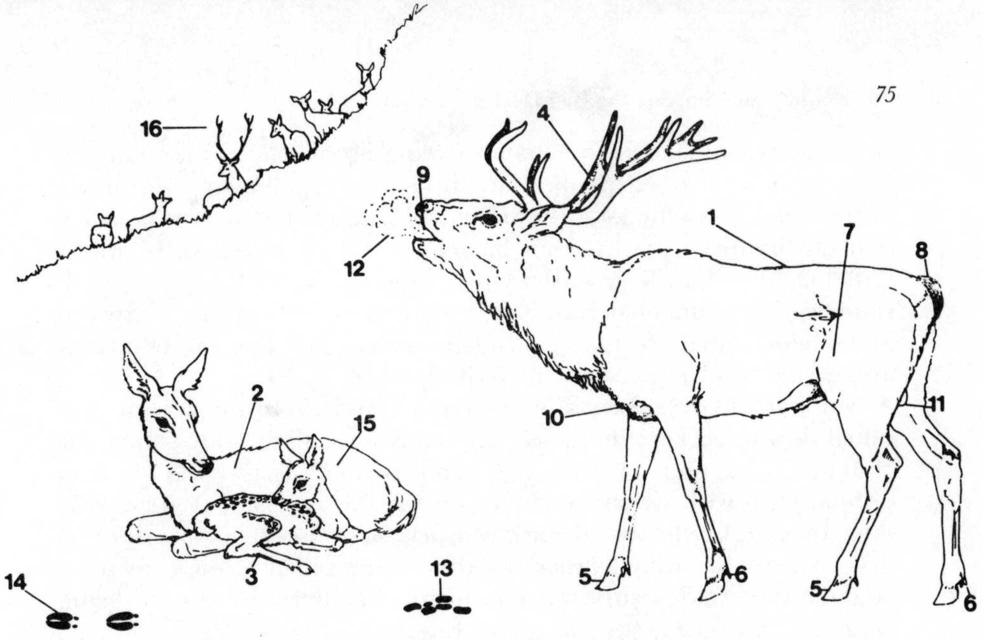

Red deer (Anciently spelt reid deer)
1 Stag
2 Hind, hinde, hynde
3 Calf
4 Antlers, attire, head, rack, trophy
5 Cleaves (toes), slot (cloven foot), talon (heel)
6 Dew claws, or surcleaves
7 Coat, hide, skin
8 Tail, flag, single
9 Grandeln, tushes (upper canines), tusks
10 Brisket, essay
11 Coddes (testicles)
12 Roar, bell, bellowing, voice
13 Droppings, fewmets, fewmishing, fues, fumes, fumet, mutes
14 Footprints, feaut, foil, foin, foyles, imprint, pace, pattern, pies, register, slotmarks, splay (spread of slot), spoor, step (interval between footprints), stride (interval between successive footprints of same hoof), trace, tracks, trail, view, voyes
15 Couched (resting), at lodge
16 Herd, hearde, heerde, hert, harem (hinds), drift, mob, parcel (hinds), roddel, soppe

Age group terminology

	Male deer	*Female deer*
Under 1 year	Calf, hinde calf, veel	Calf
1 year	Yearling	Yearling
2 years	Brocket, broket, bulloke, broacher, knobber, knobler, galloper, spitter	Brocket's sister, hearse, hearst, hearts, hert, hyrsel, jinnock
3 years	Brocard, brock, brocke, galloper, spayed, spayard, spayart, spaid, spavad, spire	Biche, hind, hinde, hynde*
4 years	Staggard, staggart, staggie, galloper	
5 years	Great soar, great stag, heavy stag (5 years and older), stag	
6 years	Hart, hert, hart of the first head	
7 years	Hart of the second head, old stag	

* A pregnant hind is called a braggard, and a hind without a calf, bluehind or yeld

with spears and shields, two men blowing horns and a stag with two hounds. A slab at Kirriemuir in Forfar would seem to indicate an untrained dog in action, for the animal is biting the tail of the stag which is being hunted by a man on horseback with a spear. In a ruined building at Balnacill in Sutherland, which dates to the seventeenth century, McConnochie states that therein is a carefully preserved monument, dated 1623, which indicates that deer hunting with bow and arrow was then a sport in Sutherland.[135]

Nothing was ever wasted in those days, and whilst the venison was salted down and kept in barrels, the skins were also highly valued for clothing, mats, tent coverings etc. and it was said that it was quite an ordinary feat with archers to shoot a deer in the ear so as not to spoil the skin. Indeed, by the seventeenth century there was an export duty on deer skins – or 'wild leather' as they were called – there being a considerable trade with the continent, the ports of export being Glasgow, Aberdeen, Inverness and Edinburgh.[135]

Time came when the bow, the spear and the sword had to give way to firearms, but it was not until the present century, when firearms became more efficient with the introduction of the modern sporting rifle, that the deerstalker was no longer accompanied on the hill by one or two deerhounds to bring down a wounded beast.

Before the use of firearms, however, it was common practice to drive deer into compounds where they could be slaughtered with the spear or other primitive weapons. Describing one of these ancient deer hunts on the island of Rhum, the Reverend Donald Maclean, in the *Old Statistical Account* of the Small Isles (1796), wrote 'On each side of a glen formed by two mountains, stone dykes were begun pretty high in the mountains and carried to the lower part of the valley, always drawing nearer, till within three or four feet of each other. From this narrow pass, a circular space was enclosed by a stone wall, of a height sufficient to confine the deer; to this place they were pursued and destroyed'. Organized deer hunts also took place on some of the other islands during the sixteenth century and one historian stated that as a result 'a thousand head were killed among the Red Hills' of Skye. Before the gun supplanted the bow, the latter certainly had one great advantage over the gun – namely that it was noiseless – so if the stalker was well concealed, several shots could be fired before the deer would become too much alarmed. Wounded deer were then despatched with the spear – a weapon which was once used against the boar and the wolf before these animals became extinct in Scotland, the former about the thirteenth century, but the latter survived until the early part of the eighteenth century.

The Reverend Dr Robertson, in the *Agriculture of the County of Perth* (1799) describes a somewhat similar method used in Perthshire. 'The natives hunted the deer by surrounding them with men, or by making large enclosures of such a height as the deer could not overleap, fenced with stakes and intertwined with brushwood. Vast multitudes of men were collected on hunting days, who, forming a ring (*Tinchell*) round the deer, drove them into these enclosures, which were open on one side. From some eminence which overlooked the enclosure the principal personages and others who did not choose to engage in the chase were spectators to the whole diversion. The enclosures were called in the language of the county *elerig*. . . . There are *elerigs* in various parts of the country.'

Bogs were sometimes used to trap deer, and in another volume of the *Old Statistical Account* mention is made of 'the bog of the high deer-trap (*Féith na h-ard Eileig*)' in Sutherland, which was 'a tract of soft boggy moor, to which in times of old the natives gathered deer, and, when entangled, they killed them.' In Strath Carron, in the parish of Kincardine, there was a deer trap known as *Eileag Bad Challaidh* 'The deer trap of the hazel-clump'.

In some districts the deer hunt seems to have been an annual event, generally held in August before the harvest so that the crofters were free to participate, and conducted under definite rules of discipline. For instance, on 1 August 1710 the Duke of Atholl ordered the men of Glen Fernate and Glen Briarachan to meet him at the foot of Ben Vurich (*Beinn a' Bhúraich* 'peak of bellowing') the following night, with a day's provision, for a deer hunt the day after. On 12 August, similar orders were sent to Blair and Struan, Kirkmichael, Moulin, Cluny, Glen Almond, Logierait, Weem, Dull and Fortingall. Invitations were sent to Farquharson of Invereye and Mackenzie of Dalmore to come with 'some pretty men' and as many dogs as they could provide. The vassals and tenants met on the Green of Blair, and on 23 August the men were drawn up on *Druim na h-Eachdra* 'the Ridge of the Expedition' at the head of Girnaig. There the orders were read out to all the officers before the tinchell was sent out, including the following:

1 That none shall offer to fire a gun or pistol in the time of the deer-hunting.
2 That none shall offer to break up a deer, or take out a gralloch, except in his Grace's presence, where they are to be disposed on.
3 That none be drunk or swear an oath.
(Charles Ferguson, *History of Strathardle*)

Driving deer to ambushed sportsmen was still being practised in Glen Tilt at the beginning of the last century, but never on such an extensive scale as those in former days when nobles went forth with all their retinue, and the whole scene had as much the appearance of a military display as of a hunting party. Parties of hillmen were sent out in advance to form a large semi-circular line in the mountains, and then move slowly forward so as to move the deer down into Glen Tilt, through which they passed before descending again into Ben-y-gloe.

There were several stations in the glen, in which the various sportsmen were concealed, and from these no one was permitted to move until all the deer had passed. These drives took place only when the wind was suitable. Under favourable conditions it was not unusual for perhaps five or six hundred head of deer to pass through the glen. After the shots dogs were used to bring down any wounded beasts. Any deer that broke back were shot at by sportsmen who had been moving forward with the beaters to cope with just such a situation, but never to fire at any deer going forward to the waiting sportsmen in the glen. It sometimes happened that those who went with the drivers had the greatest number of chances.[172]

When a herd of deer is driven quietly along, they will generally follow each other in line. Thus it is prudent for the ambushed sportsman to allow the first few deer to pass his post before raising his rifle, for if the leader is fired at, those following will probably all turn back, or take a different line. When deer are hard pressed by hounds, however, they are inclined to bunch up, which makes selection of individual beasts almost impossible, quite apart from the fact that they will be travelling much faster.

When the country was partially covered with wood, the forests were driven and the sportsmen occupied passes where they took their chance of any deer passing that way. Glengarry in Inverness-shire was one of the last localities in which such drives took place and these were still being practised there during the first half of the last century. At one time it was the practice to drive herds of deer into Loch Dulachan by a strong cordon of men, and the slaughter then took place in its waters.[172]

According to Gordon's *Earldom of Sutherland* (1630), 'In Durines . . . ther is an excellent and delectable place for hunting, called Parwe, wher they hunt the reid deir in abundance; and sometimes they drive them into the ocean at the Pharo-head, wher they do take them in boats as they list.'

A somewhat similar method of taking deer was being practised in Ireland until the late nineteenth century, when the stags in the woods of Killarney were driven into the lake, where they were either shot, or caught with ropes thrown about their antlers.

There is no doubt that some of these deer drives required immense organization. A particularly large one took place on Mar Forest (Aberdeen) in 1618, when 'five or six hundred men doe rise early in the morning and they doe disperse themselves divers wayes, and seven, eight or ten miles compass they doe bring or chase in the deere in many heardes (two, three or four hundred in a hearde) to such or such a place as the noblemen shall appoint them, then when the day is come the lords and gentlemen of their companies doe ride or go to the said places sometimes wading up to the middles through bournes and rivers; and then they being come to the place, doe lye down on the ground till those foresaid scouts, which are called the tinckell, doe bring down the deere. . . . Then after we had stayed three houres or thereabouts, we might perceive the deere appeare on the hills round about us (their heads making a shew like a wood) which being followed close by the tinckell, are chased down in to the valley where we lay; then all the valley on each side being way laid with a hundred couple of strong Irish greyhounds, they are let loose as occasion serves upon the hearde of deere, that with the dogs, gunnes, arrowes, durks and daggers, in the span of two houres, fourscore fat deere were slaine. . . .'[135]

Further north in Sutherland Lord Reay used to have a grand deer drive every August on his Forest of Reay, and upwards of sixty stags were accounted for in a day.

One of the last great deer drives on Atholl Forest of which there is any record, took place on 29 September 1800 and was attended by more than 200 tenants who formed a line of four miles in length. They surrounded about 1200 deer, but the majority broke back through the line and got away, leaving only six of their number behind killed. Drives on a smaller scale were, of course, held to a much later date, and one of these attended by Colonel Greenhill Gardyne, took place in Glen Tilt in October 1858, when 'hundreds of deer were driven in, eight or ten being killed. All the party were in the kilt and deer hounds were used'.[135]

Professor WJ Watson (1925) suggests that 'these great hunts served the Gaelic nobles as an excellent and popular preparation and discipline for warfare: they took in fact the place of our modern autumn manoeuvres'.[162]

Dogs running wild in the forest, and eagles, were always considered a serious threat to deer and both were shot on sight. As an example, on 28 June 1707 the Duke of Atholl put his signature to a Commission which gave instructions 'to shoot all dogs found in the forest and exact 20 pounds Scots from the master of each dog. As likewise we order you to kill or bring alive any eagles old or young, you can take alive or shoot in the fôrest, and for your encouragement we shall give you a warrant for killing a deer for your own use for each eagle, old or young, brought in by you, upon producing to us William Murray in Maynes of Blair his receipt for same'.[135] In 1953 when I was stalking reindeer in Norway, I found a somewhat similar arrangement in practice which enabled me to shoot one reindeer without payment in exchange for the fox I had shot during the hunt.

In addition to stalking and driving deer to rifles in ambush, a much favoured pastime in former times was coursing a 'cold' (unwounded) deer with hounds, a sport which continued until the early part of the present century but terrain, more than anything else, was the main factor which decided whether a course was worth while.

One of the earliest recorded instances of deer coursing is the account of how King Robert Bruce, during the latter part of the thirteenth century, had often hunted without success, to take a white deer. At last, in desperation, the King turned to his followers and asked whether they had hounds that could do better. At last one, Sir William St Clair, came forward and said that his two hounds, *Help* and *Hold*, would probably succeed, and this resulted in a wager being fixed between the King and Sir William, that if his hounds were successful, he would be rewarded with the gift of the Forest of Pentland Firth (Midlothian). On the other hand, if the hounds failed to catch their deer before it crossed the March Burn, Sir William would lose his head!

In due course, the deer was roused from its lair by some slower hounds, whereupon Sir William, who was following on horse, uncoupled his two hounds *Help* and *Hold* who immediately took up the chase, but could not catch up with the deer before it reached the burn, and Sir William already feared that his head was lost. Fortunately, however, *Help* leaped into the water and succeeded in heading the deer back to land where it was killed by *Hold* and *Help* just within the required boundary.

King Robert was more than true to his word and bestowed on Sir William more lands than he had promised in 'free forestrie'.

After his death, Sir William was buried in Rosslin Chapel and his effigy has a hound at his feet.[119]

As the Scottish deerhound ran by sight rather than by scent, it was essential that the dogs should have a good view of the deer both before being slipped and during the course. The preliminary, therefore, to any course was for the stalking party to get as close to the deer as possible, and with two eager hounds straining at the leash, this often entailed a far more difficult stalk than, say, a crawl up with only a rifle in hand. Fairly flat, rolling country such as can be found in parts of Perthshire, or the far north of Scotland, was the ideal type of terrain, for on such ground the deer would keep running and could be pulled down by the dogs, generally by one seizing a hind leg or flank to knock it off its balance, whilst the other dog seized the throat. However, should the deer succeed in gaining some precipitous or rocky terrain, it either succeeded in escaping from the dogs altogether or else stood at bay, its flanks guarded by some overhanging rock, whilst its antlers would prevent any frontal attack. Under such conditions, therefore, the more experienced dogs would attempt to hold the stag at bay until the stalkers arrived, whilst those of more tender years might rush in, often suffering severe injury if not death from the stag's antlers.

Scrope recalls an unusual coursing incident concerning a stalker who, whilst hunting on the island of Jura with three deerhounds, came upon three large stags. He immediately slipped all three dogs together and to his astonishment, each of them took a separate deer, which had gone off in different directions. Eventually, after a long and arduous pursuit, the stalker came in sight of one of his dogs, *Oscar* by name, which was holding a stag at bay in some long heather. The dog was lying stretched out, apparently completely exhausted, but on hearing his name shouted, immediadely sprung at the stag's throat, and a desperate battle ensued with the dog being tossed up three times into the air and severely wounded. Eventually the deerstalker, a most powerful man, was able to seize the stag by the antlers, and after a long struggle succeeded in ending the contest with his hunting knife.[172]

On another occasion, a stalking party from the island of Colonsay visited Jura on 11 August 1835 to course deer on Captain M'Neill's estate. The party took to the hill with Finlay, the stalker, proceeding about fifty yards in advance of the party who were bringing up the dogs in slips. Eventually a stag was seen about a mile away, and after a careful detour, Finlay was able to bring the party up to within about sixty yards of the stag before it became aware of their presence, and make off. Two dogs, *Buskar* and *Bran*, were immediately released as the deer set off at full speed.

The deer's first attempt was to gain some rising ground, but being closely pursued by the dogs, he soon found his only safety was in speed. However, the dogs pressed him hard, and after forcing the deer to jump down a small precipice of some fourteen feet in height, *Bran* eventually succeeded in seizing the deer by one of the hocks, whilst *Buskar* closed in, seizing him by the neck. Notwithstanding the weight of the two dogs hanging on to him, the deer continued to drag them along at quite a speed, and more than once succeeded in kicking *Bran* off. Eventually, however, the stag became exhausted and was pulled down and killed by the dogs before the stalking party reached the scene.[172]

Scrope's opinion was that the 'best sort of dog for chasing deer would unquestionably be the original Scots or Irish greyhound'. He himself, however, had some litters from a foxhound and a greyhound, the former being the father, and 'this cross answered perfectly', giving 'the speed of the greyhound, with just enough of the nose of the foxhound to answer your purpose'. Moreover, he states, 'Courage you have in perfection . . . they run mute, and when they are put upon the scent of the hart, they will follow it until they come up to him; and, again, when he is out of view, they will carry on the scent, recover him, and beat the best greyhound to fits'.[172]

At the beginning of the last century the Duke of Atholl had two such cross-bred hounds, and with these he was able to bring cold (unwounded) harts to bay.

A cross with a bulldog was once tried in the forest of Atholl, with the intention of giving the dog greater courage, but the progeny was too slow, as might have been expected, and the dogs were all killed by attacking the deer in front. It was Scrope's opinion that perhaps the greatest advantage possessed by any dog is superiority of speed, for it will keep the deer moving and run less risk of injury. A dog that has not sufficient speed for deer, following most by scent, will, after a long chase, eventually find itself confronted by a stag at bay, with his back tucked up against a rock, and in this situation no dog can possibly attack a stag with the slightest chance of success.

High couraged dogs, indeed, of any breed are always subject to accidents, either being killed or wounded by a stag's antlers, or falling over precipitous rocks in their reckless pursuit.

Another cross tried was that between a greyhound and a bloodhound, and quite successful some of these turned out to be. On Invercauld Forest (Aberdeenshire), however, it was seldom that the deer were ever driven and coursing never undertaken, unless to bring down a deer wounded by shot. The foresters used to keep small terriers which they took out stalking, and if any deer was wounded they could track it over a great distance without giving tongue, thereby causing less disturbance in the forest.

Scrope preferred to use his dogs for bringing to bay a wounded deer, seldom slipping them after a cold hart, unless he was out with the Duke of Atholl who preferred this type of sport. 'The hill-man or gillie who leads the dogs,' he writes, 'should be a very steady, clever fellow, and, moreover, a strong man; for the dogs are so eager and powerful that he who has them in the leash is frequently pulled head over heels, when he runs down hill with them. All their tackle should be strong, and regularly inspected every morning, lest the dogs should break loose, disturb the cast, and ruin your sport for the day.'

Continuing, he says, 'The dogs should be led about a hundred yards behind the deerstalker; and the leash-man should stop when he stops, and stalk him as he stalks the deer. Should the herd come in sight, he had better get them to lie down in a hole if possible, and put his handkerchief over their eyes, or they will be apt to struggle or whine, and do irreparable mischief. After the shots are fired, it is the man's duty to run up with them in the leash. . . . He then gives them up to the forester, who lays one of them on, if there is occasion; one good dog being quite sufficient to bring a wounded hart to bay.'[172]

Normally, after the shot, if the deer goes off wounded, rather than slip a hound immediately, it is prudent to keep an eye on it with the telescope to watch where it lies down. Then, after waiting a short while, the forester would either lay the dog on the scent, or take it until in sight of the quarry before slipping, and with reasonable luck the dog should soon bring the stag to bay. There are occasions, however, such as when a leg is broken, that the hound should be slipped immediately, for he can then follow on sight, and if the distance is not too great, should soon catch up with the deer. If, however, the deer is only slightly wounded, and runs off in the middle of a herd, it is really useless to slip a hound in the hope that it will be able to sort out the correct animal.

A number of different appellations seem to have been given to what is virtually the same breed – thus we have the Highland deerhound; the Scotch greyhound, the Irish wolfhound and the Irish greyhound. The colour seems to have varied between a pale yellow or even white, to a dark grey, and with a shoulder height of about 28 in. (71 cm), weighed in the region of 85 to about 100 lb. (38 to 45 kg).

By the beginning of the last century the pure bred deerhound had almost ceased to exist, and by 1839 Scrope was of the opinion that 'not above a dozen, pure deerhounds are to be met with'. Within forty years, however, 'the breed of deer-hounds which had nearly become extinct'

. . . 'had become comparatively plentiful in all the Highland districts' owing to 'the trouble taken by different proprietors and renters of mountain shootings, who have collected and bred this noble race of dogs, regardless of expense and difficulties'. At that date (1878) fifty guineas was 'not an unusual price for a first-rate dog'.[167]

Lord Colonsay and his brothers were responsible more than anyone else, for the survival and eventual revival of the Scottish deerhound. Lord Colonsay began his work about 1831, selecting the best possible stock he could find, for the sole purpose of breeding a dog for deer coursing; 'no gun was ever taken to the hill' he wrote, 'the whole done by dogs'. Soon many prominent landowners both in Scotland and in England, began to breed them seriously, and when Queen Victoria and the Prince Consort became interested in deerhounds, the deerhound was once more the companion of royalty.

However, although during the middle and latter part of the last century the number of deerhounds steadily increased, their role was soon to become one of prestige and ornament to their owner's household, for it was found that a dog that could follow by scent rather than by sight alone, was infinitely more useful in tracking down a wounded deer. So by the end of the century, the collie had become the favourite breed – or perhaps a collie-deer hound cross, which were often referred to as 'tracker dogs'.

In about 1855 as many as sixty deerhounds were being kept in kennels at Blackmount, but by 1885 the breed had been given up entirely for stalking,and collies had taken their place when required to follow up any wounded beast. By this date, also, many of the large deer forests had been split up into smaller units, and not only was the disturbance to the ground caused by deerhounds considerable, but as often as not the hounds followed the deer on to neighbouring territory, which very soon made their use impracticable except on the largest estates.

Even so, the use of deerhounds for coursing a 'cold' stag continued to be practised on Culachy Forest in Inverness-shire until about 1912, when, with the death of the owner MK Angelo, this ancient practice finally died out in the Highlands. 'The coursing on Culachy,' writes L MacNally who was stalker there for a number of years after the Second World War, 'was almost exclusively done on an extensive boggy plateau, with hard ridges enclosing it on north and south and a deer fence sealing off its west end. The stag was invariably "started" at the west end and, by the configuration of the ground, almost always was forced to turn down to where a meandering grassy-banked burn bissected the boggy plateau, flowing eastwards towards the River Tarff. With the stag's knowledge of his own habitat, the harder going of the burn's banks afforded him better going when hard pressed by the faster dogs. The procedure followed on Culachy was initially similar to traditional Highland coursing in that deer were spied, and if in a favourable position, stalked so as to get the pair of hounds as close as possible. There was this difference however . . . and this was that while the first pair of hounds and their handlers were stalking the distant deer, another two pair of hounds were posted at intervals in the burn down which the stag was almost sure to come.

'As a further last precautionary resort, at a point in the burn, near where there was a shepherd's bothy, and below which it became a rocky gorge wherein the stag might escape, an attendant was posted to turn the failing stag, if he got so far. This, I feel, denied the stag his last chance of escape to which, if he had defied the hounds so far, he was surely entitled.'[131]

Mr Angelo's hounds were not pure bred deerhounds, but had been crossed with Borzoi and weighed about 135 lb. (61 kilo), which was considerably more than a pure deerhound.

Hunting deer with a pack of hounds does not seem to have been much practised in Scotland, but H Byng Hall records at least one nobleman who occasionally foresook the rifle in order to chase a deer with his harrier pack. Apparently, the Duke of Atholl 'possessed not only a well-sized and well bred pack of harriers, with which he afforded sport and pastime to himself and neighbours in the vales immediately adjacent to his ancient castle of Atholl, but also . . . he was wont constantly to hunt from thence (Dunkeld) with the above hounds over the rich and luxuriant vale extending from Perth to the aforenamed town . . . and it was not seldom that, having secured a noble red-deer from his neighbouring forest of Atholl, and having shorn him of his graceful antlers, and conditioned him with hard food, he was turned before the hounds, almost wild from his native hills; and, under such circumstances, as may readily be supposed, frequently affording a rare gratification to those sufficiently well nerved and mounted to follow the chase over so wild a country, so difficult to cross'.[91]

Describing one of the hunts he attended, H Byng Hall wrote: 'A brief law having been granted to the stag, the pack was laid on, and, immediately taking up the scent, away they raced.

'The first portion of the run crossed an enclosed and heavy country, with tremendous fences; then came comparatively open, undulating ground, composed of strong, heathered hills; here, boggy moorland . . . then we approached hill and stony dale, then easy riding land, fir plantations, and heathered braes, without check or hindrance, till we came to a sudden halt on the banks of the Tay . . . full nine miles from the uncarting point.' The river, however, was in full spate and unfordable by man or horse, and although the stag had succeeded in crossing over to the other side and taken refuge in some dense woodland, the field could not follow, so the hunt was called off for the day. The following day, however, after crossing the river by a bridge some way up-stream, the pack was taken to the wood and soon recovered the trail. 'Chasing, however, was impossible, from the thickness of the underwood; this, nevertheless, also prevented the deer from putting forth his energies, and unharmed, therefore, he was speedily secured to fly once more before his enemies on another day.'[91]

So long as there are deer in Scotland there will always be deer poaching. In the past, although the majority of deer poachers were crofters who shot the odd beast to provide a bite for his family, there were a few, such as Alexander (Sandy) Davidson, of Craithie, Braemar (1792–1843) who made good money from his exploits among the salmon, grouse and deer of Aberdeenshire, which even at that date fetched the best prices, if sent to London.

Prior to the eighteenth century it seems that landowners did not pay much attention to estate boundaries, and it was common practice to follow game on to another estate without asking permission. In order to put an end to this practice, several of the larger landowners, which included the Duke of Gordon, the Earl of Fife and the Earl of Breadalbane put a notice in the press to the effect that anyone caught shooting without permission would be prosecuted. One of these notices appeared in an Edinburgh newspaper and stated 'The Earl of Breadalbane being desirous to preserve the game upon his estates in Perthshire and Argyllshire, hopes no gentleman will shoot there without liberty. Poachers and unqualified persons will be prosecuted'. It will be observed that a distinction is made between a 'poacher' and an 'unqualified person', but whether the latter qualified for a less severe penalty is not known.[135]

During the seventeenth century there were two noted poachers who, for many years, hunted together or separately as suited their fancy, and there was always considerable rivalry between them regarding their skill and prowess as hunters. Both bore the name of Mackerachers although how closely they were related has never been recorded. One, named Lonavey, when on his own generally hunted in the Atholl area in Perthshire, whilst Ruadh's favourite terrain was Mar in Aberdeenshire.

One season an enormous stag with a fine set of antlers was reported to be in the area, and needless to say, none were more anxious to secure the prize than Lonavey and Ruadh. For over a week the search went on, each man taking the direction he thought the stag most likely to be found in. Often the rivals would be working in sight of each other, at other times they would be far apart, and when darkness overtook them they snatched what sleep and rest they could under an overhanging bank or rock. Small trout caught in the little burns was their main food, for neither dare fire a shot for fear of scaring the big stag away.

On the eighth morning, just as Lonavey was setting out in the direction in which he expected to find the stag, which had been seen by both men late the preceding evening, he heard a shot at the back of Cairn Righ, and concluded that his rival had beaten him to the stag. With all speed, therefore, he proceeded to the spot, and it was not long before he saw Ruadh and the stag in mortal conflict. Apparently, Ruadh, so certain was he that his aim had been true, had thrown down his gun and rushed in to bleed the stag with his dirk – alas! all too soon, for there was still much life in the beast and he was badly gored by its antlers. Nevertheless, as he fell, his dirk somehow succeeded in finding the stag's heart, which fell dead above him. Ruadh, however, was in a very bad way and after gasping to his friend 'I have killed the big stag, but the big stag has killed me' immediately fell back dead.[175]

Lonavey, however, still continued his old mode of life, and for killing deer in the royal forest of Atholl, later had one of his hands cut off, the object of so barbarous a punishment being to prevent a poacher ever using the long bow again. Even this handicap, however, failed to deter Lonavey, for it was not long before he had made himself proficient with a rest on which he laid his gun barrel, steadying it with his handless arm.[175]

Probably the most romantic deer poacher of all time was R Gordon-Cumming who, by his ingenuity, was able to shoot a fine 11-pointer in Braulen Forest right under the nose of the keeper waiting for him and still got away with it.

The circumstances were as follows. The stag had been spotted by the stalker in charge of the beat where the stag was generally to be found, and as it was known that Roualeyn Gordon-Cumming was in the area, he was instructed to maintain a special watch over it. It so happened that a gentleman in the district died, and although the stalker desired to attend the funeral, he was told that he could only do so provided he saw Gordon-Cumming went also. On the day of the funeral Gordon-Cumming put on his Highland dress and with a rose in his buttonhole, walked along the road, when he met the stalker, who asked him why he was going to a funeral with a rose in his buttonhole. Gordon-Cumming's non-committal reply was that when everything was over he would leave him the rose. The stalker, assured that Gordon-Cumming was going to the funeral, changed his clothes and proceeded to the church. No sooner, however, had Gordon-Cumming got out of sight than he set off for the forest and in three hours had killed the stag and cut off its head. The stalker, having heard the shot, immediately set off in the direction of the sound, and eventually found the carcase of the stag with the rose by its side![195] Roualeyn Gordon-Cumming died in 1866.

There is no doubt that some of these men, whether killing deer legitimately on their own ground, or poaching off someone else's property, were both tough and adventurous, even to tackling an unwounded stag with nothing more than a knife as a weapon. During the summer of 1837 a forester by the name of Donald who belonged to the Chief of Clanchattan, whilst passing through the forest of Strathmashie, near Loch Laggan, saw the antlers of a sleeping stag protruding from some heather in which it was resting. Taking advantage of some cover, he crept cautiously up to the deer and with his knife held between his teeth, pounced upon the sleeping beast. Immediately the stag sprang to its feet, and made off down the rugged hillside with Donald sitting astride, and holding on to its antlers for dear life with both hands, so was unable to use his knife! Eventually, however, after dashing through a burn, the stag began to tire and it tried to ascend the mountain on the other side of the glen, and Donald was then able to snatch the knife from his mouth and plunge it into the stag's throat.[172]

The last great chief of the Macdonnells of Glengarry was another of those romantic characters who, at the beginning of the last century, would go forth in his kilt and remain in the hills for a full week, sleeping in the open air. When the stag was at bay, he would sometimes have a close engagement with him, using his gunstock, or skene-dhu and, although often in peril, was ever successful. Once, when his dogs held a stag at bay on an island in Loch Garry, no boat being at hand, he placed a knife in his handkerchief, which he bound round his head, swam out to the island and killed his stag.[172]

Glengarry was founder of 'The Society of True Highlanders' and among its aims was the renewal of the ancient Caledonian Hunt. The first hunt took place in September 1817 and extended over three successive days. According to the official report, however, 'this noble recreation produced less venison than was anticipated, though quite as many shots were fired, ball practice being less sure with most Highlanders of the present day than it was with their ancestors; yet some of the roe deer fell in capital style, at the height of their speed'. During the following year, members were content with grouse shooting, but in 1819 both red and roe were taken. 'The grand hunt, at Straidan Garry,' states the report, 'in which both hart and buck fell at the top of their speed to the single ball of the sportsmen's rifle, and the cold roe deer was taken by the high-bred deerhound by speed of foot, between the Derrys.' The Caledonian Hunt does not seem to have survived for more than three or four years, for there are no further records of any hunting after 1820.[135]

Coming to more recent times, the late Captain James Brander Dunbar, who died aged 94 on Christmas Day 1969, claimed to have inspired the story of the poaching wager in John Buchan's novel *John McNab*. In this, a sportsman shot a stag, a grouse and took a salmon all in one day on a friend's estate without being caught. Buchan based this on an exploit by Captain Brander Dunbar before the First World War, and a framed cheque in settlement of the bet hung in his study at Pitgavenny, Morayshire. It is rumoured that the scene of the exploit was Braulen, belonging to Lord Lovat.

The modern deer poacher, however, cannot be compared to the adventurous characters of men like Ruadh, Lonavey and R Gordon-Cumming, for the majority kill only for financial gain, and unless a deer can be shot near a road providing a quick getaway route for his vehicle, from which he seldom ventures far, deer on the hill are comparatively safe. Unfortunately, however, severe wintery weather drives hundreds of deer down from the inhospitable hillsides to such areas where, weakened by hunger and cold, they become easy prey for these motorized bandits.

Although I hold no brief for such men, there are some exceptions, and the resourcefulness of one did have the flavour of the exploits of R Gordon-Cumming, even though his quarry was only a hind which he had shot and left hidden in some bracken with the intention of fetching it at some later hour. In the meantime, however, the stalker having heard the shot, had found the carcase in the bracken, and taking up a position some distance away, awaited the return of the poacher.

After a time the stalker noticed a small van coming up the glen, and as it failed to reappear from out of a small clump of trees bordering the road immediately below where the hind was lying on the hill, he assumed the poacher had returned and would shortly be seen walking up the hill to collect the carcase, when he himself would then step down to the van and await the poacher's return, so catching him 'red-handed'. But no poacher appeared and after perhaps a full hour, the van was seen to drive away down the glen.

Puzzled as to what had happened, the stalker walked over to the patch of bracken and, to his amazement, found the carcase had disappeared! Apparently the poacher had realized that he might be watched, and instead of walking up to the carcase had crawled through the bracken under cover and having tied a rope to the hind had somehow managed to crawl back to his van, towing the hind with him!

I think he deserved it!

One of the most exciting and probably longest stalks of all times is described by Charles St John when he followed the 'Muckle Hart of Benmore' for a full six days before he was finally able to shoot 'him through the head' whilst standing at bay in a loch.

For some time 'a hart of extraordinary size' and cunning had been known to frequent the area around Benmore in Sutherland, and although many stalkers had sought to bring him to account, the stag – now known as the 'Muckle Hart of Benmore' – seemed to have a charmed life, and was unapproachable. One Sunday evening Malcolm, the shepherd from the shealing at the foot of Benmore, whilst returning from church, came across the track 'of a hart of extraordinary size; and he guessed it must be the Muckle stag of Benmore'. The information was immediately passed on to Charles St John who, the following morning at sunrise, set out with his dog *Bran* to try and find the stag, but all to no avail, and that evening he returned to Malcolm's shealing without so much as having set eyes on him.

On the following day, Charles St John, accompanied by his friend Donald and *Bran*, were out on the hill by dawn, but it was not until late afternoon that the object of their chase was first seen. 'He was a long way off, perhaps a mile and a half, but in excellent ground for getting at him. Our plan was soon arranged. I was to stalk him with the rifle, while Donald, with my gun and *Bran*, was to get round, out of sight, to the pass by which the deer was likely to leave the valley. My task was apparently very easy. After getting down behind the rock I had scarcely to stoop my head, but to walk up within shot, so favourable was the ground and the wind.' However, success was not to be, for Donald and *Bran* unfortunately disturbed two other stags which, in their flight, took the Muckle Hart off with them, without so much as giving either party a chance of a shot. That evening they again returned to Malcolm's shealing.

The following day – although up an hour before daylight, and searching corrie after corrie for signs of the big stag they saw nothing, and by nightfall were so far away from the shealing that they had to spend the night out on the hill, on a bed of heather, with their plaids wrapped around, and 'slept pretty comfortably'.

Their luck on Thursday was not much better, and although they repeatedly during the afternoon 'came on the fresh tracks' of their deer, he still 'remained invisible'.

On the following day Charles St John took to the hill on his own and, as subsequent events turned out, had foolishly left his dog *Bran* behind. It was not long before visibility was reduced to about twenty yards, as a thick mist slowly enshrouded the hill. Not knowing which way to go in such weather, he decided to spend the night in the mountains – but not before he was able to shoot a couple of grouse with one shot from his rifle which he 'speedily skinned . . . and took them down to the burn to wash them before cooking'. In crossing a sandy spot near the burn, he came across some deer tracks which, by their size, undoubtedly belonged to the 'Muckle Hart'. But nothing could be done until morning, so after cooking and eating his meal of grouse, he wrapped himself in his plaid and was soon sound asleep in a bed of heather.

On the following morning he soon spied a deer lying on a black hillock, and on closer examination, realized to his delight, that it was *the* stag. Approach to the beast, however, was not going to be easy, for the stag commanded a good view of the valley below, and was facing in his direction. After a long crawl a burn was eventually reached, from which he was able to approach to within about 200 yards (183 metres) of where the stag lay. When further approach was impossible, Charles St John 'watched him for fully an hour', the water up to his knees all the time. Eventually the stag rose, and after stretching himself 'went into the burn at a deep pool and standing in it up to his knees, took a long drink'. At long last the chance of a shot at the Muckle Hart of Benmore seemed likely, so let the stalker himself describe the events that followed. 'I stooped to put on a new copper cap and prick the nipple of my rifle; and – on looking up again he was gone! I was in despair! and was on the point of moving rashly, when I saw his horns again appear a little farther off, but not more than 50 yards [46 metres] from the burn. By and by they lowered, and I judged he was lying down. "You are mine at last" I said, and I crept cautiously up the bed of the burn till I was opposite where he had lain down. I carefully and inch by inch placed my rifle over the bank, and then ventured to look along it. I could see only his horns, but within an easy shot. I was afraid to move higher up the bed of the burn, where I could have seen his body; the direction of the wind made that dangerous. I took breath for a moment, and screwed up my nerves; and then with my cocked rifle at my shoulder and my finger on the trigger, I kicked a stone which splashed into the water. He started up instantly, but exposed only his front towards me. Still he was very near, scarcely 50 yards [46 metres], and I fired at his throat just where it joins the head. He dropped on his knees to my shot; but was up again in a moment, and went staggering up the hill. Oh, for one hour of *Bran*. Although he kept on at a mad pace, I saw he was becoming too weak for the hill. He swerved and turned back to the burn; and came head long down within ten yards of me, tumbling into it apparently dead. Feeling confident, from the place where my ball had taken effect, that he was dead, I threw down my rifle, and went up to him with my hunting-knife. I found him stretched out, and as I thought, dying; and I laid hold of his horns to raise his head to bleed him. I had scarcely touched him when he sprang up, flinging me backwards on the stones. It was an awkward position. I was stunned by the violent fall; behind me was a steep bank of seven or eight feet high; before me the bleeding stag with his horns levelled at me, and cutting me off from my rifle. In desperation I moved, when he instantly charged, but fortunately, tumbled ere he quite reached me. He drew back again like a ram about to but, and then stood still with his head lowered, and his eyes bloody and swelled, glaring upon me.... We stood mutually at bay for some time, till recovering myself, I jumped out of the burn so suddenly, that he had not time to run at me, and from the bank above, I dashed my plaid over his head and eyes, and threw myself upon him . . . the poor beast struggled desperately and his remaining strength foiled me in every attempt to stab him in front; and he at length made off, tumbling me down, but carrying with him a stab in the leg which lamed him. I ran and picked up my rifle and then kept him in view as he rushed down the burn on three legs towards the loch. He took the water and stood at bay up to his chest in it. As soon as he halted, I commenced loading my rifle, when to my dismay I found that all the balls I had remaining were for my double-barrel, and were a size too large for my rifle. I sat down and commenced scraping one to the right size, an operation that seemed interminable. At last I succeeded, and, having loaded, the poor stag remaining perfectly still, I went up within twenty yards of him, and shot him through the head. He turned over and floated, perfectly dead. I waded in and towed him ashore, and then had leisure to look at my wounds and bruises, which were not serious, except my shin-bone, which was scraped from ankle to knee by his horn.' After gralloching the stag, Charles St John returned to the shealing where he found Malcolm, who was subsequently despatched to recover the 'Muckle Hart of Benmore' – 'a duty which he performed before nightfall'.[167]

It is not often that a wounded stag will make any deliberate attempt to attack a human being, and so far as I am aware, the only known instance of an unwounded animal ever doing so refer to stags that have been reared from a calf by man. One such instance occurred in Ross-shire during the early part of the century when a stalker was attacked and killed by a stag which he had himself brought down from the forest as a calf and which, in consequence, knew him well. Early in the last century Dr John Mackenzie of Eileanach was attacked on Kinlochewe Forest by a wounded stag that 'rushed on three legs' at him; he replied 'with small shot, which, applied to his neck, ended matters'.[130]

In another instance in 1907, a heavy stag was shot by Mr B who, believing it to be on the point of death, discarded his rifle and went over to bleed the animal. He had no sooner laid his hands on the stag, however, when it recovered, and for some moments a struggle ensued between the stag and Mr B who had seized the antlers in an effort to prevent the stag driving home the attack. Eventually the stalker also grabbed hold of the antlers, and the two together were able to pull the beast down, and so enable it to be knifed.[79]

Even as long ago as the beginning of the last century, Dr John Mackenzie was scornful of the habits of the 'modern' stalker. 'It makes a real deerstalker sick to observe how stalking is generally managed now in the Highlands,' he wrote. 'I used always to be on the look-out ground if possible before 6 am to observe any deer which had been down feeding on the low ground, and were slipping away in the morning to their spying posts up above for the day. Now the sleepy, soft-potato fellows must have a grand breakfast ere they can stand the fatigue of the hill. The keepers are sent out very early to find the deer and mark them down for the guns, and when the soft gunners reach the ground, on horseback if possible, they are led up to the shooting spot as if to kill a cow or a sheep, getting their shot, but never forgetting the luncheon hour. When we went to stalk we were always off ere daylight. I have walked miles on the moor to reach the spying spot long before dawn.'[130]

Scrope who, by his writing, did much to popularize deerstalking in Scotland, was even more scornful of the stalker who liked his bed. 'As for sleep,' he wrote, 'he should be almost a stranger to it, activity being the great requisite; and if a man gets into the slothful habit of lying a-bed for five or six hours at a time, I should be glad to know what he is fit for in any other situation? Lest, however, we should be thought too niggardly in this matter, we will allow him to doze occasionally from about midnight till half-past three in the morning. Our man is thus properly refreshed.'[172]

Scrope was also of the opinion that the less hair the stalker had upon his head, the better. 'It is lamentable,' he wrote, 'to think that there are so few people who will take disinterested advice upon this or any other subject; but without pressing the affair disagreeably, I leave it to a deerstalker's own good sense to consider whether it would not be infinitely better for him to shave the crown of his head at once, than to run the risk of losing a single shot during the entire season. A man so shorn, with the addition of a little bog earth rubbed scientifically over the crown of his head would be an absolute Ulysses on the moor, and perfectly invincible.' Scrope was at least honest, for he admitted that 'I never did it myself'!

As to eating and drinking, Scrope's advice to his stalker was to 'be moderate in your food' for 'he should go forth light and shapy as a gazelle'. However, 'the best part of a bottle of champagne may be allowed at dinner; this is not only venial, but salutary. A few tumblers of brandy and soda-water are greatly to be commended, for they are cooling. Whiskey cannot reasonably be objected to, for it is an absolute necessary, and does not come under the name of intemperance. . . . Ginger beer I hold to be a dropsical, insufficient and unmanly beverage: I pray you avoid it!'

Scrope's idea of the model stalker was that he 'should not only be able to run like an antelope and breathe like the trade winds, but should be endowed with various other undeniable qualifications. As, for instance, he should be able to run in a stooping position, at a greyhound pace, with his back parallel to the ground and his face within an inch of it, for miles together. . . . He should rejoice in wading through torrents, and be able to stand firmly on water worn stones, unconscious of the current . . . when he loses his balance and goes floating away upon his back . . . he should raise his rifle aloft in the air, Marmion fashion, lest his powder should get wet and his day's sport come suddenly to an end. A few weeks' practice in the Tilt will make him quite *au fait* at this. . . . To swim he should not be able because there would be no merit in saving himself by such a paltry subterfuge; neither should he permit himself to be drowned . . . it is very cowardly to die'.[172]

The introduction of sheep farming during the latter part of the eighteenth century when sheep ousted the cattle from the hill farms, resulted in a great reduction in the number of deer in many localities. Needless to say, the deer poachers were not slow to take advantage of the situation, for the majority of sheep owners were only too glad to turn a blind eye on an activity which was providing additional grazing for their sheep. By 1883, however, the price of wool had fallen to well under what it had been fetching ten years previously, and before the close of the century sheep farming in the Highlands of Scotland was on its way out. The coast was now clear for deer stocks to be built up again, and with the increasing interest in stalking, more and more land was set aside exclusively for deer.

By this date much of the available stalking ground was already being snapped up by sporting tenants, most of whom came from England – and indeed, so popular had forests and moors become in Scotland by the middle of the last century, that in 1840 some of the newspapers were reporting that many sportsmen had to return south disappointed after travelling over the whole of the north in search of shooting quarters. By the 1880s one man in particular was responsible for the shortage of stalking grounds, and that was Walter Winans, an American millionaire who at one time held the sporting rights over almost a quarter of a million acres, stretching practically from Lochalsh in the west to Loch Ness and the Moray Firth in the east, and included such forests as Fasnakyle, Glencannich, Glenstrathfarrar, Glomach, Killilan, Pait and Kintail. Winans needed a large tract of country for his main interest was deer driving, which was conducted with military precision on a large scale. He was a brilliant shot and could kill stags galloping at 200 yards (182 metres) range – indeed he often preferred to walk with the beaters than wait in the butts, as this gave him more chance of a running shot at a deer breaking back through the beaters. He was a fanatic on camouflage and once had his white mare dyed grey to make her less conspicuous on the hill.

Whilst Winans was bowling over his running stags at extreme range, many other sportsmen had great difficulty in hitting a standing beast at 50 yards (45 metres), and the sheer incompetence of some of them must have been a severe trial on the patience of the professional stalker accompanying them. Quoting from the unpublished diary of George Ross, the stalker at Corriemulzie, Hart-Davis writes, 'stag after stag was missed; often a young stag or a hind was shot by mistake, and beast after beast went away wounded, with no proper attempt being made to follow it up. No doubt the inaccuracy of the Express rifles was largely to blame for the fact that so many fiascos took place, but most of the gentlemen whom Ross took to the hill seem to have been rotten shots. . . .' A typical day was 24 September 1872 when Mr Eddie had seven shots which resulted in the death of 'one Heind', and Mr Davys eight, all at stags within fifty yards, but missed each time.[96]

The first paying tenants of which there is record dates back to 1800 when Sir John Maxwell, Mr Macadem and Mr Robert Wallace took a ten-year lease of the game on Abergeldie Estate (Aberdeenshire). Twenty years later, Scottish Newspapers were reporting in August that most of the shooting quarters were being occupied by English sportsmen, whose main interest, however, at that period seems to have been grouse. In 1821 Invereshie deer forest was let to the Duke of Bedford whilst the Marquis of Huntly was the tenant at Coignafearn in 1824. Despite this growing interest in deerstalking, there were still large properties in Scotland that, apparently, did not appreciate that deerstalking had any value, and when Strathconan (Ross-shire) was advertised for sale in 1836, deer were not even mentioned in the announcement. By 1910 this fine forest was yielding about 140 stags per season.

So much for hunting and stalking the deer in the past – what of today? The high velocity, precision rifle, fitted with telescopic sight as well as replacement of the horse by mechanical transport, has completely revolutionized deerstalking. The modern deerstalker with a jeep, haflingor or snow-trac vehicle, etc. to drive him to the hill no longer need leave the lodge before 8.30 or 9 in the morning, and with the accuracy of the modern rifle and the lethal potential of present-day ammunition, the deerhound – so essential to follow up the wounded animal in the past – is no longer required. Even since 1939 there has been a noticeable change in stalking procedure, for during the inter-war years the use of the telescopic sight for deerstalking in Scotland was very much in its infancy, and, indeed, there were many stalking veterans who considered that its use made it all too easy and was, therefore, a trifle unsporting. A telescopic sight undoubtedly does make long shots at deer easier but this is not deerstalking which, if to be enjoyed as a *sport*, should be a test of fieldcraft and not marksmanship. The target is the place for the latter, but when an animal's life is at stake, the shot should be made so easy that any possible error on the part of the sportsman is reduced to a minimum. A telescopic sight does not make one shot any *straighter* – it only makes the vital target area more visible and, accordingly, more accurate shooting should be the result. Some sportsmen, however, will not use the telescopic sight because any movement of the rifle, perhaps by a side wind or, more likely by exhaustion after a long crawl on the part of the stalker, is so magnified that a miss seems inevitable. For this reason, therefore, it is a mistake to use a scope glass of higher magnification than, say, four power.

The main principles of deerstalking are, first to find your deer, select the one to go after, and then make an approach to within about 100 to 150 yards (90 to 137 metres) of it before taking the shot.

Spying for the deer is done with either a telescope or binoculars, and whilst it is easier, due to the larger field of view, to locate animals with the latter, selection of a suitable beast to stalk is best accomplished with the telescope. When deer are spotted, study the surrounding ground very carefully through the glass before attempting to see the deer with the naked eye, trying, if possible, to pick out some prominent landmark as a guide to their whereabouts, such as a big rock, rowan tree, etc.

Once the deer have been located, the approach should, if possible, be made from above rather than below, for the simple fact that the deer, normally wary creatures, expect danger to come from the valley and their gaze is generally directed in that area, relying on their noses to warn of any danger from above. Another advantage of an approach from above is that during the morning the deer, which have been feeding in the glen during the night, start to work up the hill, and by the time the stalk is complete, may well be a thousand feet or so nearer the skyline than when first seen. If a stalk is attempted from below, therefore, the deer will be moving away and the further they get up the hill, the better, in all probability, will they be able to see the ground below. On the other hand, although it will take some little time to climb the hill to get above them, once there, provided the wind keeps steady and the stalking party don't show themselves unnecessarily, if the deer haven't settled for their midday siesta, they will in all probability be moving upwards in their direction. A crawl or slide from above is, also, a far easier manoeuvre than a long, uphill crawl in full sight of deer.

On the majority of deer forests the line of approach, dictated mainly by the contours of the terrain and direction of the wind, is conducted by the professional stalker, and it is essential, therefore, that the rifle sportsman – or 'gentleman' as he is often referred to by the stalker – should follow, explicitly, his instructions and actions. If the stalker crawls with his belly pressed to the ground, he does so for a special reason and nothing will annoy him more than to glance round and find his companion, if not actually walking upright, is at least crawling on hands and knees to avoid getting wet!

When in full view of deer, with no cover at all, advance will have to be made only when the deer have their heads down whilst feeding, or if lying down, their attention is directed elsewhere. This operation is undoubtedly easier when all the deer are on their feet, for they will probably be feeding, and unless their suspicions have been aroused, there will be plenty of opportunity to advance when all heads are down or turned away. With resting deer, however, the position is much more difficult, for if the day is calm there will probably be a sitting deer facing in almost every direction. Resting deer will normally be chewing the cud, but should the jaw movement of any deer suddenly stop, it is certain that something has happened to arouse suspicion. Under such circumstances the stalking party must 'freeze'. The deer may rise to its feet to have a better look, but if assured that it was a false alarm, will generally settle down again.

In late afternoon, in sunny weather, it is often possible to use the sun's rays to dazzle the deer, whilst an approach is made over an open piece of ground. On the other hand, if the sun is behind the deer, any movement on the part of the stalking party will be more easily detected. There are numerous other do's and don'ts which will bring success or failure to a stalk. In all probability, however, it will be scent rather than sight of the stalking party that will cause a premature end to most stalks, for the wind plays funny tricks at times in Scotland's glens and corries.

Before the war the normal method of bringing in deer from the hill was by pony. A Highland pony is slow maturing, and is not really fully matured until it reaches the age of about four years, although three-year-olds may be worked on a small forest for the first year, or on home beats where the distance to the larder is not very great. On some of the larger forests, however, particularly during the early part of the season when the stags are well out, it is nothing unusual to require a pony to bring in a beast a distance of ten or twelve miles or more, and young ponies should never be asked to do such a long trip. The working life of a pony – often referred to as a garron – lasts from about three to twenty years, and sometimes even longer.

During and since the war considerable progress has been made in the design of light vehicles capable of extremely hard cross-country work, and as a result such vehicles as the Swedish 'Snow-trac' and American 'Weasel' – both track driven – and a number of smaller versions either wheel or track driven, have gradually replaced the pony, and whilst they are, in most places, considerably more efficient and speedy, a truck load of deer carcases coming in from the hill can never present the romantic picture of a pony, with a deer a-saddle and antlers silhouetted against an evening sky, which seems to epitomize the end of a successful day on the hill.

Forty years ago, the man of moderate purse and limited holiday, unless he was the fortunate guest of an owner or long lease tenant of a deer forest, had few opportunities for deerstalking in Scotland. Today this has largely changed, for during and since the last war many of the larger estates have been broken up into smaller units and many more owners, anxious to obtain some revenue from their estates, are now prepared to let these smaller forest units on short term tenancies, varying in period from perhaps a month to a week, or even a day or two in some cases. A number of hotels have also taken the tenancy of one or more forests in order to let stalking by the day or week to their guests. The Forestry Commission, who are now the largest landowners in Scotland, controlling more than a million acres, also provide stalking for both red and roe deer on a day basis.

Stalking costs, like everything else, have increased considerably during the past fifteen years, and whereas in 1964 a day's stalking from a hotel could be had for about £10, today's prices, principally due to the increase in wages and escalation in rents, will be at least £90 to £100 – a figure which does not, of course, include board. An advantage of stalking from a hotel is that the sportsman is relieved of all worries of normal tenancy agreements, principally connected with staff and transport, for the use of the stalkers, ghillies, ponies and/or mechanical transport will all be included in the cost.

As to the cost of renting a forest for the season, this varies tremendously from one estate to another and depending also on whether a lodge is provided or not. With estates keeping the venison, but accommodation provided, the average price for stalking in 1978 varied between £120 to over £200 per stag, dependent on the degree of luxury available. Thus, for example, the all-in cost required for a week's stalking from Braelangwell Lodge, Sutherland in 1978, during which six stags could be shot, was £1250. On the other hand, the rent for ten stags during a week's stalking from a lodge of more modest facilities, was £1295.

Cheaper stalking can, of course, be obtained on sheep ground, but in the majority of cases no professional stalker, ghillie or transport will be available, so the two are not really comparable.

The day or short-term tenant usually wants, quite naturally, his money's worth, and will probably wish to shoot the best head he can find. But it is obviously bad for the forest if only the worst animals are being left to breed. In any lease agreement, therefore, there should be a limit set as to the number of good heads that can be shot – say not more than one or two per cent – and perhaps a fine imposed, say of £50, for any promising young royal killed. On the other hand, there could well be a bonus of £5 for every switch killed. A day-permit holder should not normally be allowed to shoot a royal.

So much for the cost of shooting a stag in Scotland today. The next question is, should there be an extra charge for shooting trophy heads? I think there should, and quite a number of landowners who let stalking are of the same opinion.

On the continent the main charges are based on either the weight of the antlers or on its C.I.C.* international points score. Weight is not a good measurement, for it includes the weight of the skull, or at least part of it, and good antlers can be grown from small skulls and vice versa. Furthermore, the assessment of any trophy under the rather complicated C.I.C. formula is not easy for anyone not conversant with the method, and is not to be recommended.

What constitutes an outstanding Scottish red deer trophy? Any royal with an antler length of at least 82 cm (32 in.); an inside span measurement of 76 cm (30 in.) or more and a beam circumference measured between the bay and tray tines of at least 12 cm ($4\frac{3}{4}$ in.) with good, strong tines, is good, and if the length of such a trophy reaches 100 cm (about 39 in.) extremely good for a wild Scottish stag.

As a method of charging extra for any outstanding trophy shot by a tenant, I believe the following formula might be suitable and easy to work to:

1 A charge of £20 for each tine in excess of ten.
2 An increase of £10 for every centimetre the length of *each* antler exceeds 81 cm (32 in.).
3 An increase of £10 for every centimetre the *inside* span exceeds 76 cm (30 in.).

These increases would, of course, be additional to whatever basic fee per stag was being charged.

The minimum extra trophy charge, therefore, for killing a royal with an antler length of less than 81 cm, and a span of less than 76 cm would be £40 plus, of course, the basic fee.

During the 1974 stalking season, a 14-pointer was killed on Kylestrome Forest in Sutherland with the following measurements:

Length 96.5 cm (left) 97.8 cm (right) inside span 79.9 cm

* C.I.C. = Conseil International de la Chasse

Had this fine trophy been charged in accordance with the formula suggested above, the extra fee in *addition* to the basic (rent) fee for shooting a stag would have worked out as follows:

		Number	*Factor*	*Total*
Points in excess of 10 (14)		4	× 20	80.0
Length of antler in excess of 81 cm:				
left antler (96.5 – 81)	=	15.5	× 10	155.0
right antler (97.8 – 81)	=	16.8	× 10	168.0
Inside span in excess of 76cm (79.9 – 76)	=	3.9	× 10	39.0
				£442.0

When one adds to this figure the basic fee for shooting a stag which, as stated above, can vary between about £70 to over £100, the final figure is well over £500.

Probably the best Highland stag killed during the present century was a 13-pointer from Braulen Forest in Inverness-shire in 1905, and which, with an assessment of 180.73 C.I.C. points was the only Scottish head to be awarded a Gold medal at the 1971 Budapest International Exhibition of Game Trophies. Under the proposed trophy fee formula, this head would have cost about £660 to shoot.

Figures in the region of five to six hundred pounds may seem a lot of money, but compared to the four-figure prices required to shoot stags in Hungary and Yugoslavia, it is ridiculously low, particularly when one realizes that for about £660 one could shoot the *record* trophy for Scotland, whereas a large trophy stag in one of the eastern countries of Europe could well cost $20,000 – say about £10,000 – and if it happened to be a world record, considerably more.

There is undoubtedly big money in big antlers, and there is no shortage of continental sportsmen prepared to pay these astronomical prices for them. It is purely up to the sportsman to shoot the size of trophy to suit his pocket, and if he is content to shoot switches and stags bearing antlers of no great merit, then the cost will probably be under £100, which does not seem unreasonable today.

From an estimated red deer population in 1979 of about 250,000, about 36,000 to 40,000 beasts are being killed annually in Scotland, of which about 16,000 will be stags. In recent years much of this venison has been exported to Germany – a trade which by 1972 had amounted to well over 1000 tons per annum and more could have gone that way if it had been available.

Whenever output fails to satisfy demand, prices rise and during the early part of the 1973 deerstalking season, venison dealers were paying anything from 45 pence to 53 pence per lb. for carcases in the skin, with a deduction of 5 pence per lb. for any beast that had been shot in the haunch. This was more than ten times the price venison was fetching in 1966 and about 30 pence more than in 1972. Compare these prices with those of pre-war when, in 1936 the Manchester market was paying only about one penny per lb. (under half a new penny)!

During 1974 there was a big slump in venison prices and no game dealer was prepared to pay more than about 25 pence per lb. for early season stag venison, and during the hind season this fell as low as 11½ pence per lb. The reason for this dramatic slump was that at the beginning of the season the German market was in a state of uncertainty while new Export of Game regulations were being drafted and these eventually came into effect on 1 January 1975; as a result very little venison was able to reach Germany from many Scottish deer forests in an acceptable condition. For instance, every carcase 'shall be submitted within 24 hours to a licensed game exporting firm' where it must be 'officially inspected, appraised and marked accordingly' by a veterinary officer. On entry into Germany, a veterinary certificate both in English and German, must accompany each shipment, which should be in a refrigerated container. Furthermore 'skinning and dissecting at the place where the animal has been shot is prohibited' and the heart, lungs, liver and kidneys must accompany each carcase and 'be marked in such a way as to indicate that they belong to the carcase in question' and must remain 'next to the carcase until the official inspection has been concluded'.

As a result of these regulations most deer forest owners found it necessary to completely overhaul their larder facilities – and in some instances, build a completely new unit, whilst game dealers organized a daily collection of carcases from the forests in refrigerated vans so as to get the venison into their warehouses as soon as possible after coming in from the hill. Once more, Scotland's venison has been acceptable in Europe and at the commencement of the 1977 stalking season, dealers were paying an all-time high of about 75–80 pence per lb. in the skin. However, by the end of the hind season, the figure had slumped to just over half this amount, and about 55–60 pence per lb. was as much as the Scottish dealers were prepared to pay during 1978 for stag venison.

In the folk-lore of the Highlands, deer are called 'fairy cattle' and were supposed to be milked on the mountain tops by the fairies. Fairy women were also said to assume, on occasions, the shape of a deer, and Scrope relates such a transformation which took place in the forest of Gawick (Gaick) in Inverness-shire when 'Murdoch, a noted deer-stalker, went out at sunrise into the forest, and discovering some deer at a distance, he stalked till he came pretty near them, but not quite within shot. On looking over a knoll he was astonished at seeing a number of little neat women dressed in green, in the act of milking the hinds. These he knew at once to be fairies; one of them had a hank of green yarn thrown over her shoulder, and the hind she was milking made a grasp at the yarn with her mouth and swallowed it. The irritable little fairy struck the hind with the band with which she had tied its hind legs, saying at the same time, "May a dart from Murdoch's quiver pierce your side before night"; for the fairies, it seems, were well apprised of Murdoch's skill in deer killing. In the course of the day he killed a hind, and in taking out the entrails he found the identical green hank that he saw the deer swallow in the morning. This hank, it is said, was preserved for a long period, as a testimony of the occurrence.'[172]

This was not Murdoch's only adventure, for on another occasion 'he got within shot of a hind on the hill called the Doune, and took aim; but when about to fire, it was transformed into a young woman; he immediately took down his gun, and again it became a deer: he took aim again, and anon it was a woman; but on lowering his rifle it became a deer a second time. At length he fired, and the animal fell in the actual shape of a deer. No sooner had he killed it than he felt overpowered with sleep; and having rolled himself in his plaid, he lay down on the heather; his repose was of short duration, for in a few minutes a loud cry was thundered in his ear, saying, "Murdoch, Murdoch! You have this day slain the only maid in Doune". Upon which Murdoch . . . immediately quitted the forest as fast as his legs would carry him'.[172]

At times things happen that logical reasoning fails to explain, and the majority of people would undoubtedly dismiss the above events as figments that only happened in the imagination of Murdoch, and others to which similar events have occurred. A friend of mine who owned a deer forest in Sutherland, once told me of a weird experience that he and other people had encountered with a stag just prior to the Second World War. His story was so unusual that I asked him to write it down for me, together with the names of those who witnessed these strange happenings, which he agreed to do provided no names were mentioned should the account ever be published. And this was his story.

It was in August 1937, that a stag bearing only one antler of rather peculiar shape, was first seen with about a dozen other stags in a Sutherland forest. The stalker, who was accompanied by the wife of the owner of the forest, decided that the one-antlered stag should be their quarry, and as all the beasts were lying down and there was good cover for approach, it appeared that the stalk would offer no great difficulty. For about 300 yards (274 metres) the stalking party had to pass behind a hillock, but when they arrived at the place selected for the shot, although all the other stags were still lying peacefully together, there was no sign of the one-antlered stag.

A few days later the owner of the ground was stalking by himself in 'a certain Corrie which has a bad reputation' when he saw a one-antlered stag, which was lying down and which, from the description given by his wife, must have been the same beast that had given her the slip some days previously. He decided to stalk it. All appeared to be going well until, at about 200 yards (183 metres), the stag just seemed to disappear. As the beast had been pretty well in view the whole time of the stalk, its sudden disappearance naturally puzzled him. In order to make sure, therefore, that he had not, during the course of the stalk, mistaken the actual spot where the stag was lying, he started to retrace his footsteps, but he had barely gone more than about 400 yards (366 metres) when the stag reappeared in exactly the same position as before, still lying down.

A repeated stalk was made. But again, when he got to about 200 yards (183 metres) from the stag, it disappeared. This time, however, he continued the stalk and when he was about 100 yards (91 metres) from the spot where the stag ought to have been, the air, according to his description, 'became absolutely evil, despite the fact that it was a nice, bright day'. Although rather unnerved by the whole episode, he continued the stalk until, at about 40 yards (37 metres) from where the stag ought to have been, he 'could distinctly see the grass flattened as though something was lying on it'.

Anxious to get to the bottom of this, he withdrew the rifle from its cover, a careful sight was taken at the spot where it was presumed the shoulder should be, and he was just about to pull the trigger when something wrenched the rifle out of his hands and hurled it to the ground some three yards away. Thereupon 'the grass was seen to rise as if a weight had been taken off' and shortly afterwards, at a distance of about 200 yards (183 metres), the stag suddenly became visible and trotted away, and 'the air became clearer'.

Some days later, the owner of the forest, accompanied by a stalker, found the same stag on a different part of the ground with a mixed party of other stags and hinds. A stalk was decided upon and all went well until they were within about 100 yards (91 metres) of the deer, when, as on the previous occasion, 'the air seemed to become evil, although it was a nice day'. This time, however, the stag remained in view the whole time and, in due course, at about 90 yards (82 metres), a shot was fired at it, although, in the words of the owner, 'I expected something to happen'. Something did happen, for apparently the bullet went clean through the one-antlered stag and killed another beast standing some distance behind. A second shot was fired at the same range and on this occasion the bullet 'was distinctly heard to strike him but nothing occurred'. The stag ran off, but at about 150 yards (137 metres) he gave a chance for a third shot. Again the bullet was heard to strike, but again with apparently no ill-effect.

Although the stag was not seen again during the remainder of the stalking season, the stalker saw it during the winter months until February, when it disappeared altogether.

What is the explanation for this extraordinary train of events? The stag's disappearance from the resting herd in the first instance can be explained by the fact that for a short time the entire herd was lost to sight during the stalk. But what of its disappearance on the second occasion whenever it was approached closer than 200 yards (183 metres)? The owner of the forest *could* have mistaken the exact spot, and, although the grass was seen to be lying 'flattened as though something was lying on it' this *could* have been a shadow or play of the wind on grass. But what about the rifle being knocked out of his hand? Nerves, wind, imagination, or what? The owner of the forest was alone on this occasion, so there was no chance of his stalker having 'accidentally' wrenched his rifle out of his hand. Nor, unfortunately, was there any witness of this event.

And what about the third meeting with this mysterious stag which on this occasion remained in sight throughout the whole episode? The owner *may* have been mistaken in believing his first shot went right through the one-antlered stag, killing one behind, because in his excitement and apprehension he *may* have aimed at the wrong stag or perhaps missed, the bullet hitting another beast standing to one side. He was, I know, an experienced deerstalker, and I cannot believe that he would ever dream of taking a shot at an animal when he knew that another beast was standing directly behind, for unless the former was hit in some bony part of the body, the beast behind would be most likely to be hit as well. Hearing the second and third shots strike something is no sure proof that contact with the stag had been made; it could have been a peat hag, which can, at times, make the firer jump to wrong conclusions. By this time one can appreciate the emotion of the man behind the rifle and even the most experienced shots sometimes have 'stag fever' when even an easy shot will be missed.

One thing is certain, however, and that is that none of these shots had any effect on the animal; otherwise it would not have been seen on the ground for the next three or four months. What eventually became of it will never be known. Whenever the subject was subsequently raised with the stalkers they all seemed strangely silent on the matter.

Not so very far away from the forest where these events occurred lies Kildonan, in Sutherland, and on this ground a somewhat similar event occurred before the First World War. In the days before the railway passed through the Kildonan Strath, it used to be visited by stags from the Duke's grounds at Langwell. One big stag – known locally as the *Piper* by virtue of the fact that his left antler, growing down over his cheek and then turning up again, somewhat resembled a pipe – visited Kildonan for three successive years, and although the Kildonan stalkers had several good chances of killing him, all tried without success. At last, in exasperation, Norman Fraser observed: 'This stag has a charmed life, he is either an evil spirit or protected by a witch, and nothing but a silver bullet will have any effect on him. If lead would kill him, he was dead long ago.'[157]

Accordingly some silver bullets were made in Edinburgh (witches were supposed to have no power over silver) and everything was in readiness for the *Piper*'s return to Kildonan during the next season. Unfortunately, the *Piper* did not keep his appointment, having it was subsequently discovered, been poached by a shepherd on the Braemore ground – and I have no idea whether he used lead or silver bullets.

Chapter VII
Stag Hunting on Exmoor

Although by the beginning of the thirteenth century Exmoor, extending to about 80,000 acres, was reserved as a royal forest, it was not really until about the beginning of the eighteenth century that stag hunting in its more modern form really began. At that time the second Duke of Bedford was hunting deer from Tavistock, and another gentleman, by the name of John Walter of Stevenstone, was doing likewise around Torrington and Hatherleigh, but whether either ever brought their packs on to Exmoor is doubtful.

The first person, therefore, who was to take any real interest in hunting on the moor itself was Lord Walpole (later to become Lord Orford) who probably started to hunt the deer about 1724, but it was not until a few years before his death in 1750 that he had become a lessee and warden of the forest. By 1740 a pack of hounds was also being hunted by Edward Dyke of Pixton, who himself died in 1746. Dyke was followed by Sir Thomas Acland who, in 1767, bought the forest lease from the Lord Orford and hunted hounds until 1775, when Colonel Basset of Watermouth took over the mastership. The pack then became known as the North Devon Staghounds, and for the next fifty years there was regular hunting. Then, in 1824, the pack was sold to a German who, during the following year, took hounds back with him to Europe. For the next three years, therefore, no hunting took place during which time the deer were shot by all and sundry. In 1827 Sir Arthur Chichester raised a scratch pack of foxhounds with which he hunted the deer for the next six years, but when in the spring of 1833 he had to give up hounds, the poacher again resumed his works of destruction.

Hunting was resumed again in 1837 when Dr C P Collyns, author and sportsman, organized a pack which, for the first time, became known as the Devon and Somerset Staghounds, but this, in turn, failed from want of funds in 1842.

When Collyns gave up, the Hon. Newton Fellowes kept hounds going for a further six years when Sir Arthur Chichester again took over for one season only (1848). After this season the pack seems to have been disbanded, and during the next six years deer were hunted only by visiting packs such as Mr Luxton's Harriers (1850 and 1851), Mr Carew's Foxhounds (1852–3) and two packs of hounds normally used to hunt the carted deer.

Then, in 1855, Mr M Fenwick Bisset, a Berkshire gentleman who had come as a tenant of Lord Carnarvon at Pixton Park, near Dulverton, formed a pack and from that date onwards, Exmoor has been regularly hunted by its own pack of hounds – the Devon and Somerset Staghounds.

Mention must also be made of four other packs of staghounds that have operated in the vicinity of Exmoor during the past seventy years. In 1896, owing to deer damage in the southern part of the county, a pack had been formed by Sir John Heathcoat-Amory of Knightshayes Court, Tiverton, to hunt the country south of the railway line from Taunton to Barnstaple. This pack, known as Sir John Amory's Staghounds, was hunted by Sir John's sons until abandoned in 1915. For the remaining years of the war, however, Sir John Amory's country was hunted over by a scratch pack organized by Mr Charles Slader of South Molton, and when he retired, a new pack, known as the Tiverton Staghounds, was established under the mastership of Mr J Yandle. This pack is still operative.

Five years after Sir John had formed this pack, Mr E A V Stanley of Quantock Lodge established a pack to hunt the deer which had latterly grown plentiful in the Quantock Hills. This pack, which became known as the Quantock Staghounds, hunted regularly until the First World War caused its disbandment. Fortunately, however, Colonel (later Sir) Dennis Boles, the Master of the West Somerset Foxhounds, stepped into the breach and kept the pack going at his own expense until 1931, when a committee took over. Like the Tiverton Staghounds, this pack is also still operative.

In the same year as Mr Stanley was organizing the Quantock Staghounds another pack, the Barnstaple Staghounds, was being formed, under the joint mastership of Captain Ewing Paterson and Mr A Clarke to hunt the north Devon country in the west, but within four years it had to be abandoned. Apparently in 1908 an attempt to re-form this pack was made by a Barnstaple grocer by the name of Ashton, but after three seasons the Barnstaple Staghounds closed down for good. In addition to these local packs, Mr Peter Ormrod was invited to bring down his staghounds from north Lancashire and during his one season in the south (1904–5) accounted for twenty deer.

During the early thirties, the autumn stag hunting season generally terminated about 10 to 15 October, but now the large stags are hunted from August until about 23 October, thus leaving about a week to ten days break before the hind hunting season commences on 1 November and this is continued until the end of February. There then follows a break of about a fortnight before the spring hunting season for the young stags (three- and four-year-olds) commences and this continues until the end of April.

During the nineteenth century it would appear there was no hunting during the winter months. Stag hunting began on 10 August and continued for about a month, ending on the occasion of Barnstaple Fair at the beginning of September. Then about a month was devoted to hunting hinds, but at the beginning of October all hunting was suspended until 8 April, when hinds were again hunted until 4 June, by which date, of course, many would be heavy in calf and indeed, within about a week of calving.

By the beginning of the last century the seasons were altered slightly, the stags being hunted until about the middle of October, followed by a short winter hind season until about 10 November and a spring hind season commencing in late March or early April and finishing about 24 May. Lord Graves was very critical of extending the hunting season into some of the winter months, for in a letter to Viscount Ebrington (26 June 1812) he stated that by doing so 'half the season thrown away and hunting so late in the year crippl'd and kill'd the hounds'. Expanding on this point of view he stated 'the pack should *never* run after the last week in *October* or even *so late* if the weather proves severe. You otherwise lose your best hounds by the chill of the water which occasions violent convulsions, and terminates the life of the poor animal almost immediately. The only remedy on this occasion is frequent and profuse bleeding'. He was also of the opinion that 'a *young male deer* should never be run, such a chace kills the hounds and horses, or renders them unserviceable for a fortnight, without killing the light galloping deer you pursue'. He appreciated that 'an old stag is more difficult to find or indeed to be harbour'd', and on that account he recommended that tufting should commence '*at eight o'clock* instead of ten and eleven' as was the practice.[85]

Seasons and customs have changed considerably since Lord Graves's day, and although hind hunting is carried on throughout the mid-winter months, and young deer are hunted in the spring, neither have produced the casualties or mortality he forecast.

The spring hunting season for hinds continued until 1862, when it was abolished during the mastership of Mr F Bisset, who was never very fond of it because in spite 'of all efforts to single out a barren hind, it too often resulted in the death of one heavy in calf. Indeed, stocks were getting so low that in 1857 Mr Bisset had turned out four stags and three hinds obtained from Lyme Park, Cheshire.

The result of its cessation was a rapid increase in the number of deer and within ten years of its abandonment, deer stocks had increased from about sixty to five hundred head. Mr Bisset was now faced with the problem of trying to reduce, rather than increase deer stocks and on some occasions no fewer than four deer were being killed a day. The county was said to be simply swarming with deer, and matters were considerably aggravated by an outbreak of rabies among the pack in 1878, so hunting had to be restricted and all affected hounds killed. Shortly afterwards there were further cases so that the whole pack had to be destroyed. Even this step was not successful in eradicating the trouble, for in 1879 fresh cases occurred in the newly formed pack and four hounds were destroyed and hunting temporarily suspended. During these years of restricted hunting, the stock of deer had, of course, had an opportunity of further increasing and by 1880 were said to have 'got out of control'.

In 1883 the experiment was made of hunting four days a week during the stag hunting season, but the number of deer killed was not thereby much increased, so the practice was not continued. It was also found that hunting on so many occasions was too great a physical strain on hunt officials owing to the distances and long hours involved. The main reason for the steady increase in deer during this period seems to be that insufficient attention was being paid to the killing of hinds – the very same cause that made the deer stock soar in Scotland during the inter-war period.

Once again, at the beginning of the 1884 season, rabies struck, the first victim being a puppy which had come from a kennel where there had been previous cases of rabies. A second puppy was similarly afflicted, so there was nothing to be done but to destroy all the puppies, seven and half couple in total, and this course fortunately prevented the disease spreading to any of the older hounds. Four hounds were lost, however, during the 1884 season by falling over the cliffs.

However, the stock of deer in the West Country continued to mount, and in the Quantock coverts in particular, the number of big stags in 1895 was said to be 'very great'. About seven years later Archibald Hamilton estimated their numbers in the whole of the Exmoor country to be about 1500.[93]

Deer, particularly the stags, can cause immense damage to farmers' crops and but for the farmers' love of the chase they would never be tolerated. In a root field, for instance, a stag will pull up root after root, and after tasting it with but one bite, will cast it aside. A hind, on the other hand will often take several bites at a root without dislodging it, before passing on to the next. They are very fond of oats, and just before harvest time will often make their headquarters in an oat field. It is for this sort of damage that a deer damage fund – which was started about the turn of the century – exists, the money for which is provided by individual donations, sums ranging from about 50p. to over £100.

The deer in the Barnstaple area were, apparently, causing most anxiety, and the difficulty of dealing with them was increased because hounds were prevented from entering certain of the best holding coverts owned by Miss R Chichester who was opposed, not so much to stag hunting as to the killing of anything, even to the extent of rats and rabbits. Eventually, however, a subscription pack was formed in 1901 to hunt the Barnstaple area, which meant that there were now four packs of staghounds operating in the Exmoor country, and at the time were accounting for about 250 deer. At least the increase in deer population had been arrested and during the next few years a slight decrease was becoming apparent. This was continued until the outbreak of the First

World War by which time the Barnstaple pack had already ceased to operate.

Between the two wars the three packs – Devon and Somerset, Quantock and Tiverton (previously Sir John Amory's) – continued to hunt their respective areas and killed, on an average, about 200 deer each season, of which the Devon and Somerset would account for just over half – namely about fifty-one stags and sixty-six hinds per annum, a figure which is slightly above that which the pack is taking today (about 100).

During the late war the deer of Exmoor were considerably disturbed by military activities, for this wild domain was obviously well suited for not only manoeuvres with tanks but also artillery firing and shooting ranges. To a large extent, therefore, the deer were driven from the moor to seek sanctuary in the more sheltered and cultivated areas where they found living conditions much easier. Unfortunately, this close association with the farmers' crops soon brought them into trouble with the owners and numerous complaints were reported to the hunt of deer damage. Control of deer stocks by hunting alone was found to be inadequate, and so the hunt, in collaboration with the local Pest Officers and War Agricultural Committee, through whom damage by deer was generally first reported – organized deer drives during which the deer were shot with shotguns. Between 1939 and 1941 no fewer than 1057 deer were killed in this manner.

Since the war the deer slowly drifted back to their former haunts, and by 1951 it was probable that the total stock of deer in the West Country was approaching its pre-war level – in fact, in certain districts such as around Dunkery, there was such a plethora of deer that in addition to hunting, deer drives were again organized in the spring of 1951 by the Devon and Somerset Staghounds, with the result that during the 1950–51 season some 210 deer were either shot or taken by hounds in the West Country, not to mention others that were doubtless poached or shot elsewhere.

Even today, hinds are too plentiful in some districts, which result in urgent requests from local farmers for a greater cull to be taken than is possible by hunting. In consequence a number of deer drives are organized by the Devon and Somerset Staghounds during which the deer are moved by hounds, under the control of the huntsman, to a few selected marksmen who, unfortunately, still prefer to use the shotgun with S.S.G. shot rather than a rifle. It is claimed, however, that very few wounded deer do escape, because the hounds are used to follow up any suspected of having been hit.

At the present time the Devon and Somerset Staghounds hunt three days a week from early August until the end of April, except for a short interval of about ten days at the end of October between the cessation of the autumn stag season (warrantable deer) and commencement of the hind season, and about a fortnight at the end of the hind season before starting with the spring stag hunting season (three- and four-year-olds).

The Quantock Staghounds, however, hunt only twice weekly, which is also the practice of the Tiverton Staghounds when after hinds but for stags, three outings per fortnight is considered sufficient.

During the season it is estimated that about 184 deer are killed (stags and hinds) as follows:

	Devon & Somerset Staghounds	*Quantock Staghounds*	*Tiverton Staghounds*	*Total*
Autumn stags	24	8	6	
Spring stags	12	15	9	
	36 + 4 *	23	15	78
Hinds	60 †	20	26	106 †
Total	100	43	41	184

* Casualties – other than by hunting.
† Includes a certain number of casualties and also hinds killed during deer drives.

This total, which compares very closely to the highest number killed by the Devon and Somerset prior to the First World War (179 stags and hinds during RA Sanders' mastership 1895–1907) does not take into account deer that are poached or those killed legitimately by farmers on their land, so it could well be that the total deer casualties in south-west England are something over 200. I am informed *in litt* by Mr ER Lloyd (former hunt secretary) that in his opinion the total deer population has 'not altered significantly over the last twenty years, and that although there are certainly too many hinds in three or four districts, overall the numbers are satisfactory and just about stand at an acceptable level in the country as a whole'. It would appear, therefore, that the deer population in the area falls somewhere between 1200 and 1500 head.

So much for some of the history of the deer of Exmoor and the staghound packs that hunt them. Let us now consider how the hunt is conducted.

It is probably true to say that during the autumn stag hunting season the 'official' known as the harbourer plays the most important role, for without his assistance staghunting would be very unselective. For instance, it is only during the autumn that the older stags (five years old and upwards) are hunted, for the three- and four-year-old stags will not be hunted until the spring. Between these two male deer seasons, the hinds, as mentioned previously, will be hunted. In a locality where there are many deer about it is obviously not difficult to find an animal to hunt, but the chance of it being a *warrantable* stag (five years old and upwards) during the autumn season would not be very great. The quarry for the day, therefore, has in normal circumstances, already been decided upon and located well before hounds meet, and on the harbourer's shoulders falls this exacting task.

On the day prior to the meet the harbourer will be found in the district of the advertised meet making enquiries from local farmers etc. as to the location or movement of any deer in their neighbourhood. It may be that some deer are making a nightly raid on crops, or perhaps a local forester has been in the habit of disturbing deer when going about his work in the woods. Acting on any information he receives, the harbourer visits a number of localities where deer have been reported, and from an examination of the deer's slots (hoof prints) will be able to decide whether the deer is old or young, male or female, and act accordingly. It is seldom, particularly in the autumn when the trees, foliage and bracken are in full leaf, for deer to be seen during the middle part of the day, so having selected both from slot marks and local report, a likely quarry for the following day, an attempt must be made to not only see the animal but also ascertain where it is in the habit of lying up during the daytime. Unless the informant is well known to the harbourer, the slot mark will probably prove to be the most reliable information, for the size of a stag's antlers, like the fisherman's lost fish, is often much exaggerated in the telling.

In former days, it would appear that the harbourer used a hound to track deer from their night feeding ground to where they were lying up for the day. These hounds – called limers because they were kept on a *liam* or leash while the deer was being tracked – did not appear to be of any particular breed. Their main qualification was to have a good nose to follow a deer scent, and under no circumstances give tongue. During the seventeenth century, however, it would appear that a bloodhound or 'suit hound' was used, and it was the practice of the harbourer to 'rub the nose of his hound with vinegar for quickening his scent'.[169]

Once the harbourer has decided on a likely animal, his next task is to try and view it. This can sometimes be done, if the wind is right, by taking up a position overlooking the area where the stag was wont to feed in the evening. With luck, the stag will appear before darkness falls, and if appearances confirm that the stag is warrantable, then the harbourer will slip away without disturbing the animal, only to return to the area at dawn the following day to see, if possible, the stag returning to its day lying-up place. Sometimes the stag has already departed before first light, but by following the slot marks, the harbourer will be led to the wood in which the stag has taken refuge. Under no circumstances will the wood be entered but a detour of the complete wood will have to be made in order to ensure that the animal has not passed right through, and gone to lie up elsewhere. Early morning mist or fog undoubtedly increases the harbourer's difficulties and on such occasions slot marks will probably be the only guide.

During October when the rut is at its peak, the stags are very restless and will seldom remain in one position for long. If undisturbed, however, a stag with hinds seen at dawn will not be very far away when hounds meet later in the morning. Unattached wandering stags also travel considerable distances at this time of year, and the harbourer is ever on the lookout for such an animal – which as often as not will first reveal its presence by a roar.

Having decided where the stag has bedded down for the day, or if running hinds, the herd is likely to be found, the harbourer will make his report to the Master at the meet, and subsequently accompany the huntsman, with four or five couple of selected hounds called tufters, to where the stag has been harboured. If the whole pack was used to rouse a harboured stag in woodland, the chances are that several other deer would be roused as well, and the hounds, dividing in to small groups, would start hunting a number of deer, which would be chaotic. Indeed, during the last century when Mr Newton Fellowes was Master (1842–8) tufting for the deer was omitted and the coverts were drawn by the whole pack which caused the death of many an unwarrantable deer.

If a single stag has been located on open moorland, however, it is then sometimes possible to lay on the pack without prior tufting but such occasions are rare. 'The chief requisites for a tufter,' writes Hewett, 'are the best of noses, tongue, staunchness and discipline – the last because it must be possible for the huntsman to stop him with a rate off the wrong deer, and off the right one when they have got him away, so that the pack can be laid on. Once the harboured stag is roused, the harbourer's work is finished, and the whole responsibility passes to the huntsman.'[109] Unlike hunting the carted deer, once the deer has been roused by the tufters, it is unnecessary to give it any 'law', for the time interval between rousing the deer and informing the Master is quite sufficient to allow the deer to collect its wits and get under way. In fact, the sooner the pack can be laid on, the better.

Stag hunting has always been a favourite pastime in France, and there is little doubt that many French methods found their way into stag hunting here, the system of tufting being one.

The procedure of tufting is carried out by the huntsman and harbourer, both on horseback, along with the tufters entering the wood with the intention of rousing the stag which has been harboured there. Outside the wood the whip, and one or two experienced members of the hunt will be posted so as to spot the deer when it emerges. If one was stalking the deer with the intention of getting within shot, the direction of approach would have to be upwind, otherwise the stag would wind the approaching party and make its departure unseen. In tufting, however, direction of approach is really immaterial as the most important thing is to drive the stag into open country where the pack can be laid on and a good hunt ensue. Quite often young deer or hinds, also bedded down in the wood, may be roused before the object of the search has been seen but good tufters will immediately abandon the chase of such deer on command, and continue the search for the harboured animal. Old stags, once bedded down, will be loathe to leave their bed, and on days of little or no scent, it is often the sight of an antler tip above the undergrowth that will first betray the squatting stag's presence to the huntsman or harbourer.

Undoubtedly the most famous harbourer was Fred Goss who, during his twenty-eight years' service under seven Masters, was said to have harboured over 1200 stags. Fred Goss was harbourer to the Devon and Somerset Staghounds from 1894 to 1921, and his experiences during these years are well described in his book *Memories of a Stag Harbourer*. On one occasion, whilst searching in vain for a deer which he knew was harboured in a wood near Hawkridge, he 'became aware of an enormous swarm of flies buzzing round the brambles at one particular spot'. Thinking there must be a reason, he clambered down the bank and beat the undergrowth with his hunting whip. 'Thereupon up sprang the stag and leaping the fence nearly jumped right over the huntsman who was riding along the ditch inside.'[84]

'The first essential in slotting,' writes Goss, 'is to learn to distinguish the slot of a stag from that of a hind. Up to the age of two the differences are slight and differentiation difficult, though even at that age an expert can frequently detect the slightly broader toes that indicate the male. From two upwards the differences become increasingly clear. The toes of a hind are long and narrow. Their slots are smaller, shallower, more pointed and, on account of lighter weight, less sharply defined and altogether more "lady-like" than those of stags, which have broad square toes and large and weighty heel marks. The front slots of a good huntable stag, which are those by which I always judge, should be square, with the toes well blunted and worn back from constantly alighting on them in jumping. . . . Each claw of a good warrantable stag should be at least an inch wide, but the measurement of the slot as a whole will depend to some extent on the soil in which it is planted.'

Slot marks also give a good indication as to age, for 'elderly stags, like elderly men, walk somewhat differently from young ones, and a slot with toes turned outwards always indicates age'. A good sign of an old stag, whether the slots are large or not, 'is a difference in the length of the two claws of one foot, one claw being sometimes a good deal longer than the other'. Also, the relative positions occupied by the fore and hind slots are of importance when stags are walking. 'In young stags they practically coincide, that is, the hinder slots falls into the fore slot so that it almost covers it. In older stags the hinder slots falls slightly more behind.'[84]

Slot marks, however, can be most misleading, too, at times, for the size of slot from the same animal will differ considerably dependent on the texture of the ground, the softer the soil the larger the impression which, to the inexperienced eye, might elevate a three- or four-year-old to a much older animal. The most exact slot size is reproduced on hard ground or even a metalled road. The hooves of the forefeet are larger than the hind feet and give, therefore, a larger slot mark. Generally speaking, also, the larger the set of slots the larger the deer, stags normally having larger hooves than hinds. But as in most things connected with wildlife, there are exceptions and stags with small slot marks or a hind with larger than average have been recorded.

Occasionally, in a period of prolonged drought when the ground is baked bone dry – or perhaps after a heavy fall of rain, existing slot marks become filled with water thus making it impossible to tell whether they were fresh or old – the experienced harbourer has to look for other signs. 'On one very wet morning,' writes Goss, 'when slotting was difficult, I noticed some rape stems that had been bitten off where deer had been, were still green. The green colour told me the stems could not have been exposed to the hot sun that had been shining the day before, and proved conclusively that the rain-filled slots in the field had been recently made. Droppings sometimes form important guides. From hinds they fall separately and resemble those of a sheep. From stags they fall in clusters and are much bigger. The degree of hardness and dryness of droppings affords indication of their freshness or otherwise.' My native tracker in Africa, when tracking buffalo, used to stick his bare toe into their droppings to test the temperature – but I cannot see the West Country harbourer going to this extreme!

Racks – the gaps deer make in fences whilst travelling between their feeding ground and the woods – should also be carefully examined, not only for slot marks but also for hair left on the undergrowth etc., as the deer pass through. If a particular rack is in regular use there will be such a mass of slot marks that it will often be difficult to tell their freshness or class of deer using it. In such circumstances, Goss says, 'it is a good plan to erase some of them with the point of a stick, so that fresh ones can be detected without any trouble the next morning when the presence of a stag has to be finally confirmed. Care must, however, be taken not to interfere in any way with the rack itself, for in summer-time when food is plentiful and easily come by, deer are very suspicious, and any disturbance of the fence where they pass through, such as the dislodgment of a stick or two, will often put them off. In winter when food is scarce, they become bolder and less particular.'[84]

Spring hunting after the young stags is carried on in much the same manner as for the autumn stags, but harbouring at this time of year, when the trees are bare of leaf and there is little ground foliage, is, of course, very much easier. The young stags use their legs rather than their wits, and often provide long runs.

During the four months' hind hunting season, harbouring a particular deer is unnecessary. Hinds are usually found in herds, and the real difficulty is to separate a huntable beast from the herd, so that it can be properly hunted, and prevented, if possible, from joining other deer. A huntable hind is one that is at least two years of age. H P Hewett recalls an occasion when 'hounds started with over a hundred deer afoot, and about half of them hinds, but the huntsman nevertheless succeeded in taking one of them. It was a triumph of team work by the huntsman, his hounds and his whipper-in'.[110]

Continuing, he states, 'The whipper-in has an even more important part to play in hind hunting than in stag hunting, continually stopping hounds off fresh deer, viewing deer and spotting if there is a well-run hind among them – sometimes he has a hunt on his own with part of the pack whilst the huntsman carries on with the rest.'

Although the harbourer, therefore, is not employed in hind hunting, the prudent Master will always make enquiries before the meet and ask a knowledgeable local to report on the movement of any hinds in the area, and if possible, 'bring deer to the meet', i.e. tell him where he can find without delay.

The tufters – perhaps seven or eight couple – are then cast into the wood or combe where it is known some hinds are probably to be found, and as soon as a single hind breaks away from the rest, the pack is laid on as quickly as possible. If local reports have been accurate, the tufters are frequently running their deer within thirty minutes of the meet which, during the months of November to January, are at 10.30 am.

Generally speaking, hinds give a faster run than stags and seem to have more stamina. On the other hand, they seem loathe to leave their home ground, and whilst a stag will often make for a definite point, hinds are inclined to take a more circular route, often finishing not far from where roused. This is particularly the case early in the season when she has left a calf behind, and in such circumstances is ever on the lookout for transferring the pack to run other deer, so she can slip back to her calf.

Frequently a hunted stag will go through a herd of hinds, or cattle in an attempt to confuse the pack, or he may push up a young deer from the bracken to take his place.

Another ruse of a hunted deer – particularly a stag – is to 'beat the water', i.e. follow a stream for quite a long distance without touching a bank. Indeed, there are several recorded instances where a deer has kept to the water for three miles or even more. In such circumstances scent is often lost, and it may be a splash on a stone, or perhaps a slot mark on some muddy ground that will tell the huntsman where the deer has left the water.

Sometimes a deer will go upstream, jump out on the bank and after following it a short distance, once more jump back into the water. Occasionally a deer will sink itself in a pool under a bank throwing its head back with little but the muzzle showing above water level, and in such instances hounds have been known to pass by without winding it.

At times it would appear that deer, when taking a line, will run just as readily down- as up-wind. This is particularly noticeable during the early stages of a hunt, when the deer may be trying to join up with some companions known, perhaps, to be in a certain area. Sometimes a deer will appear to loiter before hounds, letting the pack approach to within, perhaps, 200 yards before attempting to put on any pace. Stags are frequently seen to take a brief wallow (mud bath) whilst being hunted, and a beaten stag will frequently lie down and flatten itself, as close to the ground as possible like a hare, trusting that this ruse will make the hounds over-run him. As often as not the lair will be reached by a huge sideways leap with the intention of breaking the scent line.

Points, and actual running distances of hounds, have undoubtedly been much exaggerated by some of the earlier historians, but during the season 1959–60 and the one following, hounds ran a $15\frac{1}{2}$-mile point in the former season and a 14-mile point in the latter, which were reliably estimated at about 22 miles and 30 miles respectively as hounds ran.

In the winter, weather conditions on Exmoor can be very severe indeed, and coupled with the shorter daylight hours, hind hunting is a more arduous and exacting sport than the autumn stag hunting. Fog is always a menace and throughout the stag and hind hunting seasons many a day has been lost or spoilt on this account.

The majority of deer, particularly the stags, are killed in water. A stag at bay chooses, if possible, a spot where he can stand and the hounds must swim. In such a position he is very difficult to approach, more particularly if his back is protected by a bank or rock, thus ensuring that hounds can only approach from the front. If forced to swim, hounds may succeed in getting on to a deer's back and this very occasionally may result in a hind being drowned but seldom, if ever, a stag. Having brought the deer to bay, the final kill is not for the hounds, and every effort is made to keep them clear, for an imprudent hound can be seriously damaged by a blow from the stag's antlers or forefoot. Occasionally during the last century, a deer was lassoed and taken alive for transfer elsewhere, but in the majority of cases it was despatched with a knife, formerly by slitting the animal's throat, so that the young hounds could be blooded in order 'that they may the better love a *Deer*, and learn to leap up at his throat' but, since 1879, with a deep heart thrust through the chest.

Before the stag could be knifed, however, it was necessary to force the head back so that the neck and chest were exposed. This was accomplished by a rope noose – or the thong of a whip would do as well – being twisted round the antlers while the animal's attention was directed on the hounds and when this had been accomplished, two members of the hunt who had been waiting for this moment, each seized one antler which was held back along the stag's back, thus enabling the huntsman to knife the deer. It is unwise to seize the antlers when the stag's head is down, such as when threatening hounds, otherwise there is danger of being thrown over the stag's head.

At one time, however, it would seem that any hunt servant could run in behind the stag at bay and either hamstring it, so as to make him fall, or stab him to the heart with a sword thrust *behind* the shoulder, and the reward for this act was to receive the head and skin of the deer.

Despite the strength of a stag at bay, however, remarkably few accidents have occurred resulting in injury to the huntsman. Lionel Edwards recalls an incident that happened in 1925 when a little two-year-old, with 'uprights' only, charged the huntsman in Red Cleeve. 'This youngster was run-up by two or three couples. The huntsman was with the smaller lot of hounds, and, finding this animal run-up with these few hounds, he endeavoured to take him. On his dismounting, this gallant little beast, knocking over the intervening hounds, charged and, in spite of several heavy blows from the hunting-crop, his antlers got home in Ernest Bawden's leg just above the knee. He then faced the huntsman, intending, doubtless, to charge again,' but a farmer came to his assistance, and the deer was overpowered.[70]

The same authority also recalls an earlier occasion when two horses were gored by a stag. Very tired, a stag 'was being chased up a narrow lane by the pack, with the huntsman following behind. Presently, owing probably to the steepness of the hill being too much for him in his exhausted state, he charged back again down the lane, meeting the huntsman, S Tucker, going up. The latter's grey horse was badly gored by the stag as it passed, a shocking wound being caused. The stag then met a stranger, who hastily fell off as his horse was in turn attacked. As this horse galloped off riderless the stag struck it in the buttocks repeatedly'. The stag was eventually taken and killed.

It would seem that the change from slitting the deer's throat to a heart thrust was a result of a visit by the Prince of Wales in 1879, who, when the stag was brought to bay, was invited by Arthur Heal, the huntsman, to administer the final *coup de grâce*. Describing this historic event, H J Marshall writes, 'The Prince, grand sportsman that he was, consented and at once dismounted. Then he accepted, from the hand of Arthur, the latter's formidable clasp hunting-knife with blade extended ready.

'A thrill of terrific excitement and expectation ran through the assembly of horsemen as they stood and watched the Prince deliberately wade into the stream and, without hesitation, drive the knife deep straight to the heart of the stag.'[133]

This method, apparently, aroused the interest of all concerned and was, as the Prince explained to Arthur Heal, the method always employed at the royal forest of Balmoral. All agreed that it was more humane than slitting the throat, and thereafter this method was adopted.

Today, however, a bayed stag is always despatched with either a shotgun or humane killer, and whilst a hind is *normally* killed in similar fashion, on occasions a knife may still be used. If the humane killer, which is now always carried not only by the huntsman but also by the Master and whipper-in, has to be used, it is still necessary for the stag to be physically held by its antlers so that the weapon can be held against the deer's forehead – otherwise it is ineffective.

Of the two weapons, provided the deer can be so held, the humane killer is the best in the hunting field, for not only is it more portable on horseback than a shotgun, but it is much safer to use. With the latter great care must always be exercised for fear of shooting a hound, and whilst such an event would probably not make the headlines, when a hunt follower is shot it certainly does! Not so long ago, after a deer had been despatched, the shotgun was laid on the ground, the safety catch apparently not having been applied. A hound, running over the gun, happened to tread on the trigger which discharged the second barrel, peppering one of the followers, but fortunately not too seriously. Such an incident only shows that one can *never* be too careful when handling firearms.

Even during the seventeenth century it seems that the deer was sometimes finally disposed of with a shot. 'Gallop in roundly,' advised R Blome, 'and kill him with your *Sword* or *Gun* before he has time to turn head upon you.'[19]

After the deer has been killed it will be bled and paunched – (gralloched) in much the same manner as is practised in Scottish deerstalking, the former to make the venison more palatable for human consumption, whilst the latter will be given to the hounds as their 'reward', and speedily consumed. The heart is given, where practicable, to the owner or occupier of the land on which the deer is killed, whilst the liver and kidneys will be given to the helpers present at the time of taking the deer, priority being given to anyone who gets wet pulling the deer from the water. The carcase itself will be sent back to the district where the deer was originally found, and the venison distributed among the farmers who had probably 'fed' the deer and been the sufferers from any crop damage.

The head (antlers) is always returned to the kennels by the venison distributor and in the majority of cases, after being set up on a wooden shield, with suitable inscription on the frontal bone, will be presented by the Master to a farmer or landowner in the hunt country. By the terms of the Mastership Agreement, heads may not be disposed of outside the hunt country. On rare occasions it has been presented to some notability attending the meet, such as to the Prince of Wales in 1879. Another recipient of the deer's head was a Mr George who stripped off his clothes and swam out to recover the carcase of a stag that had been drowned by hounds about a hundred yards out from the beach near Rodney. 'Streaking', therefore, is nothing new, and if it finds a place in the Guinness Book of Records, Mr George must be accredited as the first 'hunting streaker'!

The hide is the perquisite of the huntsman, as were also all hind heads in former times. Today the hind heads are not considered of any value and are disposed of.

The slots (hooves) are generally awarded to keen members of the hunt or to visitors who are present at the kill. The tusks (two canine teeth) may be similarly disposed of. They make attractive scarf pins or cuff-links, etc., and in stalking in Europe are much prized by continental sportsmen.

Lord Graves gives a list of monies which it was the custom to pay various people connected with the hunt's sport. In the first place a guinea (105 pence) was generally given to the farmer on whose land the harboured stag had mostly fed. A similar reward went to the harbourer himself. Another guinea went 'to the farmers who ride the Chase and are at the death of the stag'.[85]

The footman who assisted in securing the stag likewise received a guinea, but the farmer who had stopped the tufters was given only half-a-crown (12½ pence) for his trouble. Any person who took home the couples got a shilling (5 pence) for what, on many occasions, was a long journey. This was five times less than the reward to the man who carried the stag's head home. The person who removed the stag's carcase was paid according to the distance.

For hind hunting, the amounts were slightly less. For instance, the harbourer of a hind received five shillings (25 pence) whilst the reward for the footmen at the death of a hind was half-a-guinea (52½ pence). Anyone who secured and took care of a stray hound was paid half-a-crown (12½ pence), and at certain meets a sum of two shillings (10 pence) each was given to the men who were posted in the Bray or Bratton waters – a measure which apparently was 'of essential service if you wish to kill a deer, and should never be neglected when you tuft Bray Ball or Reepham Bottom'.[85]

Half-a-guinea (52½ pence) was paid annually to Mr Bryant's tenant, for permission to go through his meadow adjoining the New Town Bridge, 'as the passage through this person's field cuts off the angle made by ascending to the house in the middle of the hill and descending again to the bridge'. A farmer could also claim the payment of £1 for damage done to his fields by horsemen when tufting for a stag, but it was seldom claimed except by those who objected to stag hunting.

It would appear, also, that during the eighteenth century it was the custom to fine any person who left the field before the stag had been killed but I have been unable to discover the amount. Hollowing a wrong deer was also a crime 'of the greatest magnitude'.

Another curious custom which, in former times, doubtless produced no small monetary reward to the huntsman is described by R Blome as follows: After the kill 'the Huntsman presents the person that took the *Essay* with a drawn Hanger, to have a Chop at his *Head*, and after him, everyone hath a chop if it is not cut off; and generally the *Huntsman* or *Keeper* is provided with such a *Hanger* as is not over Sharp, that there may be the more Chops for the gaining more *Fees*, everyone giving him a *Shilling* [5 pence] at least'.[19] A blunt hanger would, therefore, bring a huntsman quite a good income!

Deer have been taken in strange places. More than one has jumped on to the roof of a house that has been situated under a hill, and one even managed to get into a first floor bedroom. Deer swim well, and quite a number have taken to the sea and finished up in the Bristol Channel. The usual locality for taking to the sea is in the neighbourhood of Porlock Weir. Commenting on this, Fortescue writes, 'The deer must be taken if possible when they go to sea, or they will go there every time they are pursued. So a boat has to be procured, the deer captured, blindfolded, and taken to the shore, whether fit or unfit to kill, to scare them from taking to it again. Not infrequently the deer beat the boat; sometimes they beat the right boat and are captured by some Channel craft. One deer so captured off Porlock was carried alive to Appledore, where the Receiver of Wreck [!] declined to allow her to be sent anywhere without the permission of the Master. Mr Bisset thus recovered her and turned her out once more.'[77]

On another occasion, about 1820, the stag, after a run of two and a half hours, took to the sea near Glenthorne and swam out to sea for some distance whilst the field watched helplessly from the shore, there being no boat available to follow. A trading vessel happened to be going down Channel and seeing the deer, a boat was lowered and the deer eventually captured and hoisted on board. The trader then sailed off. Some months later it transpired that the captured stag was taken to Cardiff and there sold.

A somewhat similar occurrence took place in 1838 during the hind hunting season. On this occasion the captured hind was taken to Bristol, where she was exhibited in the market place to the curious at sixpence ($2\frac{1}{2}$ pence) a head.[52]

Generally speaking when a deer takes to the sea, unless the pack has been close on its heels, it is seldom that more than a couple of hounds will follow. It is said that salt water carries little scent, and in consequence hounds will follow a swimming deer only as long as it remains in sight. Sometimes when a deer has been recovered by boat, one or two swimming hounds have been picked up as well, but being exhausted pay little attention to the deer sharing the boat with them.

Describing the taking of a stag at sea, Jeffries writes, 'They [the boatmen] throw a rope round the stag's antlers and draw him on board, and immediately tie his legs. A stag seems an awkward animal to get into a boat, but they manage it without much difficulty and bring him ashore to be killed. The huntsman, as before observed, always kills, that he may be sure it is a warrantable deer of proper age; if it proves not to be mature, the stag is let go . . . the boatmen receive a guinea for bringing in a stag and half a guinea for a hind.'[116]

During the inter-war period the motor boat replaced the rowing boat, and this considerably speeded up the taking of a deer that had taken to the sea. With the motor boat it was no longer necessary to take the deer on board, and during the early thirties the general procedure was to slip a rope over the stag's antlers, or round the hind's neck, and then drive the boat at full speed for a few minutes, with the result that the deer's nostrils were pulled under the water and the animal drowned. By 1930 this practice had ceased, and for many years the boatmen at Porlock Weir possessed a humane killer provided by the hunt to use at such times. Occasionally, also, once roped, the deer was knifed and the carcase then taken ashore.

On rare occasions, hounds that have followed a deer to sea have been drowned, and Richard Jefferies mentions a case of some hound carcases being washed ashore in Cardiff harbour.[116] In 1926 the following letter from the Earl of Dunraven appeared in the *Daily Mail*:

Sir – It may interest readers to know that some sixty years ago a stag that had been hunted into the sea by the Devon and Somerset Staghounds actually swam across the Bristol Channel.

It landed on the coast just under the park here (Dunraven Castle, St Brides Major, Glamorgan), to which it obtained access by ascending an almost impassable track up the cliff which is there over a hundred feet high and very steep.

There is no record of the exact place where the stag took to the water, but it is believed to have been near Porlock, and, in any case, the journey would not have been far short of twenty miles.

This would seem an incredible distance for an animal to swim, but the probability is that the stag rested on the Nash Sands, which are uncovered at low water, and went on again when forced to do so by the rising tide!

In Scotland red deer have several times swum across the Kilbrannan Sound from Arran to the Mull of Kintyre, but this is well within their capabilities for the distance is under four miles.

I understand, however, that today few deer take to the sea, and largely as a result of public opinion against the use of a boat to assist its capture, when it does occur hounds are called off and the deer allowed to escape.

The cliffs overlooking the Bristol Channel can also be a hazard and whilst they have undoubtedly been the salvation of many a deer finding refuge therein, others have fallen to their deaths, accompanied, perhaps, by one or two hounds which have been following closely.

In addition to animal casualties, it would appear that these cliffs have also claimed at least one human life, for H Byng Hall records an occasion when a young girl and her lover, whilst riding along the cliff top, roused a stag from the heather which resulted in her horse taking flight and dashing off in the direction of the cliff only to stop abruptly when the frightened animal perceived its perilous position. Unfortunately its rider was thrown from the saddle, over the edge of the precipice and dashed to death on the rocks below.[92]

During the stag hunting season it is seldom that hounds will draw again after a kill – but with hinds, a second beast is sometimes taken.

Just over a century ago, however, following the abandonment of the spring hunting in 1862, deer became so plentiful that during the 1870s on several occasions a brace of stags were killed in a day, and on at least one occasion from Cloutsham, in 1875, four hinds were accounted for.[77]

About this period it was the practice to take alive hinds and young male deer for subsequent release in the Quantock Hills. Even today, it is quite usual for three to be taken in a day's hind hunting.

In former times it was, apparently, the custom to drink the stag's health after it had been killed, but so far as I am aware, the practice disappeared some time during the latter half of the nineteenth century. Describing this ancient custom Nimrod, in the *Sporting Magazine* (*c.* 1824) wrote, 'In more chivalrous times . . . the head of the deer, after a good run, was produced in the evening with a silver cup in his mouth, out of which the favourite toast was drunk. The custom is still kept up by the huntsman, whippers-in, farmers and others, and the operation is performed in the following manner. The cup is placed in the stag's mouth, secured with a cord to prevent its falling out. When it is filled to the brim, each person who is to drink it holds a horn in each hand, and brings it to his mouth, when he must finish it at one draught and then turn the head downwards, bringing the top of it in contact with his breast to convince his companions that he had drunk it to the dregs, otherwise he will be subject to a fine.'

History was made on 10 March 1970 when the three packs joined forces in Crowcombe village, the intention being to hunt some deer which were frequenting Slaughterhouse Combe. Eventually the tufters of the Quantock Staghounds got the deer moving, and when stopped near the Stowey Road, the pack, consisting of six and a half couple from the Devon and Somerset Staghounds, and an equal number from the Tiverton Staghounds were laid on, finally to take their deer on Lady's Edge at 3.45 pm. Three hundred and twenty horses were counted leaving the meet, which was attended by some three thousand people on foot.

The occasion for this historic event was to provide some unusual manifestation of support for stag hunting, for at that time there was a private member's bill before Parliament to prohibit coursing and stag hunting. The Chairman of the Devon and Somerset Staghounds, Sir Bernard Waley-Cohen, made a speech at the meet and the event received considerable publicity on all television news channels that evening. When the private bill failed, it was adopted officially by the Labour Government at the time which, however, omitted stag hunting from the terms of the bill. There seems little doubt, therefore, that the Crowcombe meet did contribute largely to this decision.

For over forty years there has been a continuous campaign against stag hunting raised, in the majority of cases, by people or organizations who have neither knowledge nor experience of the subject. 'It has become apparent to us,' stated the Scott Henderson *Report on Cruelty to Wild Animals* (1951), 'that many people who think they know what takes place obtain their information from propaganda issued by organizations who, in turn, rely to a surprising extent on Press reports of particular items which, in their turn, are based on misconception. . . .'[103]

The controversy has, in the main, been waged between the rival factions – the supporters of stag hunting and the abolitionists – and in consequence opinions are inclined to be biased, with the result that the argument has tended to be focused on the ethics of hunting rather than the control and future of deer in south-west England.

The claim, often put forward, that stag hunting with hounds is the *only* satisfactory way of controlling the deer population in this part of England, is not borne out in practice, because occasional deer drives still have to be held to kill surplus stock, particularly hinds. Anti-hunting supporters can argue that, since some deer have to be shot, complete control should be effected by shooting. Such a thing is of course possible, but whether the farmers, deprived of their favourite sport of hunting, would tolerate *any* deer at all on their land is extremely doubtful.

It must not be forgotten that but for the re-establishment of the Devon and Somerset Staghounds in 1855, and the great interest and pride in the deer taken by farmers and landowners, who maintained this attitude throughout two world wars, there is little doubt that the red deer of Exmoor would by now have been near to extinction. How near they came to this is shown only too well by what happened during the years hunting was suspended. Paradoxically, therefore, the deer owe their existence to being hunted by staghounds, and since the latter are unable to control their numbers in some areas to an accepted level, a few deer have to be shot as well. No-one could complain about this, but what is a matter of concern is the manner in which they are shot, i.e. with a shotgun, using S.S.G. shot.

This weapon is quite definitely not satisfactory for an animal as large as a red deer, and as stated in the Scott Henderson Report, its use 'must inevitably be accompanied by a great deal of suffering'. In many countries it is illegal to use shotguns on deer, but its use in this country is still legal, provided the weapon is not less than 12-bore and the shot size no smaller than S.S.G. (*Deer Act* 1963). S.S.G., however, is not lethal against red deer at ranges in excess of about 15 yards (14 metres), and it is because of the difficulty of moving deer to within this range that much cruelty must result. Brenneke rifled slug or lethal ball, instead of S.S.G. shot, would be preferable and is used extensively and effectively on wild boar in Europe, but this ammunition can only be produced under a Firearm Certificate and has had very little use in this country.

Ten years ago the shotgun was the weapon generally used by the Forestry Commission for deer control work, principally against the small roe deer, but now it has been replaced by the rifle. Is it not time the rifle should also replace the shotgun in south-west England? One of the arguments against the use of the rifle in this part of England is that of danger to human life. This is just not true, for many hundreds of deer are shot by rifle in far more populated parts of England without incident. The best times to shoot deer in wooded country are dawn and dusk – times of day, particularly the former, when few people are astir. Times of day, in fact, when the harbourer goes about his work. The solution would be to have a few specially appointed keepers or wardens responsible for the control of deer in specific areas. When the hounds met in these areas the appropriate warden could then either act as harbourer or be in a position to give the harbourer some really reliable information about any stags in his area.

The National Trust control a large portion of Exmoor and it would seem logical, therefore, that in the National Park area anyway, they should be responsible for the deer. Would it not be possible, therefore, for some of their personnel to be employed during the winter months on deer control work? Even if this suggestion is not practicable, some solution *must* be found so that any surplus deer are only killed by experts armed with rifles of suitable calibre. In many parts of England local Deer Control Societies exist for the sole purpose of supplying personnel (unpaid) for deer control work on estates unable to do it themselves. Until such time as trained keepers are available for this type of work, would not this be an interim solution, and proceeds from the sale of the venison could even be directed to hunt funds.

Chapter VIII
Hunting the Carted Deer

Although at one time hunting the wild deer was being practised in many parts of England, the Enclosure Acts and the spread of agriculture gradually put an end to this form of hunting. So a substitute had to be found, and George III (1760–1820) is generally credited with being the first monarch to hunt a deer from a deer cart.

In hunting the fox, hare or wild deer, the aim is always to kill the animal; in hunting the carted deer the main consideration is to avoid killing or even harming the quarry. The deer should never be touched by hounds but, particularly with young deer having their first run, casualties do sometimes occur due to the struggles of the animal whilst being taken. Once initiated to the sport, however, many deer have run for upwards of ten seasons, during which time they may have given more than thirty runs without suffering any harm. Such a deer was *Mabel*, a hind belonging to the Oxenholme Staghounds which ran for seven seasons without so much as a scratch before being sent to retirement in Gowbarrow Fell park. I understand, however, that hinds are, perhaps, more likely to injure themselves than stags, whilst stags at times are inclined to become sulky and will not run. This is one of the reasons why the havier – a castrated stag – has often been found to be more satisfactory, not to mention the more obvious advantage that should it be left out there is no fear of him breeding with any of the wild deer in the district. Furthermore, a stag that has been to rut is no good for hunting until well into December so it is really necessary to hunt haviers during November and early December. When full stags are hunted, the antlers have to be removed, not only to facilitate their capture and make them less dangerous when taken, but also to enable the deer to be carried about in the deer cart. Moreover, Lt.-Col. Frank Byers of the Co. Down Staghounds, told me (*in litt.* 1964), 'that when there are a large number of stags in the park – say about 22 to only a dozen hinds – it is prudent to remove the antlers from all the stags prior to the rut, otherwise there will be some casualties'.

A carted deer enthusiast once said, 'The science of stag hunting lies in the management of the deer; the rest is a matter of a bold, fast horse and an adhesive buckskin.' Lt.-Col. Harvey – obviously influenced by some previous writing by Lord Ribblesdale – considered that successful stag hunting depended more upon the condition and humour of the deer than in scent or the type of country over which the deer is hunted. There 'is always scent enough for hounds to hunt a carted deer upon days when they could not own a fox', he wrote. 'The scent of a deer is much sweeter. Country, of course, ranks very high. . . . But the condition and temperament of your deer – for perhaps it is temperament rather than humour – come before country. Given these, and given anything approaching a decent country within a two-mile radius of your turnout – surely a very moderate postulate – you are right. An amicable deer will have you out of the bad country in a twinkling. Upon the other hand . . . the condition and temperament of the deer – certainly their condition – sometimes prevent them being taken. . . . Taking the deer is, of course, the proper conclusion of a day's stag-hunting. . . . It is nice, too, after a good run, to be able to bid good-night to your good deer comfortably housed in the best loose box about the place, up to his knees in long wheat straw.'[98]

Apropos scent, whilst Mr Jorrocks considered that there was 'nothing so wonderful as scent 'cept a woman', Christy was of the opinion that ladies with scent were out of place in the hunting field as also cigar smoke. 'By their loud talk, perhaps, right up to the covert side, and with every other man smoking the second half of his Corona, and with ladies bedecked with large bunches of Parma violets . . . plus a liberal supply of French scent, they turn the hunt into a farce.' On one occasion a member of the field unwisely remarked to the huntsman that there was no scent, and the prompt reply was that 'there'd be plenty if it were not for them stinking violets!'[48]

One of the advantages of hunting the carted deer is that the blank day can generally be eliminated although it is *just* possible that both deer taken to the meet may prove to be non-runners. However, it is seldom that this does occur. The pace is also, generally, fast and the duration of the hunt not too time consuming, so like the drag hunt, it is admirably suited to the business-sportsman whose leisure hours are rather limited.

The science of hunting the carted deer lies in the management and selection of the deer, for just as there are 'horses for courses' so are some deer better suited for hunting in, say, hilly or boggy country. Deer, like women, are unpredictable in their behaviour! Some deer will keep to the roads, others will run up and down the fences and be loathe to leave the field where uncarted, or even fail to run at all until the hounds have practically caught up with them. Catching the deer as soon as possible, however, is not the sort of sport the field are looking for, for unless the deer has given them at least an hour and a quarter's run, they quite rightly feel that they have not had their money's worth. Whilst it is obviously desirable that the deer should be taken, the success of a carted deer hunt does not depend on the capture of the deer, but on the run that it has given. Should, however, the deer be taken within the first hour it is most probable that a second deer will be enlarged.

Some deer seem to quickly understand what is required of them. During the days of the West Surrey Staghounds (*see page 38*) there was a

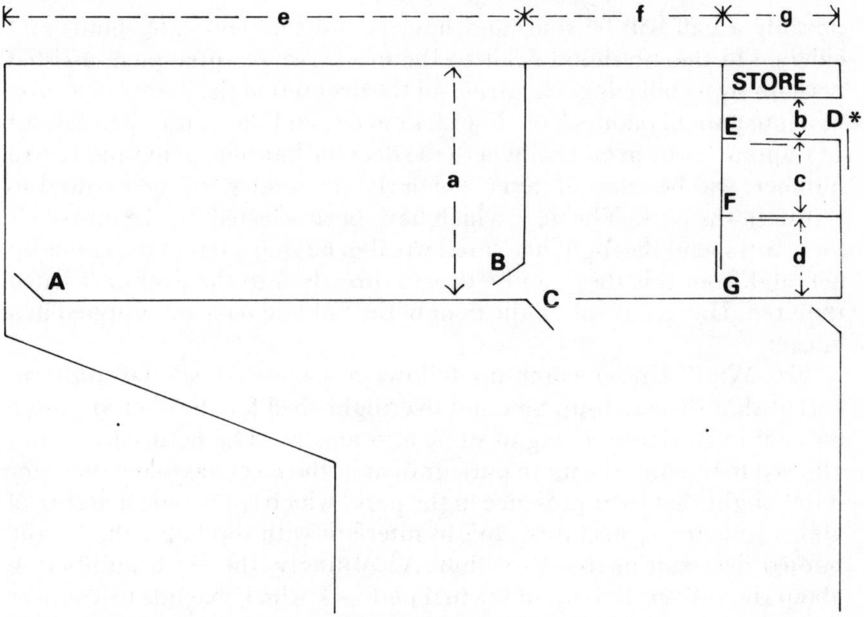

Co. Down Hunt catch-up pens (not drawn to scale)

Pen measurement	*Door widths*
a = 42 feet (12¾ metres)	A = 6 feet (1¾ metres)
b = 2½ feet (¾ metre)	B = 4 feet (1¼ metres)
c = 11 feet (3⅓ metres)	C = 4 feet (1¼ metres)
d = 11 feet (3⅓ metres)	D = 2½ feet (¾ metre)
e = 246 feet (75 metres)	E = 4 feet (1¼ metres)
f = 33 feet (10 metres)	F = 4 feet (1¼ metres)
g = 11 feet (3⅓ metres)	G = 4 feet (1¼ metres)

* Exit for loading deer into cart.

havier called *Master Walter* which, no matter where uncarted, always made a point straight back to the paddocks and on all but three occasions, arrived there before hounds. It is remarkable, also, how often a carted deer, no matter where enlarged, will make for the same line of country, and eventually be taken on several different occasions in the same locality.

The Norwich Staghounds used to catch up their deer for hunting on the morning of the meet, whereas the two Irish hunts catch them up on the previous day. This involves catching up the whole herd in an enclosure in order to select the individual deer which will be enlarged for hunting. The season lasts from about October to the end of March, and as meets generally take place twice a week during this six month period, by the end of the hunting season the deer in the enclosure will be getting fairly accustomed to the catch-up procedure.

For instance, in the Montalto enclosure, which extends to about thirty acres, the Co. Down Staghounds keep some fifty-two deer, of which possibly a half will be stags and haviers and the remainder hinds and calves. On the afternoon prior to the meet, two or three men, assisted perhaps by a collie dog, will drive all the deer out of the main enclosure, first into a small paddock of about four acres, and then into a pen (about 154 square yards in extent) where the deer for hunting, generally two in number, will be selected, after which the remainder will be allowed to return to the park. The deer which have been selected for the morrow's meet will spend the night in a small wooden hut adjacent to the catch-up pen and from this they can be driven directly into the deer cart when required. Hay is strewn on the floor of the hut and oats are supplied in a bucket.

The Ward Union catch-up follows a somewhat similar pattern, except that the catch-up pen and overnight shed for the deer are more palatial in structure, being of stone and mortar. The herd, also, is not allowed to re-enter the main park until after the meet has taken place for it is thought that their presence in the park, which is a wired enclosure of about 10 acres (4 hectares), might interfere with the hunt, should the hunted deer run in that direction. Accordingly, the herd, numbering about thirty deer, remain in the first paddock which extends to just over 1 acre (½ hectare), being separated from the main park and surrounding countryside by a 9 foot (2¾ metre) fence of corrugated tin. At one time, when the deer were kept at Slane Castle, it was the practice to leave the deer selected for the season's hunting in this enclosure throughout the six months of the hunting season, and needless to say, the whole area within the fence soon became a sea of mud without a blade of grass to nibble. The deer, therefore, had to be artificially fed throughout the time they remained in this enclosure. Even at Montalto throughout the winter months it is the practice to put roots and oats down for the deer daily in the main enclosure, but the Ward Union only feed their deer when caught up. In former times, in addition to the deer being 'highly fed', they were also 'being constantly exercised in order that they may be in thoroughly fit condition when required'.[30] The Norwich Staghounds used to feed their deer on oats, dairy-nuts, mangle and hay all the year round, and they also had the run of a good 14 acre (5¼ hectare) paddock, portions of which would be shut off in rotation so that some part of it was always being rested.

Opinions seem to vary as whether stags, haviers or hinds give the best runs, and whereas both the Norwich and Mid-Kent Staghounds generally used to prefer the hind for hunting, the Irish packs favour male deer. Both the Ward Union and Co. Down do on occasions, however, hunt the hind and some very good runs have been had. The preference as to what animal gives the best hunt seems to be very much a personal one, for whereas Mr Henry Bothway of the Norwich Staghounds always liked a havier meet, he tells me that Tom Thackery would hunt only hinds.

Whether a stag or havier gives the best run seems to depend very much on the age of the deer. The Ward Union, for instance, start hunting their stags at about four to five years old, and after hunting them for a season or two, the stags are castrated and will then be hunted for a further six to eight years as haviers. This has been done because after about six years, stags are inclined to become vicious and difficult to handle. Other male deer are castrated in their first or second year, and from a humane point of view I am certain this is preferable. Indeed I would strongly recommend two stud stags being kept until they are about twelve or fourteen years of age and then shot rather than being operated on. When the stud stags had reached the age of about twelve years then would be the time to obtain from outside a fresh stag of say, about four years of age, which in due course would take over stud duties. All male deer born in the park would then be castrated in their first year, and the pack would hunt only the havier or hind. Castration is performed either by strangulation or removal of the testicles, the Ward Union preferring the former method, but the Co. Down are definitely of the opinion that removal by knife is best.

Stags are normally gelded in September when their testicles have dropped. Castration is generally accomplished when the stags have been rounded up for removal of the antlers, which will take place in September when the antlers are hard.

The antlers are sawn off. It appears that if the antlers are removed from a stag in September at the same time as he is castrated, there is another growth of antler almost immediately and although never free of velvet, by February this new growth may well be some 20 inches (51 cm) in length with, perhaps, a fork on top and a short brow or bay point – the latter being the more common. If a havier with such antlers is selected for hunting, then the antlers will have to be cut off – an operation which causes a certain amount of blood to spurt from the antler cores. Tar is immediately daubed on the antler stumps and this both quashes the blood flow and acts as an antiseptic. No further antler will grow, but small cups sometimes appear on the velvet covered antler stumps of gelded deer, and these will often be shed in the spring.

It seems unwise to hunt a deer before it is at least four years old, for most young deer will not give in and stand at bay when they have had enough, but keep on running. These young deer, when eventually taken, may seem all right for a few weeks, but in due course a number frequently die, presumably from heart strain. A number of years ago the Co. Down obtained – one September – some deer from Warnham, mostly three and four year olds – which they attempted to run about four months after their arrival at Montalto. The result was fatal, and almost all the deer which had been hunted died. Since that date several other consignments of Warnham deer have been received by the Co. Down, who now keep them for about eighteen months before giving them a run and no further casualties have occurred. Lt.-Col. Cunningham was of the opinion that deer from England require this length of time to acclimatize themselves to Northern Ireland, but personally, I believe the casualties which the Warnham deer suffered were not due to any lack of acclimatization but from being hunted too young.

The number of times a deer is run in a season seems to vary between hunts, and whilst it was seldom that the Norwich Staghounds would run the same deer more than twice a season, the Ward Union have sometimes turned out the same animal on three or four occasions.

The hunting season generally starts about the end of September or early October, and continues until the end of March. Given good weather, there may well be at least forty to forty-five meets in a season which means that there must be at least twenty huntable animals in the enclosure if the same animal is not to be run on more than two or three occasions. Both the Ward Union and Co. Down meet twice per week during the season.

Two deer are generally taken to the meet in the deer cart, but unless the first deer has given a run of less than about an hour, it is seldom the second deer will be enlarged. When an outlier is to be hunted, then probably only one deer will be taken to the meet.

It would seem preferable to uncart the stag upwind, and this practice was certainly favoured by Charles Davis, who was once huntsman of the Queen's Hounds before resigning his post in 1866. No fox or wild deer in its right senses will go upwind for one moment longer than compelled to do so. It is recorded that with the Queen's Hounds it was the custom for the first whip to be told off to 'ride' the deer for the first few hundred yards, so as to head him in the desired direction.

Every season a few deer are left out, and the number may vary from perhaps two or three to as many as eight or ten. If a deer is left out it is generally given about a fortnight before an attempt is made to re-take it. During this period the movements of the animal will be studied, for it must be properly harboured before being hunted again. Some deer make their own way back to the park – others become very elusive and a few have successfully remained at large for two or more seasons. At one time it was the practice of the Ward Union to enlarge a few deer for subsequent hunting as outliers, but this is not practised today by either of the two surviving packs of carted staghounds. One of the oddities of carted deer hunting terminology is that the deer – be it stag, havier or hind – is always referred to as the 'stag'.

The amount of law given to a deer after enlarging from the cart seems to vary from about five to fifteen minutes, according to the day and the deer. Indeed, some deer – particularly hinds – require hardly any law at all, and even if given a few minutes will sometimes wait in the next field until the hounds are in sight. On a cold and frosty day shorter law is generally given than on a mild and muggy one.

A good deer should give a run of at least an hour and a half before standing at bay. The site chosen for the 'bay' varies between the traditional pond or stream to a yard or even a kitchen or front parlour!

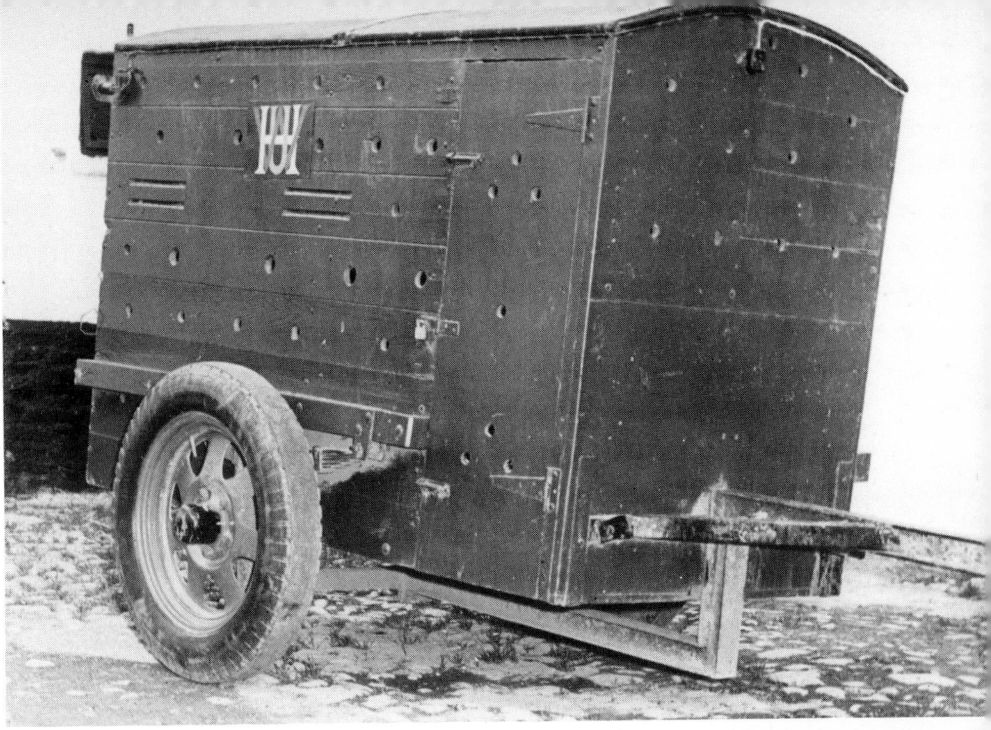

12 Ward Union Hunt deer cart

13 Interior of Ward Union Hunt deer cart

14 The Ward Union Hunt – stag being enlarged from the deer cart

15 A Ward Union Hunt stag, with antlers removed, pauses to decide which line to take

16 Stag being bayed in water by the Co. Down Staghounds

17 Hounds moving off from Montalto, Ballynahinch, after a meet of the Co. Down staghounds during January 1966. Joint Masters: S.J. Martin and T.H. Moore

18 *Above* The Co. Down Hunt deer cart
19 *Right* The Co. Down Hunt deer cart, with a boat on top used to recover deer that take to water

20 The stag being enlarged from the deer cart – Co. Down Staghounds

21 Deer in the Montalto deer paddock, belonging to the Co. Down Hunt

22 Red deer at the rut

23 Nervous work; a deerstalker of the nineteenth century taking a close-in shot (from *Deerstalking in the Highlands of Scotland* by Lt.-Gen. H. Hope Crealock.) The illustration depicts the stalker using the prone form of his companion as a rifle rest, whilst the ghillie has thrown his cloak over the hound to prevent it seeing the deer and is endeavouring to hold it down

24 Bringing in a stag on Invercauld Forest, Aberdeenshire

25 Mechanized transport is fast replacing the pony for bringing in deer. Transport varies from the large Snow-Trac, capable of bringing in at least four stags, to . . . **26** *Below* The Gnat, and . . . **27** *Bottom* The Snow-tric, the smallest of all

Occasionally a deer – particularly a havier – will stand in the open, but most deer like to get their backs into a corner or under a bank.

Some deer run better than others, and a deer which gives a good show on its first outing before hounds will not necessarily turn out the best in later years. Indeed, *Baldarra*, one of the Ward Union deer, which achieved fame as a havier, ran badly as a stag (*see page 70*). Generally speaking, however, both stags and haviers can give equally good runs, although Mr Bothway of the Norwich Staghounds was of the opinion that the latter ran stronger and straighter.

Occasionally, a stag which has been an outlier all summer and autumn, will be taken in full antler, and under such circumstances, as soon as the deer has been roped, his antlers will be cut off before it can be loaded into the deer cart.

Some deer develop a tendency to keep to the roads when running and when any animal develops this habit it generally has to be disposed of. The mass of cars, however, which nowadays follow the meet, has probably done a lot to discourage this habit which seems to have been more prevalent among the deer at the beginning of the century than it is today.

When the deer stands at bay it is very seldom that it is molested by hounds. As soon as possible it is taken by a rope, a loop being thrown over its head, with a knot to prevent it pulling tight and so throttling the deer. An official of the hunt will then put his arm round the neck of the deer, and with someone walking on each side of it, the deer will be escorted to the deer cart. It is important that the arm should be placed round the neck from the top rather than underneath, for should the deer struggle, a broken neck might result. The lower jaw of the deer should also be gripped with the thumb or finger placed in the deer's mouth, taking care to see that it is clear of the deer's back molars – otherwise, as once happened with the Ward Union – the unfortunate hunt official may find himself minus a finger! The size of the rope for 'the take' seems to vary between window cord thickness (Norwich Staghounds) to about $\frac{3}{8}$ in. (1 cm) diameter (Co. Down Staghounds).

Sometimes the deer is brought to bay in a pond or under a river bank. To meet this eventuality, the Co. Down carry on the deer cart, a long bamboo 'fishing rod' of about 12 feet ($3\frac{1}{2}$ metres) in length and from the end of this rod the noose can be slipped over the deer's head. The animal is then drawn back to the bank where it can be handled in the normal way. Occasionally the deer takes to the sea, or swims out on some lake, and as much of the Co. Down Staghound country is bounded by the sea, a boat is always carried on top of the deer cart. If the sea is calm the deer can generally be taken quite safely, but should it be at all choppy, the animal may be drowned. In recent years the Ward Union have also lost one or two deer in this fashion, but when one of their deer does take to sea, a boat has to be borrowed, as one is not carried about on the deer cart.

Deer carts are of no fixed pattern, and whilst in former times they were drawn by horses, today the tractor, lorry or Landrover provides the motive-power. Prior to the abandonment of the Norwich Staghounds, their two deer were taken to the meet in separate crates loaded on to a trailer which was towed by a Landrover. The Co. Down have their deer box loaded on to the back of a light lorry whilst the Ward Union tow their box behind a tractor.

The deer boxes of the two Irish hunts each have two compartments for the deer, but arranged differently, for whereas in the Co. Down box the compartments run side by side down the length of the box, the division in the Ward Union box is arranged horizontally.

In the Co. Down box each deer enters by way of the right-hand compartment – the first deer to enter being driven by way of a communicating door at the front of the box, into the left-hand compartment. This deer, which will be the first one to be hunted, will then be facing the rear of the box. The communicating door, which acts on a slide, will be shut and the other deer driven into the right-hand compartment, after which the back door will be closed. When the deer in the near-side compartment has been enlarged for hunting the communicating door will be opened and the second deer driven from the off-side into the near-side compartment. This deer will now be facing the back of the deer box ready for enlarging should it be required, and the offside compartment is now vacant to receive the hunted deer after taking. When loading the deer into the box it is essential to have the window at the end of the off-side compartment closed, as the light may cause the animal to try and jump through with possibly injury to itself. Light, however, coming through the window at the end of the nearside compartment is a help in persuading the deer to pass through the communicating door into the near-side compartment.

In fox hunting you have the cub-hunting season in which to introduce the young entry to the sport. The 'training' of hounds is to teach them to 'bay' or 'hold up a deer at bay' – if not taught to do so when the deer stops they will lose interest and if the huntsman is not up, will either hang around or probably wander away. When trained, hounds will bay a deer and stand round it until taken. Lt.-Col. Cunningham tells me that he has known this to happen in rough country when it was over an hour before any of the field arrived – the deer stood and all hounds remained there. Deer will stand for hounds but not for people round them – generally speaking well-trained hounds will not go nearer than 6 or 7 yards (5 to 6 metres).

In carted deer hunting the usual practice when training hounds is to take them on a laid trail of about two or three miles which will finish in a yard wherein a deer is tethered. Here the hounds will learn that the hunt should end with a deer standing at bay. It has been the practice of some hunts to tether an old or unwanted deer, and after the hounds have bayed it, for the deer to be despatched with a humane killer so that its entrails can be given to the pack. If the deer is shot with a gun or rifle, however, experience has shown that the noise of the shot is likely to so upset the pack that they will not, subsequently, approach to nearer than about 30 yards (27 metres) of a deer at bay. I am informed however, by some Masters, that to shoot a deer over hounds during the training period is quite unnecessary, and most hunts just allow the new entry to bay the deer in the enclosure for a few minutes. It should be remembered that in hunting the carted deer, the first and last aim is to avoid killing or even harming the deer, so there doesn't seem to be much point in giving the young entry a thirst for blood. Both the Ward Union and the Co. Down, however, feed their hounds entirely on raw flesh, of which there seems to be no shortage in Ireland.

Some hunts in the past have tried rearing a deer calf and allowing it to mix freely with hounds as it was thought that if the pack became accustomed to the deer they would be less likely to harm one at the 'take'. The deer, however, often becomes very tame and it is doubtful if much advantage is to be gained by this practice.

In order to avoid any chance of the hounds biting the deer when at close quarters, Christy stated that he used to 'tush' all the hounds' teeth and found this very effective.[48] It was the practice, also, of the Norwich Staghounds before their disbandment, to remove the canine teeth from their hounds as pups. A similar practice is followed by the Ward Union but not the Co. Down.

It is, however, rare for the deer to be killed or even harmed by the hounds. Very occasionally – perhaps every other season – a deer will get damaged by running into wire or drowning at sea, but on the whole it is remarkable how well the deer seem to come through a hard hunt. Occasionally a deer may be a little stiff the following day, but a few days in the park will soon remedy this.

At times deer are taken in strange places and under strange circumstances. On one occasion with W Angerstein's Staghounds, the stag took refuge in a farm house. On arrival at the farm, members of the hunt 'found the proprietor's wife and daughter standing in the garden in a great state of alarm'. In answer to Jack Hickman's (the huntsman) inquiries they said that just as they were sitting down to dinner the stag trotted into the 'keeping room' and had frightened them dreadfully, so they had run to safety in the garden. 'Don't you be frightened, marm,' said Hickman, 'I'll soon have him out,' and forthwith dismounted and entered the house where, however, he remained so long that one of the field were deputed to go in and see what he was about. He found Hickman seated on a corner of the table munching a Norfolk dumpling, well soaked in rich gravy, on the point of a fork, and the stag standing peaceably in the corner. With the aid of the newcomer the deer was quickly housed in an out-house and Hickman, cap in hand, went back to see the ladies. With profuse apologies he assured them that the stag had done no harm, except, to his great sorrow, of having eaten one of the dumplings. 'But, there, Lor' marm, what can you expect? The poor dumb thing don't know no better.'[98]

Lt.-Col. Harvey also mentions that R Barkley, who told him the above story, once had a claim from Suffolk of 16 shillings (80 pence) for some ducklings which the deer had eaten!

On another occasion Mr Barkley, whilst hunting near Cretingham, was confronted by a rather aggressive young woman who demanded 5 shillings (25 pence) from him in compensation for the hunt having killed her 'gran-mother'! According to the young woman, 'the poor old dear was a-sittin' in her chair, when them beastly dorgs and a great savage lookin' brute of an animal came a bouncin' in at the door and frightened the poor old dear so, that she fell down all of a fit and there she now lay'. Having paid the woman her 5 shillings Mr Barkley hurried to the old woman's home to see if she was really dead, and was relieved to find that with the aid of some sloe gin her life was restored.[98]

During the early part of the last century (1809) a stag, hunted by Captain Darell's hounds, ran across a regimental parade ground just as the Norwich Squadron of Light Horse Volunteers were concluding their drill, and the Volunteers at once joined in the chase. 'This must have been am amusing scene,' comments Harvey, 'our Norfolk Yeoman in their bearskin crested helmets, red coatees and curved sabres, breaking the ranks, in spite of the restraining language of their squadron leader, and galloping for all they were worth in the tail of the hunt. They must, alas, have only witnessed the end of a good hunt, as from Mulbarton [where the parade ground was] to Mangreen [where the stag was taken] is no distance, but no doubt they thoroughly enjoyed themselves, and it served as a good finish to the uninteresting drill of those days.'[98]

Miss Muriel Bowen records a number of amusing events that have happened to the Ward Union Staghounds. On one occasion at Batterstown, the stag jumped through a mulled glass window into a Mrs Delaney's kitchen. In flight the stag cleared the table where two maids were having their dinner; heaven knows the effect of the uninvited guest on the two diners! 'Another stag was taken in a kitchen at Dunshaughlin, which was full of crockery and not a single piece was broken!'[20]

On two occasions a stag has run to bay in licensed premises, 'and it proved an appropriate choice for on each occasion, having got so far, the field decided to call it a day!'

One of the most amusing incidents followed a meet at Ashbourne in 1949, whence a stag, enlarged for the first time, found refuge in a lake on Mr Walkinson's farm off the Dunshaughlin road. Describing this event, Miss Bowen writes: 'Determined to take the stag, Mr Malcolmson sent to Ashbourne for a rubber dinghy. Depositing his spurs and scarlet coat on the bank he set forth to get his quarry. All efforts to lasso the stag failed, but the spirit of gallantry and adventure continued to burn strong on the bank. Top hats and coats came off, and several followers essayed to swim, or wade, their way into the lake, which had several feet of mud at the bottom. Still no luck!

'It looked as if they would have to call it a day when jockey George Wells, jumped from his horse, ran along the trunk of a tree which had fallen into the lake, and dived into the water. Grasping the stag, he guided in to the edge. Cheers went up from what had now swelled to several hundred onlookers, but in the excitement nobody was quite sure whether George Wells arrived at the brink astride the stag, or not. At any rate, nobody was more pleased than Mrs Wells to see them both emerge. After this episode the deer was sent back to the deer park at Slane Castle, as one hunt member said: "One swimming canter is quite enough for a Saturday afternoon!"'[20]

More recently (14 December 1963) the Fermac Beagles, under the mastership of Mr RA McIlwaine, following a meet at Drumlough crossroads, came into close proximity of the Co. Down Staghounds who were hunting an outlier from Saintfield. After the beagles had been taken back to kennels Mr McIlwaine found that the stag was being held at bay in a garage at the rear of the Royal Ulster Constabulary Barracks, and so unaided, he got his arms round the neck of the deer and held it for about fifteen minutes until the arrival of the deer cart. Mr McIlwaine now shares with his father the distinction of having taken a stag single-handed at the end of a day hunting hares.

Chapter IX

Fallow Deer Hunting in Britain

Although fallow deer hunting with hounds has been practised in Britain for many hundreds of years, and is still done so today by the New Forest Buckhounds, remarkably little has been written about this activity. This is in marked contrast to books on stag hunting in the West Country – a sport which undoubtedly has more public appeal than buck hunting. Nevertheless, an old fallow buck is a worthy quarry for any pack of hounds, and although they may not give such good points as the red deer stag they are, in many respects, just as difficult to hunt, and are up to all the tricks of the trade.

Opinions vary as to whether it was King Canute or William the Conqueror who first designated the New Forest – which in those days bore the name of Ytene – as a royal hunting reserve. Whoever it was, organized deer hunting in the New Forest did not really commence until 1883 when the Hon. Gerald Lascelles established the New Forest Deerhounds under the mastership of Mr Lovell of Hinchelsea, and for about thirty years this pack hunted both red and fallow deer of either sex. The latter were – and have always been – the most numerous. During the First World War the red deer were almost wiped out, and as the hunt started to concentrate their activities on fallow bucks, the name was changed to its present one – the New Forest Buckhounds.

At what date the fallow deer were first introduced to the New Forest is not known. It is reasonable to suppose, however, that all the woods along the south and south-east coast of England would have been the first areas selected for their introduction to Britain by the Romans – or whoever was initially responsible for bringing the species to England from the continent. Prior to the formation of the New Forest, local hunters probably kept the stock of deer well in check but when it became a royal hunting preserve, which automatically brought it under the jurisdiction of the harsh forest laws, then not only was all hunting banned except for a privileged few, but every encouragement was given to raise the deer stocks to their highest possible level.

However, from time to time various special relaxations of the law allowed a few privileged subjects to hunt deer in the forest, and the following extracts quoted by Hutchinson from Woodward's *History of Hampshire* are of interest. 'William Briwer had many privileges in the New Forest. On July 3, 1219, the bailiffs of the forest were ordered to let his dogs chase bucks in the forest up to Michaelmas.

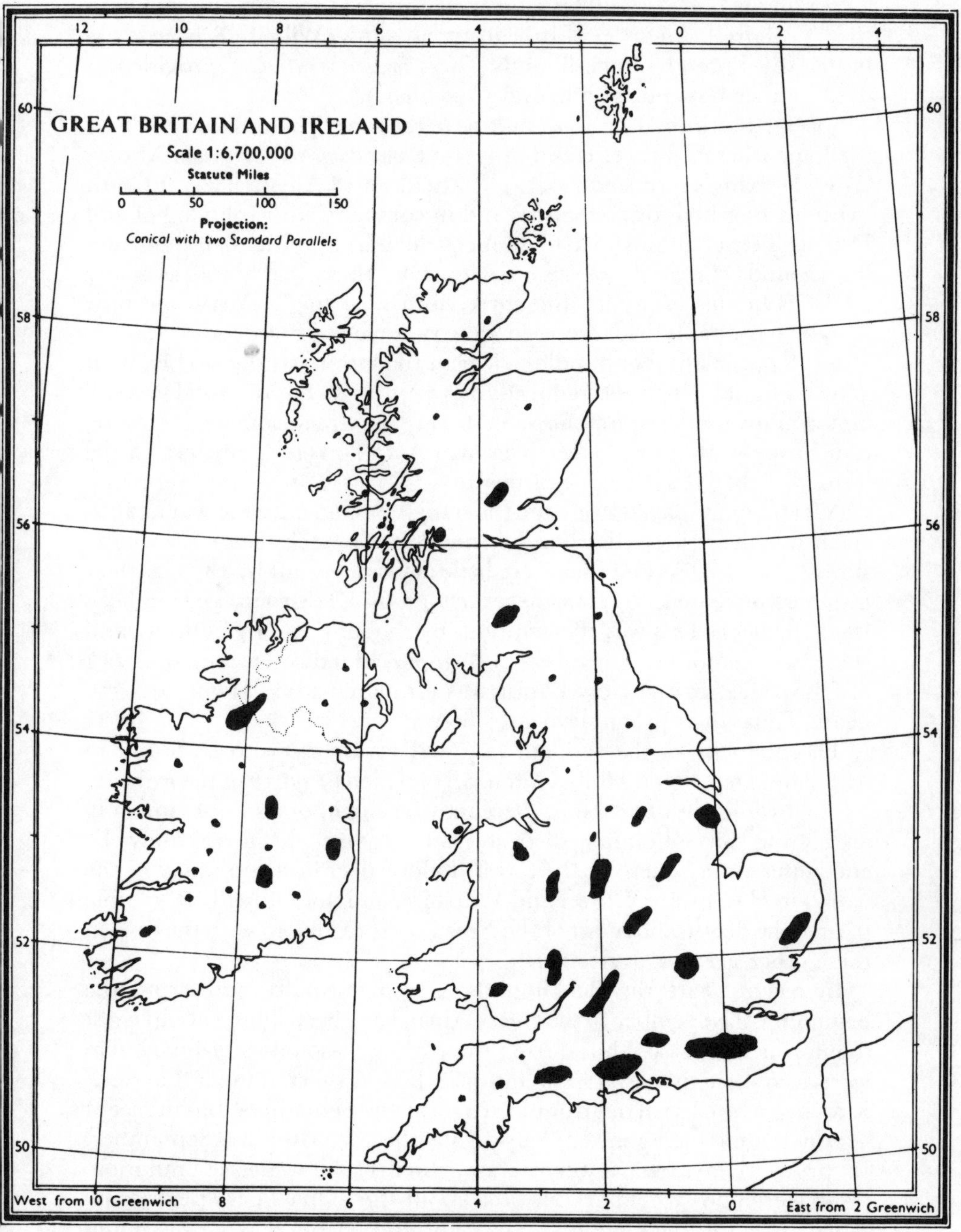

The approximate distribution of fallow deer in Great Britain and Ireland. The existence of fallow deer in many areas is due to escapes from deer parks. Apart from buck hunting in the New Forest, Hampshire, the control of fallow deer elsewhere is by shooting

'Again on July 8, 1222, his dogs were privileged to run after bucks in the New Forest. An order of July 30, 1223, allows William Briwer to use in the New Forest his buck-hounds (*Canes damericos currentes*) provided he used neither bow nor greyhound (*leporarium*).'

Special discrimination was made as to the type of hound that could be used, for whereas Briwer could only use *Canes damericos currentes*, Master Guy, the King's huntsman was permitted, on 18 August 1227, to hunt 'with his stag-hounds, *Cervericiis*' and in company with John le Fol and John le Berner, huntsmen to Hubert de Burgh, with their stag and buckhounds, *Cervericiis et damericiis* to 'take thirty harts and as many bucks'. On this occasion 'the three huntsmen might carry one bow apiece' – probably because their quarry included red deer.

By 1845 the number of fallow deer in the forest was said to be about 4582 – a figure which was reduced to 3552 in 1846, but this total was still far too many for the commoners. Such were the circumstances, therefore, that brought about the Deer Removal Act of 1851. A new era in the history of the New Forest had begun.

A few deer managed to escape the slaughter, and once the war against them was over those that had fled the forest to seek refuge elsewhere, slowly returned. At first they were little in evidence but by 1870, as their numbers increased, so it was necessary to kill a few every year to keep them in check. This was effected both by shooting and by hunting, and these two methods of control are still employed today. In 1892 the stock of fallow deer in the New Forest was estimated to be about 200–250 head. Today it is probably nearer 800 or so.

The majority of the resident fallow deer are often to be found in Milkham, Denny and Holly Hatch, all of which lie north of the railway, but following a hunt or shoot, there may be a temporary influx into any area from an adjoining district. Fallow deer, however, may be encountered anywhere in the forest. Fallow deer occur in many of the woods in Hampshire, Dorset and Wiltshire, and undoubtedly from time to time the deer wander out of the New Forest to join up with the deer in these other areas and vice versa.

In recent years the Buckhounds, which normally hunt from the beginning of November to the end of April, have been killing about eight to nine bucks a season, but during the 1952–3 season twenty-nine bucks were accounted for in sixty-two hunting days. A short summer 'Fat Buck Season' *can* be carried out from 11 August to 30 September, but in recent seasons hounds have gone out only during the last fortnight of September. In pre-war days, when there was a bigger fallow deer population, the Buckhounds would account for about thirty-five bucks per season. Since 1918 the Buckhounds have only hunted buck as it was found that practically no sport could be had with the does. In addition to the deer killed by the forest keepers and the Buckhounds, an unknown number are killed on freehold land within or adjoining the Perambulation.

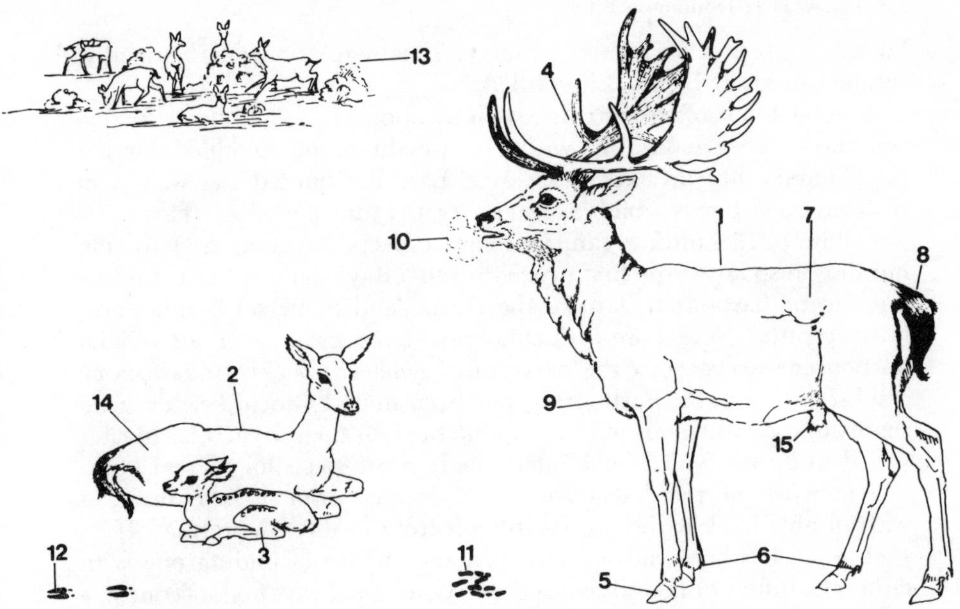

Fallow deer

1 Buck, bucke, gres
2 Doe, dae, doo
3 Fawn
4 Antlers, attire, head, rack, trophy
5 Cleaves (toes), slot (cloven hoof), talon (heel)
6 Dewclaws, ergots, os, surcleaves
7 Coat, hide, skin
8 Tail, flag, single
9 Brisket, essay
10 Groan (sound) troat, voice
11 Droppings, cotying, croties, fewmets, fewmishing, fues, mutes
12 Footprints, foil, foin, foyles, slotmarks, spoor, trace, trail, view, voyes
13 Herd, brace, leash
14 Couched (resting), at lodge
15 Brush (penis), pensel

Age group terminology

	Male deer	*Female deer*
Under 1 year	Fawn	Fawn
1 year	Yearling	Yearling
2 years	Pricket	Pricket's sister, teg, tegg
3 years	Sorel, sorrel, spade	Doe*
4 years	Soar, soare, sore, sour	
5 years	Bare-buck, buck of the first head	
6 years	Buck, great buck, great head	
7 years	Full-headed buck	

* Pregnant doe – braggard

Having hounds that are steady and remain on the line of not only fallow buck, but one particular buck, is the whole essence and skill of buck hunting. Unfortunately, due to some rules introduced by the Forestry Commission during the past few seasons regarding the age and colour of the deer to be hunted, hounds are being spoilt by having to be stopped and taken off animals which scentwise to *them* are absolutely right, but for reason of colour – something which cannot be explained to hounds – are not permissible quarry. This regulation has, naturally, resulted in fewer bucks being killed.

A good buck of present day weighs about 14 stone clean, which compares very favourably with the weight of bucks killed by the Buckhounds fifty or sixty years ago. Lascelles quoted the weight of thirteen good bucks which averaged 13st. 13lb. (87.75kg.) (clean).

Fallow buck hunting can, in some respects, be compared to stag hunting in so far as the first procedure to a day's hunt is for a suitable buck to be harboured. Unlike the Devon and Somerset Staghounds, however, the New Forest Buckhounds have never had an official harbourer and ever since the last century, when the Buckhounds became a subscription pack, harbouring has been done by local keepers who report to the huntsman of any suitable buck in their area. The Master will then decide which buck offers the best prospects for a good hunt.

The work of the harbourer is to locate, prior to the meet, a warrantable buck without disturbing it from its daytime retreat. If no such buck has been harboured, then the chance of finding one with either the tufters or hounds is not great. One can always find, of course, a younger buck – but it is the six-year and older bucks which are particularly sought after. On the other hand, particularly during the early autumn when the older bucks are often separated from the herd, if a buck has been close-harboured by the keeper, it is sometimes possible to lay the pack on to him without first using the tufters. It is all a question of circumstance.

Since buck hunting takes place between the months of August and April, it will be appreciated that harbouring, due to the amount of thick undergrowth, is much more difficult in the autumn than in early spring, particularly during a period of dry weather when it is almost impossible to see slot marks. Quite apart from seasonal undergrowth, wooded terrain considerably restricts spying, but on more open land, be it moorland, hill or agricultural, it is often possible for the vigilant dawn watcher to see deer returning from their night feed to some favoured covert, where they will lie up for the day.

When the harbourer has seen a buck enter some covert, he will give it time to settle and bed down before venturing further. After allowing, perhaps, half an hour, a wide detour of the wood will then be made so as to make sure that the deer has not passed through, and if no slot marks are found leaving the wood to suggest that this has happened, the keeper will then be able to return home for a late breakfast before reporting at the meet the whereabouts of the buck to the Master.

Fog and early morning mist, even if the terrain is fairly open, will often make it impossible to see any deer returning to covert, and on such occasions the keeper will then have to rely on 'slotting'. Slotting is a science of its own, for a good keeper, by slot marks alone, should be able to tell whether the beast has passed recently, whether it was a buck or a doe – and if the former, approximately what age by the depth and size of the impression. On hard ground, although the imprint will correspond almost exactly to the size of hoof, if the ground is at all rocky or lacking in bare earth or sandy places, such slots will be extremely difficult to discern. In snow or soft clay etc. the reverse is the case, but one must be guarded against the conclusion that the animal is bigger than it really is, for under such conditions slot mark sizes are always exaggerated.

In thick cover one may occasionally spot a good buck lying down among bushes and bracken. There is no question that the buck has not seen you also, and has probably heard you coming for some time previous, but as is the nature of fallow deer many beasts, particularly the older and craftier ones will, like a hare, remain couched in the hope of escaping detection. Under such circumstances it is fatal to stop and look, but if one continues to walk past as though nothing had been seen, the deer will probably not move.

Some bucks are extremely cunning and as a case in point, Sir George Thursby, who was Master of the Buckhounds for some twenty-five years (1910–36) gives the following account.

'A buck with a curious and very distinctly formed head, was harboured by Slightam . . . at Hampton Ridge. I hunted this buck and lost him. Later on, he was again harboured by Slightam, who saw him some way off, and not appearing to have noticed him rode his pony on as if he had not seen him, and reported him to me later in the day at the Meet. On getting to where he had been seen, he had vanished.

'A third time he was harboured by Slightam on the same ground. This time he was so far away that he felt certain that the buck would not be disturbed, in fact, doubted if he himself had been seen. He came to the Meet, reported and assured me that this time I would be sure to find him, but on getting there he had vanished once more.

'On the fourth occasion Slightam harboured him in Amberwood about a mile away and instead of being alone, he had a pricket with him. This time I did find him with the tufters, and the two deer ran out to Hampton Ridge, all along the top, over the open, past the long patch of gorse. I could see them all the time as I was galloping parallel to them. The pricket was in front of him, when suddenly the buck butted him in the hind-quarters, sent him off and himself lay down in the heather, whilst the tufters went on with the pricket. I had them stopped and brought back to where I had seen the buck lay down. This time, after a clinking hunt and long point, we killed him, and I really was quite sorry.'[187]

Following a satisfactory report of the whereabouts of a good buck from one of the keepers, the huntsman will take the tufters to try and locate the buck, and if he is with other deer, get him separated and moving on his own. A tufter's essentials are that he must have a good nose, great perseverance, give tongue continuously, and above all be obedient, for he is liable to be frequently stopped and laid on a fresh line if necessary. The tufters, generally consisting of about three couple of

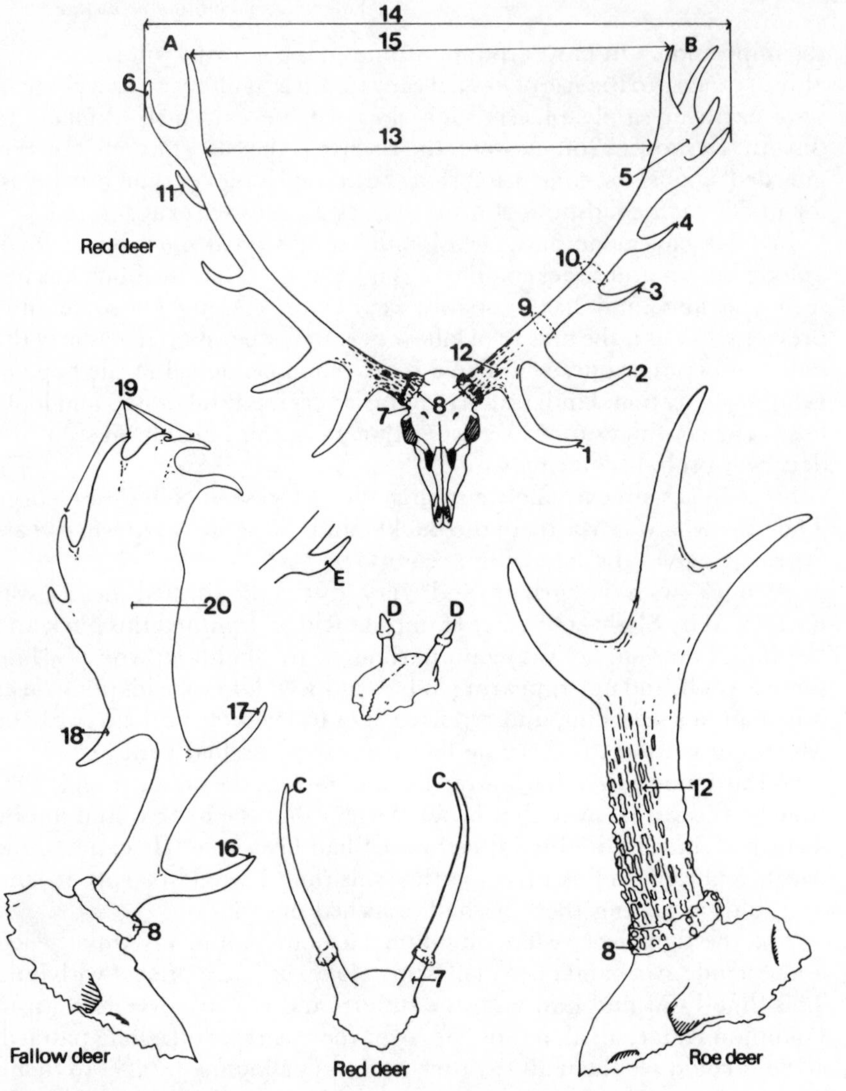

The antlers, head or attire of a deer

1 Brow point or tine, first antler, antler, ollanaich	Double brows	Rights
2 Bay point or tine, beas, biz-antler, fur-antler, sur-antler		
3 Tray point or tine, trey, trez, royal-antler, sur-antler royal, shoulder point		

4 Sur-royal point or tine, fourth point
5 Crown, croches, crockets, cup, tops, troachings, troches
6 Forked top
7 Pedicle, pillar
8 Coronet, bur, burr, coronel, mowse, mules
9 Beam, lower
10 Beam, upper
11 Offer, snag
12 Pearling, knobs, glitters, gutters, spines (of roe antlers), furrows, ridges
13 Inside span

14 Spread
15 Tip to tip
A Off-antler, right antler
B Near-antler, left antler
B–8 Length
A–8 Length
C Dags, spikes, spires, uprights
D Bossets, knobs, buttons
E Point, tine, real spurs (on roe antlers)

Fallow buck antlers
16 Braunch, brow tine
17 Advancer, forward tine, tray tine
18 Back antler, black antler, rear tine
19 Spellers, spillers, top points of fallow buck head
20 Palm, palmated top

hounds, are capable of hunting a cold buck, and only when the selected deer is on his own will the main pack be sent for and laid on. From then on the hunt follows the general pattern of a deer hunt, much of which is conducted in thick cover and as often as not, only the music of the hounds will reveal to the followers the progress of the hunt. A buck, when first roused, will generally circle round looking for other deer before taking off, but when he does go, provided he has been separated from other deer, then is the time to stop the tufters and lay on the pack. The following account by James Lewis describes a typical hunt after a buck that had been harboured in Applesdale Inclosure '[The tufters] moved about as fast as they drew, and working on to their buck they gave sporadic peals of music as they took up the gradually strengthening line. The buck did not try to make for the open; but after he had been rattled around for about half an hour he was obviously on his own.

'The pack was sent for. They were brought up past Roe Cottage and laid on in Roe Inclosure. The buck had got into the part of this wood where there is plenty of thick scrub, and hounds had a tough job combing it. Then the buck moved to a more open part of the covert. With this move he had forfeited his advantage. His protagonists were in their element. The peat of the bogs and the pine needles were wet.

'There was one anxious moment when hounds settled. Then *Pirate* had the line, and there was no respite. The pack was pushed on and on, back and forth, whichever way he turned, with no let up. Hounds were together with no jealousy. The pace was hard and fast, but the buck would not make a point. We came to the edge of the open commons and some does, though there may have been a buck among them, took some hounds away over Buckherd Bottom. They were brought back, and after a long delay they picked up their buck in Red Shoot Wood.

'Here again the undergrowth was thick, and the buck twisted about. It was now after four o'clock. Hounds, though no less keen, nor any less persistent than they had been at one o'clock, were nevertheless hunting a line that was petering out fast. They were stopped by Linford Brook and the buck, which when last seen looked as though he had had all the running that he could take, was unaccounted for.'[122]

One of the longest runs enjoyed by the Buckhounds occurred in April 1923 when a buck jumped out of a bush in the open at the corner of

Bentley Wood. 'The pack' writes Lionel Edwards, 'ran fast via Holly Hatch, Sloden, Slufters, Bentley Wood, Oakley, Roe Wood, Picket Post, High Town and thence alongside the railway to Holmersley, being set up and taken at the edge of Sway village. 12 mile point and 26 miles as hounds ran. Time 3 hours.'[70]

Occasionally, before the pack can be laid on, the tufters will conduct the complete hunt themselves. One such occasion happened in March 1924 when a buck was found in Hinchelsea gorse by two couple of tufters, and a great hunt followed, which ended with the deer being pulled down in the stream at Moyles Court after a ten mile point – time one hour twenty minutes.[70]

As an example of the type of strategy a buck will resort to in order to throw off hounds, Lionel Edwards once saw a buck run to a flock of sheep, and gallop to and fro among them in order to foil his line before going on. Hounds could make nothing of it, but unfortunately for the buck he forgot that the field could quite well see him far below, as they came off the top of the Downs, and his trick was of no avail. All the same, the buck escaped in the end, as he ran 'to herd'.

When a buck takes to cultivated land, he is much more difficult to hunt across plough than fox, for if there is much of it the pace of the hounds will be reduced to a crawl. When brought to bay a fallow buck is not such a formidable opponent as a large West Country stag, but occasionally a too adventurous hound will get hurt or even killed. Gerald Lascelles recalls one such instance when a hound called *Wanderer* got severely handled by a buck, being caught, when swimming, against the high bank of the stream and badly punished; though he did not at the time seem seriously hurt, and came home well enough with the pack, he was afterwards very ill, and seemed to have suffered from blood poisoning from the hurt of the buck's horns – at any rate, it took him the whole summer to recover, and he lost every hair he had on his body before he recovered.'[120] Didn't Turberville (1576) once say:

If thou be hurt with horne of Harte 't will bring thee to thy bier,
But leeches' art can bore's hurt heal; thereof thou needst not fear.

Prior to 1952 the knife was generally used to despatch the buck after it had been brought to bay by hounds but following the recommendations of the Scott Henderson Report of the Committee on Cruelty to Wild Animals (1951) this has been replaced by a humane killer. Seldom, if ever, will a hound approach the deer, but will stand around baying. Should a hound attempt to go in, a buck is quite capable of driving him off. A fallow buck, when nearing the end, normally twists about for the last ten minutes or so, and this gives the hunt staff an opportunity to place themselves around the area so that they can immediately jump off their horses when the deer stands at bay or lies down. He is then shot with a humane killer, and the time lag between the deer standing at bay and being despatched is probably about two or three minutes. Two humane killers are always taken out.

Unlike red deer, a hunted buck will not stand at bay in water. Sometimes, during a hard run, a hunted buck will pause momentarily to 'sit' or roll in a wet pool as if to refresh itself before continuing.

During Sir George Thursby's mastership it was seldom that two deer were hunted in one day, his reason for not doing so being as follows: 'If you have lost your hunted buck and start drawing for a fresh one, hounds will think you are still trying for the hunted one, so naturally take no notice of fresh deer. If you encourage them to hunt the fresh deer, you are undoing all you have been teaching and drilling into them ever since you entered them. If you have killed, hounds know that they have completed their job and generally the Hunt horses have had all that they want, and certainly do not want another possible two hours' hard galloping. So the order is HOME, but it is hard to make some of the field understand this.'[187]

Appropos the scent from a hunted deer, Sir George Thursby is convinced that if a buck has been tufted for some time 'he will in consequence, carry a scent different from that of a fresh deer, and thus by laying the pack on to the scent of a deer that has been run for some time by the tufters, they are taught to recognise the scent that they are required to hunt. In this way, even if the hunted buck does join fresh deer, hounds should be able to carry the line through that of the fresh deer.' A hunted deer, however, will seldom run long with fresh deer, and although, while this occurs, hounds may run more or less silent, once the deer have separated they will throw their tongue again. Mute hounds are not good for buck hunting. Sir George Thursby once had a hound that would come back and bay at him when the rest of the pack changed course.[122]

Sir Dudley Forwood, who was a former Master of the Buckhounds, confirms *in litt.* Sir George Thursby's remarks concerning the scent of a hunted deer, and suggests that 'the breaking away from the herd during the tuft would seem to coincide with this change of smell, for it is at this point that your old hound running with the tufters will suddenly join in, giving tongue with the remainder of the tufters, having not done so previously.' Sir Dudley once had an old liver and white hound called *Warspite* that would go forward in front of his horse, give tongue, then look up at him before taking up the line.

A remarkable exhibition of foxhound adaptability is recalled in *Sporting Reminiscences of Hampshire*. A Mr Land of Park House, Hambledon, kept a pack of foxhounds with which all the summer in the forest of Bere, he hunted deer. In the autumn, however, he changed to hunting foxcubs, and within two or three days, the same pack would stick to their fox, and actually go through a herd of deer they had hunted in the summer!

During the latter part of the seventeenth century and a good many years before the establishment of the New Forest Buckhounds, Lord

Rivers was hunting a pack of buckhounds from Rushmore in Cranborne Chase. Meets took place in summer and seem to have invariably been fixed for 4 pm, thus allowing the sportsmen to have a hearty lunch at 2 pm before setting out on the chase. An evening meet in summer had its advantages, particularly during hot weather, for at this time of day fallow bucks are more easily found, and having rested all day, will be empty and capable of giving better sport. The cooler air of the evening is also more pleasant for both horse and hound which may be involved in any hard physical work, and as the dew falls, scent generally improves.

It was also the custom to meet every season on 29 May – known as King Charles's Restoration Day – and members of the hunt carried oak boughs in their caps as a mark of loyalty. Young male deer were hunted in order that any young hounds could be introduced to the sport – a practice which was termed 'blooding the hounds', whilst the young deer killed was referred to as the 'blooding-deer'. It was also claimed that the venison from any deer that had been thoroughly hunted was far superior to that from a beast that had been shot without a run. Judges seem to have been particularly fond of both buck hunting and venison, and many succeeded in arranging their Circuits to correspond to the Meet Calendar.

William Osbaldiston had this to say of buck hunting during the eighteenth century. 'In buck-hunting, the same hounds are used as in running the stag. In forests and chases, as they lie at layer, so they are hunted. In parks, where they are inclosed, the sport is not so diverting by reason of the great change and foil, unless they break out and run the country, which they seldom do; but deer that lie out, though near the park, make, in general better chases than forest deer.'[152]

It would seem, however, that on occasions extremely unsporting and cruel tactics were resorted to 'in order to facilitate the chase', for the keeper would often 'select a fat buck out of the herd, which he shoots to maim him, and then he is run down by the hounds'.

As to the method of hunting the buck, Osbaldiston states that 'the company generally goes out very early for the benefit of the morning; sometimes a deer is ready lodged; if not, the coverts are drawn till one is roused, or sometimes, in a park, a deer is pitched upon and forced from the herd; then more hounds are laid on to run the chase, and if you come to be at a fault, the old staunch hounds are only to be relied upon till you recover him again'.

After the deer has been taken and the gralloch given to the hounds as a 'reward', 'everyone has a chop at his neck, and the head being cut off is shewed to the hounds to encourage them to run only at male deer, which they see by the horns, and to teach them to bite only at the head; then the company all standing in a ring, one blows a single death, which is succeeded by a double *recheat* from the whole, when they conclude the chase with a general hollow, and depart the field to their several houses, or to the place of meeting.'[152]

It would seem that a fair amount of buck hunting, both within the deer forest and in the open forest, was being practised in Ireland during the seventeenth and eighteenth centuries, and this is fully described in Stringer's excellent little book *The Experienced Huntsman* (1780). Stringer was not only a good writer but also a most successful huntsman, having killed some '500 brace of bucks' in Ireland. True, much of his hunting was done in parks and in one season alone he killed '54 brace of bucks, and four brace of stags' in Lord Conway's parks at Portmore in the north of Ireland. Other parks in which Stringer hunted included Lord Massareen's in Antrim.[181]

A great many park deer escaped into the open countryside during the troubled years of 1688–9, and by the end of that century 'there was hardly any place, either mountain or low-land, that had not plenty of fallow deer, although now (1780) they are almost destroyed'.[181]

Buck hunting seems to have taken place during the summer and autumn months – in fact almost the very months when the Buckhounds of modern times have a complete rest from hunting. 'An old buck (if in a good country where he lies quiet) will be good venison by the 20th. of May', wrote Stringer, 'and continues in good season, till the 14th of September or longer, if a dry season a buck of the first head, or sore (4-year old buck), will be in season till the 20th. or 27th. of September'. However, autumn hunts gave the best sport for 'an old deer does run harder and make a better chase in September, than any of the three months before; he being then better in wind, and not filling his paunch so, as in the three months of June, July and August'. The doe was hunted from August onwards, 'and if a dry winter, and good pasture, will be tolerable venison till February' – about the time the present day Buckhounds give up hunting the doe.

As to the custom of castrating and spaying bucks and does respectively in parks in order to improve the venison, Stringer gives this advice. 'Take a male fawn, and geld him, and he shall never have any horns, he is called a heaver, and in some grounds very rarely ever good venison, unless very old; take a Buck (five year old) and geld him ... these are called gelt Bucks, and commonly prove very high venison.'

'Take a female fawn, and splay her, and when she comes to be six years old, she will be very high venison, and generally much larger than any other doe.' This opinion was based on the experience of having 'splayed fifty brace of fawns in a season, for several seasons together' and killing them after they had attained the age of five or six years.

Stringer also said it was a great mistake to hunt park fallow deer too frequently, as the venison steadily deteriorated, and as a case in point mentioned that in the year 1700 Sir Edward Seymour and his son came to Portmore from England, bringing with them twenty couple of hounds for hunting the parks at Portmore which extended over 3000 acres (1214 hectares) being 'very well stocked with red and fallow-deer'. For eleven weeks commencing on 3 June, they hunted every second or third day until 18 August – perhaps thirty days in all, and during this period 'they killed with the said hounds twenty brace of Bucks, a leash of Stags, by fair hunting; the very first deer they killed was high venison, and so were all they killed for fourteen or twenty days; but the venison declined from the very beginning of hunting; so that in *August* the oldest deer in the park were become so thin, that they could scarce be venison'. Too much hunting in parks during the months of June and July will also kill a number of fawns, and at any time of the year, unless the park fences are extremely good, will encourage escape.

As to hunting a buck in a park, Stringer considered it something that 'every pretender can perform' provided he had good 'staunch hounds; for they are not troubled with finding, nor can they (without being very unmindful of their business) lose a Deer, and if they do lose him, parks are commonly such sort of ground as that you cannot fail to find him again'. Quality rather than quantity in number of hounds was the essence of successful park hunting, and Stringer himself used only six couple, and his advice was 'that you can never be too kind, nor reward a hound too well, when he sticks to his game, hunts well, and performs his business right; nor can you reasonably be too churlish to a hound, or whip him too much when he commits a fault'. During the month of June Stringer suggests that the scent of a male deer differs little from that of a doe or fawns, and your greatest difficulty will be to keep hounds on male deer only – 'good staunch park hounds will (when a deer comes to the herd) cast up and try round the herd by their noses and if they find the deer not gone off, will pick it towards the herd, but your rude young hounds will run riot, that is, violently at view into the herd, and so every hound have a several deer; in such a case, one man must mind the hunted deer, and the rest must rate the hounds'. For such occasions, Stringer suggests that you should have 'several men both on horseback and afoot, with good whips, and each a pair of couples at his belt; so that when any of your young hounds change, whoever is near them, must spare no pains to rate them, and alight and couple them, and beat them severely, so as they shall have cause to remember it'. . . . No case of Spare the rod and Spoil the hound with this huntsman, who sums up by saying that 'the fewer the hounds the surer the kill, especially in a park or forest; when changes are plenty, a great many hounds breed confusion in such places'.[181]

When it came to hunting the wild fallow, Stringer's advice was to 'cause all your hounds, except your staunch finders, to be harled, and led two or three hundred paces behind you as aforesaid, and so go on foot with such hounds as you can depend on for finding'. Having reached the area where the buck is expected to by lying, 'there uncouple your finders, and if they flourish or cry any thing, take pains to find the view [slot marks] by which you may immediately know what sort of deer it is'. . . . An old buck often lies up in company with a pricket or younger buck, and if the latter is roused by hounds he will generally stand 'if he have any old deer with him, or if the hounds come suddenly on him, when he hath run a little from the place, he will stand and look back, all these are certain tokens that he hath company, and if so, it is certainly an old deer, for when it happens that an old deer rouzeth first, (unless a hound be very near him) he will not go away without the young deer, but will beat him up with his head before he goes off'.[181]

As often as not Stringer used 'but four couple of hounds, which really (if good) are better for killing or finding than twenty couple'. It is most important, however, that 'a huntsman should keep as near his hounds as he can, for nature hath taught a deer several shifts, both in his lodgings and hunting'. The huntsman should also 'be well mounted and ride very light in your apparil, both for your own and horse's ease; for if a man have a great deal of clothes on him, he is not able to ride or run on foot if occasion serve, therefore in a cap, waistcoat, breeches and a pair of light thin boots or rather shoes, lest he come to ground where he cannot ride, and must trust to running on foot'.[181] Fallow buck hunting in Ireland was undoubtedly tough going in those days.

As in former days in England there was quite a ceremony attendant to the death of a deer. 'Whoever happens to be first in at the fall of the deer, ought to seize him by the beam and keep off the hounds, gently, with the words *warr haunch*, and hollow the whoop to give notice to the rest of the company if they chance to be out; then the chief keeper or huntsman that is there ought to present a knife to the first gentleman that comes in at the fall to cut his throat, then to call the hounds to the blood, and if any of the company be yet out, to touch his horn, and to hollow to call them in; next, the chief keeper or huntsman aforesaid ought to present a knife to the chief person of quality or gentleman, to take say of the deer, then paunch him and give the hounds that, and then to strip the skin off the neck of the buck and present his hanger to a third gentleman to cut the buck's head off, which should be scored and scotched with a knife, so as the hounds may tear it off the easier, and let one take it by the beams, and call all the hounds to it, hallowing and encouraging them, and while they are pulling and tearing, blow a *recheat* to them to encourage them; then the keeper or huntsman aforesaid should take some of the blood, and offer it to every gentleman to blood them withal, some will have it rubbed on their faces, others will wash their hands in it, then all the gentlemen keepers, and huntsmen that carry horns, stand round the deer and blow the death or mort, and all at once give the whoop, hollow, then the keeper or huntsman aforesaid must wait on, or enquire of the gentleman whose concern it is to dispose of the venison . . . as to the fine morsels, viz. the tenderlings (if his head be tender), his tongue, the roots of his ears, his caul, his dulcets, his hinch-pin, and part of his liver, lap them up in a clean handkerchief.' He makes no reference, however, as to the ultimate disposal of these 'fine morsels'.

If any hound had difficulty in distinguishing between the scent of a buck and a doe, Stringer suggested the following treatment. 'The very best way to amend that fault in such a hound, or any hound that covets to hunt a female deer is when a Buck is down before you, cut his throat, call the hound to his mouth, and let him smell his breath, and take bread or cheese, and put it in the Buck's mouth (while he is yet living) and give it to the hound, and let him smell at his pizzle, and rub cheese or bread on his pizzle, and give him to eat; and cut off his tenderlings if his head be tender, and give him to eat; likewise, cut off his head and let him pull first at the roots or remains that are left of his tenderlings; and then turn the head, and let him take satisfaction of it, and forget not to clap, cherish and encourage him, with such words are you use to your hound in finding, and by doing so two or three times, you will find him to amend his faults.'[181]

None of this pagan ceremony is attendant to modern buck hunting in the New Forest, and even the custom of blooding has lately been discontinued. On the death of a buck, presentation of the head to one of the followers is made by the Master or huntsman in the Master's absence, whilst slots are likewise distributed, the younger generation being given preference.

Coursing fallow deer with specially trained dogs was a favourite sport in some English parks, such as Eastwell in Kent and Woburn in Bedfordshire, and some of these dogs were so well trained that once having caught hold of their deer, they would hold it by the ears until the keepers arrived to take charge of it. So far as I am aware no British park today use hounds for deer coursing.

At the beginning of the present century, however, coursing fallow deer was still being practised at Woburn Abbey by the present Duke's grandfather, the 11th Duke of Bedford, with a breed of hound which had been trained to capture fallow buck alive during the winter months. Apparently it was the custom to use these hounds for capturing either bad or aged beasts for fattening up in a shed for venison, or old bucks with exceptional heads who were to receive preferential treatment as regards feeding and shelter during the winter months in order that their life might be prolonged for breeding purposes. The procedure was as follows. A deer would be selected by the Duke and pointed out to one of the mounted keepers. The keepers would then attempt to separate this particular beast from his companions, and when this was done, the hound or hounds, which had been bringing up the rear in a specially constructed hound-van, would be slipped out at a suitable opportunity, and would then course the deer until it turned to bay. They would then seize the deer by the ear and hold it down until the keepers arrived to rescue the deer from them. This was accomplished by one of the men seizing the buck by a hind leg whilst others pulled the hounds away. The buck, having its legs tied together, was placed in a cart and driven away to the paddock or enclosure where it would be released little the worse for its experience.

Accidents were rare, but occasionally unavoidable. If a buck refused to turn to bay it might be seized by a hind leg and so severely damaged that it would have to be destroyed. Occasionally a buck would run into iron railings and break a leg or its neck, whilst others would run into one of the ponds in the park and be drownwd when overtaken by a fast swimming hound. Ice was also a hazard and when thin ice covered the ponds they were given a wide berth.

Occasionally a buck would evade capture by refusing to be separated from the herd, at other times by jumping a high fence, or even by reversing the operation and chasing a yellow-livered hound away! About a hundred bucks were caught annually in this manner. Various kinds of dogs were tried, the most successful combination being a cross between a bull-mastiff and a greyhound bitch.

During the last century deer were coursed on a large scale in both Godmersham and Eastwell parks in Kent so as to be caught up for fattening as venison. The system followed practically identical lines to that employed for coursing fallow buck at Woburn only sewels – lengths of cord on spindles, to which turkey feathers had been knotted at about 2 foot (60 cm) intervals – were much used at Eastwell.

The hounds used at both Eastwell and Godmersham were described as being 'smooth-haired powerful greyhounds' and by coursing alone, approximately sixty deer at the former park, and fifty at the latter were taken annually. There is a record of sixteen bucks having been taken at Eastwell in a single day without mishap.

During the present century muzzled greyhounds were used at Calke Abbey park in Derbyshire for capturing fallow fawns. Their method of capture was to knock the fawn down, and then prevent the youngster from regaining its feet by lying down on top of it until the keeper arrived to take charge.

At Eridge Park, Sussex, too, a similar method for catching deer required for venison was practised right down to 1914. In former times hounds specially trained to catch deer in this manner were often referred to as 'hart-hounds' or *lévriers*. They resembled, and had the speed of, a greyhound, and hunted purely on sight or 'by view'. In coursing deer – especially red deer – Turberville (1576) said that hounds used for this purpose were divided into the following three leashes – Teasers, Sidelaies and Bucksets, which were set at the deer in turn.

Today when it is necessary to catch up park deer, if nets or catch-up pens are not available, the air gun or crossbow firing a tranquilizing dart has now taken the place of the coursing hound.

Chapter X

Roe Deer Hunting in Britain

Roe deer hunting with hounds has been much neglected in Britain during the past few centuries, and at the present time there is not a single pack hunting them. On the continent, however, roe hunting in France has always been a popular sport and at the beginning of the century there were over eighty packs hunting this animal and during the year some fifteen hundred roe were being taken. Today there are about fifty packs.

Very little has been written about this form of hunting, and as this small deer, except by accident, has not been regularly hunted by any pack of hounds since early in the century, it is to the record book that one must search for any history or account of this much neglected sport.

Of early roe hunting, Nicholas Cox has this to say. 'They are most easily taken in the woods. When they are chased, they desire to run against the Wind, because the coldness of the Air refresheth them in their Course; and therefore they who hunt them place their Dogs with the Wind. They are often taken by the counterfeiting of their Voice, which the skilful Huntsman doth by the Assistance of a Leaf in his Mouth.

'This Beast is very easie to hunt. . . .

'When they are hunted, they turn much and often, and come back upon the Dogs directly; When they can no longer endure, they then take Soil, as the *Hart* doth, and will hang by the Bough in such Manner, that nothing shall appear of them above Water but their Snout, and will suffer the Dogs to come just upon them before they will stir.'

After being taken by hounds, 'if he hath not Beavy-grease on his Tail when he is broken up, he is more fit to be Dogs-meat than Mans-meat!'.

'The Hounds must be rewarded with the Bowels, the Blood, and Feet slit asunder, and boiled all together. This is more properly called a *Dose* than a *Reward*.'[57]

Snaffle in his monograph on *The Roedeer* (1904), which has now become extremely scarce, devotes five short chapters to hunting roe with hounds, and much of the history of roe hunting during the last century has come from this source.

Although formerly plentiful in many parts of Britain, by the eighteenth century this small deer had completely disappeared from all counties in England except those in the extreme north and north-west. How was it, therefore, that the roe, once tolerably abundant, should

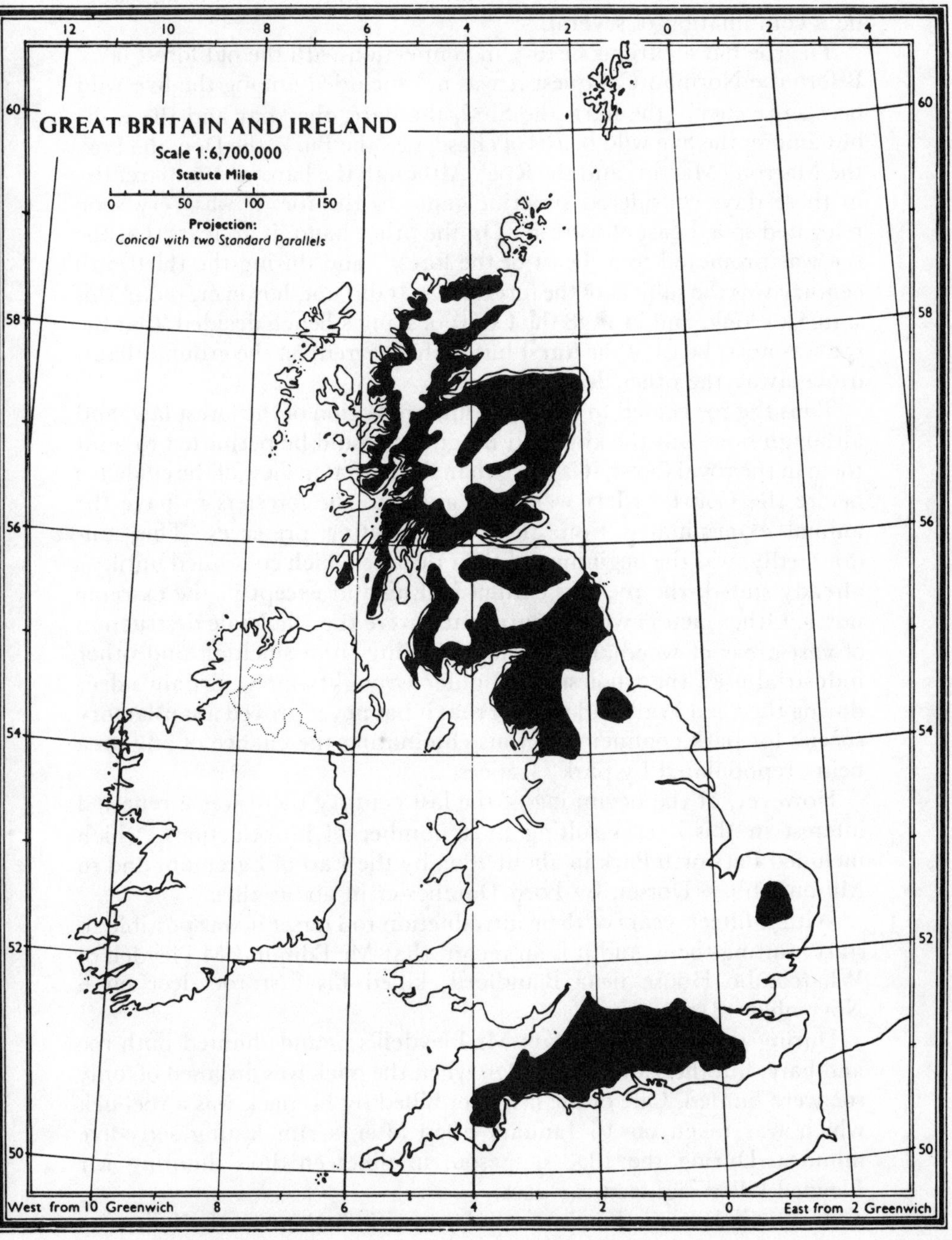

The approximate distribution of roe deer in Great Britain. In both England and Scotland roe deer are no longer hunted by hounds, but are shot either by stalking, from a high seat or during a drive. There are no roe in either Wales or Ireland have come so near to extinction is difficult to find, for it would appear to be a combination of several.

The roe has a curious history in connection with the old forest laws. Before the Norman Conquest it was not included among the five wild beasts of venery (the hart, the hind, the hare, the boar and the wolf) but among the five wild beasts of chase, i.e. 'the Buck, the Doe, the Fox, the Matron (Martin) and the Roe'. Although the hare was, apparently, in those days considered superior game to the roe, it was very soon relegated to a 'beast of warren'. On the other hand, it appears that the roe was promoted to a 'beast of the forest', and during the thirteenth century was the subject of the forest laws. It did not, however, retain this status for long, and in 1338 the Court of King's Bench decided 'that the roe was not a beast of the forest but of the warren, on the ground that it drove away the other deer'.[189]

Thus the roe ceased to enjoy the full protection of the forest law, and although none but the king and his guests would be permitted to hunt them in the royal forest, it is more than likely that in view of the evidence before the Court, orders would be given to the foresters to have the animal exterminated from the royal hunting preserves. This, undoubtedly, was the beginning of their decline which continued until, as already stated, the roe was extinct in England except in the extreme north. Other factors which contributed were the wholesale destruction of vast areas of woodland for ship building, iron smelting and other industrial uses; the wholesale slaughter wrought among Britain's deer during the Civil Wars and the fact that it has never proved a satisfactory species for park confinement, thus eliminating the chance of any area being repopulated by park escapees.

However, at the beginning of the last century there was a renewed interest in this deer resulting in a number of introductions, which included Petworth Park in about 1805 by the Earl of Egremont and to Milton Abbas, Dorset, by Lord Dorchester in about 1800.

Within fifteen years of their introduction to Dorset it was possible to start hunting them, and it is on record that Mr Edmund M Pleydell of Whatcombe House near Blandford, killed his first roe deer on 6 November 1815.

During the next three years Mr Pleydell's hounds hunted both roe and hare, but thereafter until 1829 when the pack was disposed of, only roe were hunted. One of the last deer killed by his pack was a roebuck which was taken on 16 January 1829 after a run lasting sixty-five minutes. During the 1828–9 season, in nineteen days' hunting Mr Pleydell killed eighteen roe deer.

A contributor to the *Sporting Magazine* (1824) gives the following account of the type of sport provided by Mr Pleydell's hounds. 'The kennel is spacious and extremely well built. The huntsman is William Rice, who has lived all his life in the Pleydell family, and hunted the Harriers in Mr Pleydell's father's lifetime, the hounds having been kept in the family for more than a century. The pack consisted of eighteen couple of dwarf foxhounds and a few moderate-sized harriers. With one or two exceptions, a prettier pack I have never seen. They finished the season in the second week in April, having killed fourteen brace of deer. In the middle of the season they killed six times following, each producing a good run, from three hours to three hours and a half. The covers are drawn in the same manner as for a fox. At first, the roebuck runs short, and does not care to keep very far from the hounds, and will allow itself to be surrounded by them; but when once it takes to the open it will run for more than two hours before it is taken. It is remarkable that foxes and hares are occasionally chopped, but the roebuck scarcely ever, their agility and strength enabling them to evade the hounds. None, not even the oldest buck, has been known to stand at bay, but will allow itself to be taken without an attempt to defend itself.'[176]

Mr Henry Symonds, of Goswell and Milton St Andrew, who later hunted with a pack known as Mr Harding's Mountain Harriers, describes an extremely good run he had on 5 April 1828 with the Pleydell pack.

'They threw off at Elcombe Wood, and in about ten minutes a fine buck was viewed going over the opposite hill in gallant style for Escombe, through which it passed and made for Turnwood. Here he remained a few minutes, and then broke over the downs into the Vale of Blackmoor to Ibberton where, being headed by some labourers, he ascended the hill and, skirting Ibberton Park, ran to Houghton Wood, passed through that extensive covert, and turned through the enclosures of M. Davis Esq., to a coppice at some distance, near Darweston. Thence he made for Elcombe, and again attempted the hill, but, his strength failing, he turned back into covert and passing directly through, broke on the other side, and the whole pack (with the exception of one couple of hounds) ran into him in view in a short furzy brake on the down, after a run of one hour and forty minutes without a single check, and the greater part, particularly in the open country, at speed.'[176]

About the time of the disbandment of Mr Pleydell's pack, Mr James Harding was hunting a pack of hounds – generally referred to as the Mountain Harriers – from his home at Higher Waterson near Puddletown in Dorset – and this pack didn't seem to mind what it hunted so long as it could run. Thus on 8 November 1830, they killed a fallow deer, whilst on 19 March 1831 they accounted for a very mixed bag – a fox, a roebuck and two hares. It would appear, however, that it was primarily in the months of March and April that this pack hunted roe.

During the next few years the Mountain Harriers had several notable hunts of an hour or more duration – and on such occasions it would appear that hounds were either stopped before actually coming to terms with the deer or the deer was captured without being harmed by hounds and subsequently released. For instance, on 5 April 1835 hounds hunted and lost a deer in pouring rain after a hunt lasting one hour

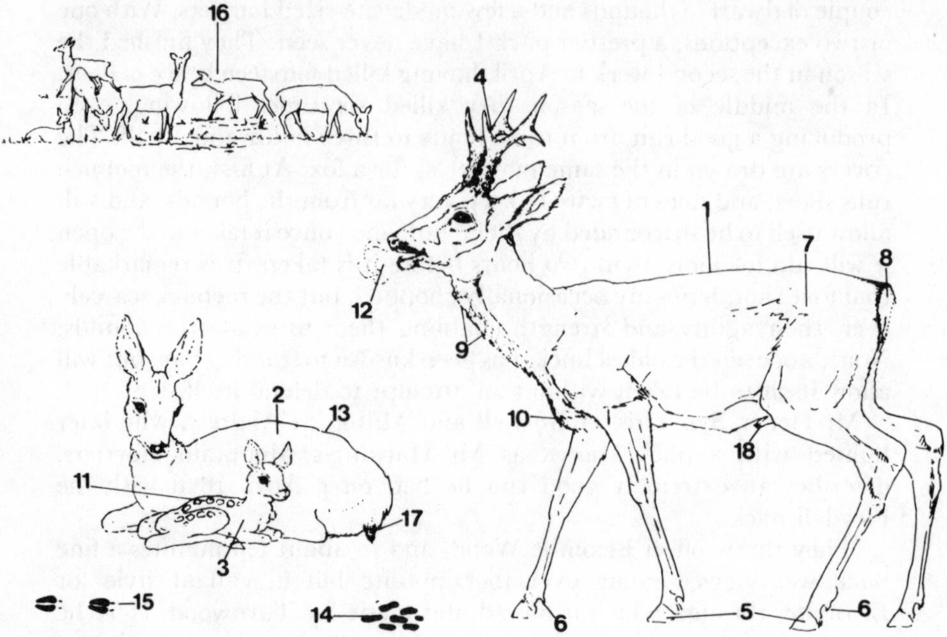

Roe deer (Anciently spelt ra, raa, rae, rais, rays, roo, raibukes)

1 Buck
2 Doe, dae, da, daa, dais, doo
3 Kid, gyrle
4 Antlers, attire, head, rack, trophy
5 Cleaves (toes), slot (cloven foot), talon (heel)
6 Dew-claws, ergots, os, surcleaves
7 Coat, hide, skin
8 Rump patch, eyres, target
9 Throat-patch, gorget
10 Brisket, essay
11 Spotted, pomeled
12 Bark, belloweth, voice
13 Bedded (resting), also couched
14 Droppings, croties, fewmets, fewmishing, mutes
15 Footprints, feaut, foil, foin, foyles, imprint, pace, pattern, register, slot marks, splay (spread of slot), spoor, step (interval between footprints), stride (interval between successive footprints of same hoof), trace, tracks, trail, view
16 Beuy, beve, bevy, bey (collective term for six or more roe deer)
17 Tush (anal) – (doe, in winter pelage)
18 Brush (penis), pensel

Age group terminology

	Male deer	*Female deer*
Under 1 year	Kid	Kid, gyrle
1 year	Yearling	Yearling
2 years	Gazelle	Gazelle, girl, girle, gyrle
3 years	Brocard, hemule hemuse, heimuse, heinuse	Doe
4 years	Roebuck of the first head	
5 years	Fair roebuck	

thirty-five minutes – this particular deer having previously, on 11 November 1834, given the pack an extraordinary run of just over two hours. On 12 April 1836, however, a three-year old buck was killed near Houghton Wood after a first class run without a check, lasting an hour and five minutes.

Another deer, known as the 'barren roe doe' gave the hunt a couple of fine runs before coming to an untimely end. On the first occasion (22 February 1836) she kept hounds running for two hours fifty minutes before being taken uninjured in the turnpike road opposite Holnest Farm house.

Two months later (15 April 1836) the Mountain Harriers had their second great run after the 'barren roe doe'. On this occasion the deer, after being found in Upcerne Wood, ran before hounds for almost two hours before jumping the iron gate fence into Melbury deer park where Mr Harding, seeing the distressed state of the deer, stopped hounds. Thus ended a splendid run of at least eighteen miles.

Unfortunately there was a sad sequel, for some people in the park, on seeing the distressed deer, ran after her and soon caught her under the windows of Melbury House. The deer, however, managed to escape but whilst attempting to jump a twelve-foot high wall, fell back and broke her back.[176]

The Mountain Harriers gave up roe hunting about the end of 1838 following which there does not seem to have been any roe hunting in Dorset for nearly twenty years. By this time they had become extremely steady on the line of the hunted deer as was proved by the occasion when they ran a roebuck right through Charborough Park in which there were nearly 600 fallow deer, finally killing their buck in Lytchett High Wood after a run lasting sixty-eight minutes.

Also in Dorset, during the 1830s, Mr Drax of Charborough hunted for about eight seasons, roe deer with a pack of hounds which it is believed had previously belonged to Mr Pleydell. Mr Drax – who Captain Radclyffe describes as an extraordinary man, as nearly mad as he could be – also kept two other packs – one for stags and the other for fox, and these he kept going for about thirty seasons.

About the middle of the last century roe hunting in Dorset was once again revived when Mr Radclyffe of Hyde Park, Wareham, formed a pack which is recorded to have killed nearly forty roe in the two seasons of 1856 and 1857. Each season provided a memorable run. On 6 April 1856 following a meet at Tolpuddle, hounds went into Milborne Wood where it was known a very fine buck was making its headquarters. Milborne Wood, however, belonged to a certain Mr Farquharson who was very jealous of anyone keeping hounds or interfering with his covers in any shape or form. The deer was duly roused, and leaving the wood it took a line to Dewlish Park where a gentleman shot both barrels at it but without effect, before the deer re-entered Milborne Wood. However, it did not remain there long, and was eventually pulled down on Tuck's

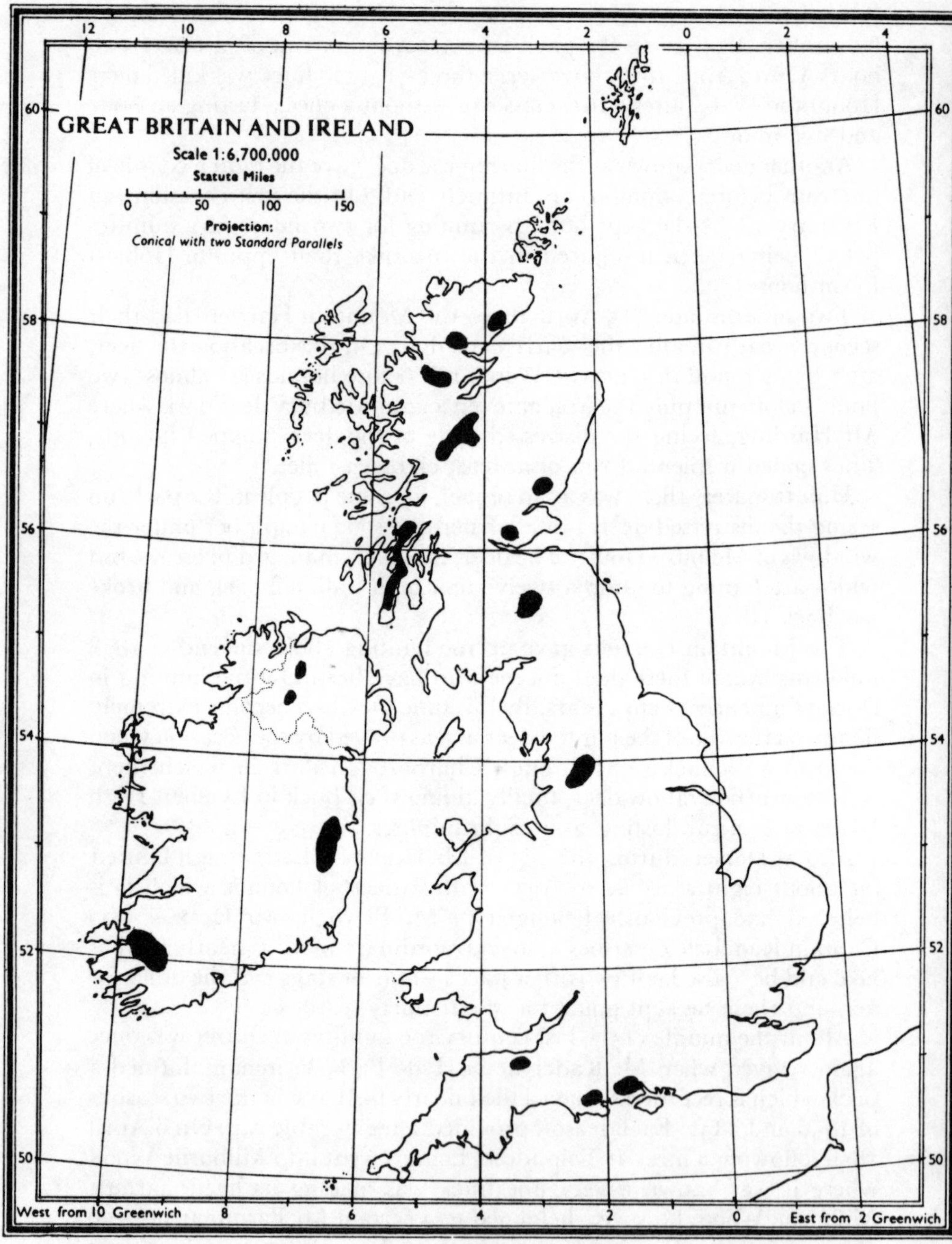

The approximate distribution of sika deer in Great Britain and Ireland. As the map shows, sika deer are not as widespread as fallow. It is over fifty years since sika were last hunted with hounds, all control today being done by shooting

Down near Cheselborne Village.

The longest run without doubt, however, was after a deer which broke away from Lytchett High Wood on 3 April 1857 and ran a distance of about twenty-five miles before being taken some four hours ten minutes later under Julian's Bridge, near Wimborne, where it had taken refuge.

Hunting roe with hounds seems to have been continued in Dorset until the First World War, the last 'Master' to do so being Miss Guest who tells me (*in litt.*) that it was nothing then to see 'groups of thirty or forty together, in the Grange Woods which lie between Cerne and Sherborne'. The Earl of Ilchester seems to have given up roe hunting some years prior to this.

Occasionally in the past it would seem that the New Forest Buckhounds used to make a special effort to hunt roe deer, some of which have given the hunt extremely fine runs. One such occasion was on 3 January 1896 when following a meet at Markway, it was decided to draw with the pack for the Clumber roebuck which had last been hunted three years previously on 6 March 1893. The buck was found in Aldridgehill, and taking off in the direction of Clumber and Bolderwood, he finally led the pack into the Franchises where hounds were stopped owing to growing darkness. The actual point was eight-and-a-half miles, but the distance covered was more than double. The buck was later found dead. About three years later the New Forest Buckhounds had another long run after a roebuck in the Wilton country, finally killing close to Draggons Road Station after a run lasting about three-and-a-quarter hours.[176]

In 1904 the Seavington Harriers, following a meet at Chillington Down on 22 February, found a roe in Chaffcome Wood, which after circling around for some time, finally took off and after crossing Cricket Park and swimming the ornamental water in the park, made off in the direction of Potwell Copse, where hounds killed their deer. Thus ended an exceptionally fine run and a ten-mile point.

At the turn of the century the Ripley and Knaphill Harriers were also hunting roe in Swinley Forest, near Windsor but how long this practice continued is not known. It was, apparently, the custom at the end of the hare hunting season to have a meet or two after roe, and the following is an account of one such day (*Sporting Notes and Sketches*, 1899).

The meet was between Ascot and Aldershot. 'Keepers hovered about, giving bits of fresh information. One knew of a red-deer, an "outlier" from the Queen's. There was some talk about a fallow-buck. But the roe-deer were the main topic of conversation. A farmer had seen a roe-doe at feed upon his farm. . . .

'Coming near to Bagshot Park, hounds burst into sudden cry and, immediately after, a roebuck leaped across the road. Scent was useful for sudden flashes: for a consecutive hundred yards it could not be carried, and fresh deer perpetually diverted the attention of the pack.'

The hunt lasted all day until the evening, and although at times it seemed that the deer must be taken, it 'slipped back into some covert of the fern, and another took his place and responsibilities. Once . . . the roe was just before the pack . . . so beat that he nearly lay down in the road. But he climbed the hedge into the wood and, when a few moments later the pack reached the place, scent had vanished utterly'.

More recently Richard Prior records a more successful hunt when, 'in the nineteen-thirties a bobbery pack roused a buck in Odstock Copse on the outskirts of Salisbury, and ran it into Blandford where it was killed in a garden, a distance of nearly twenty miles'.[158] During the same period the Lunesdale and Oxenholme Staghounds, which hunted both wild and carted deer in Westmorland (*see page 225*) found the roe which were increasing in numbers in the southern part of the Lake District, a decided nuisance, and on numerous occasions caused the pack to be split. In the majority of cases hounds were stopped before coming to terms with the deer.

Although roe hunting with hound and horse does not seem to have ever been practised in Scotland, deer coursing was certainly once a favourite pastime. Sir Walter Scott in *Waverley* has this story.

'For until the shooting season commences, I would willingly show you some sport; and we may, God willing, meet with a roe. The roe, Captain Waverley, may be hunted at all times alike; for never being in what is called *pride of grease*, he is also never out of season, though it be a truth that his venison is not equal to that of either the red or fallow deer.' Prior to the course, it would appear that about half-a-dozen boys – which he calls 'Gillie-white-foots' were destined to beat the bushes, which they performed with so much success that, after half-an-hour's search, a roe was started, coursed and killed'.

Snaffle quotes from an article by 'W' in *The Field* describing how roe coursing was carried out in Scotland about the turn of the century. 'We found a roe in the big woods down by the lake' he wrote, 'and after a long and difficult chase through the woodlands the hounds forced him out on the top side, and though we had three men posted at different points with all the running dogs, he succeeded in escaping unobserved. However, the hounds stuck to the line, and carried it over the highest hill on the moor, about three miles away. The roe then swung to the left over the march and through one of our neighbour's coverts, then down on to the road by the loch and, as luck would have it, back to our own ground and into the same wood where we had first found him. Here the four hounds had a difficult bit of hunting, and it was marvellous how they managed to stick to him so well, but they did it somehow, and drove him down on to the lake shore again and along the edge of the lake for about half a mile, when he turned up the hill again through the wood. We had viewed him once or twice in the wood, and knew we were not very far behind him, but at this point the hounds checked, and we all had serious fears that we should lose him. However, my friend, who acted as huntsman, with a singularly lucky cast downhill, hit it off again, and hounds ran right away from us along the side of the hill. Taking the two lurchers with me, I went along the road, telling the men with the greyhounds to go to the top again on the chance of his facing the open. As luck would have it, he doubled back through the top of the wood and broke quite close to them, and they slipped both dogs; but directly these began to press him, abandoning his point, which was evidently a distant plantation, he turned back into the wood and came straight down the hill, having shaken off one dog in the undergrowth. The other was still after him, and drove him straight towards me through a thin bit of wood, but at last he crossed an open space amongst the birch trees not sixty yards away. I immediately slipped the lurchers, and he did not go very much further before they ran into him.'

After describing several similar runs, 'W' says that although 'we did not, of course, kill many roe, we had a lot of sport with our small pack'. On several occasions they tried to kill a roe with hounds alone, but apparently never had any success for 'the real use of the hounds was to force the quarry into the open for which purpose they are preferred to beaters, who are often difficult and expensive to obtain in remote parts of Scotland'. I wonder what 'W' would think of the £5–£8 daily wage expected by the modern beater of today?

More recently, Sir John Buchan-Hepburn recalls that on an estate in the Lake District, where he was acting as agent, his employer 'had three couple of cross-bred hounds, blood-hound X foxhound. These hounds were trained to hunt up and down the woods and drive the deer out on to the open ground where the guns were posted, so that when the deer came out there was a chance to get a shot at them. Hounds very rarely came out of the wood themselves whilst in pursuit of the deer, but carried on to find another. Our procedure was as follows: At a given time the keeper who had charge of the hounds was told to let them out and put them into the wood. About an hour before this, the guns started off in order to be in position and ready before the hounds were let out. . . . We found that the early morning was the best time and that it was useless to continue after mid-day. Say hounds were unkennelled at 8 am we started off at 7 am to get to our positions and there waited until we heard hounds running towards us.'

Once on the open ground, it seems that the roe seldom went far, for 'their main idea seemed to be to get back to the wood as soon as they considered it safe to do so'. The best bag, for six rifles, was eight roe.[34]

Snaffle mentioned 'that there is a good deal of roe-coursing in Dorsetshire, but it does not afford much test of the merits of the greyhound. The usual method is to locate the deer in a small and detached covert, and then beat this out towards a point where the coursing party is stationed. Once a roe is fairly away and separated by men from the woodland, the hound soon pulls it down'.[176]

Hounds of one sort or another were also used to drive roe to guns, and

Harry Harewood recalls the following incident. 'In March 1831 Captain Chalmers of Auldbar, in Scotland, gave a grand *chasse* in his woods, which abound with these beautiful little animals. Ten couple of highly-bred harriers were selected for the purpose of rousing the roes, and the shooters were placed in certain parts of the openings where the deer were expected to cross. Six double guns obtained chances; and the result was fifteen head of deer killed and two wounded.'[95]

A more sporting method of taking roe which, although practised in Scandinavia, is seldom done in Britain, is to go *roe baiting*. This method, which is quite unlike the old form of bear or badger baiting, consists of hunting a particular buck by one man armed with a rifle and accompanied by a single hound. Sometimes the hunter takes up his position on a track often used by the beast being hunted, and the hound is released with the object of circling the roe back past the concealed sportsman.

The best sport with roe is undoubtedly the stalk with rifle at early dawn or in the evening, particularly during the summer months when the countryside is looking its best. Shooting from a high seat that has been placed at some point of advantage in the forest can not only be rewarding and selective, but in certain terrain near human habitation, can often be the only completely safe method of using a high powered rifle – the *only* weapon that should be used on deer. Alas, far too many roe deer are still being shot with shotguns during the course of a deer or game bird drive. Whatever method is used, one should always have a hound available to find a wounded beast in cover, for even when mortally wounded by a heart or lung shot, deer will often run off up to a distance of perhaps 100 yards (90 metres) before collapsing in dense undergrowth. A good dog will often prevent an hour or two of worrying search, which may well end in failure even though the beast is lying dead not so very far away. Various breeds of dogs have been successfully used for this task, and although two of the most favoured breeds on the continent are the German short-haired pointer and the Vizslas, almost any breed, provided it has a nose, can be trained. I personally have had considerable success with yellow labradors, and my present one will often indicate the presence of a deer in thick cover, or over the crest of a small hill by stopping dead in his tracks and pointing with his nose in the direction of the deer.

Chapter XI
Deer Legislation in England

It would seem that King Canute (1016–35) was probably the first monarch to issue any game laws – though at that period the wild beasts of the forests were not specifically called 'game' but forest beasts. Indeed it was not until 1389 that there was any mention of the word 'game' in an English statute.

The word 'game' is an indefinite word, and seems at various times to have had various meanings. Generally speaking, game may be said to be those animals and birds which are the object of sport. Nevertheless, there is no general definition of 'game' when it appears in the various statutes that have been passed to protect it. Each statute has its own definition. For instance, deer are not included among the list of game to which the *Game Act* 1831 applies. Deer are, however, included in the list of game for which the *Game Licences Act* 1860 applies, making it necessary, therefore, for anyone wishing to shoot wild deer to hold a current Game Licence. This, however, is legislation of the nineteenth and twentieth centuries; for the moment we are considering legislation as it affected Britain at the time of Domesday.

Before the reign of King Canute, all wild beasts and birds were assumed as belonging to the king and no other person might kill or hunt them. In 1016, however, King Canute, who was a Dane, granted at a Parliament held in Winchester a *Charta de Foresta*, and one of the quaint clauses of this Charter stated that 'he that doth hunt a wild beast, and doth make him pant, shall pay ten shillings. If he be not a free-man, then he shall pay double; if he be a bond-man, he shall lose his skin'. Death or loss of a limb was also the penalty for killing any of the King's deer by a bondman but bishops, abbots and barons were permitted to hunt all beasts of the forest, provided they were not royal beasts (stags) – if they did, they would have to 'make satisfaction at the King's Pleasure'.

A number of Forest Officers were appointed to see that law within the royal forests was observed, and these included four chief men called *Pagened* – later known as Verderers – Ealdermen and Tineman, the latter becoming Foresters or keepers and Regarders. If at any time, a man offer force to a Verderer, should he be a free-man then the punishment was loss of such freedom. A villain, however, lost his right hand, whilst any subsequent offence of a like nature incurred the death penalty. If a Regarder was struck in anger, the punishment was the same as though a royal beast had been killed.

To all **VERDERS, FORESTERS, REGARDERS,** *and other Officers, of* **The Forest of ESSEX,** *otherwise called* **The Forest of WALTHAM:** *in the County of* **ESSEX.**

WHEREAS by the Forest Laws, for the Preservation and Quiet of the WILD BEASTS, with their Fawns, the Forest ought to be DRIVEN Yearly, Fifteen Days before *Midsummer*, and Fifteen Days after:——THESE are therefore to require You to assign a certain Day for the DRIVING of the said Forest, and to give Notice to all Officers, and others concerned in such Drifts, to give their Assistance, and also to the Owners of such Beasts and Cattle, as shall be found then commoning upon the said Forest, to come and challenge their Beasts, and take them away, or else to seize them as Strays for the Use of the Warden:—AND for your so doing, this shall be your sufficient Warrant.

Dated 15th June — **1824**

[illegible] Verd.

for W. P. T. Long Wellesley **WARDEN.**

[illegible]

J. Robinson, Printer, Essex Press, Romford

Notice posted in 1824 ordering Waltham Forest to be cleared of cattle etc., for the 'Fence Month' – the season of fawning

The Charter also made certain regulations about dogs in the forest. It was forbidden for any 'mean person' to keep a greyhound, but so long as 'their knees be cut before the Verderers of the Forest' – which made them unable to chase deer with any speed – then it was permissible for this breed of dog to be kept by a free-man, who could also keep one with the knees uncut, *provided* he lived at least ten miles from the bounds of the forest. Should, however, any 'uncut' greyhound be found, the owner would have to pay twelve pence for every mile within the ten mile limit. Any such dog, however, found actually within the forest, would be confiscated and the sum of ten shillings paid to the King. (This mutilating of dogs was variously called Hambling or Hocksynewing but when the operation was later changed by the *Charta Foresta* of 1224 to cutting off three claws of the forefeet, it became known as lawing or expeditating of dogs.) Small dogs, called Valteres and Ramhundt, were however, allowed within the forest without having their knees cut, for it was considered that they did not constitute any real danger to the deer. They had, however, to be kept under the owner's control.

Should, however, such a dog – through the negligence of its master – run wild and perhaps bite a wild beast in the forest, then if the owner was a 'mean man', recompense, according to ancient law, was £10 – a free-man, however, had to pay 'twelve times a hundred shillings'. On the other hand, should the dog have bitten 'a Royal beast, then he shall be guilty of the greatest offence'.

The law did, however, provide 'that every man might take his Venery in his own ground, so long as he refrained from taking the Venery of the King in his Forest'.

During the next thirty years or so the forest laws remained materially unaltered and it was possible for people to hunt on their own ground, provided they did not trespass in the royal forest. All this, however, was soon to change, for following the Conquest and during the reigns of the four Norman monarchs, private hunting grounds practically disappeared as William I, the Conqueror (1066–87), and subsequent monarchs laid claim to the sole and exclusive hunting rights over large areas of forests such as New, Dean, Windsor and Sherwood. Indeed, at one time there were no fewer than sixty-nine forests, thirteen chases and seven hundred and fifty parks in England in which deer and other forest beasts were protected by the harsh forest laws. It was these forest laws which, because they were so abused by the officers of the Crown, did so much to estrange the monarch from his people. Of William I it was said that it was better to be one of his deer than one of his subjects, so harsh were the punishments given to offenders against the forest laws, which even included death to the owner of a dog that should bite a stag. So unpopular, in fact, was he at his death that it is said his corpse was denied a burial until the ground was paid for where he was interned. He was succeeded by his son William Rufus who, if anything, dealt even more cruelly with any offender found hunting in the royal forest. It seems only justice, therefore, that this King should have lost his life by a shooting accident whilst hunting in the New Forest.

Manwood described a forest as 'a certain Territory of Woody grounds and fruitful pastures, privileged for wild beasts and fowls of Forest, Chase and Warren, to rest and abide in, in the safe protection of the King, for his princely delight and pleasure. . . .'[132]

Adjoining the forest there might be a certain tract of land which was once part of the forest but had later been disafforested. This land was known as a purlieu, and although in general the forest laws still covered these disafforested areas, according to Manwood those who had woods and lands of freehold within the purlieu to the yearly value of forty shillings by the year, were able to keep greyhounds. Should any wild beast of the forest be found within the woods and lands in the purlieu, it could be chased by the greyhounds towards the forest. At all times, however, the pouralee man, as he was called, had to observe the following six lessons:-

1 That he do begin his chase in his own Purlieu.

2 That he do not forestall nor kill the wild beasts with any engine.

3 That before his dogs enter the Forest, he do repell and call them back again.

4 That in no sort he do pursue his dogs into the Forest, except that they fasten upon the deer first, and that the deer do draw the dogs into the Forest, and then kill the same.

5 That he do hunt with no more company but his own servants.

6 That he do hunt no unseasonable deer.

Besides the forests there were other tracts of land, defined only by bounds, called chases. The only difference between these and forests was that they could be held by a subject, and on account of this, any offences committed therein, were generally punishable by the common law and not by forest jurisdiction. Some of these chases, such as Dartmoor, had once been the property of the Crown, and had, therefore, been a forest in every sense of the word. When, however, the land passed by royal grant into the hands of a subject, it was considered to have lost many of the attributes of a forest.

In addition to the forests and chases, there was still a further class of unenclosed land, called warren, wherein the public had a right to hunt wild animals, though occasionally the 'public right' was restricted by some special royal grant. Normally, however, the word 'warren' denoted that the public had the exclusive right of hunting and taking certain beasts on a certain piece of land, or denoted the land over which such privilege existed. Grants of free-warren over land outside the royal forests were made by the King to both private individuals as well as to religious bodies, and anyone who had no such licence was not permitted to hunt over the warren without the owner's permission, under penalty of £10. It was permissible, however, to continue following a hunted deer over such land, as deer were not included among the 'beasts of the Warren', which only included the hare and the cony. It is of interest to note, however, that after a time the roe deer was relegated from a royal forest beast to a 'beast of the Warren' on the ground that it drove away the other deer (*see page 152*).

From the royal forests, chases and warrens as well as elsewhere, the parks, one by one, were fenced off by pales or a wall. In certain forests there might be several such parks, whilst in others only one, but whenever the park fell within the forest boundary, forest law prevailed, whilst in those which lay outside, offenders were punishable by common law.

Many parks were held throughout the country by subjects under a Crown Licence, which sometimes included permission to erect deer-leaps or salteries (Saltatoria). A deer-leap was a low fence or bank in the main park fence, over which the wild deer from the adjoining forest could easily jump into the park, but once inside they were unable to return because of a steep upward slope or wide ditch inside the park fence. Occasionally, owners of parks within or adjacent to a forest deliberately constructed deer-leaps without any royal licence, and there are numerous records of deer-leaps being presented to the Justices in Eyre – as the courts for dealing with the pleas of the forest in any particular county or group of counties were called – who generally ordered their removal should the deer-leaps be considered to constitute a threat to the forest. Probably the last park in England to exercise the privilege of a chartered deer-leap was Wolseley Park in Staffordshire, and to this day remains of the deer-leap can be seen on the edge of Cannock Chase.

In ancient documents mention is frequently made of 'hayes' – a word derived from the Saxon meaning, literally, a hedge. Hayes would appear to differ from parks in that they were not intended for the permanent preservation of the deer but as a means to entrap them in some small enclosure from which they could be later transferred to a proper deer park. There is little information about the size of these hayes, but the haye of 'Donnelie' which belonged to the Earl of Mellent, measured half a mile square. At the time of the Domesday Book there were thirty-one parks and more than seventy hayes in England.

For many years no one could form a park without a special licence being obtained from the Crown, and although in 1404 attempts were made to abolish this law, it was not until after the Restoration (1660) that licences became unnecessary.

During the next hundred years or so, the severe forest laws continued with more and more land being converted into royal hunting grounds as each succeeding monarch 'did dayly increase and make more new Forests, and more in the Lands of their subjects, to the great hindrance and impoverishing of their subjects'.[132]

These despotic proceedings were not confined solely to royalty, for when the fashion for park making became general among people of wealth, the same treatment was often meted out to any small holding that interfered with the park boundaries. John of Salisbury, a writer of the twelfth century, gave his views on Norman tyranny when he wrote:

In our time hunting and hawking are esteemed the most honourable employments, and most excellent virtues by our nobility; and they think it the height of worldly felicity to spend the whole of their time in these diversions; accordingly they prepare for them with more solicitude, expense and parade, than they do for war; and pursue the wild beasts with greater fury than they do the enemies of their country. By constantly following this way of life, they lose much of their humanity and become as savage, nearly, as the very brutes they hunt. . . .
Husbandmen, with their herds and flocks, are driven from their well cultivated fields, their meadows, and their pastures, that wild beasts may range in them without interruption. . . . If one of these great and merciless hunters shall pass by your habitation, bring forth hastily all the refreshment you have in your house, or that you can readily buy or borrow from your neighbour; that you may not be involved in ruin, or even accused of treason.

At last, however, King Henry III (1216–72), put an end to the practice of requisitioning more and more land for the exclusive hunting of the monarchy and by the *Charta Foresta* of 1224 – often referred to as the Charter of the Liberties of the Forest – all such woods that had been requisitioned by King Richard and King John and turned into royal forests, were immediately disafforested.

Undoubtedly the most important decision among the many changes in forest law brought about by this Charter was that 'no man from hence forth shall lose either life or member for killing of our Deer'. Instead, any person convicted of taking venison 'shall make a grievous fine, if he have anything whereof to make fine; if he have nothing to lose, he shall be imprisoned a year and a day; and after the year and a day expired (if he can find sufficient sureties) he shall be delivered. And if not, he shall abjure the Realm'.[132]

The Charter also provided that if any archbishop, earl or baron was passing through one of the royal forests he was entitled 'to take and kill one or two of our deer, by the view of the forester if he be present, or else he shall cause one to blow an horn for him, that he seem not to steal our deer'.[132]

There was a change, also, in the practice of hambling (also called lawing) of dogs. In addition to reducing the number of forests where it was necessary for dogs to be lawed at all, the Charter changed the mutilation from cutting the knees to cutting off the three claws of the front feet – and this operation could be performed only by an officer appointed by the Court of Swanimote which had considered the Inquisition of the Regarders, following their view of the forest. The manner in which this operation had to be done was described in the Charter as follows: '. . . one of his fore-feet [is placed] upon a piece of wood eight inches [20cm] thick, and a foot square [900sq cm], then one with a Mallet, setting a chizel of two inches [5cm] broad upon the three claws of his fore-foot, at one blow doth smite them clean off; and this is the Manner of expeditating of Mastiffs'. This practice, which made it impossible for the dog to chase a wild deer with much speed, was instituted for the 'quiet and safety of the Wild Beasts' and related to every man's dog living within or near the forest. As before, small dogs were permitted without being expeditated.

Originally, this lawing was intended for mastiffs, but it was generally applied to all dogs of sufficient size and speed to chase the deer. To ensure lack of size and speed, a special large stirrup was kept in some forests such as the New Forest and Blackburnshire Forest, and any animal that could squeeze through it was exempt from lawing.

The fine for having kept a large dog, such as a mastiff, not expeditated near the forest was only 3 shillings (15 pence), and it would appear that quite a number of people were prepared to take the risk of not being found out. If, however, any dog that had not been expeditated happened to hurt or kill a wild beast of the forest, then the owner, in addition to paying the above mentioned fine and having the dog confiscated, was also punished according to the severity of the offence. If, however, the dog had been expeditated, the owner was exonerated of all blame. In purlieus and other places, however, that had been disafforested, a dog could be kept without being expeditated.

If any deer was found dead, and its meat was not fit 'to be eaten of the best sort of people', the carcase was given to the Lazar-house (poor house). If, however, the venison was in good condition and the beast happened to be a royal beast, then since the deer 'was the King's beast alive, and the killing of him hath not altered the property, and then the same being the King's, his Justice of the forest may dispose of it at his pleasure. . . .'[132]

It was also a crime to take off the skin of a deer that had died of the murrain, and anyone convicted of so doing 'shall pay the Price of the Skin, and be amerced'. It would appear that foresters were expected to hang up on the trees of the forest the carcases of those deer that had died of the murrain and always to keep a strict record of those that thus perished.'[56] At a later date it became customary to burn the carcase. In mediaeval England 'murrain' was the generic term for almost every known form of disease that affected cattle as well as deer. In 1334 upwards of 500 deer died of 'murrain' in the forest of Pickering, whilst in the Forest of Rockingham during the sixty years period between 1420 and 1480 it was estimated that over 1400 head of game succumbed to this disease.

In 1235 certain Lords tried to get a statute passed whereby the punishment for trespass in their parks should be 'proper imprisonment' but it was contrary to the wishes of Henry III so that statute was deferred (Stat. Mert. 20 Hen. 3–1235).

Forty years later, however, the question of trespass in parks and ponds came up again, and as a result, the penalty for trespassers was 'three years imprisonment, and after shall make fine at the King's pleasure (if he have whereof) and then shall find good surety, that after he shall not commit like trespass. And if he have not whereof to make fine, after three years imprisonment, he shall find like surety; and if he cannot find like surety, he shall abjure the Realm' (Stat. Westm. 1.3 Edw. 1:1275, c. 20).

Trespass in forests, chases, parks and warrens was again the subject of a further statute during the reign of Edward I and as a result, any 'Forester, Parker or Warrener' who happened to kill any trespasser who tried to evade arrest 'with force and arms' was exonerated from blame. Nevertheless, if any forester, parker or warrener 'by reason of any malice, discord, debate or other evil will had before time' killed any person for alleged trespass 'when of a truth they did nothing' . . . 'the death of such persons shall be inquired' and justice done 'according to the Law and Customs of our Realm' (Stat. 21, Edw. 1. 1293).[83]

At this period the hunting seasons for the various species of deer were as follows:

The time of grace of a Hart, or Buck, beginneth at Midsomerday and lasteth till Holy-Rood day (24 June to 14 September).

The Season of the Hind, or Doe, doth begin on Holy-Rood day and lasteth till Candlemas (14 September to 2 February).

The Season of the Roebuck beginneth at Easter and lasteth till Michaelmas (about end of March to 29 September).

The season of the Roe (doe) beginneth at Michaelmas and lasteth until Candlemas (29 September to 2 February).

In addition to the proper hunting seasons, there was also a 'Fence Month' – sometimes called 'Defence Moneth' – which lasted from 'fifteen days before Midsomer . . . until fifteen days after Midsomer, which is upon Saint Cyril's day' (9 June to 9 July) during which time the forests were to be left completely quiet so that the female deer could raise their young undisturbed.

During the fourteenth and fifteenth centuries there were a number of statutes concerned with the preservation of game in the royal forests but the majority concerned themselves only with the illegal taking of various species of birds and fish rather than deer.

During this period, every person not having a greater annual revenue in land than one hundred pence, was obliged to have in his possession a bow and arrows, with other arms offensive and defensive. Furthermore, those who had no possessions but could afford to purchase such arms, were commanded to have a bow with sharp arrows if they dwelt *without* the royal forests, but if within the forest area, the arrows had to be round-headed, so as to prevent them being used with any effect against the king's deer. These round-headed arrows were also called bolts, and could be used with both longbow and crossbow.[182].

During the reign of Richard II (1377–99) there was passed the first of many Acts designed to keep the pleasures of the chase as the prerogative of men of property, as the following quotation suggests only too well. 'For as much as divers Artificers, Labourers and Servants and Grooms keep Leverers [Greyhounds] and other dogs, and on the Holy Days when good Christian people be at Church, hearing Divine Service, they go hunting in Parks, Warrens and Connigries of Lords and others, to the very great Destruction of the same, and sometime under such colour they make their assemblies, conferences and conspiracies for to rise and disobey their Allegieance; It is ordered and assented that no manner of Artificer, Labourer, nor any other Layman, which hath not Lands or Tenements to the value of 40 shillings by Year, nor any Priest, nor other Clerk, if he be not advanced to the value of 10 pounds by Year, shall have or keep from henceforth any Leverer [Greyhound] or Lerce [Hound] or other Dog to hunt; nor shall they use Ferrets, Heys, Nets, Harepipes, nor Cords, nor other Engines to take or destroy Deer, Levers [Hares] and Conies, nor other Gentlemen's Game upon pain of one Year's Imprisonment' (13 Ric. 2, c. 13. D. 1389). This, it will be noted, was the first statute in which the word 'game' was expressly mentioned – it was also 'the first "qualification act" forbidding persons not of a certain rank in Society or whose income from land did not amount to forty shillings per annum, "to take or destroy deer, hares, conies or other gentlemen's game".'[228]

During the next four hundred years or so there were no fewer than fifty Acts of Parliament passed concerning the possession, killing and vending of game. During this period the value of the qualification seems to have kept pace with the increasing value of heritage and movables. For instance, during James I's reign (1603–25) it was necessary to have £40 in heritage, £80 in life rent or £400 in movables before being qualified to kill pheasants or partridges (7 Jac. I. c. 11. 1609). An Act during the reign of Charles II (22 Car. 2, c. 25. 1670) increased the qualification to £100 per annum in heritage; or £150 of leasehold. In 1831, however, the qualifying Statutes were repealed by the *Game Act*, and now any person may kill game in Britain who holds an Excise licence for that purpose.

By the beginning of the sixteenth century, however, deer stocks, both red and fallow, were being decimated by deer poachers who were using 'nets called Deerhayes, and Buckstalls, and stalking with beasts, to the great displeasure of our Sovereign Lord and King'. Accordingly it was made an offence for anyone who did not own a forest, chase or park to have in his possession 'any Nets called Deerhayes, or Buckstalls'. A month's grace after the passing of the statute was given, but thereafter a fine of £40 was 'forfeit for every Month they are so kept'. Nor was it allowed to stalk a deer by using a Bush or Beast – i.e. a stalking horse –

under forfeit of the same penalty (Stat. 19 Hen. 7 c.11:1503).[83]

A number of other statutes for the preservation of game followed during the sixteenth century, the most important of which were the Statute of 1533 – the first to provide any close season period for the taking of wild fowl but deer were not included (Stat. 25. Hen c.8.1533) – and the Statute of 1541 which concerned itself with all matters appertaining to the ownership of guns and crossbows etc., together with certain technical details as well as places where such weapons could be used, and the type of game for which individual licences would be granted (Stat. 33. Hen. 8 1541). One of the provisions of this latter Statute was that no person or persons, no matter 'of what estate or degree soever he or they be, shall from or after the said last day of June, command any of his or their servants to shoot in any cross-bow, hand-gun, hagbut or demy-hake of his or their said Masters, or of any other persons, at any Deer, Fowl or other thing, except it be only at a butt or bank of earth, or in the time of war . . . upon pain to forfeit for every such offence ten pounds'.

The seventeenth century saw a number of Statutes for the better protection of deer becoming law. This was a period when deer stealing was accompanied by considerable violence whenever the offenders were confronted by the deer keepers, and in order to restrict the number of people entitled to take deer an Act was passed in 1603 which made it illegal for anyone who had an Inheritance of less than '£10 per annum, a Lease for Life of £30 per annum, or be worth £200 in Goods, or be the Son of a Baron, or Knight or Heir apparent of an Esquire . . . 'to keep' a Greyhound, or other Dog or Net, to kill or take Deer' and anyone found committing such an offence 'shall be committed to Prison without Bail, unless he immediately pay forty shillings to the Use of the Poor where the Offence was committed, or be apprehended'. The Act also made it illegal for anyone to 'sell, or buy to sell again, any Deer, on Forfeiture of ten shillings for each Deer, to be divided between the Prosecutor and the Poor . . .' (1 Jac. 1. 1603).[83]

Two years later there was a further Act which made it illegal for anyone without the owner's consent, to 'kill or chase any Deer or Conies in Parks or inclosed Grounds, in Pain to suffer three Months Imprisonment, and to pay treble Damages to the Party grieved to be assessed by the Justices before whom he shall be convicted after the said three Months expired, and to be bound with two good sureties to the good Behaviour for Seven Years, and to remain in Prison till he find such sureties'.

This Act also entailed anyone who owned lands 'worth £100 a Year' to take for his own use any gun, bow or crossbow etc. from a 'Person not having £40 per Annum in Lands, or £200 in Goods, or some inclosed Ground used for Deer or Conies, worth forty shillings per annum at least', who was apprehended for using such weapons on his land.

This Act, however, did not apply to any park or enclosed ground which might be made in the future without licence from the King 'nor to any Offence concerning the chasing or killing of Deer in the Day-time, but to such Offences only as shall be committed in the *Night*' (3 Jac. 1. 1605).[83] The implications of this last paragraph, not unnaturally, encouraged certain 'malefactors . . . to chase, hunt, kill and destroy Deer in the daytime, by colour of the said Proviso . . .' and accordingly this section of the Act was repealed in 1609 and as a result 'all and every such person and persons so offending shall for every such offence pay and satisfie unto the party grieved the summ of ten pounds of current money of England, or else treble damages and costs at the election of the party grieved' (7 Jac. 1. c. 13:1609).

In 1661 there was a further Act 'to prevent the unlawful Coursing, Hunting or Killing of Deer' which provided that anyone 'that course, kill, hunt or take away Red or Fallow Deer in any ground where Deer are kept, without consent of the owner . . . shall forfeit £20 to be levied by Distress . . . one Moiety [half] to the Informer, the other to the owner of the Deer; and for want of Distress shall be committed to the House of Correction for six Months, or to the Common Gaol for a Year, and not be discharged till Security given for their Good Behaviour for one Year after their Enlargement' (13 Car. 2. c. 10.1661).[83]

Despite these Acts, deer poaching continued unabated, and the penalties provided by existing legislation were 'found by daily experience not to be sufficient to deter divers, lewd, sturdy and disorderly persons, who confederate together in great numbers, making amongst themselves as it were a brotherhood and fraternity, whereby if any of them shall be discovered and convicted, which seldom happens, because of their great force and clandestine manner of combination, then by a common contribution (for the most part) advance and pay, for such persons so apprehended, the pecuniary penalties (which are but small) inflicted on such offenders', so a new Act, entitled *An Act for the more effectual Discovery and Punishment of Deer-stealers* was passed in 1692, the main provisions of which were as follows:

> If any Persons shall unlawfully course, hunt, take in Toils, kill, wound, or take away any Red or Fallow Deer, in any Forest, Chase, Purlieu, Paddock, Wood, Park, or other Ground inclosed, where Deer are, have, or shall be usually kept, within the Realm of England or Dominion of Wales, without the Consent of the Owner or Person chiefly entrusted with the Custody thereof, or shall be aiding or assisting therein . . . shall forfeit for every such Offence the sum of £20. And for each Deer Wounded, Killed or Taken the sum of £30 to be levied by way of Distress upon the Goods and Chattels of every such Offender, under the Justice or Justices hand, before whom convicted; one third to the Informer, another to the Poor . . . and the other to the Owner of the Deer.

Failing to meet the fine, 'they shall be imprisoned a Year, and set in the Pillory an Hour on some Market Day in the Town next the Place where the offence was done'.

This Act also gave Constables, in possession of a Justice's warrant, power to search the houses of anyone they suspected of being implicated in deer poaching, 'and if any Venison, Skin of Deer or Toyles be found, shall carry such offender before a Justice of the Peace,' and failure to produce a satisfactory explanation as to how he came into possession of the above, would make him liable to the same penalties as would be inflicted for killing a deer (3 & 4 Will. & Mar. c.10. 1692).

The following is the wording of a warrant to search after venison and deerskins.

To the Constable

By virtue of an Act of Parliament made in the third and fourth of King William and Queen Mary, These are to authorise and require you, on Sight hereof, to enter into and search the Houses, Outhouses, (as for stolen goods) and all other Places belonging to suspected Person or Persons, within your Precints, to have in their Custody any Venison or Skins of Deer, not being lawfully qualified; and if on Your Search, you shall find Venison or Skins of Deer, then you are presently to bring such Person or Persons, in whose Custody the same shall be found, before me or some other of his Majesty's Justices of the Peace for this Country, to be proceeded against for such offence, according to Law.

An interesting case arose when a man who was charged under the 1692 Act with deer stealing in a purlieu of a forest, objected on the grounds that in this particular purlieu, deer were not usually kept, but only in the adjacent forest, and therefore did not fulfill the requirements of the Act, which stated 'If any person shall unlawfully course etc. any red or fallow deer in any forest, chase, purlieu, paddock etc., where deer have or shall be *usually kept*, without the consent of the owner. . . .' The defendant claimed that a purlieu was a place where by law deer cannot be kept, it being disafforested as well, and one of the tasks of the ranger was to drive any deer out of the purlieu back into the forest.

Another objection was that the defendant was, apparently, the owner of the purlieu and, therefore, presumably had the right to chase the deer out of his ground. Nevertheless the conviction was confirmed.[81]

During George I's reign (1714–27) there were a number of new Acts passed for the preservation of game in England, three of which were directly concerned with illegal killing, or taking away of deer from forests, chases and parks.

The first of these, the Act of 1719 (5 Geo. I. c.15:1719), was passed in order to make more effectual the Act of 1692 for the discovery and punishment of deer stealers, and a most important section of this was to make provision for any keeper or officer of the forest 'in breach of the Trust reposed in them' to be fined £50 for each deer killed or taken away illegally, the sum 'to be levied by way of Distress upon his or their Goods and Chattels, to be distributed as the Forfeitures in the Said Statute are to be distributed; and for want of such Distress, that then he or they shall suffer Imprisonment for Three Years, without Bail or Mainprize, and be set in the Pillory for Two Hours, on some Market-Day in the next adjoining Town. . . .'

In the same year another Act was passed (5 Geo. I. c.28.1719) which increased the penalty for illegal killing of deer within a park or enclosed ground from a fine of £30 to transportation for seven years 'to some of His Majesty's Plantations in America'. This Act, however, did not repeal or alter any previous law for the punishment of deer stealers, but any offender punished by the above mentioned Act could not be prosecuted, under any other Act, for the same offence.

Four years later, the Act of 1723 (9 Geo.I.c.22:1723) provided that anyone who appeared armed and with their faces blackened and otherwise disguised in any forest, park or other ground where deer were kept, were liable to 'Suffer Death . . . without benefit of Clergy'.[83]

It would appear, however, that the provisions of the Act of 1723 did not extend to the unlawful coursing, hunting, taking in toils, killing, wounding or taking away any red or fallow deer that were being fed or kept in open forests or chases where deer are usually kept, but only to such as were inclosed within pales, rails or other fences. Offenders against the former, therefore, were only punishable by the Act of 1692 which inflicted only a pecuniary penalty. An Act was therefore passed in 1736 which provided that any persons convicted a second time of hunting, and taking away, of deer out of unenclosed forests or chases, would be transported to one of His Majesty's Plantations in America for the space of seven years in the same manner as other offenders convicted under the 1723 Act. Should any such person return to any part of Great Britain or Ireland within the said seven years, he shall be adjudged guilty of felony, and shall suffer death 'without the benefit of clergy'. The Act also provided the same punishment for any person who entered with arms, a forest or chase, whether it be enclosed or not, or a park wherein deer are usually kept with intent to hunt deer, and when apprehended happened to cause bodily harm to the keeper or other servants (10 Geo.2.c.32:Sect.7.1736).

Nineteen years later a further Act was passed to make the above mentioned Act 'perpetual', and also to make 'the more effectual Punishment . . . of Persons unlawfully hunting or taking any Red or Fallow Deer in Forests or Chases; or beating or wounding the Keepers or other Officers in Forests, Chases or Parks'.

In 1755 there had been an Act passed to prevent the reckless burning of gorse, furze and fern in forests and chases, thereby destroying not only the cover necessary for the deer and other game, but also much valuable timber as well, when the fire got out of control. It became necessary, therefore, for anyone wishing to burn such undergrowth, to obtain 'the licence or consent' of the owner or proprietor. Failure to do so would incur a fine, on conviction, of 'any sum not exceeding five pounds, nor less than forty shillings' – one half of which would be paid to the informer and the other to the use of the poor of the parish where the offence was committed. Failure to find the money might incur 'sale of the offender's goods and chattels' or a spell in the common gaol 'for any time not exceeding three months, nor less than one month'

(28.Geo.2.c.19.Sect.3.1755).

On the question of burning heath, as long ago as the twelfth century during Henry II's reign, some men in Surrey 'were fined 100 Marks for burning of *Heath* for it spoileth the Layer of the Deer and disturbs them'.[145]

During the eighteenth century, in order to deter poachers from entering the woods the man-trap came into use. This was a large gin trap with a moveable flat pan set centrally between a pair of opposing steel jaws, which were either straight or curved, held by a catch connected with a spring at each end. The trap, about 6ft. 4in. (190 cm) in length, was hidden among the bushes or covered with leaves. Anyone treading on the pan released the catch, the jaws springing together and catching the intruder by the leg about 12 in. (30 cm) from the ground. The usual type of man-trap had large spikes set at intervals along the jaws, which sometimes had a toothed edge, but there was also a so-called 'humane' trap with plain jaws.

Poachers often used to strap wooden slats to their legs, inside their trousers, to protect them from the most severe injuries, but even then, the strength of the springs was such that a trapped leg was probably broken. The use of man-traps was prohibited in 1827.

During the reign of George III (1760–1820) there were two Acts concerned with the illegal hunting, shooting and stealing of deer etc., the first in 1776 (16 Geo.3.c.30) and the second in 1802 (42 Geo.3.c.107) the latter repealing the former and increasing the penalty imposed by the former for the above offences, from a fine not exceeding £10 nor less than £5 for the first offence, the sums of which would be doubled on every conviction after the first, to transportation for seven years.

During the nineteenth century there were a number of new laws for the preservation and taking of game, some of which are still in force today. These included *The Night Poaching Act* 1828 (9 Geo.4.c.69) – which remains the law on poaching at night to the present day – and *The Game Act* 1831 (1 & 2 Will.4.c.32) which abolished all the old game laws except *The Night Poaching Act.* In neither Act, however, are deer specifically mentioned in definitions of 'game'. The former Act applies to the entire country whilst *The Game Act* 1831, which was primarily to legalize the sale of game, and thereby make it an article of commerce, to England and Wales only.

The most important Act was undoubtedly the *Game Licences Act* 1860 for it applies to everyone in the United Kingdom except the royal family and a gamekeeper appointed on behalf of Mer Majesty, who wishes to kill game (23 & 24.Vict.c.90; 1860). 'Game' includes not only those birds and beasts which are set out in the 1831 *Game Act* definition, but also *deer.* This Act repealed the duties on game certificates and certificates to deal in game, and imposed, in lieu thereof duties on excise licences and certificates for the like purposes. A full annual Game Licence, referred to as a Red Licence, expiring on 31 July no matter when taken out, now costs £6. Licences for shorter periods can, however, be taken out, namely a Green Licence (1 August to 31 October), and a Blue Licence (1 November to 31 July), both of which cost £4. An 'occasional licence' costing £2 can also be taken out. It runs for fourteen days, including the day of issue and day of expiry. A Game Licence authorizes the holder to sell game to a game *dealer* whose licence costs £4 and is valid until 31 July each year. No licence, however, is needed by a dealer in England to sell wildfowl, snipe, pigeons, woodcock, rabbits or *deer*.

It is also necessary for a gamekeeper to hold a licence, and this costs £4 no matter when taken out; it likewise expires on 31 July. The holder of a gamekeeper's licence may only shoot game on his employer's land or shoot. If he wishes to kill game elsewhere he should possess a proper Game Licence.

Game Licences are obtainable from any post office which transacts Money Order business or at the offices of the local Authority. It is an Excise Act, the money it raises being directed to the County Authorities instead of, as formerly, to the Exchequer.

A Licence to kill game does not authorize any person to purchase, have in his possession, use or carry any firearm except as permitted by the *Firearms Act* 1968, and a firearm or shotgun certificate must be obtained in respect of any firearm for which it is necessary to hold such a certificate.

A Game Licence is, therefore, required by anyone deerstalking anywhere in Great Britain, the only exception being killing deer on *enclosed* lands by the owner or occupier, or with his permission.

In a recent case – Jemmison v. Priddle (1972) 2. W.L.R. 293, it was held that for the purpose of the *Game Licences Act* 1860, farmland is 'enclosed land': Jemmison was shooting deer with permission on B's farm. He, however, killed a deer on Priddle's farm where he did not have permission to shoot, and also shot a second deer – this time on B's land – but it also ran on to Priddle's land before falling dead. Jemmison was charged with killing game without a licence contrary to Section 4 of the Act. He contended that he was shooting deer with permission on enclosed land and so was within exception 5 of Section 5 of the Act. The Justices found that the land in question was not enclosed land, being ordinary farmland and not a place where deer were artificially accumulated. Jemmison appealed and it was held, dismissing the appeal, that 'enclosed land' for the purposes of the Act meant land other than moorland, but that as Jemmison had no permission to shoot over Priddle's farm he was guilty of an offence under Section 4 in respect of the first deer, but not in respect of the second deer as this was shot on land where he had permission to shoot.

It is, however, unnecessary to have a Game Licence for hunting deer with hounds.

Prior to the passing of the *Game Licences Act* 1860 the amusement of hunting and fowling was ultimately made a subject of revenue in 1784 when every sportsman was required to pay two guineas annually – subsequently increased to three guineas in 1791 and a further ten shillings in 1812, for a Game Certificate which authorized him to kill game.

In 1861 the *Larceny Act* (24 & 25. Vict. c. 96) was passed and until repealed entirely under the *Theft Act* 1968 (16 & 17 Eliz.2 c.60) provided in Sections 12 to 16, as well as, to a lesser extent by the *Deer Act* 1963, the only measure of protection given to deer being killed by the poacher. Under the *Larceny Act*, Section 12, it was an offence to chase, wound or kill deer in the unenclosed part of any forest, purlieu or chase. The penalty for a first offence was a fine of up to £50 whilst for a second, and any subsequent offence, a similar fine and/or up to two years' imprisonment was imposed. At one time, if the offender had been a male under the age of sixteen, he could have been whipped.

An owner of a dog which broke loose and hunted deer without the consent of its master, would not have been liable under this section, but if it could be proved that he knew his dog was in the habit of chasing deer, and yet permitted it to be at large in or near a forest, he might have been liable in an action for any damage the dog had done. Forest, in this section, means only a legal forest. There are many districts which have long been disafforested, and preserve only the name. The New Forest is now practically the only unenclosed forest which has preserved much of its original character, and in which deer are still preserved.[197]

Section 13 provided a similar penalty for anyone chasing, wounding or killing a deer in the enclosed part of any forest, or on enclosed land – i.e. a deer park – where deer are usually kept. The definition of what constituted an 'enclosed part of any forest' was tested in a case in 1847 when the Court decided that an enclosure erected in the Forest of Dean for the protection of timber, consisting of a ditch and bank which were sufficient to prevent cattle getting into it, but over which deer could pass in or out as they pleased, was held to be an 'enclosed part' of the forest.

Under Section 14, any person in possession of any deer or part of a deer such as head or skin, etc., or any snare or device for catching deer, who could not satisfactorily account for his being in possession of it could, on summary conviction, be fined up to £20. A Court also had power to summon before it every person through whose hands any deer or part thereof had passed unlawfully and inflict punishment on each person.

Under Section 15, any person who set snares or other devices for taking deer or breaking down deer fences etc., was liable to a fine not exceeding £20.

Section 16 authorized deerkeepers and their assistants to demand from trespassers on any forest or land where deer are usually kept, any gun, snare or engine, or any dog brought there for the purpose of taking deer. If these were not surrendered, they could be seized. Resistance and injury to the keepers or their assistants entailed a fine and/or imprisonment of up to two years, with or without hard labour.

The *Larceny Act* 1861, which as already stated, has now been repealed by the *Theft Act* 1968 applied only to England and Wales and did not cover deer roaming the country at large. However, it should be noted that Section 32 (1) and Schedule 1 of the latter Act expressly preserve the provisions of the *Larceny Act* relating to deer, whilst the provisions of Section 4 of the *Theft Act* cover the theft of tame deer.

In the year following the *Larceny Act*, the *Poaching Prevention Act* was passed, but deer were not included in the list of 'game' for 'all the purposes of this Act be deemed to include' (25 & 26 Vict. c.114.1862). It was unfortunate that this was so, for this Act enabled the police to stop poachers and search them on the highways.

Nor were deer included in the list of 'ground game' for which the *Ground Game Act* 1880 applied (43 & 44 Vict. c.47). This was an Act for the better protection of occupiers of land against injury to their crops from ground game (rabbits and hares).

Three years later the *Customs and Inland Revenue Act* 1883 was passed, the main purpose of which was to alter the date of expiry of Game Licences from 5 April to 31 July – and this expiry has remained in force ever since (46 & 47 Vict. c.10).

Before leaving legislation of the nineteenth century, mention should be made of the *Deer Removal Act* of 1851 (14 & 15 Vict. c.76) which referred only to the New Forest. Towards the middle of the last century there was considerable agitation from people in the area that deer stocks were getting too numerous and causing considerable damage. In 1830 the stock of deer in the New Forest was estimated at about 5417 and although by 1850 the figures had been reduced to only 2000, this was still considered to be 2000 too many, so in the following year the *Deer Removal Act* was passed which decreed that all the deer had to be removed from the forest within two years. 'No effort was spared to bring this about,' wrote Lascelles. 'At first the great bulk of them were simply shot down. But as they became scarcer and wilder, all sorts of means had to be adopted. Nets were used, and the deer were driven into them, set at well-known tracks and paths throughout the woods: hounds were freely employed to drive the deer into the nets and up to the guns posted in likely places. Finally, hunting pure and simple had to be resorted to, and a deer when found was run down by the bloodhounds each keeper used to assist him in his duties. At the end of two years, the Act had been carried out as far as was possible in a densely wooded country like the New Forest.'[120]

Wild deer are subject to the same common law rules as other wild game, and the occupier of any land, provided he has not let the sporting rights to any tenant, is entitled to shoot any deer found wandering over his land. Although it is necessary, with certain exceptions, to hold a Game Licence to shoot a wild deer, it should be remembered that deer

FOREST OF ESSEX,

Otherwise called

Forest of Waltham.

Unlawful Enclosures and Trespasses.

BY an ACT passed in the last Session of Parliament (52 Geo. III. Chap. 161.) Reciting, That the Number of Unlawful Enclosures, Encroachments, Purprestures and Trespasses in the Royal Forests, have of late years been much increased, and the Fences of many such Encroachments, and the Houses and Buildings erected thereon, though at different Times abated and thrown down by the Keepers or other Officers of the Forests, have again been reinstated by the Trespassers, who originally made them, or by others subsequently occupying or claiming the same; and that it is expedient that effectual Provision should be made for the Prevention of such Offences, and for the Punishment of the Offenders:

It is Enacted, That *all such Unlawful Enclosures, Purprestures, Encroachments, and Trespasses,* which shall have been wilfully made, or caused or procured to be made, by any Person or Persons, in and upon ANY Forest, or shall be wilfully held, occupied or made use of by any Person or Persons subsequently occupying or claiming the same (except such as have been legally demised, or in respect of which any Treaty for a Demise shall or may be pending) *shall be enquired of in the Court of Attachments* of the Forest; and the Person or Persons guilty of *making, continuing or renewing* any such Unlawful Enclosure, Purpresture, Encroachment or Trespass, *shall be prosecuted for the same* in the same Court, and *may be fined* for every such Offence, in any Sum not exceeding *Twenty Pounds:* And every such Unlawful Enclosure, Purpresture, Encroachment or Trespass, *shall be abated or thrown down* by the Officers of the Forest.

AND by the same Act, It is further ENACTED, That every Under Keeper of the Forest shall, before the holding every Court of Attachments, carefully *Survey* such Part or Parts of the Forest as shall be within his Walk, and shall *take an account of all unlawful Enclosures, Purprestures, Encroachments and Trespasses whatever* there, and shall *at every Court of Attachments* make and deliver *a true Return and Presentment of all such unlawful Enclosures, Purprestures, Encroachments and Trespasses,* and at what Time or Times and in what particular Part or Parts of the Forest, and by whom, any such unlawful Enclosures, Purprestures, Encroachments and Trespasses, have been made, done or committed: And every such Under Keeper shall at the time of making or delivering his said Return or Presentment, *make Oath,* that to the best of his Knowledge, Information and Belief, no unlawful Enclosure, Purpresture, Encroachment or Trespass, hath been made, done or committed, or then exists, other than such as are contained and described in the Returns or Presentments so made and delivered.

The UNDER KEEPERS of the several Walks are required to proceed forthwith in making SURVEY of all such unlawful Enclosures, Purprestures, Encroachments and Trespasses, as have been made, done or committed at any time within *Twenty Years* last past within the said Forest of ESSEX, and to make Report thereof, that the same may be presented at the next Court of Attachments which will be holden for the said Forest at the King's-Head Inn at CHIGWELL, on Monday the Twenty-first Day of September 1812, so that the Offenders may be proceeded against by due Course of Law.

By Order of the Lord Warden,

Steward's Office,
East Heynalt Lodge,

T. E. TOMLINS,
Steward.

Printed by Luke Hansard & Sons, near Lincoln's-Inn-Fields, London.

Notice concerning unlawful enclosure in the forest of Waltham are not specifically included in the definition of game, so in any lease of game shooting, it is important that if deer are to be included, it should be definitely stated. A tenant who killed deer that were reserved to his landlord would render himself liable to an action for breach of covenant or agreement.[125]

If deer are kept in an enclosed ground or deer park – presumably with a deer-proof fence – where they are fed and preserved, they come within the same category as cattle and to steal them would be a felony.

The owner or keeper of a lawful deer park is justified in shooting any dog running after deer in it. On one occasion an action was brought against an owner of a deer park who had killed a brace of greyhounds whilst chasing deer in his park. One deer had been killed by the dogs, and to prevent further casualties the defendant had killed them. In reply, the plaintiff claimed that the deer, when first seen, was outside the park feeding on his own land. Accordingly he had let loose the two greyhounds to chase it off his land. The deer, when pursued by the dogs, returned to the park where it was caught and killed, despite the plaintiff's efforts to stop the dogs entering the park. Judgement was given for the defendant.[145]

The property in deer passes, in general, to the heir and not to the executor. However, if deer have been so tamed as to acquire the character of personal property, then they pass to the executor. This was decided in a court case during the last century when trover (common-law action to recover value of personal property wrongfully taken or detained) for deer in a park was brought by executors against the heir, and recorded by H W Woolrych (1858) as follows: 'The deer belonged to a park in the possession of the Earl of Abergavenny. The evidence for the plaintiff was, that the park consisted of about 900 acres [360 hectares], containing much fern, brake and gorse. The deer had the range in the old park. They were attended by keepers and fed in the winter with hay, beans and other food. The does were marked, and the fawns marked. There was a selection of the deer at certain times for the purpose of fattening them for consumption, or for sale to venison dealers. Deer sometimes, though rarely, escaped over the fences. They had of late been sold generally, like sheep, or other animals, for profit. For the defendant it was contended, that this was an ancient park, that notwithstanding any new additions, the old boundaries were still visible, and that the deer were generally in a wild state. The plaintiff answered, that although vert, venison and inclosure might originally have belonged to this park, it had ceased to bear that character, and that the deer had ceased to be animals *ferae naturae*.'

Although the finding of the court was for the plaintiff, following a new trial the verdict was reversed and judgement given in favour of the executors. During the hearing it was stated that some of the deer were kept in stalls and whilst some of them would be found to be tame and gentle, others were quite irreclaimable in the sense of temper and quietness.[231]

Tame deer, on the other hand, as distinct from 'escaped park deer' are, in the opinion of Nicholas Everitt 'as much a species of private property as sheep, so that if a tame deer strays on to another man's land he has no right to shoot or take it against the real owner, and if he does so he may be prosecuted for stealing, though, unless it was shown that he knew it to be a tame animal, it would be difficult to secure a conviction if the plea were set up that the shooter imagined it was a wild one'.[72] Presumably, therefore, if the animal was wearing a collar, as is frequently the custom with someone's pet deer, this would be proof enough that it was a tame animal. When it was the custom to hunt the carted deer in England, presumably this animal could also be claimed to be 'tame' by the hunt who owned the deer. Even if the shooter's plea that he only shot the animal in the belief that it was a wild one is upheld, if it is subsequently proved that the deer was, in fact, a tame one, then the carcase would belong to the owner of the live deer. If, however, the deer was proved to be a wild one, then the carcase would belong to the shooter or person on whose land it was shot.

Apropos the shooting of a wild deer by a trespasser, Everitt (1910) has this to say. 'If a wild deer is found upon an ordinary farm and there shot by a trespasser, the occupier has no criminal remedy against the trespasser, but may, of course, bring a useless and expensive common law action for trespass. On the other hand, the trespasser has no right to the carcase, which belongs to the occupier of the land (unless the general sporting rights belong to the landlord or some other person). If, however, neither the trespasser nor the whereabouts of the carcase are discovered till the former and his friends have consumed the venison, the occupier of the land will be chagrined to find that he has no satisfaction but a right of action for damages against (probably) a man of straw.'[72]

Everitt then describes an incident in which a farmer client of his was about to shoot a fat doe grazing on one of his pastures, when a shot rang out, and the deer fell dead. A moment later a well-known poacher was seen to approach the carcase, but on seeing the farmer, ran off.

The farmer was anxious to prosecute the poacher for stealing, but was advised that nothing had, in fact, been stolen and even if the poacher had removed the carcase it would only be theft if it could be proved beyond reasonable doubt, that the deer was truly a *wild* one and not a tame one. If the latter, then the owner might come and claim the carcase, and if this had already been consumed and was, therefore, not available, then its value.

After inquiries in the neighbourhood it was subsequently shown that the deer had, in fact, escaped from a deer park some forty miles distant, and although the farmer then tried to persuade the keeper of the park or its owner to prosecute the poacher for shooting a 'tame' deer, his request was, wisely, turned down for it could not be claimed that the deer in the park fulfilled the description of 'tame' and accordingly, once outside the park, could be treated as a 'wild' animal. The keeper appeared to be interested only in recovering the skin, so the sequel to this incident was that the carcase was cut up and equally divided between the farmer who claimed it, the policeman who carried out the investigation work, the butcher who removed and cut up the carcase and, strangely enough, the poacher himself, much to the objection of the farmer.

Wild deer, like game, have never been the subject of property at common law and it was no offence to kill them on another's land, the only remedy of the occupier of such land being a common law action for trespass. Various provisions have from time to time been made by Act of Parliament to protect the interest of deer preservers, but the older statutes were repealed and replaced by the *Larceny Act* 1861 (Sections 12 to 16), details of which have already been given. In 1968, however, the *Larceny Act* was also repealed entirely by the *Theft Act*.

Ownership of deer contained within a park fence remains so long as the deer remain within that fence. Once outside, ownership ceases. The *Agriculture Act* 1947 (10 & 11 Geo.6.c.48) includes deer with foxes, moles and wood pigeons, as an agricultural pest, and the Minister of Agriculture may, therefore, by his delegate, the County Agricultural Executive Committee, direct the owner of a deer park to take certain measures to ensure that his deer did not escape. The Act, in fact, looks upon the owner of the park as having some measure of control over the deer within the park – a 'qualified ownership'. Any ownership involves responsibility, but once a deer has escaped, ownership of that particular animal ceases and the owner of the park cannot be held responsible for any damage the deer may do to farmers' crops outside the park. The escaped deer now belong to him on whose land they happen to be, and any farmer is at perfect liberty to shoot them as he would marauding rooks or pigeons. The only possible exception to this could be a tame deer – and in particular one wearing a collar as mentioned. The Close Seasons provided by either the *Deer Act* 1963 or the *Deer* (*Scotland*) *Act* 1959 and amendments, do not apply to *marauding* deer.

As regards damage by deer, the *Agricultural Holdings Act* 1906 (6 Edw.7.c.56) stated that where the tenant has sustained damage to his crops from game (which include deer), and he himself has not the right to kill the game, he 'shall be entitled to compensation from his landlord for such damage if it exceeds in amount the sum of one shilling [five pence] per acre of the area over which the damage extends, and any agreement to the contrary, or in limitation of such compensation, shall be void'.

The amount of compensation payable under this section shall, in default of agreement made after the damage has been suffered, be determined by arbitration, but no compensation shall be recoverable under this section unless notice in writing is given to the landlord as soon as may be after the damage was first observed by the tenant and a reasonable opportunity is given to the landlord to inspect the damage.

Where the right to kill and take game is vested in some person other than the landlord, the landlord shall be entitled to be indemnified by such other person against all claims for compensation.[156]

The *Agricultural Holdings Act* 1948 (11 & 12. Geo.6. c.63) likewise made provision for compensating tenants in respect of damage to their crops by 'game', which is defined for the purpose of the Act as pheasant, partridge, grouse, blackgame and *deer.*[228]

There is, however, no legal liability upon a hunt, be it foxhounds or staghounds, for compensation to be paid for poultry killed by foxes or damage to crops etc., by deer. In practice, however, the Devon and Somerset Staghounds, since about the turn of the century, have run a deer damage fund, out of which about a thousand pounds or more will be paid annually for compensation to farmers for deer damage or for the purchase of wire to prevent such damage.

Undoubtedly the most important Act of the twentieth century, so far as deer are concerned in England, is the *Deer Act* 1963 which was 'to provide close seasons for deer; to prohibit the killing and taking of deer by certain devices and at certain times and to restrict the use of vehicles in connection with the killing and taking of deer; and for purposes connected with the matters aforesaid'. This Act only applies to England and Wales, for by the time it became law, the *Deer* (*Scotland*) *Act* 1959 was already in existence.

One would have thought, therefore, that since close seasons for red deer were already in existence in Scotland before details of the *Deer Act* 1963 had been finalized, there would have been some attempt at conformity – but this, unfortunately, was not the case. Indeed, the subject of close seasons for deer in Britain as a whole was made even more confusing by *The Deer* (*Close Seasons*) (*Scotland*) *Order* 1966, which extended the close season to other species of deer in Scotland but again, the dates selected were largely at variance with those operating in England at that date.

The close seasons, set out under Schedule I in the *Deer Act* 1963 and applicable only to England and Wales, are as follows:

	Stag/Bucks	*Hinds/Does*
Red deer	1 May to 31 July inc.	1 March to 31 October inc.
Fallow deer	1 May to 31 July inc.	1 March to 31 October inc.
Sika deer	1 May to 31 July inc.	1 March to 31 October inc.
Roe deer	No close season *	1 March to 31 October inc.

* (Now provided under a new act – see below)

It will be noticed that the Act did not provide any close season for roebucks – nor for the other species of alien deer which are now firmly established in a feral state in England – namely the muntjac and Chinese water-deer, both natives of China. However, the *Roe Deer* (*Close Seasons*) *Act* 1977, which came into force on 1 November 1977 now provides the roebuck in England and Wales with a close season which runs from 1 November until 31 March inclusive. Recently a new bill to replace the existing *Deer Act* 1963 has been before Parliament but unfortunately after a successful passage through the House of Lords during 1977, was subsequently defeated on an objection in the Commons. Briefly, the main provisions of the new bill were to provide close seasons for those species of deer not fully covered under the existing Act; the eventual ban on the use of shotguns for deer control; greater powers given to the police and courts for enforcement with much increased fines and penalties for offenders; and a better control on the sale and purchase of venison.

Fines for any offence under the *Deer Act* 1963 have, of course, now been increased, under the *Criminal Law Act* 1977, up to £500 and if tagging of deer carcases, as suggested on page 197 ever came into force, this would control the sale and purchase of venison, thereby reducing deer poaching. The most serious setback, however, following the defeat of this bill is that the ban on the use of shotguns for deer control – an activity which causes considerable suffering, particularly to the larger species of deer – still seems a long way off.

With certain exceptions, the *Deer Act* 1963 makes it illegal to shoot deer at night – i.e. between the expiration of the first hour after sunset and the commencement of the last hour before sunrise. However, a diseased or wounded deer, or one marauding 'any cultivated land, pasture or enclosed woodland' may be killed by any person at any time of day or night, or even during the recognized close seasons *provided* that 'he is the occupier of that land, pasture or woodland, or that he acted with the written authority of the occupier' and that proof can be given that such action was necessary for the purpose of preventing serious damage to crops and property.

Apropos the shooting of a deer that was alleged to be marauding crops, a case recently came up before the courts – Trail v. Buckingham (1972) 1.W.L.R.459, in which it was held that it is no defence to a charge of shooting deer during the close season that it was damaging crops on land *adjacent* to that on which it was shot. It would appear that Buckingham, having seen damage caused by a deer to a crop on his cultivated land, went into an adjoining wood and shot a red deer hind during the close season. He was charged with contravening Sections 1 and 4 of the *Deer Act*, and he raised a defence under Section 10 (3) of the same Act 'that his action was necessary for the prevention of serious damage to crops . . . on that land'. On appeal it was held that on the true construction of Section 10 (3) 'that land' meant land on which the shooting took place; and that since the defendant's crops were not growing on the land on which the shooting took place, there was no defence.

The Act then turns to unlawful weapons and methods for killing or taking deer, such as the use of any net or snare, or of 'any arrow, spear or similar missile' and 'any missile, whether discharged from a firearm or otherwise, carrying or containing any poison, stupefying drug or muscle-relaxing agent'. However, an exception to this is that 'a licence may be granted to any person by the Nature Conservancy exempting that person, and any person acting with his written authority' so that nets, traps, stupefying drugs and so on can be used for catch-up deer 'for the purpose of removing deer from one area to another or of taking deer alive for scientific or educational purposes'. It is also illegal – except on enclosed land by the occupier, or with his written authority, to fire at a deer 'from any mechanically propelled vehicle' or to use 'any mechanically propelled vehicle for the purpose of driving deer'.

Certain firearms and types of ammunitions are also made illegal, and these are summarized in Schedule 2 'Prohibited Firearms and Ammunition' as follows:

Firearms

1 Any smooth bore gun of less gauge than 12 bore.

2 Any rifle having a calibre of less than .240 inches or a muzzle velocity of less than 1700 foot pounds.

3 Any air gun, air rifle or air pistol.

Ammunition

4 Any cartridge for use in a smooth bore gun other than a cartridge purporting to be loaded with shot none of which is less in diameter than .269 inches.

5 Any bullet for use in a rifle other than a soft-nosed or hollow-nosed bullet.

The Act gave the police power to arrest without warrant anyone suspected of having committed an offence and anyone convicted of an offence under this Act is liable 'to a fine not exceeding £20 or, in the case of a second or subsequent conviction, to a fine not exceeding £50 or to imprisonment for a term not exceeding three months, or to both such fine and imprisonment'. Under the *Criminal Law Act* 1977, however, the maximum fine for an offence under the *Deer Act* 1963 is now increased to £500.

The following Acts relevant to deer legislation in England and Wales are still extant:

Title	**Date**	**Reference**
Game Licences Act	1860	c.90
Agriculture Act	1947	c.48
Agricultural Holdings Act	1948	c.63
Deer Act	1963	c.36
Theft Act	1968	c.60
Firearms Act	1968	c.27
Roe Deer (Close Seasons) Act	1977	c.4
Criminal Law Act	1977	c.45

A summary of the legal position connected with deer in England and Wales today is as follows:

1 *Game Licence*

Anyone shooting wild deer of any species must hold a Game Licence (*Game Licences Act* 1860).

2 *Firearms*

(a) Smooth-bore gun (shotgun) of 12 bore gauge or greater, firing a cartridge loaded with shot, none of which is less in diameter than .269 inches (S.S.G.).

(b) A rifle with a calibre of not less than .240 inches or a muzzle energy of not less than 1700 foot pounds, firing a soft-nosed or hollow-nosed bullet (*Deer Act* 1963).

3 *Time of Day*

(a) Except in case of marauding crops or forestry on *enclosed* land, deer may be shot only during the period commencing one hour before sunrise and ending one hour after sunset (*Deer Act* 1963).

(b) It is legal to shoot deer on a Sunday.

4 *Close Seasons*

Wild deer, except when marauding agricultural ground or woodland, may not be shot during the following close seasons:

	Stags/Bucks	*Hinds/Does*
Red deer	1 May to 31 July	1 March to 31 October
Fallow deer	1 May to 31 July	1 March to 31 October
Sika deer	1 May to 31 July	1 March to 31 October
Roe deer	1 Nov to 31 March	1 March to 31 October

Note: On page 183 reference is made to an unsuccessful attempt to introduce a new deer bill to replace the existing *Deer Act* 1963. This bill, in revised form, is again (1980) scheduled to be reviewed by Parliament. Apart from providing a close season for both sexes of muntjac and Chinese water-deer to correspond to that for all other female deer in England, existing close season dates for all species remain unaltered.

Chapter XII
Deer Legislation in Scotland

There can be no doubt that the Scottish kings, like the Norman sovereigns of England, had their forests in which they exercised exclusive hunting rights, but the origins of some of the old forest laws cannot be traced. Indeed it is not until James I of Scotland (1424–37) who himself was a keen sportsman, had returned from his long captivity in England, that game preserving in Scotland really started to take shape.

In the old Scottish statutes there are numerous provisions referable to deer which show the importance which was attached to all that related to the matter of the chase, and the severest punishments, even death itself, were denounced against offenders.

Deer stealing, particularly from a deer park, has always been treated as a very serious crime, for it was considered that anyone who entered a park to take deer did so in the full knowledge that he was taking someone else's property, and was probably an individual who might just as well carry off domestic stock or a horse, as deer from the park. A number of statutes, therefore, directed against deer stealers were passed during the fifteenth and sixteenth centuries, and one of these provided that 'nan man hwnt, schut, nor sla dere nor Rais' without special licence of the owners, under pain of theft (Act 1474, cap. 16, A.P.S., II, 107).* This Act also prohibited the slaying of deer until 'thaj be a yer aulde'. By the Act of 1503, the slaying of 'parkit dere or Rais or Raibukis of lordis propir wodis', i.e. the slaying of park deer, or roe or roebucks in woods that are the property of lords – was declared to constitute a matter of criminal prosecution, the penalty for which was a fine of £10 'togidder with ane mendis of the partij according to the skath' – that is to say, the party that did the damage had to pay compensation commensurate with the damage he did (Act 1503, cap. 12, A.P.S., II, 242). If the offenders were under age, their fathers had to pay for each of them the noble sum of 'xiij s & iij d' (approx. 67 pence) or else deliver the child for a whipping.

The statutes of 1535 and 1587 were also directed against the illegal shooting of deer in a park, the latter Act in particular, ratifying the older Acts, especially those of 1567 and 1581 because they had had little effect, and added that 'the slayeris and schuittaris of hart hynde da ra hairis cunningis [rabbits] and vtheris beistis . . .' without licence or permission of the owners was similar to horse and oxen stealing, and the

* Note: A.P.S. = Acts of Parliament for Scotland.

offenders would be punished accordingly (Act 1587, cap.43, A.P.S.,III, 453). In 1567 deer-slayers had to suffer for their first offence forty days' imprisonment should they have no goods to forfeit; and for the second offence, the loss of the right hand.

It was also forbidden under the Act of 1594 to hunt within the bounds of six miles of any of the royal parks or forests, or of any of the royal castles or palaces, under the penalty of £100 Scots. This money was, apparently, equally divided between the informer and the King (Act 1594, cap.20,A.P.S.,IV,67).

On the question of property of escaped park deer, Alexander Forbes Irvine (1856) had the following to say: 'Deer, when confined in a park or enclosure, having lost their natural liberty, became the property of the proprietor of the ground, and if they escape, it would seem that the original owner retains his right of property as long as he continues the pursuit, but subject, of course, to the penalties of trespassing at the instance of the owner through whose land he passes. The destruction of deer while confined in a park would no doubt be viewed as theft, and punished accordingly; where, however, the deer have escaped from confinement and are again roaming at large, the shooting of them would be punishable by fine, although not as theft.' Irvine also quotes another opinion which stated that as soon as deer 'get free from their confinement, he who shall have first laid hold of them, *after the former proprietor has given over the pursuit acquires their property*'.[114]

The Act of 1579 imposed a fine of £10 for the breaking down of a park fence for the first offence; £20 for the second and £40 for the third. If the offenders had not sufficient goods to pay, they were to suffer imprisonment for eight days, and to be fed on bread and water for their first offence, fifteen days for the second, and for the third offence, the penalty was 'hanging to the deid' (Act 1579, cap.22, A.P.S., III, 145).

With regard to the illegal killing of deer on the open hill or forest, the Act of 1424 provided that 'stalkaris that slais dere that is to say harte hynde daa or raa . . .' shall, on conviction, 'pay to the king x I s . . .' (forty shillings) (Act 1424, cap.13,A.P.S.,II,7).

Shortly after this it would appear that firearms started to appear in Scotland, and in order to prevent their use in hunting, even stricter laws were passed. Thus the use of firearms was prohibited by the Act of 1551 and any person found using that mode of killing game should lose his life and forfeit his moveable goods (Act 1551, cap.21, A.P.S., II, 488).

This offence was afterwards made punishable with less severity, but even so, under the Act of 1567, which dealt mainly with the use of culverin, crossbow or handbow, an offender would forfeit all his moveable goods. If, however, the offender happened to be a vagabond who had no goods, he was to be imprisoned for the space of forty days for the first offence whilst the second offence would incur the loss of his right hand (Act 1567. cap.17, A.P.S., III, 26). Thirty years later the Act of 1597 ratified all the previous Acts against the shooting and taking of deer with weapons and appliances.[114]

Whether anyone ever suffered the death penalty for shooting a deer is not recorded, but it appears that these statutes were never, at any time, strictly enforced, for the judges, owing to the severity of the penalties, were averse to put them into execution.

None of these Acts appear to have been formally repealed, however, but they gradually went into disuse and have long been obsolete. Indeed, the Act of 1685 permitting the use of 'fowling pieces' was the first indication that firearms were to be allowed for hunting (Act 1685, cap.24, A.P.S., VIII, 475).

An old statute of Robert III of 1400 prohibited the taking of deer and hares in time of snow, under the penalty of 6s. 8d. Scots, without remission. The Act of 1474, mentioned above, also provided 'that na man sla dais nor Rays nor deir in tyme of storme or snaw, or sla ony of thair kyddis quhill thaj be a zer aulde, under the payn of xli . . .' (Act 1474, cap.16, A.P.S., II, 107).

These provisions against the slaying and hunting of does and roes in time of snow were subsequently ratified by the Act of 1621, which ordained that the contraveners of the Act were 'to be vnder the payne of ane hunderethe poundis money Toties quoties (for each offence) as they salhappin to Contravene the same' (Act 1621, cap.32.A.P.S.IV,629).

During the sixteenth and seventeenth centuries the great landowners were much troubled by deer poachers, and in some forests deer were reduced to almost vanishing point. Much of the poaching at that period was, however, to provide something for the pot, for the peasants had little else to subsist on. Such poaching is, perhaps, excusable, for wild life was never intended to be for the exclusive benefit of the wealthy. Poaching such as occurs today, however, for commercial gain is an entirely different matter.

By the end of the sixteenth century, due to excessive poaching, the forests along the border with England were rapidly losing their game, and in an effort to curb the activities of the poacher, an Act was passed on 6 March 1600 which enacted that all defaulters should be 'held to mak payment of the sum of three hundred merks* for every deer so to be shot and slain, the one-half to his Majesty, and the other half to the dilater and avower'.[135]

Between the years 1474 and 1607 there were a number of other statutes relative to deer in Scotland, but all have long been in desuetude.

In order to preserve the pastime of hunting, an Act was passed at the close of the sixteenth century, which prohibited the sale of any deer under a penalty of £100 on the buyer and seller, failure to pay the fine being scourging (Act 1600, cap.34, A.P.S, IV, 236). Sixteen years later keepers of forests were holding courts for trying persons guilty of slaying

---

* 1 merk Scots = 13s. 4d. ($66\frac{1}{2}$ pence).

deer, the penalty for 'landed men' being 500 merks (about £330), whilst unlanded men had to pay 100 merks (about £66) *toties quoties* (Act 1617, cap. 18, A.P.S., IV, 547). This was ratified by the Act of 1621 (cap.32, A.P.S., IV, 629).

In 1685 there was an interesting statute which again forbade the shooting of deer and roe in time of snow, but in addition made it illegal to buy or sell deer for a period of seven years (Act 1685, cap.24, A.P.S., VIII, 475).

As mentioned in Chapter XI certain rights and privileges were granted in England for the preservation of game in forests, chases, parks and warrens. It would appear, however, that these 'privileged places' have never existed in Scotland, and the qualified right to kill game cannot be separated from the ownership of the land except by statute.[156]

In 1744 a fine of £20 Scots was imposed by the Skye lairds for killing a deer 'without permission from the heritors', whilst at a later date a fine of £20.stg. was imposed on the slayer of a deer on Arran.

The question of forest rights and privileges in Scotland was decided in the case of the *Duke of Athole* v. *Macinroy* in 1862 (24D.673). Macinroy was a proprietor of lands adjoining, held in feu of the Duke, but not included in the ancient forest of Atholl owned by the Duke. The Duke sought to have it declared that he was entitled to enter on Macinroy's land for the purpose of killing deer, or at least for the purpose of driving back any deer that had strayed from the royal forest. It was concluded that the right to hunt and kill deer is not *inter regalia*.

The decision in this case showed (1) that a proprietor of land might breed and protect deer on his own lands; (2) that the right to hunt and kill deer is not, and never was, an exclusive prerogative of the Crown; (3) that apart from the game certificate, the only restriction on a proprietor to hunt and kill deer on his own land was imposed by the Act of 1621 (cap.31), which provided that 'no man hunt or haulk at anye tyme heirefter quha has not a pleughe of land in heretage', which meant as much land as he could plough in a year with a horse or oxen, i.e. about a hundred acres (40 hectares) or a little more.* This Act was expressly repealed by the *Statute Law Revision* (*Scotland*) *Act* 1964 (Eliz.2 cap.80).

This case, therefore, dispelled the erroneous idea which generally existed in Scotland early in the last century, that deer were the property of the Crown, and they were no different to other wild animals, and belonged to the person on whose land they happened to be at any one time.

---

* *Note:* 'According to Balfour "ane pleuch sould contene viii oxengang, the oxengang sould contene xii aikers, the aiker sould contene iiii rudis." But although this may have been a rule in measuring land antiently, it will not be found to correspond with the measurements specified in the charters'. (*Bells Dictionary of the Law of Scotland* (3rd edn) vol.2., pp.316–17).

Deer and roe are specially mentioned in the *Game (Scotland) Act* 1832 and arising out of this Act, an interesting case, Macdonald v. Maclean came up in 1879 (6 R. (J) 14) when it was decided 'that entering or being on land without leave of the proprietor for the purpose of carrying away the dead body of a stag, there being no proof that the persons so entering had anything to do with killing it, was not an offence within the meaning of the Day Trespass Act'.[156]

The circumstance of this case, which created considerable interest among the deerstalkers, was as follows: John Maclean, gamekeeper, Kilmorie and two others, were charged with trespassing in the day-time on the lands of Corriebhruadarain, being part of the Macdonald deer forest. It appears that on 2 October 1878 a gamekeeper, while out stalking in the forest, heard shots. Suspecting something wrong, on the following day he went to the corrie and saw Maclean and two others carry a dead stag from the bottom of the corrie, place it on the back of a pony, and carry it off. They were three hundred yards within the boundary of the forest. They had no guns or dogs, and no shots were heard on that day. There was, therefore, no proof as to who had killed the deer, but it would appear that the men, who were accompanying Maclean, were doing so under the instructions of the tacksman of the adjoining property, taking with them a pony to remove the stag. The question submitted for the opinion of The High Court of Justiciary was:

> 'Is the "entering or being upon land without leave of the proprietor" for the purpose of taking away the dead body of a stag, there being no proof that the persons so entering had anything to do with the killing of it, an offence within the meaning of the first section of the Act?'

The question was answered in the negative by the Lord Justice-Clerk who said:

> 'A man trespassing in search or pursuit of game, etc., within the meaning of this provision, is a man whose object is to capture or destroy a living wild animal. . . . The trespass not *unico contextu*, but after an interval of time to secure a wild animal which another has killed, may go to shew complicity, but is not the offence set out in the statute.'[156]

In another case which occurred in 1810, a joint proprietor was found entitled to drive off deer from common pasturage contrary to the will of his co-proprietor.

As mentioned, the *Game Licences Act* 1860 (23 & 24, Vict. cap.90) applies to the whole of the United Kingdom, and it is, therefore, illegal for anyone to stalk or shoot wild deer in Scotland without being in possession of such a licence under a penalty of £20. It is also an offence to assist in any manner in the taking or killing of deer unless a Game Licence is held.

From 1784 to 1860 it had been necessary for anyone wishing to kill game to be in possession of a Game Certificate, the cost of which was, initially two guineas. This was increased to three guineas in 1791, and to £3 13s. in 1812 – a figure at which it remained until replaced by the *Game Licences Act* 1860. It is of passing interest to note that deer were not specifically mentioned under the list of game for which it was necessary to hold a Game Certificate, but presumably were covered by the phrase '*any* game whatever'.

Prior to the *Game Licences Act* 1860, the *Game* (*Scotland*) *Act* 1832, sometimes referred to as the Duke of Buccleuch's Act, was passed, the main purpose of which was to provide more effectual ways of dealing with deer poaching in that period. In this Act, which applied only to Scotland, deer and roe are specifically mentioned, and anyone found in pursuit of same was liable to a fine not exceeding £5 together with costs of conviction – or if in default of payment of penalty and costs, to imprisonment with or without hard labour, for any term not exceeding two calendar months (2 & 3 Will.4. cap.68, 1832).

Although deer and roe are, as stated above, included in this Act, in the clause empowering the arrest of offenders, deer and roe are omitted from the enumeration in the trespass clause. 'Whether this omission is intentional or otherwise,' commented Porter (1907), 'it is impossible to say; and whether if a person was found trespassing in search of deer or roe only, the omission would preclude his being warned off the land, or his apprehension on refusal is, in the absence of any authoritative decision, equally difficult to determine.'[156]

Nor did this Act, like the *Game Act* 1831 which applied only to England and Wales, repeal any of the preceding statutes, 'except,' commented Porter, 'in so far as they were inconsistent with its provisions and hence arises much of that confusion which is so perplexing to those engaged in executing laws.'[156]

At this period it was illegal to sell game anywhere in Scotland for an Act of 1600 had prohibited 'ony persone quhatsumeuir within this realme, in onywayes To sell or by ony fastane reid or fallow deir dais Rais hairis . . .' (Act 1600, cap.34, A.P.S., IV, 236). Indeed it was not until 1860 that the sale of game was permitted in Scotland, though the *Game Act* 1831 had already legalized its sale in England and Wales.

Despite the increased interest in deerstalking during the second half of the last century, and early part of the present century, it was, perhaps, a little surprising that no legislation went through Parliament to give deer greater protection against poachers or indeed, setting aside any close seasons for them during the breeding season. Venison, however, was not valued too highly during this period, and apart from a limited amount of poaching for the pot – or an odd stag poached for its trophy – there was really little to encourage any large-scale poaching for financial gain.

During the late war years, however, when meat became scarce and rationed, venison came into its own, and many thousands of deer were taken by poachers. As a result, there was considerable agitation for the introduction of a bill to not only strengthen the law against deer poaching, but also to prevent the cruelty which is attendant upon the methods of modern gang poaching. Accordingly, in April 1952 a *Poaching of Deer (Scotland) Bill* was discussed and had a second reading in the House of Lords. Unfortunately this bill was among the four Government bills which were crowded out before the summer recess, and this particular bill was not proceeded with subsequently.

In the meantime, however, a Deer (Close Season) Committee had been appointed by the Secretary of State for Scotland, under the chairmanship of Sheriff R H Maconochie, with the following remit: 'To consider the desirability of introducing a close season or seasons for deer in Scotland and the manner in which, and the safeguards for agricultural and other interests under which, any close season or seasons they may recommend should be made effective; and to report.' On 27 October 1954 the long awaited report was finally published following which, Mr James Stuart, the Secretary of State for Scotland, stated in reply to a question in the House of Commons, 'I have received a report signed by the majority of the Committee and a separate report signed by a minority of three members. In view of the considerable differences of opinion desclosed in these reports, I have come to the conclusion regretfully that the introduction of legislation at the present time would achieve no satisfactory result.'

Despite this setback the question of suitable legislation was still being pursued by a working party and eventually the *Deer (Scotland) Act* 1959 had a successful passage through the House and became law on 14 May 1959. This Act, states the preamble, was to further the conservation and control of red deer in Scotland; to prevent the illegal taking and killing of all species of deer in Scotland; and for purposes connected with the matters aforesaid.

The Act had five parts as follows: Part I. Conservation and Control of Red Deer; Part II. Close Seasons. Part III. Prevention of Illegal Taking and Killing of Deer. Part IV. Enforcement and Procedure. Part V. Supplementary.

In order to implement Part I, a Red Deer Commission was formed with power 'to advise in the interests of conservation any owner of land, on the application of such owner, on questions relating to the carrying of stocks of red deer on that land'. The Commission have power to require from any owner or occupier of land, a return of the number of deer of each sex killed, and unless such information is supplied within thirty-six days, or if the information given is knowingly or recklessly false, in a material particular, then a fine not exceeding £20 can be imposed in the first instance, or in the case of a second or subsequent conviction, to a fine not exceeding £50, or to imprisonment for a term not exceeding three months, or to both such fine and imprisonment.

If in any area, red deer are coming on to agricultural land, woodland or garden and are 'causing substantial damage' to crops, etc., the Commission can authorize in writing a competent person to kill such

28 Spying for deer on West Benula deer forest, Ross-shire

29 Homeward bound after a successful day's stalking on a Sutherland deer forest

30 High seat overlooking a ride. They are used for shooting deer in woodland, and give safe shooting over flat ground

31 Stag at bay in the river Exe; Tiverton Staghounds, season 1964–5

32 Devon and Somerset Staghounds opening meet at Cloutsham

33 Hunted hind clearing a high wire fence

34 Stag at bay; Devon and Somerset Staghounds

35 Hunted stag with long brow tines; the big Dunkery stag, October 1952

36 *Above opposite* The Berks and Bucks Farmers' Staghounds enlarging their stag on the Downs above Hampstead Norris in 1933

37 *Below opposite* The Berks and Bucks Farmers' Staghounds at the opening meet at Little Stoke Manor, near Wallingford, Berkshire, October 1934

38 *Above* A stag frequently gives a leap in the air after enlargement from a deer cart

39 The Ward Union Hunt; the stag shortly after enlargement

deer, if the owner of the land or person having the sporting rights has shown that he is unable or unwilling to deal with the situation.

Where the Commission are satisfied that red deer have caused damage to agriculture or forestry in any locality, and that to prevent further damage they should be reduced in number or exterminated, they must consult with the owners of the land and try to obtain agreement on the measures to be carried out. Failing agreement, or if the agreed measures are not being carried out, the Commission shall make a 'control scheme' which will specify not only the control area, but also the number and also, if necessary the sex and class of animal to be killed. Time limits within which the owners or occupiers are to take such measures will also be prescribed.

Before any control scheme comes into operation, it must have confirmation by the Secretary of State. Any person who refuses or wilfully fails to comply with any requirement laid upon him by a scheme shall be liable, on summary conviction, to a fine not exceeding £50, and in the case of a second or subsequent conviction to a fine not exceeding £100 or to imprisonment for a term not exceeding three months or to both such fine and imprisonment. In such circumstance the Commission shall undertake the Control Scheme themselves, if they are satisfied that it is still necessary to do so.

Any person authorized or required by the Commission to kill any red deer under the provisions of Part I of this Act is *not* required to obtain for that purpose a licence to kill game.

Part II provides the following close season for red deer only, and was dated to come into operation on 21 October 1962:

Red deer stags	21 October to 30 June
Red deer hinds	16 February to 20 October

Provision was made, however, for the Secretary of State to fix close seasons for other species of deer in Scotland and this was eventually put into effect by *The Deer (Close Seasons) (Scotland) Order* 1966, which provided close seasons for fallow, roe and sika deer to come into effect from 16 February 1966 as follows:

Fallow deer	Male: 1 May to 31 July	Both dates inclusive
	Female: 16 February to 20 October	
Roe deer	Male: 21 October to 30 April	Both dates inclusive
	Female: 1 March to 20 October	
Sika deer	Male: 1 May to 31 July	Both dates inclusive
	Female: 16 February to 20 October	

Part III of the *Deer (Scotland) Act* 1959 concerns itself with poaching, and the illegal killing of deer either at night or by illegal weapons. As regards poaching, any person found guilty of such an offence shall be liable on summary conviction to a fine not exceeding £20, and on a second conviction £50 or three months' imprisonment, or both, as well as the forfeiture of any deer illegally killed by him or in his possession at the time of the offence.

With the exception that an occupier of agricultural land or of enclosed woodlands may kill deer on such land during the hours of darkness, the Act made it illegal for anyone else to kill a deer between the expiration of the first hour after sunset and the commencement of the last hour before sunrise. This Section 33 – subsections (2) and (3) – was subsequently repealed and replaced by Section 2 subsection (2) of the *Deer (Amendment) (Scotland) Act* 1967 which permitted night shooting of deer by a person acting 'under the authority of or at the request of the Commission. . . .' By Section 23 (2) it also makes it illegal to take or kill deer otherwise than by shooting, and shooting for the purpose of the Act means discharging a firearm, as defined in the *Firearms Act* 1937; other than a prohibited weapon. Any person guilty of an offence against either of the above shall be liable on summary conviction to a fine not exceeding £20, and in the case of a second or subsequent conviction to a fine not exceeding £50 or to imprisonment for a term not exceeding three months, or to both such fine and imprisonment. It is of interest to note that contrary to the normal Scottish rules of evidence, an offence under Section 24 can be proved on the evidence of only one witness.

If two or more people act together to unlawfully take or kill deer each person shall be liable, on summary conviction, to a fine not exceeding £50 or to imprisonment for a term not exceeding three months, and in the case of a second or subsequent conviction, to a fine not exceeding £100 or to imprisonment for a term not exceeding six months or to both such fine and imprisonment. If the conviction is on indictment, then each person is liable to a fine not exceeding £500 or to imprisonment for a term not exceeding two years or to both such fine and imprisonment.

Part IV describes the procedure for the enforcement of the provisions of the Act, such as powers of search and seizure by the police, apprehension of offenders, forfeiture of vehicles, disposal of deer etc., whilst in Part V, *Supplementary*, an interpretation of the two previous parts is given as well as certain exceptions, such as the killing of deer on any arable ground, garden or woodlands etc., during the close season. This provision is to be construed as one with the *Agriculture (Scotland) Act* 1948, a number of sections of which, so far as they related to red deer, were repealed by the *Deer (Scotland) Act* 1959 (*see page 195*). References to 'deer, roe' in Section one, and 'deer' in Section four of the *Game (Scotland) Act* 1832 were also repealed.

Subsequently, the *Deer (Amendment) (Scotland) Act* 1967 amended Sections 15 and 33 of the *Deer (Scotland) Act* 1959 so as to:

(a) give the Red Deer Commission a right of entry upon land for the purpose of taking a census of red deer,

(b) permit the shooting of marauding red deer at night by officers or servants of the Red Deer Commission acting under the Commission's authority under Sections 6 of the 1959 Act, and

(c) permit the shooting of deer of any species during any statutory close season for that species if authorized in writing by the Secretary of State for some scientific purpose.

The *Deer (Amendment) (Scotland) Act* 1967 also provided for any occupier of enclosed land or woodland to authorize, in writing, for another person to kill marauding deer on such land during the close season period.

Damage by the depredation of deer has long been a subject of complaint by crofters and other tenants in the neighbourhood of deer forests, as they had no right to kill the deer without the consent of their landlords, and had no right of action against anyone for the damage done by the deer which, being wild animals free to roam from one estate to another, were not the property of any particular person.

Section 2 of the *Agricultural Holdings Act* 1906 – subsequently repealed and re-enacted, as regards Scotland, in Section 9 of the *Agricultural Holdings (Scotland) Act* 1908 – provided that, where the landlord did not allow (in writing) the tenant to kill the deer, the tenant should be entitled to compensation from him for any damage caused by the deer.

Deer, however, were not included in *The Ground Game Act* 1880 nor in the *Ground Game Amendment Act* 1906, and in order to include deer under 'ground game' Mr Dundas White introduced to the House in 1913, the *Ground Game (Inclusion of Deer) (Scotland) Bill*. In an attached memorandum it was pointed out that most of the complainants for damage caused by deer were poor men who could not face the cost, direct and indirect, of arbitration proceedings, so provision was made in Section 10, subsection (3), of the *Small Landowners (Scotland) Act* 1911, that in the case of small landowners under that Act the Land Court should be substituted for arbitration. The *Ground Game (Inclusion of Deer) (Scotland) Bill* proposed to put deer on the same basis as ground game, so that the person whose property they depredated might have the remedy in his own hands, and the owners of deer forests, in their own interests, would take adequate steps to prevent the deer invading other people's cultivated land. This bill, however, was never passed.

Some thirty-five years later, however, the *Agriculture (Scotland) Act* 1948 gave the occupier of an agricultural holding or of enclosed woodlands – and any person authorized by him in writing – the right 'to kill and take, and sell or otherwise dispose of the carcases of, any deer found on any arable land . . . etc'. as well as giving the Secretary of State powers to authorize the reduction in number of deer in any area where they were causing damage. This latter right, however, was not to be exercised 'at any time between the tenth day of April and the sixteenth day of October in any year; or between one hour after sunset and one hour before sunrise'. This Act also enabled the Secretary of State to give notice in writing to the owner of any land 'to make a return in such form as may be prescribed showing the number of deer of each sex which to his knowledge have been killed on the land during such period (not exceeding five years) immediately preceding the service of the notice as may be specified therein, and also a return showing the number of deer of each sex which he estimates to be on the land'. Failure to make the required return within thirty-six days after the service of the notice, or making a false return 'in any material particular' could incur a fine not exceeding £50.

Subsequently Sections 39–42 of the *Agriculture* (*Scotland*) *Act* 1948 so far as relating to red deer, as well as Section 43 subsection (2), and Sections 44–47 were repealed by the *Deer* (*Scotland*) *Act* 1959, and the provision for dealing with marauding deer incorporated in Part I (Conservation and Control of Red Deer) in the above mentioned Act (*see page 192*).

For a few years following the *Deer* (*Scotland*) *Act* 1959 there was a slight diminution in deer poaching but this was due mainly to a lessening in the demand for venison rather than as a result of the Act itself, though would-be poachers were undoubtedly seeing how the increased powers of the police would 'interfere' with their activities. About this time, however, a new avenue for the disposal of venison was being developed – namely the export of venison to Germany, whose demands for this form of meat seemed inexhaustable. Once more, out of season deer killing started to increase, not only by poaching gangs but also by owners of property on to whose land the deer wandered in winter time, and could then be shot quite legally as 'marauders'. On one estate alone during the winter of 1965–6 over a thousand deer were killed by a contractor who had been called in to deal with some animals that had entered a forestry plantation. In the hope of providing some control on the disposal of venison, the *Sale of Venison* (*Scotland*) *Act* 1968 required that every dealer in venison should not only be registered but should also keep a proper register in which should be entered all purchases and receipts of venison together with, if possible, particulars as to the sex and species of deer. Price particulars, however, were not to be included. The register can be inspected by any person with the written authority of the Secretary of State or the Red Deer Commission and any registered venison dealer who fails to comply to keep such a register, or knowingly makes a false entry shall be guilty of an offence and liable on summary conviction to a fine not exceeding £20.

Unfortunately, not all venison reaches the licensed dealer and quite a lot of business in the home trade is done for cash with hotels etc. Furthermore, it is not difficult for a dealer buying venison from a 'doubtful source' to overlook the purchase in the register, for at present there is no means of checking that entries in the register correspond to the number of carcases received.

Since the passing of this Act, venison prices have fluctuated from about 50 pence per lb. for carcases in the skin during the autumn of 1973, and although during the following season prices had fallen to about half, by the beginning of the 1977 season some dealers were prepared to pay as much as 75 to 80 pence. This figure, however, was not maintained and by February 1978 the price for hind venison had fallen to about 40 pence per lb. Eighteen months later the price had risen to about 65 pence to 75 pence per lb. at the beginning of the stag stalking season.

Unfortunately, these high prices have encouraged the excessive slaughter of deer, particularly during the close season period, for alleged marauding, and it has been estimated that the number of stags now being killed out of season varies between 10 and 20 per cent of all stags shot in Scotland. If one assumes that about 16,000 of the 36,000 to 40,000 deer that are being killed annually in Scotland are stags, then the total 'out of season' stags killed must amount to about 2000 to 3000 animals. At 75 pence per lb. this represents over £250,000 revenue. One of the reasons for price fluctuation has been the flooding of the German market with venison, not only from New Zealand and the Eastern bloc countries but also some 500 tons of reindeer meat.

Poaching and out of season killing of deer is nothing new or unique to Scotland – it is practised throughout the world where game still survives. Some countries, however, have been able to tackle the problem more effectively than others, and we should, therefore, take heed of what remedies have been proved successful elsewhere and try them here.

One system which has proved effective in Germany and elsewhere in Europe is the tagging of deer carcases and if a similar scheme was applied here I am convinced it would go a long way to ease the present serious situation.

I first became acquainted with the tagging system in 1951 and on my return to this country I prepared a short paper on how the scheme works, for the late Duke of Bedford to present to the House of Lords during the second reading of the *Poaching of Deer* (*Scotland*) *Bill* on 13 March 1952.

This is how I think a tagging scheme should operate in Great Britain:

1 A deer carcase can only be accepted by a game dealer if it has the official tag of the forest on which it was shot. If applied to all species of deer, a different colour of tag should be available for each species.

Every proprietor would need the official metal tag which could only be stapled to the ear or limb of every deer carcase by means of special pliers, whether it was hanging in his larder for subsequent disposal to friends or disposed of to a game dealer. The tags would not only be serially numbered but would also bear the official number or prefix of the estate in question. It might also be desirable to have the date the beast was killed punched on to the tag in the same manner as many dairies date the metal caps on milk bottles. Once the seal of a tag has been broken it would be useless.

2 *Licensed* game dealers would only be permitted to accept *full* carcases so tagged – and those tags would have to remain on the carcase in the refrigerator until it was cut up. If any licensed game dealer was caught

trafficking in untagged carcases, or holding any carcase in his refrigerator with the seal broken, unless some satisfactory explanation was forthcoming he could be heavily fined and his licence to deal in game withdrawn.

3 There must be some authority to operate the scheme. If applied to Scotland only, it could be run by the Red Deer Commission. Otherwise it will be necessary to form a deer control association which could also take over the work of the Red Deer Commission.

4 It will be the duty of every estate that holds a resident stock of deer to provide details to the controlling body of the stock figure of deer by sexes at, say, 1 April, and also the number of male and female deer it planned to shoot.

5 If, in relation to stocks, the cull plan is approved, the appropriate number of serially numbered tags will be issued to each applicant.

If, during the season, it is found desirable to kill more deer than originally planned, then a further application will have to be made for additional tags, with reasons for doing so.

6 Within ten days after the end of the appropriate shooting season for each species and sex, each proprietor will have to submit a report of the number of deer that have been killed and any unused tags be returned. At the same time details will be given of how the carcases have been disposed of and the name and address of the game dealer to whom they have been sent. Information will also be supplied of the number of carcases that have been cut up privately for giving away to friends etc., and for these carcases the tag, with seal broken, will have to be returned.

7 If, during the winter, marauding deer of either sex have to be killed either out of season or on ground not normally occupied by deer, the owner of such ground will have to apply for 'X' number of tags to cover the number of marauding deer it is intended to kill and reasons given for doing so. If approved, the necessary tags – valid for, say, four weeks – will be supplied and at the end of this period any unused tags will have to be *returned* together with a statement as to the number of marauders killed and to whom the carcases have been disposed.

Under no circumstances are tags transferable.

8 Twice a year each licensed game dealer will have to make a return to the controlling body giving the number of carcases, by species and sex, that have been received during the season together with the number of carcases still held at that date.

9 Each licensed game dealer will be required to keep an accurate register of purchases and sales, and such registers will be examined periodically, along with refrigerators, larders, etc., to see that no untagged carcases are present.

Venison, of course, from other species of deer such as roe, fallow and sika deer also find their way to the game dealer. As different open seasons operate for these deer, as well as red deer in England, the dates for return by proprietors will have to be altered to meet the circumstances.

At present, as already mentioned, not all venison reaches the larders of the licensed dealer, and quite a lot of business in the home trade is done for cash with hotels, etc. This is an obvious loophole in any venison disposal scheme, and can be eliminated by making it illegal for hotels and restaurants etc., to purchase venison from anyone except a licensed dealer.

Although for many years the Red Deer Commission have voiced the opinion that 'circumstances in Scotland are such that a system of tagging could not be operated satisfactorily', it did seem that at last (1974) there might be a change of opinion in this quarter, for Lord Arbuthnott, then Chairman of the Red Deer Commission, in an article on *Venison Sale Safeguards* (The *Field*, 11 April 1974) stated that 'carcase tagging has now become a national issue in the minds of many people in England and Scotland', and was in favour of a trial scheme being put into operation. To date, unfortunately, although six years have now elapsed, no such trial scheme has yet materialized. It is, in my opinion, the only easy method that will solve the problem.

Although the *Deer (Scotland) Act* 1959 increased the powers of the police when dealing with poachers, it did nothing to assist or alter the procedure required to be taken in accordance with the provisions of *The Game (Scotland) Act* 1832 by which a stalker or proprietor could apprehend a poacher. Just how limited these powers are was well illustrated by the following incident which happened whilst I was stalking on a west coast forest in 1973.

About midday, whilst we were watching a rather nice royal rounding up some hinds near the Common Grazing march, the young ghillie, who had remarkably good eyesight, suddenly remarked that there was a 'funny looking deer' to the left of the beasts we were watching. On putting the glass on the object it turned out to be a man, carrying a rifle, who was working his way up the burn in the direction of the deer. At the time he was, perhaps, some 400 yards (360 metres) from the deer and about half a mile from us.

As soon as he disappeared round the shoulder of a small hill, my stalker and ghillie set off at the double in pursuit, leaving me behind not only to look after *Sandy*, my labrador, who generally accompanies me stalking, but also all the impedimenta likely to reduce their speed on the hill, such as rifle, sticks, telescopes and sandwich bag, etc. I could also keep a watch on the hill opposite to see which way the man might take should they fail to find him.

Only for a brief moment after their departure did the figure come in to view again, and when the deer moved over the skyline he started to retrace his footsteps in the direction of the Common Grazing land.

For the next half hour or so I did not see anything, and had just started to eat my sandwiches when a shot was heard. Another half hour elapsed before the stalker and ghillie re-appeared, and I noticed that the former was carrying a rifle.

When they rejoined me I was told that they had, apparently, got to within about 200 yards (180 metres) of the man with the rifle, who had by then reached the Common Grazing ground. A request to hand over the rifle was refused and when a round was put into the breach the stalker had dived in, grabbed hold of the rifle and pulled the trigger so that the live round was fired into the air. The rifle was then, at least, safe!

There followed a struggle as an effort was made to wrest the rifle from the man's grip, but owing to the sling being wrapped round his wrists, this was not easily accomplished. Eventually the ghillie joined in and after cutting the straps with his knife, the rifle was seized. The man was recognized as a local crofter and when requested to accompany the stalker back to the lodge in order to make a statement, he refused.

On returning to the lodge ourselves, we immediately telephoned the police to report the incident and make arrangements to hand over the rifle. Imagine our surprise when we were informed that the gentleman had already telephoned to say that whilst hunting foxes on the hill, he had been assaulted and his rifle stolen!

Apparently, only the previous day the police had granted him a Firearm Certificate to use a rifle against marauding deer *on his croft* and for *control of vermin* on the Common Grazing land. When first seen approaching the deer, he was definitely on the deer forest proper and had, therefore, no legal right to carry a rifle there, even after foxes, but by the time the stalker caught up with him he was back on Common Grazing land.

In due course the stalker received a summons to appear before the court at Dingwall on a charge of assault against Mr X and I was requested to attend as a defence witness.

In his summing up the Sheriff said he had been impressed by the evidence of the accused, and he also thought that the stalking party had quite genuinely believed that Mr X was poaching deer, and therefore the accused, quite rightly, went after him. Mr X on the other hand, was quite adamant that he was only after foxes.

It has been suggested, the Sheriff continued, that when first seen, Mr X was some 300 yards (270 metres) beyond the watershed which marked the boundary between the forest proper and the Common Grazing and was, therefore, on land for which his Firearm Certificate did not apply. Quite apart from the fact, however, that it was always difficult to know *exactly* where boundaries defined only by a watershed lay, it was really immaterial to this particular case, for the point where the alleged assault took place was indisputably on the Common Grazing land where Mr X had every right to be.

Continuing, the Sheriff said that the accused's lack of knowledge of the manner in which it was lawful for a gamekeeper to tackle a poacher had resulted in a demand – quite wrongly in the circumstances – for the rifle to be handed over, and when that request failed, physical force to seize it had been resorted to. The defence had submitted that there was no struggle until Mr X had worked the bolt of his rifle, and only then did the accused close in to fire the rifle. Working the bolt and putting a live round in the breach may, therefore, have acted as provocation for the accused to act more zealously than he might otherwise have done. Nevertheless it was appreciated that in the circumstances, it was probably the wisest and safest course to fire the rifle into the air.

It was wrong, also, for the accused to have made a request to Mr X that he should accompany the stalking party back to the lodge. No private citizen, except under conditions of serious crime, is entitled to arrest anyone, and an attempt to do so could amount to a breach of the peace. All that he was empowered to do under the *Game (Scotland) Act* 1832, Section 2, was for the name and address to be taken and a request to quit the land. Moreover, in this particular incident, even that was unnecessary for the man was a local crofter well known to the ghillie.

The Sheriff believed, however, that the stalker's action was undoubtedly due to inexperience and over-zealousness and so, whilst he found the charge proved, he was admonished.

There is no doubt that when a crofter is granted a Firearm Certificate for a rifle by the police for use on both his croft and Common Grazing, the implications of such authorized use should be most carefully studied by anyone who may have the sporting rights over the latter. The rights on the Common Grazing, I understand, are regulated by the Common Grazing Committee, and in certain areas where the interests of both crofters and landowners overlap, by agreement between the two parties concerned. If such an arrangement, therefore, exists between landlord and Common Grazing Committee that there shall be no use of firearms whatsoever on the Common Grazing, then the possession of a Firearm Certificate by a crofter would still *not* permit him to use his rifle on such land. It is equally important that any such agreement existing between landlord and the Common Grazing Committee should be brought to the notice of every crofter who is in possession of a Firearms Certificate – otherwise any offender might genuinely claim that any such clause in his Firearms Certificate made such action legal. Under such circumstances, it would be unlikely that there would be a prosecution.

The following are relevant to deer legislation in Scotland:

Title	**Date**	**Reference**
Game (Scotland) Act	1832	c.68
Game Licences Act	1860	c.90*
Deer (Scotland) Act	1959	c.40
The Deer (Close Seasons) (Scotland) Order	1966	No. 56
Deer (Amendment) (Scotland) Act	1967	c.37

* repealed in part.

Title	**Date**	**Reference**
Sale of Venison (Scotland) Act	1968	c.38
Firearms Act	1968	c.27
Sale of Venison (Forms etc.) (Scotland) Regulations	1969	No. 794 (S.63)

A summary, therefore, of the legal position connected with deerstalking in Scotland today is as follows:

1 *Game Licence* Anyone stalking wild deer of any species must hold a Game Licence (*Game Licences Act* 1860).

2 *Firearms* Provided the weapon is one 'as defined in the *Firearms Act* 1937, other than a prohibited weapon' there is no restriction *in Scotland* on either the calibre of the rifle or bore of shotgun that may be used – nor in the case of the latter any restriction in the size of shot loaded into the cartridge.

3 *Time of Day* Except in cases of marauding, deer may be shot only during the period commencing one hour before sunrise and one hour after sunset.

4 *Close Seasons* Wild deer – except when marauding agricultural ground or woodlands etc., – may not be shot during the following close seasons:

	Male	*Female*
Red deer	21 October to 30 June	16 February to 20 October
Roe deer	21 October to 30 April	1 March to 20 October
Fallow deer	1 May to 31 July	16 February to 20 October
Sika deer	1 May to 31 July	16 February to 20 October

Historical Register of Deer Hunting Packs & Establishments

1 Alphabetical List

2 Description and History

Allen-Jefferys' Staghounds

Counties in which hunt mainly operated: Somerset and Dorset
Period of hunt's existence: *c.*1895
Kennels: Seavington, near Ilminster
Pack: Fifteen couple of black and tan hounds, 22–23 in. (56–58 cm): a special breed of the Master
Deer paddock: Seavington, near Ilminster, in which about twelve deer were kept
Masters: 1898 Jefferys C Allen-Jefferys

History: This pack, which was established in 1895, hunted 'over a fine flying country, nearly all grass . . . in Somersetshire and Dorsetshire, within the limits of the Seavington country . . . and the limits of the Blackmore Vale, Cattistock and Taunton Vale Territories'.[7] The owner of this pack was also Master of the Seavington. The favourite centres for meets were Ilminster, Yeovil, Crewkerne and Taunton.[7]

Sir John Amory's Staghounds

See Tiverton Staghounds.

Anderson Staghounds

A private pack of staghounds was kennelled near Hendon in Middlesex during the late 1830s. It was hunted by Mr Anderson himself.

Angerstein's Staghounds

Mr William Angerstein kept a pack of staghounds at Weeting, near Rugby,

Northampton, for a number of years about 1870. In 1872 he brought his pack to Norfolk where it hunted under the title of the Norfolk Staghounds. In 1876 Mr Angerstein relinquished the command of the pack in favour of Captain Haughton.

Sir Jacob Astley's Staghounds

County in which hunt operated: Norfolk
Period of hunt's existence: 1815 to 1823
Kennels: Burgh Hall, near Melton Constable
Master: Sir J Astley

History: This pack was started by Sir Jacob Astley in about 1815 and for about eight or nine seasons hunted deer before changing to fox in 1823.

Balmoral Staghounds

During the early part of the last century a pack of staghounds was maintained at Balmoral, but was discontinued soon after 1860.

Barnstaple Staghounds

County in which hunt operated: West Devon
Period of hunt's existence: 1901–5; 1908–9
Kennels: Brinsworthy, Fremington (1901–5); Barnstaple (1908–9)
Pack: Twelve to fifteen couple
Masters:
1901–3 Captain Ewing Paterson and Arundel Clarke
1903–5 Major Penn Curzon
1908–10 B Chester

History: This hunt was established in 1901 to hunt the district in which deer from Exmoor had become increasingly numerous, It was given up in 1905 but re-started in 1908 with a guinea minimum subscription and no cap being taken. Meets generally took place twice a week.

Hounds were owned by a committee, the Master having no guarantee.

The country lay in Devon west of Lynton railway, most of it being hilly with a good deal of woodland. It was shared by the Barnstaple and North Devon Harriers.

Duke of Bedford's Staghounds

During the eighteenth century the second Duke of Bedford hunted the wild deer of Exmoor with a pack of hounds which were kept at Tavistock. During his lifetime, the principal haunts of the deer were in Holt Chase and in the coverts on the bank of the Tavy, the Tamar, the Teign, the Dart and the Torr rivers, on the sides of Dartmoor. When they ran they often went to sea in Torbay.

The fourth Duke of Bedford kept his pack of deerhounds in Bedfordshire, and history relates how, on 13 October 1743, a stag was roused in Wooton Woods near Bedford, and ran for six hours without a check, during which it was estimated that hounds had covered about sixty miles!

Berkeley Staghounds

Thomas Moreton Fitzhardinge Berkeley and his brother Grantley hunted the carted stag with a pack of hounds which were kept at Cranford, the family seat. The brothers were the officers of the hunt, together with Mr Henry Wombewell, all wearing the orange tawny livery of the family. The pack, which probably didn't exist for more than a few years, was given up about 1830 when Mr Grantley Berkeley went to hunt the Oakley.[14]

Berkhamsted Staghounds

Counties in which hunt operated: Hertfordshire and Buckinghamshire
Period of hunt's existence: 1870–1920*
Kennels: The Common, Gt. Berkhamsted
Pack: About fifteen to sixteen couple of hounds
Masters:
1870–1901 Richard Rawle
1901–8 John Rawle
1908–? W H Dickinson

History: When, in 1870, Sir Clifford Constable gave up his staghounds in Yorkshire, Mr Richard Rawle and Mr Dan Bovingdon bought the hounds and brought them south to Hertfordshire to form the Berkhamsted Staghounds, the first meet being held on 6 March of that year.[27]

To commence with, the pack hunted fallow buck, but subsequently changed to red deer.

The Hertfordshire and Old Berkeley (East) Foxhounds hunted over the same country as the Berkhamstead Staghounds, which at times were invited to districts far out of their normal country. The Berkhamsted Staghounds was a subscription pack owned by the Master. Meets took place on one day only per week (Wednesday).

Berkshire and Buckinghamshire Farmers' Staghounds

Counties in which hunt operated: Berkshire and Buckinghamshire
Period of hunt's existence: 1901–39
Kennels: Formerly at Binfield Grove, Bracknell, but moved to Highway, Maidenhead in 1908. In 1919 Kennels were moved to Beenham's Farm, Waltham St Lawrence, and in 1923 again moved to Cookham Dean, in Berkshire.
Pack: About twenty to twenty-two and a half couple of hounds
Deer paddocks: Formerly at Binfield Grove, Bracknell, but moved to Highway, Maidenhead in 1908, where the deer generally numbered about twenty to twenty-five.
Masters:
1901–7 Sir Robert Wilmot, Bart
1907–14 F W and A H Headington
1914–19 E W Shackle and A H Headington
1919–34 Major E W Shackle
1934–7 Major E W Shackle and H J Colebrooke
1937–8 Major E W Shackle
1938–9 Miss Iris Bennett and N B Ducker

---

* 'Drifter' in *Horse & Hound* says it ceased to exist before the First World War.

History: The Berks and Bucks Harriers were, in 1901, converted into staghounds when the Royal Buckhounds were abolished.

The hunt operated over most of the country formerly hunted over by the Royal Buckhounds in parts of both Berkshire and Buckinghamshire. The most northerly meet took place at High Wycombe, and the most southerly at Woking. Uxbridge was about as far east as the hunt went, whilst the most westerly point was Twyford. In all, the hunt covered some 300 square miles of country, which was also shared by the Garth Foxhounds in the south-west part, the South Berks in the west and the Old Berkeley West in the northern part. Meets took place on Tuesdays and Fridays, the best centres being Maidenhead, Bracknell, Wokingham, Windsor, Ascot, Amersham and High Wycombe.

The Berks and Bucks Farmers was a subscription pack, with a minimum subscription of £21 (1938) and non-subscribers being capped.

Broadley's Staghounds

County in which hunt operated: Warwickshire
Period of hunt's existence: c.1840

History: Very little is known of Mr Broadley's Staghounds except a reference to the fact that they were brought to Ireland from Leamington in 1840 and hunted, as a subscription pack, for a few years by Lord Howth before being sold to the Dublin Garrison (*see page 248*).

WP Burton's Staghounds

County in which hunt operated: West Suffolk
Period of hunt's existence: (under title of WP Burton's Staghounds), 1906–11 (*see also page 250*).
Kennels: Edgehill, Ipswich
Pack: Twenty couple of hounds
Deer paddock: Nether Hall, Bury St Edmunds
Master: WP Burton

History: This pack was originally formed by Sir (then Mr) E Walter Greene in 1864,* but after several changes of mastership, including a nineteen year suspension of stag hunting (1870–89), the pack eventually came under the control of Mr WP Burton in 1906.

The deer, up to thirty in number, were kept at Nether Hall, Bury St Edmunds, the residence of Sir Walter Greene.

This was a private pack owned by the Master, with no subscription, all expenses being defrayed by him.

Lord Carrington's Bloodhounds

In 1880 Lord Carrington bought from Lord Wolverton his pack of bloodhounds. They were not a success with their new owner, and after only one season he parted with them to the Comte le Canteleu, who intended to use them for deer and wild boar.

---

* British Sports & Sportsmen *Hunting* volume, gives this date as 1891.

Carrow Abbey Hounds

County in which hunt operated: Norfolk
Period of hunt's existence: c.1766–83
History: This hunt existed during the latter part of the eighteenth century and, it seems, hunted everything that offered itself, be it deer, fox or hare. During the Holt Jubilee week in January 1783, a deer hunt was arranged for the Monday and Thursday, a fox hunt on Tuesday and Friday, and a hunt after the hare on Wednesday and Saturday, with a grand Ball arranged for the Thursday night (*see page 42*).

Castleacre Hounds

County in which hunt operated: Norfolk
Period of hunt's existence: c.1853
Kennels: Castleacre
Master: Stephen Abbott

History: This was initially a pack of harriers which occasionally hunted deer – presumably outliers or park escapees. Ultimately, however, they received 'a draft from Lord Rothschild, and hunted deer after Christmas'. The hunt never advertised their meets and was probably a farmers' subscription pack.[98]

Castleside Hounds

County in which hunt operated: Durham
Period of hunt's existence: c.1850
Master: Mr Richardson of Woodlands Hall, Consett

History: For a period of about eight to ten years in the late 1840s and early 1850s Mr Richardson had a pack of hounds to hunt the roe deer in the large woodlands south of Castleside, known as Lord Bute's plantation. The roe, however, did not prove a satisfactory quarry, and the pack changed over to hunting foxes.

Cheltenham Staghounds

County in which hunt operated: Gloucestershire
Period of hunt's existence c.1838–49
Masters:
1838 Committee
1844 Committee
1849 F Theobold

History: Little is known about this pack except that its favourite centres for meets were Northleach, Pewsdown, Cleave Village, Beeches' Pike, The Pheasant, Birdlip, Brockhampton, Shipton, Teddington Hands.[80] Meets took place on Mondays, Wednesdays and Fridays.

Cheshire Staghounds

This pack, which had its kennels near Nantwich in Cheshire, was being hunted in the late 1830s by Mr Shakerley, with Joseph Maiden as huntsman.

Sir Arthur Chichester's Staghounds

Three years after the sale of the North Devon Staghounds in 1824 to a German sportsman, Sir Arthur Chichester formed a scratch pack and for six years hunted the deer of north Devon and Somerset before disposing of the pack in the spring of 1833.

Four years later, after a period of no organized hunting in this part of England, the Devon and Somerset Staghound pack was formed and before it, too, was temporarily disbanded in about 1849, Sir Arthur Chichester took over the mastership for about one season (*see page 214*).

Chillingham Staghounds

A private pack of staghounds was kennelled at Chillingham Castle in the late 1830s, with Lord Ossulston as Master and John Cole, huntsman in 1839.

Cleveland Staghounds

County in which hunt operated: Durham
Period of hunt's existence: c.1844
Kennels: Raby Castle
Master: 1844 Duke of Cleveland

History: Little is known of the activities of this hunt, except that T Flint acted as huntsman to his Grace in 1844 (*The New Sporting Almanack*).

Sir Clifford Constable's Staghounds

County in which hunt mainly operated: Yorkshire
Period of hunt's existence: c.1839–70
Master: Sir Clifford Constable, Bart

History: Little information is available concerning this private pack, which operated from Sir Clifford Constable's home at Burton Constable in Yorkshire. The quarry could have been either red or fallow deer, for in the park there were, in 1867, about 160 red deer and 350 fallow deer. Favourite meets were held at Wyton Tollbar, Ridgmont, Sproatley, Hedon, Lelley and Coniston in the East Riding of Yorkshire.

When the pack was disbanded in 1870 it was taken south to form the Berkhamsted Staghounds (q.v.). In 1839 the pack was said to be bloodhounds.

Common Hunt

In its early existence, the Easter Hunt (q.v.) was generally referred to as the Common Hunt.

Colonel R P Croft's Staghounds

Counties in which the hunt mainly operated: Middlesex, Hertfordshire and Bedfordshire (1912–14), Essex (1920–26)
Period of hunt's existence: 1912–14; 1920–26 (see above)
Kennels: Farnhams Hall, Ware
Pack: About twenty couple of hounds
Deer paddock: New Road, Ware. About twenty deer were kept in the paddock.

Masters:
1912–14 Major R P Croft
1920–26 Lt.-Col. R P Croft

History: The Enfield Chase Staghounds (q.v.), after Major R P Croft had taken over the mastership in 1912, were frequently referred to as Major R P Croft's Staghounds. Hunting was suspended during the First World War years but when hostilities ceased Colonel R P Croft took over the mastership of the Essex Staghounds in 1920 and hunted the pack privately for about six years.

Tommy Crooks's Staghounds

County in which hunt operated: Essex
Period of hunt's existence: c.1847

History: Little is known of this small private pack which was kept by Tommy Crooks for hunting deer in Essex. Tommy Crooks was a butcher in Chelmsford.

Dalgety's Staghounds

County in which hunt operated: Hampshire
Period of hunt's existence: c.1926
Kennels: Overton
Pack: Twenty couple
Master: A W H Dalgety (Master of Vine Foxhounds)

History: This is a private pack which hunted the Vine area, but through the courtesy of some neighbouring and other Masters, days were arranged in their territory also. Hounds normally hunted three days a fortnight.[12]

Notice of this pack did not occur in any subsequent directories.

Captain John Darrell's Staghounds

Apart from the fact that Captain John Darrell hunted a pack of staghounds in Norfolk, c.1809, nothing is known of this hunt.

De Burgh's Staghounds

This private pack of staghounds, which had its kennels at Drayton in Berkshire, hunted the carted deer during the late 1830s. In 1839, following the death of Mr De Burgh, Mr Crosby acted as both Master and huntsman.

Lord Derby's Staghounds

Counties in which hunt operated: Surrey, Sussex and Kent
Period of hunt's existence: c.1800 to 1851
Kennels: The Oaks, Woodmansterne
Master: 14th Earl of Derby, with Jonathan Griffith as huntsman

History: During the early part of the nineteenth century, the 14th Earl of Derby formed a pack of staghounds to hunt much of south-east England with boundaries north up to London and south to the sea, practically from London to Brighton, with east and westerly boundaries from Guildford to Tonbridge, and although various other packs hunted over portions of the same ground, the boundaries from a stag hunting point of view were practically limitless.[27]

All deer were bred at Knowsley Park near Liverpool in Lancashire, where fresh blood from Lord Fitzwilliam's park at Wentworth in Yorkshire had occasionally been introduced.

During Lord Derby's association with the pack, it was his custom to send all his horses, hounds and deer back to Knowsley for the summer – the animals travelling by road, and covering about twenty-five miles a day.[3]

In 1851, when Lord Derby gave up his hounds, a committee was formed, and the pack became known as the Surrey Staghounds.

Dering Deerhounds

During the early part of the last century, a pack of staghounds was kept at Surrenden Dering Park, Pluckley in Kent, but just how long this pack existed or what type of deer it hunted, is not known. It appears to have been disbanded in about the middle of the last century, and some of its descendants formed the foundation stock of the Mid-Kent Staghounds which were founded in 1868 by Mr Tom Rigg (q.v.).

Devon and Somerset Staghounds*

Counties in which hunt operates: Devon and Somerset
Period of hunt's existence: from *c.*1775, and still extant
Kennels: Exford, Somerset
Pack: Forty-five couple
Masters:

1775–85 Colonel Basset
1785–94 Sir Thomas Dyke Acland
1794–1802 Colonel Basset
1802–3 Lord Fortescue
1803–10 John Worth
1810–12 Lord Graves
1812–18 Lord Fortescue
1818–24 Stucley Lucas
1827–33 Sir Arthur Chichester (scratch pack)
1837–42 C P Collyns
1842–8 Hon. Newton Fellowes
1848–*c.*1849 Sir Arthur Chichester
1855–81 M Fenwick Bisset
1881–7 Lord Ebrington (fourth Earl Fortescue)
1887–93 C H Basset
1893–5 Colonel J F Hornby
1895–1907 R A Sanders (later Lord Bayford)
1907–9 E A V Stanley
1909–11 Captain A S Adkins
1911–14 Major Morland Greig
1914–15 A committee
1916–18 W Badco
1919–35 Colonel W W Wiggin

* Prior to 1837 the pack was known as the North Devon Staghounds.

1936–9 Major S L Hancock
1939–40 Major S L Hancock and Miss B K Abbot
1940–46 Major & Mrs S L Hancock and Miss B K Abbot
1946–8 Miss B K Abbot and Mrs S L Hancock
1948–9 Miss B K Abbot, Mrs S L Hancock and M C Houlder
1950–51 Miss B K Abbot and M C Houlder
1951–3 H P Hewett and Mrs E C Lloyd
1953–5 Mrs D A Cox and Colonel L M Murphy, O.B.E.
1955–7 Captain and Mrs Cox
1957–8 Mrs D A Cox
1958–63 Colonel L M Murphy
1963–9 Major N H Hambro and R H Nancekivell
1969–72 R H Nancekivell and S J Westcott
1972–4 R H Nancekivell
1974–6 Mrs N Harding (formerly Mrs D A Cox)
1976–80 Mrs N Harding and M E Robinson

History: Although deer hunting was being practised in south-west England before 1775, it is from this year that the history of the Devon and Somerset Staghounds really commences, although it was not until 1837, some sixty-two years later, that it was officially known by this title.

From 1775 until the pack was disposed of in 1824, it operated under the name of North Devon Staghounds (q.v.) and then following a period of three years in which there was no organized deer hunting, Sir Arthur Chichester formed a scratch pack which hunted the deer in the area for six years before being disposed of in 1833. Once again there was no hunting in the area and as before, the deer were much reduced by shooting. However, in 1837 C P Collyns organized a pack which, for the first time became known as the Devon and Somerset Staghounds, but this, five years later, looked as though it would have to be abandoned for lack of funds. However, in 1842 the Hon. Newton Fellowes took over and managed to keep hounds going for a further six years, followed by, for one season only, Sir Arthur Chichester. After this, the pack seems to have been disbanded.

However, in 1855 Mr M Fenwick Bisset of Pixton House formed a pack and from this date onwards Exmoor has been regularly hunted by its own pack of staghounds – the Devon and Somerset Staghounds.

Meets take place on three days per week, the large stags being hunted from August until about 20 October, and the young stags (three and four year olds) in the spring (middle March to end of April). Hinds are hunted from 1 November until end of February.

The annual subscription (1979–80) varies from £130 for one subscriber to £260 for a family and guests hunting from the house. If, in addition to the subscriber, only one member of the family hunts, the subscription is £185. The subscription for car followers is £37–50.In each case VAT is added. There is a cap of £20 per day except for regular subscribers of adjacent hunts who pay a cap of £15 per day for stag hunting, and £10 per day for hind hunting.

The best centres for this hunt are Exford, Minehead, Porlock, Dulverton, South Molton, Winsford, Withypool and Wootton Courtenay.

E Dewing's Staghounds

County in which hunt operated: West Norfolk
Period of hunt's existence: c.1818–27
Master: Edward Dewing

History: In the year 1818 a pack of hounds was kept by Edward Dewing of Guist which hunted deer, hare or fox. When deer hunting, fallow buck seems to have been its principal quarry and about 1823 there were several notices in the *Norwich Mercury* announcing meets 'to run a buck'. Mr Dewing died in 1827.

Co. Down Staghounds

Counties in which hunt operates: Down, Meath, Louth and Kildare
Period of hunt's existence: Since 1881 and still extant
Kennels: The Kennels, Ballynahinch
Hounds: The pack today, consisting of black-and-tan and Dumfriesshire foxhound cross, numbers approximately twenty-five couple, as compared to thirty-four couple at the end of the last century. The dog pack is preferred and on hunting days about eleven and a half couple will be taken out.
Deer paddock: Montalto, Ballynahinch. About fifty red deer (twenty stags and thirty hinds) normally kept in the paddock (thirty acres). The main source of supply over a long period of years has been Warnham Park, Sussex.
Masters:

1881–7	Captain R B Ker, D.L.
1887–91	Alex H Gordon, D.L.
1891–2	Captain R B Ker, with A H Gordon as Deputy Master
1892–4	Marquis of Downshire, with A H Gordon as Deputy Master
1894–6	A H Gordon, D.L.
1896–1903	Frank Barbour
1903–4	R W Lindsay
1904–6	David Ker, D.L.
1906–7	Captain Hugh Montgomery
1907–14	S B Combe
1914–15	Captain A F Charley
1915–21	A committee, with J Hurst acting as Master
1921–6	Major D Dixon
1926–8	Robert Dunville
1928–30	Sir Joseph McConnell, Bt., & F W Workman
1930–32	F W Workman
1932–3	A committee
1933–9	Commander K C Kirkpatrick
1939–43	A committee
1943–5	A committee (Acting Masters, J Hurst & Granville Nugent)
1945–6	A committee (Acting Master, Cdr. K C Kirkpatrick)
1946–7	Major J Corbett and Captain G Clark
1947–50	Major J Corbett
1950–2	Lt.-Col. James G Cunningham, O.B.E., D.L.
1952–7	Lt.-Col. James G Cunningham, O.B.E., D.L., and A Willis

1957–62 Lt.-Col. James G Cunningham, O.B.E., D.L., and SJ Martin
1962–72 SJ Martin and TH Moore
1972–5 TH Moore and G Bryson
1975–8 G Bryson
1978–80 G Bryson, J Coburn, G Wilson and S Carson

History: The Co. Down Staghounds were established in 1881 by Captain RB Ker, D.L., who had previously hunted the pack as harriers with an occasional day after fallow deer. It would seem that in that year Captain Ker brought his hounds to an invitation meet of the Downe Hunt and we read that the hunt gave about £30 towards the maintenance of the Staghounds. In 1881 the difficulties of hunting the red deer were overcome, and this species of deer has been their quarry ever since.

During the last twenty-five years the Co. Down Staghounds have purchased fifteen stags and two hinds from Warnham Park in Sussex, the latter, along with a stag, being received in 1963.

The country over which the hunt operates is a fine, sporting one, chiefly pasture and no large woods.

The annual subscription (1979–80) is £130 for members hunting two days per week, or £100 for one day per week. For farmers the annual subscription is £70, whilst for children under 18 years of age the amount is £30. Visitors pay £20. The cap for everyone is £5.

1st King's Dragoon Guards Staghounds

County in which hunt operated: Norfolk
Period of hunt's existence: 1893–5
Kennels: Norwich
Master: Captain CL Bates

History: The 1st King's Dragoon Guards relieved the 8th Hussars at Norwich in July 1893, and immediately took over the pack of staghounds which they ran for two seasons before handing over to the 7th Dragoon Guards in 1895. The second season appears to have been spoiled by frost, but some good sport was enjoyed during 1893–4.

2nd Dragoon (Scots Greys) Staghounds

Counties in which hunt operated: South Norfolk and Suffolk
Period of hunt's existence: 1842–3
Kennels: } Not known, but possibly at Bramford, near Ipswich where
Deer paddock. } the previous Regiment had kept them
Master: Lord William Hill (2nd Dragoons – Scots Greys)

History: This pack was taken over from the 13th Light Dragoons, and for a season (1842–3) was hunted by Lord William Hill, a captain in the Regiment. Lord William Hill seems to have been quite fearless in the saddle – and this eventually cost him his life, for mounting a horse which his groom had complained about as being quite uncontrollable, the beast bolted and passing under a low bough of a tree, Lord William Hill was struck a blow on the forehead from which he never regained consciousness.

What became of the hounds subsequently is not recorded, but the pack does not seem to have passed on to any succeeding cavalry regiment.

7th Dragoon Guards Staghounds

County in which hunt operated: Norfolk
Period of hunt's existence: 1895–8
Kennels: Mousehold, Norwich
Pack: Twenty-four couple of hounds
Deer paddock: Mousehold, Norwich. The deer in the enclosure generally numbered about twenty-two.
Master: Captain H S Follett

History: In the autumn of 1895, the 7th Dragoon Guards moved into Norwich and immediately took over the pack of staghounds from the 1st King's Dragoon Guards which they continued to run until relieved in 1898 by the 7th Hussars.

13th Light Dragoon Staghounds

Counties in which hunt operated: Southern Norfolk and Suffolk
Period of hunt's existence: 1841–2
Kennels: Bramford Mill, near Ipswich
Pack: The hounds were collected from various sources, which included nine couple from Wales, some of which were the smooth, Welsh type; a couple from the Royal Buckhounds which had proved too slow for His Majesty's pack; two couple from H Villebois and two and half couple from the Essex and Suffolk Hunt.[98]
Deer paddock: Bramford, near Ipswich
Master: Captain J Anstruther Thomson

History: Quoting from the *Reminiscences of Colonel Anstruther Thomson*, Lt.-Col. Harvey (1910) gives the following record of the formation of this pack:

'October 1841. At Ipswich in the autumn, we decided to have a pack of staghounds. All the fellows in the Regiment entered into it cordially, and all the gentlemen of the county gave us permission.'

As mentioned above, hounds came from a number of sources and the pack probably numbered about fourteen and a half to fifteen couple. The deer, both red and fallow, were also collected from a number of sources, and the subscription seems to have amounted to £139.[98]

Drax Roebuck Hounds

County in which hunt operated: Dorset
Period of hunt's existence: c. 1830–38
Master: Mr Drax of Charborough, Dorset

History: When Mr E Morton Pleydell gave up his pack of hounds in 1829 they were taken over by Mr Drax, who hunted them for about eight or nine seasons.

Dunston Staghounds

Little is known of this pack which was run by John Gurney and Mr Long. It operated in East Anglia and seems to have lasted until about 1779.

Easingwold Staghounds

Little is known of this pack apart from the fact that it operated in the middle of the last century in Yorkshire, and in the year 1865 had a great run after a deer from Bossall Wood to Nunburnholme.

East Antrim Staghounds

County in which hunt operated: Co. Antrim
Period of hunt's existence: (as staghounds): 1906–*c.*1920. (This pack still exists as harriers)
Kennels: Brookfield House, Doagh, Co. Antrim
Pack: Varied bedween twenty-nine couple in 1912 to twenty-two couple in 1920. The hounds were described as Studbrook Harriers.
Deer paddock: About five deer were kept in the paddock
Masters:
1906–7 Richard Cecil
1907–20 James Craig

History: The East Antrim was founded in 1895 to hunt hares and to run drag, and during the first ten years of its existence, Sir Thomas J Dixon, Bart, J.P., acted as Master. In 1906, when drag hunting was given up, Mr Richard Cecil purchased a new pack of staghounds and a number of deer, hunting them in 1906–7.

The country, which lay to the north of Belfast Lough, was principally pasture with little wood and no bog. The sea bordered it on the east.[29]

Prior to the First World War, hunting took place on two days per week, the Saturday meet being reserved for stag and the Wednesday meet for hare. After the war the hunt gave up hunting the deer and continued as a harrier pack.

Easter Hunt

County in which hunt operated: Essex
Period of hunt's existence: The twelfth or thirteenth century to *c.*1865

History: In former days it was the practice for the citizens of London to accompany the monarch on an annual Easter hunt in Epping Forest. Just when this festive occasion was first promulgated is not very certain but it has been suggested that it may have been during the reign of Henry I (1100–35), or failing that, during the reigns of either Richard I (1189–99) or of Henry III (1216–72). Originally, in Henry I's time, it was called the Common Hunt – but by the beginning of the nineteenth century it was generally referred to as the London Hunt. It would seem that for this annual event the Epping Hunt hounds were used.

Eccles Hunt

Sir James Flower's Staghounds (q.v.), which hunted in south-eastern Norfolk during 1834–7, were sometimes referred to as the Eccles Hunt.

Enfield Chase

Counties in which hunt operated: Middlesex, Hertfordshire and Bedfordshire
Period of hunt's existence: 1885–1912 thereafter known as Colonel Croft's Staghounds (q.v.).

Kennels: The pack, prior to 1899, was kept at Enfield Court. Then from 1899–1905 it was moved to Hadley Green, Barnet after which the kennels were at High Canons, Shenley (1905–7). From 1907–8 the pack was kept at Beeson End, Harpenden but the following season hounds were moved to Pursley, Shenley. In 1913 the pack was transferred to Farnham's Hall, Ware.
Deer paddock: The deer paddocks were located with the kennels (see above). In 1905 both a deer paddock and a stag paddock are mentioned in Baily's *Hunting Directory* as being located at Shenley. When the deer were kept at Enfield there were about eighteen in the paddocks. After their transfer to Shenley the number was increased to about twenty hinds and one stag. At the outbreak of war the number of deer was about twenty-five.
Masters:
1885–99 Colonel A P Somerset, C.B.
1899–1901 Captain J Hills Hartridge
1901–3 C Arnold (Acting as Master for a committee)
1903–4 Captain A Hill, M.P.
1904–7 W Walker
1907–12 D D Bulger (Acting as Master for a committee)
1912–13 Major R P Croft, J.P., D.L.
(*see also* Colonel R P Croft's Staghounds)

History: The Enfield Chase Staghounds were established in 1885 by Colonel Somerset. About 1907 the hunt was near disbandment but at the last minute was resuscitated by Mr D D Bulger, who took over the mastership. It was Coaten's opinion that the Enfield Chase Staghounds were 'the best of the Metropolitan stag-hunts, because it is good country, for which early rising in Town is not necessary'.[50]

This pack of staghounds hunted by invitation in Middlesex, Hertfordshire and Bedfordshire, there being hardly any wire. Convenient centres for hunting were Potters Bar, Hatfield, St Albans, Hertford and Ware. Prior to Christmas the hounds were generally hunted three days per week, but thereafter twice weekly.

The Enfield Chase Staghounds was a subscription pack, the subscription in 1898 being fifteen guineas, which had increased to £21 by 1912. Cap for non-subscribers was one guinea. The hounds and deer were the property of the Master, and after the First World War the hunt seems to have taken the name of its Master and become known as Colonel Croft's Staghounds.

Epping Forest Staghounds

Little is known of this pack which appears to have hunted deer during the early part of the nineteenth century under the mastership of John Conyers, who was also Master of the Essex Foxhounds.

Epping Hunt

This hunt operated during the eighteenth and early nineteenth centuries, being disbanded in 1806 or 1807 when Lord Middleton bought the pack and sent it to Yorkshire. Both red and fallow deer were hunted, hounds being kept at Loughton Bridge.

Two famous Masters of the Epping Hunt were Joseph Mellish, who was killed by a highwayman in 1798, and his brother William, who hunted the pack until it was taken over by Lord Middleton.

Long before the Epping Hunt came into being, it was the practice for the citizens of London to accompany the monarch on an annual hunt, which took place on Easter Monday. During the Epping Hunt's existence, the pack was used for this annual event.

Essex Farmers

County in which hunt operated: Essex
Period of hunt's existence: From 1911 to 1914, under the title of Essex Farmers. Prior to 1911 this pack was known as the Essex Staghounds (q.v.) which was formed in 1831.
Kennels: Sturgeons, Writtle
Deer paddock: Sturgeons, Writtle
Master: During the time the hunt was known as the Essex Farmers (1911–14) it was hunted by a committee with Theodore Christy as Master.

History: In 1911 the Essex Staghounds, which had been formed in 1831, changed its name to Essex Farmers. The country, which lay wholly in Essex, was shared in parts with the Essex, Essex Union and East Essex Foxhounds.

Essex Staghounds

County in which hunt operated: Essex
Period of hunt's existence: 1831–1914 and 1920–26
Kennels: Originally at Myles's, but by the end of the century hounds were being kept at Mill Green Park, Ingatestone. In 1899 the kennels were transferred to Meghills, Leaden Roding, where they remained for two seasons before being moved to Writtle in 1901. From 1908 to 1910 the pack was kept at Matching Green, but when the pack became known as the Essex Farmers they returned to Sturgeons, Writtle. After the war, kennels were for a time at Farnhams Hall, Ware.
Pack: During the present century it would seem that hounds were never bred at the hunt's kennels, as a new entry was received each year from drafts of various local fox hunts.[48]

After the war the pack consisted of about twenty couple.
Deer paddocks: During the early part of the present century at Sturgeons, Writtle, but after the war the deer, about twenty in number, were kept at New Road, Ware.
Masters:
1831–43 Sheffield Neave
1846–7 Lord Petre
1851–67 Hon. Frederick Petre
1867–85 Hon. Henry Petre
1885–99 Sheffield Neave
1899–1901 W H Pemberton Barnes
1901–8 A Jackson
1908–11 John Balfour
1911–14 Committee, with Theodore Christy as Master
1920–26 Lt.-Col. R P Croft, J.P., D.L.

History: The Essex Staghounds were established in 1831 by Mr Sheffield Neave to hunt the carted deer in Essex. This pack, apart from two short breaks between 1844–5 and 1847–50, continued to hunt the carted deer until 1914, although in 1911 the title of the hunt had been changed from Essex Staghounds to the Essex Farmers' Staghounds. In 1920 Lt.-Col. R P Croft took over the pack and hunted it privately for about six years.

The country lay wholly in Essex, with the best centres being Ongar, Chelmsford, Dunmow and Harlow. The Rodings, over which the pack hunted, was generally considered to be the best plough land in the country.

The pack was a subscription one, with non-subscribers being capped £1.

Sir James Flower's Staghounds (Eccles Hunt)

County in which hunt operated: South-eastern Norfolk
Period of hunt's existence: 1834–7
Master: Sir James Flower

History: During its four years' existence this pack, consisting of sixteen couple of hounds, hunted carted red deer.

Richardson Gardner's Staghounds

In 1877 Colonel Richardson Gardner formed a staghound pack at Cowley Manor but little information is available except that Mr Jack Hickman, who had previously been huntsman to Mr Angerstein's Staghounds in Northampton, and later in Norfolk, was taken on as huntsman and remained there for two seasons before moving to the Surrey Staghounds.

Garrison Staghounds

County in which hunt operated: Co. Dublin and adjacent country
Period of hunt's existence: *c.*1840–1854
Masters:
Captain Forrester
Captain Armit
The Hon. W Hutchinson

History: In 1840* Lord Howth brought over Mr Broadley's Staghounds from Leamington and hunted them himself until his wife's death in 1848. The pack was then sold to the Dublin Garrison, and became known as the Garrison Hounds – a pack which soon earned the reputation of being one of the fastest in the country.
amalgamated with the Ward Hounds and became known as the Ward Union Hunt – the second part of the name being derived from the name of an inn – The Union.

Gerard's Staghounds

County in which hunt operated: South Lancashire
Period of hunt's existence: *c.*1810–1913

* Muriel Bowen gives this date as 1842.[20]

Kennels: Formerly at Garswood, but since 1895 at Wrightington Hall, Appley Bridge
Pack: About twenty-five to thirty couple of hounds, a proportion of which were home bred with a Welsh cross
Masters:
*c.*1810–26 Sir William Gerard*
1826–54 Sir John Gerard
*c.*1880(?)–1913 The Hon. R G Gerard-Dicconson

History: The Gerards of Garswood, Ashton-in-Makerfield, hunted the south-west portion of Lancashire for many generations, and for very many years the family owned and kept a pack of hounds. Sir William Gerard, who was Master of the Badsworth from 1811 to 1814, had a pack of hounds kennelled at the Old Hall. On his death in 1826 he was succeeded by his brother, Sir John, who kept the pack going until his death in 1854, at which date, according to Sir John's last wishes, the pack was destroyed. There is no doubt that Sir John's pack did, on occasions if not always, hunt the deer, for there is mention of his pack taking a deer in the Mill Brook at Newton after a long run.

The country was then taken over by Major F Gerard who formed a pack of harriers in 1859, known as the Aspull Hunt. In addition to this pack of harriers, however, it seems that the Gerard family kept two other private packs, one for stag and the other for fox.

When Major F Gerard died in 1883, the Hon. William (later second Baron Gerard) took over the mastership, and the Aspull Harriers, coming to Garswood, took that name. All three packs were then hunted by Sir William's brother, the Hon. R Gerard-Dicconson and occupied the same kennels. It is recorded, however, that the introduction of fresh hound blood by the purchase of the Stalybridge Harriers introduced rabies in the pack, and over twenty couple had to be destroyed.

In 1889 Lord Gerard handed over the harrier pack to the Hon. R J Gerard-Dicconson who was then hunting the Gerard staghounds as well as the foxhounds. He, however, found the hunting of three packs too much, and so transferred the harriers to a committee, the pack reverting to its former name of Aspull Harriers, with kennels at Whittle-le-Woods, near Chorley. The staghounds, however, were kennelled at the Gerard-Dicconson residence, Blackleyhurst, near Garswood, and hunted the country from the Mersey in the south to the Ribble in the north. In about 1895 on succeeding, through the death of his uncle, to the Wrightington Estates, he built new kennels and transferred the pack there.

The Gerard Staghounds hunted fallow deer of the black variety, the animals being perfectly wild and showing good sport. During its latter years the same pack seems to have been used for both deer and fox hunting.

---

* It is not known for certain, whether Sir William's pack hunted deer, hare, fox or all three.

Walter Greene's Staghounds

County in which hunt operated: West Suffolk
Period of hunt's existence: 1864–70; 1889–1900 (*see also page 52*)
Kennels: Nether Hall, Bury St Edmunds
Pack: Sixteen couple of hounds
Deer paddock: Nether Hall, Bury St Edmunds where about twenty deer were kept
Master: E Walter Greene

History: This private pack was formed in 1864 by Mr (later Sir) E Walter Greene, and continued until 1870, when the pack was temporarily suspended whilst Mr Greene took over the mastership of first, the Suffolk Foxhounds, and then the Croome. In 1889* he returned to Suffolk and re-established his pack of staghounds which he hunted until handing over the deer and hounds to Mr F Riley-Smith in 1900.[27]. For the subsequent history of this pack (*see page 237*).

Mr Greene's Staghounds shared the country over which three other packs hunted portions – namely the Suffolk, the Essex and Suffolk, and the Newmarket and Thurlow Foxhounds.

Gunton Staghounds

County in which hunt operated: Norfolk
Period of hunt's existence: *c.*1854–6
Kennels: Gunton, near Cromer
Deer paddocks: Gunton Park, near Cromer
Master: Charles Harbord, fifth Baron Suffield

History: This pack was started by the fifth Lord Suffield about 1854 for hunting anywhere in the county of Norfolk.

In 1856, owing to local agitation from farmers, and others, in the district, it was decided to establish a pack of foxhounds, Lord Suffield being invited to act as Master. In that year, therefore, the Gunton Staghounds relinquished hunting the stag in Norfolk, and became the Norfolk Foxhounds.

During the existence of the Gunton Staghounds, meets took place on Tuesdays and Fridays, and included the following places: Westacre High House, Swafield, Drayton, Aylsham, Bawdeswell, Sall, Frettenham, Stoke, Felmingham.[98]

James Harding's Mountain Harriers

County in which hunt operated: Dorset
Period of hunt's existence: *c.* 1829–38
Kennels: Higher Waterson, near Puddletown
Master: James Harding, *c.*1829–38

History: Little is known about this pack except that, although in its later years it principally hunted roe deer, it also hunted, on occasions, fox, hare and fallow deer.

---

* Baily's *Hunting Directory* gives this date as 1891.[7]

Lord Howth's Staghounds

In about 1840 Lord Howth, of Howth Castle, Baily near Dublin, brought over a pack of staghounds from England, and with the help of a subscription from the local military, hunted them himself until 1848, when the pack was acquired by the Dublin Garrison and became known as the Garrison Staghounds.

4th Hussars Staghounds

County in which hunt operated: Norfolk
Period of hunt's existence: 1883–5
Kennels: Denmark Farm, Sprowston, Norwich
Pack: Twenty-five couple of hounds
Masters:
1883–4 Captain S W Follett
1884–5 W P Wilson Todd

History: Following Mr R A Barkley's resignation in 1883, the Norfolk Staghounds and deer were handed over to the 4th Hussars Regiment which was stationed at Norwich, and for the next two seasons the hunt became known as the 4th Hussars Staghounds.

The 4th Hussars commenced their first season up to Christmas by using the pack as draghounds, but this ceased at Christmas 1883, and from then on it was employed solely as staghounds.[98] Some good sport was enjoyed and in particular with a deer called *Zulu* and a havier. Some of the best hunting seems to have taken place in the spring.

7th Hussars Staghounds

County in which hunt operated: Norfolk
Period of hunt's existence: 1898–1900
Kennels: Mousehold, Norwich
Deer paddock: Mousehold, Norwich
Master: Colonel The Hon. R T Lawley

History: This regiment relieved the 7th Dragoon Guards at Norwich in the spring of 1898 and took over the running of the staghounds. For two winters the followers enjoyed good sport. The regiment was then posted to South Africa, and with their departure ended the military's interest in running the staghounds, for shortly afterwards the War Office placed a ban on regimental packs of hounds. The pack was, therefore, handed over to the county, and they became a subscription pack under the new title of Norwich Staghounds (q.v.). Meets took place on Mondays and Thursdays, also on Fridays after Christmas. No foxhound packs hunted over the same country.

8th Hussars Staghounds

County in which hunt operated: Norfolk
Period of hunt's existence: 1890–93
Kennels: Norwich
Masters:
1890–92 Captain D E Wood
1892–3 Major R L Clowes

History: The 8th Hussars took over from the 20th Hussars in 1890 and hunted the pack for three seasons before handing over to the 1st Dragoon Guards in July 1893.

19th Hussars Staghounds

County in which hunt operated: Norfolk
Period of hunt's existence: 1886–8
Kennels: Norwich
Master: Captain M Wright

History: The 19th Hussars came to Norwich in the autumn of 1886 and immediately took over the pack of staghounds which, during the previous two seasons, had been hunted by the 4th Hussars.

The Regiment was stationed at Norwich for only a year and on its departure handed the pack over to the 20th Hussars.

20th Hussars Staghounds

County in which hunt operated: Norfolk
Period of hunt's existence: 1888–90
Kennels: Norwich
Master: Captain R J E Oliver-Bellasis

History: This regiment, on relieving the 19th Hussars in the autumn of 1888, immediately took over the pack of staghounds, which they ran for one season before handing over to the 8th Hussars.

Inwood Buckhounds

County in which hunt operated: Dorset
Period of hunt's existence: 1913–*c.*1921
Kennels: Inwood
Master: Miss Guest

History: The Inwood Buckhounds were started as a private pack by Miss Guest in 1913 to hunt the wild roe deer in the district. During their existence hounds met twice a week. During the latter part of the war the pack hunted fox.

The Ladies' Hunt

County in which hunt operated: Essex
Period of hunt's existence: *c.*1760

History: During the latter part of the eighteenth century Earl Tilney's hounds were sometimes referred to as The Ladies' Hunt because of the number of the fair sex who followed them. The occasion seems to have been the Easter Monday hunt which was followed by a dinner and ball.

London Hunt

This is an alternative name for the Easter Hunt (q.v.).

Lunesdale and Oxenholme Staghounds

County in which hunt operated: Westmorland principally, but also north Lancashire. This area is now known as Cumbria.

Period of hunt's existence: 1871–1939 (deer hunting commenced in 1888)
Kennels: Endmoor, near Kendal
Pack: About eighteen couple of hounds
Deer paddocks: Prior to the First World War at Oxenholme, where about forty red deer were kept. After the First World War the deer were kept at Rigmaden Park, Kirkby Lonsdale. During this period, however, there were plenty of wild deer in the district.
Masters:
1871–88 C H Wilson (harriers only)
1888–94 C H Wilson (hare and deer alternately)
1894–1918 C H Wilson (deer only)
1918–30 J R Heaton (deer only)
1930–39 Miss F Weston

History: The Oxenholme Hunt was started in 1871 and for the first seventeen years hunted hares which, although plentiful at first, started to become extremely scarce. Then, on 9 February 1888* a comparatively new departure was made when a red deer was enlarged at Low Bleaze and stag hunting was begun. From 1888 to 1894 hare and stag were hunted on alternate meet days, but in November 1894 the livery of green of the Oxenholme Harriers was replaced with the scarlet livery of the staghunter and from that date the career of the Oxenholme Staghounds really commenced.[59]

During the latter part of the last century, when the pack – then known as the Oxenholme Staghounds – were hunting both hare and stag, they consisted of a cross between the old Southern Harrier (the blue mottled harrier) and the rough Welsh foxhound, crossed again with the bloodhound by Mr Charles Wilson, who was Master 1871–1918. They were big, powerful hounds but rather slow. They were, however, well adapted for the country, which consisted chiefly of grass, moorland and open fellside, with a fair amount of rough wood.

When Mr J R Heaton took over the pack in 1918, all these hounds had been sold and for a time the country was hunted with the Vale of Lune Harriers, at which time it became known as the Lunesdale and Oxenholme Staghounds. Using the harriers as foundation stock, Mr Heaton crossed them with foxhounds, Cotley harriers, Scarteen black and tan, rough Welsh and blue mottled harriers, as well as recovering some of Mr Wilson's old stock. As a result, two packs were formed, one to hunt deer and the other hare.

Unfortunately, when hunting was suspended during the Second World War years, there was no-one to take an interest in the deer, and as a result their population was sadly depleted by shooting and other methods. Thus, when hostilities ceased, insufficient deer remained to make it worth while for the staghounds to be re-formed.

The hunt was a subscription pack, the minimum subscription in 1930 for a member being £20 with a cap being taken for the Deer Damage Fund. Ten years previously the subscription had been £25. The best centres were Kirkby Lonsdale, Milnethorpe and Kendal.

* Bailey's *Hunting Directory* gives this date as 1887.[7]

Duke of Marlborough's Deerhounds

During the middle of the eighteenth century, the Duke of Marlborough had a pack of deerhounds which hunted primarily in Oxfordshire. On 25 November 1748 this pack had a very fine run during which hounds covered about fifty miles.

Mid-Kent Staghounds

County in which hunt operated: Kent
Period of hunt's existence: 1868–1962
Kennels: Hounds have been kennelled at a number of places. At the end of the last century the kennels were at Wateringbury but in about 1910 they moved to Boughton Monchelsea. In 1913 the hounds were taken to Smarden but by 1930 they had once more returned to Boughton Monchelsea. More recently the kennels were at Mount Ephraim, Faversham.
Pack: Prior to the First First World War the pack generally consisted of about twenty-four couple but by 1920 only ten couple of hounds remained. During the latter years it was kept at about twenty couple.
Deer paddocks: At the beginning of the present century the deer were kept at Wateringbury but by the end of the First World War they had been moved to Boughton Place, Maidstone, where they remained until the hunt was disbanded in 1962. The number of deer in the paddock, which extended to about seven acres was about twenty to twenty-five red deer, the majority of which were hinds.
Masters:

1868–74	T Rigg
1874–5	A Warde
1875–83	C F Leney
1883–6	H Leney
1886–8	R A Barkley
1888–92	Colonel J T North
1892–4	G P Russell
1894–1909	A Leney
1909–13	G B Winch
1913–20	Lt.-Col. G B Winch and Brig.-Gen. T M S Pitt
1920–21	H Buckland
1921–4	Brig.-Gen. T M S Pitt
1925–7	Captain G Mitchell
1927–39	Captain E S Dawes
1939–48	Captain E S Dawes and W Day
1949–57	W Day and H M Allfrey
1957–60	A committee (Joint Acting Masters – K R Betts and C M Ramus)
1960–62	K Betts

History: The Mid-Kent Staghounds were established in 1868 by Mr Tom Rigg who, as a private pack, first started with hare, but within a year or two of its formation, his pack was hunting fallow deer, and before he handed over the mastership in 1874 to A Warde, red deer had replaced the fallow (*see page 29*). At this stage it became a subscription pack. For the next ninety years red deer remained the quarry of this pack, hinds being the usual type of animal to be uncarted, as well as any outlying deer of which there were quite a number dotted around the countryside.

Their country lay in mid and east Kent, extending to about forty square miles, and the best centres included Headcorn, Pluckley, Tenterden and Appledore.

In May 1962 it was decided to disband the Mid-Kent Staghounds. Their country was shared by the Ashford Valley Foxhounds, and a certain amount of rivalry had always existed between these two hunts. In order to give its members the best possible opportunity to continue hunting over the same country, the Mid-Kent Staghounds placed all its assets and capital at the disposal of the Ashford Valley Foxhounds, who took some of their hounds, the remainder being given to neighbouring packs. The few deer that remained in the paddock were given away to ornamental parks. During the last few years of its existence, the Mid-Kent Staghounds had obtained most of their deer from Warnham Court Park, near Horsham in Sussex, one consignment in 1948 consisting of one three-year-old stag and twelve hinds.

The hunt met on Wednesday and Saturday, the annual subscription (1950) being twenty guineas with a cap of three guineas.[13] The deer and hounds were the property of the hunt committee.

Lady Mary Wortley Montagu's Staghounds

Little is known of Lady Wortley Montagu's Staghounds, except that she frequently hunted her pack in Richmond Park about 1680.

Mountain Harriers

This pack – better known as James Harding's Mountain Harriers – hunted roe in Dorset during the early part of the last century (*see page 223*).

New Forest Buckhounds

County in which hunt operates: Hampshire
Period of hunt's existence: Deer hunting in the New Forest commenced in about 1854, but it was not until 1883 that the New Forest Deerhounds became a regular subscription pack. It is still extant, changing its title to Buckhounds during the First World War.
Kennels: New Park, Brockenhurst
Pack: Twenty couple of about 25 to 26 in. (63 to 66 cm) hounds
Masters:
Private pack
*c.*1854– *c.*1858 Buckworth Powell
1858–83 Francis Lovell
New Forest Deerhounds
1883–93 Francis Lovell
1893–4 Edward Walker
1894–5 E Walker and E F Kelly
1895–1901 E F Kelly

1901–8 O T Price
1908–10 G J Thursby and Major Timson
1910–*c.*14 Sir G Thursby, Bart
New Forest Buckhounds
*c.*1914–36 Sir G Thursby, Bart
1936–8 Sir John Buchanan-Jardine and A Dalgety
1938–40 H J Colebrook and Miss Colebrook
1940–41 A committee
1941–2 H J Colebrook and Mrs Collins
1942–4 No hunting
1944–7 A Dalgety and Lady Daresbury
1947–9 H J Colebrook
1949–50 A committee
1950–58 Lt.-Col. Sir Dudley Forwood, Bart., C.M.G.
1958–73 A committee, with acting Master Donald Egremont
1973–8 A committee, with acting Masters Mrs K D Millar and Mrs L D Vickery
1978–80 A committee, with acting Master Mrs K D Millar

History: Following the *Deer Removal Act* of 1851 a number of privately owned packs operated in the New Forest to help keep the deer under control. One of these was owned by Mr Buckworth Powell who, with a few couple of hounds, hunted the deer only during the months of August and April. In about 1858 Mr Francis Lovell was hunting deer in the forest but by this date considerable friction existed between the various packs then hunting fox and deer in the forest, and also the covert shooters. This continued until 1883 when the New Forest Deerhounds really came into being as a regular subscription pack, Mr Francis Lovell being appointed Master. Regular meets took place from August to April, the months of October and February being excluded. During the First World War years the hunt started to concentrate its activities on fallow bucks so the name was altered to the New Forest Buckhounds.

At the present time meets are held twice a week on Mondays and Fridays, with an occasional bye-day on Wednesday.

Although there are four species of deer running wild in the New Forest – red deer, roe deer, fallow deer and sika deer – hounds hunt only the fallow buck. Control work on the does and other species of deer is done by shooting.

Subscriptions vary according to the amount of hunting to be done during the season. The cap for visitors (1974) was £2.50 with 50p field money for all mounted followers. The country is much the same as that hunted over by the New Forest Foxhounds.

The best centres for this hunt are Ringwood and Brockenhurst.

New Forest Deerhounds

Prior to taking on the name of New Forest Buckhounds in about 1914 when the hunt concentrated its activities on fallow buck hunting, the pack was known as the New Forest Deerhounds, and hunted all species of deer then in the New Forest, but primarily red and fallow deer.

Norfolk Staghounds

County in which hunt operated: Norfolk
Period of hunt's existence: 1844–51, 1872–86
Kennels:
Witchingham: 1844–51
Weeting: 1872–6
Masters:
1844–5 Charles Kett Thomson
1845–51 Henry Kett Thomson
1872–6 W Angerstein
1876–7 Captain Haughton
1878–83 R A Barkley
1883–5 4th Hussars (*see page 224*)
1877–8 C T Hoare
1885–6 R A Barkley

History: Although the first mention of these staghounds is in 1844, it may well be that the pack was one and the same as that which Lord William Hill had hunted with the 2nd Dragoons (Scots Greys, q.v.).

After the Thomson regime, although other packs of staghounds, such as the Gunton Staghounds, operated in Norfolk, no pack seems to have carried the name of Norfolk Staghounds until 1872 when Mr William Angerstein, whose residence was at Weeting, brought a pack of hounds from Rugby to hunt in Norfolk under this title.

In 1876 Mr Angerstein relinquished the command of the pack in favour of Captain Haughton, but in the following year he also handed over the mastership to C T Hoare. In 1878 Mr Hoare gave up and the pack, which prior to this date had been privately owned, became a subscription one under R A Barkley. For the next few years the pack became known as the Norfolk and Suffolk Staghounds (q.v.) until in 1883 Mr Barkley handed them over to the 4th Hussar Regiment, by which name the pack became known for the next two years. In 1885 the 4th Hussars left Norfolk and were relieved by the 13th Hussars who, however, did not wish to take over the hunt. Accordingly, Mr Barkley once more stepped into the breach and for one season only (1885–6) the pack was once again known as the Norfolk and Suffolk Staghounds.

Norfolk and Suffolk Staghounds

County in which hunt operated: North Suffolk and southern Norfolk
Period of hunt's existence: c.1873, 1878–83, 1885–6
Kennels: 1878–83, Palgrave, near Diss
Deer paddock: 1878–83, Palgrave, near Diss
Masters:
1873 Charles Chaston
1878–83 R A Barkley
1885–6 R A Barkley
See also Norfolk Staghounds

History: This pack was formed by Mr Charles Chaston in about 1873 but under him it does not seem to have survived for more than about a season. Charles Chaston, who was also Master of the Waveney Harriers, seems to have been quite a character for he tried to combine both harriers and stag hunting on one and the same day, wearing a different uniform for each sport. On occasions the pack was referred to as the Waveney Staghounds.

For the next few years packs operating in Norfolk seem to have been variously described as either the Norfolk and Suffolk Staghounds, or just simply Norfolk Staghounds, by which name the pack under the masterships of W Angerstein (1872–6), Captain Haughton (1876–7) and C T Hoare (1877–8) were generally known. When R A Barkley, however, took over (1878–83 and 1885–6), it received the full title of Norfolk and Suffolk Staghounds.

North Devon Staghounds

Counties in which hunt operated: Devon and Somerset
Period of hunt's existence: 1775 until 1824
Masters:
1775–85 Colonel Basset
1785–94 Sir Thomas Dyke Acland
1794–1802 Colonel Basset
1802–3 Lord Fortescue
1803–10 John Worth
1810–12 Lord Graves
1812–18 Lord Fortescue
1818–24 Stucley Lucas

History: The North Devon Staghounds were formed in 1775 by Colonel Basset, and for the first twenty-six years or so of its existence the pack was maintained and hunted at the personal cost of each succeeding Master. In 1803, however, when John Worth took over the mastership, it became a subscription pack, until 1812 when Fortescue again hunted the pack privately. It reverted to a subscription pack in 1818 under the mastership of Stucley Lucas.

In 1824 the pack was sold in London to a German who, in the following year, took it back to Europe with him. After the sale of the pack there was no hunting for three years, during which time the deer were much reduced by shooting.

North Walsham Harriers

This pack occasionally hunted deer during the late 1850s (*see page 47*).

Norwich Hunt

Little is known about the activities of this hunt, which was supported by the Norwich Sportsmen's Society under Mr Sturt towards the end of the eighteenth century.

Norwich Staghounds

Counties in which hunt operated: Principally in Norfolk, but also in north Suffolk

Period of hunt's existence: 1900 to 1963
Stag hunting in Norfolk dates from a very early period, but it was only from 1900 that the hunt assumed the title of Norwich Staghounds. For seventeen years prior to this date it had been a private hunt owned by each cavalry regiment stationed at Norwich, and in consequence bore the name of the regiment. Prior to that date packs of staghounds had operated in East Anglia under various titles, including Norfolk Staghounds, and Norfolk and Suffolk Staghounds.

The following packs (*see also the separate entries*) were probably most closely associated with the Norwich Staghounds during the last century before it assumed this title, although gaps and a certain amount of overlapping of years does occur:

1818–27 Edward Dewing's Staghounds
1815–23 Sir Jacob Astley's Staghounds
*c.*1821–9 The Westacre Staghounds
1834–7 Eccles Hunt
*c.*1837–41 H Villebois' Staghounds
1841–2 13th Light Dragoon Staghounds
1842–3 2nd Dragoon Scots Greys Staghounds
1844–51 Norfolk Staghounds
*c.*1853 Castleacre Staghounds
1854–6 Gunton Staghounds
*c.*1873 Norfolk and Suffolk Staghounds
1872–8 Norfolk Staghounds
1878–83 Norfolk and Suffolk Staghounds
1883–5 4th Hussars Staghounds
1885–6 Norfolk and Suffolk Staghounds
1886–8 19th Hussars Staghounds
1888–90 20th Hussars Staghounds
1890–93 8th Hussars Staghounds
1893–5 1st King's Dragoon Guards Staghounds
1895–8 7th Dragoon Guards Staghounds
1898–1900 7th Hussars Staghounds

Kennels: In a number of places, generally at the residence of the Master. By 1903 they were being kennelled at Brooke Lodge, Norwich; at Mousehold, Norwich in 1904 and more recently at Suton, Wymondham. Since 1953 the pack was kennelled at Wacton House, Long Stratton.

Pack: About twenty-two couple of hounds

Masters (Since the hunt became known as the Norwich Staghounds):

1900–1 Major H S Follett
1901–2 Charles A Fellowes
1902–3 Bertram W A Keppel
1903–22 John E Cooke
1922–3 J A Keith
1923–6 J A Keith and Lt.-Col. R W Patteson
1926–31 J A Keith
1931–2 Mrs J A Keith
1932–44 Miss Sybil Harker
1944–6 A committee
1946–53 Lt.-Col. B S Gooch and S J Cole

1953–62 Brevet Colonel B S Gooch and Miss Sybil Harker
1962–3 Brevet Colonel B S Gooch

Deer paddocks: For many years the deer were kept at Brooke Lodge, Norwich, where their number was about twenty-five. From about 1932 to 1942 they were kept at Rackheath Park near Norwich, and more recently in a 14-acre paddock at Winfarthing, Diss. Rackheath Park was enclosed about 1850, and the enclosure at Diss was in 1947.

The deer: Stags for stocking the hunt's enclosure were obtained from a number of sources, including Richmond Park, Surrey and Ashridge Park, Hertfordshire. Hinds were obtained from Blickling Park, Norfolk and Warnham Park, Sussex. In fact, for over sixty years there have been traces of Warnham blood in the deer hunted by this pack (*see page 49*).

History: Although stag hunting in Norfolk dates from a very early period it was only when the cavalry regiments stationed at Norwich relinquished ownership of the pack in 1900 that it became known as the Norwich Staghounds. Apart from outliers, the pack hunted carted deer – a sport which had been practised in Norfolk since 1793.

About the turn of the century both stags and hinds were being hunted, but during its latter years hinds and haviers only were hunted.

Prior to the First World War the annual subscription was £10 (farmers £5) but in its latter years the amounts were increased to £50 (families £75) with a £3 cap. Mondays and Thursdays were the usual hunting days, and the hunt operated all over Norfolk, wherever invited. Much of the country was shared with the Dunstan Harriers, but there were no foxhounds.

Prior to 1939 the Norwich Staghound pack had been bred from some of the best hunting blood in England, which included strains from the West Norfolk, Brocklesby, Puckeridge and Heythrop hunts. Unfortunately, during the war the pack had to be put down, with the result that when hunting was resumed in 1946 a fresh start had to be made with an unentered draft of five and a half couple which had been obtained from Ireland. In due course, however, further drafts were obtained from some of the leading foxhound packs in the country, and these included Pytchley, Seavington and York and Ainsty, as well as three couple of unentered black and tan hounds from Sir John Buchanan-Jardine's Dumfriesshire pack, and as a result a good working pack was built up again.

In 1963 the Norwich Staghounds gave up hunting the carted deer and changed to a drag on one day, hunting the fox on the other day, with the intention of eventually getting a foxhound pack going.

Lord Orford's Staghounds

Little is known about this private pack of staghounds which was kept at Houghton by Lord Orford (Sir Robert Walpole) in about the middle of the eighteenth century. It operated principally in East Anglia (*see also page 41*).

Peter Ormrod's Staghounds

County in which hunt operated: Lancashire
Period of hunt's existence: 1899 to early twentieth century

Kennels: near Scorton
Pack: Twenty to thirty couple. A lot of Welsh blood in the pack with a slight strain of Old Southern. Many were blue-mottled or tan ticked. Dogs stood about 25 in. (64 cm).
Deer paddock: Wyresdale Park, Scorton where 'over 100 red deer and a herd of fallow' were kept.[7]
Master: Peter Ormrod

History: This was a private pack established by Peter Ormrod of Wyresdale Park, Scorton, in 1899. They were noted, it was said, 'for their wonderful music and hunting qualities'. The pack hunted twice a week.

In 1904 Mr Ormrod took his staghounds to Oare, Brendon where he built them temporary kennels and by invitation of the Master of the Devon and Somerset, hunted hinds on Exmoor.[9] Assisted by his north-country kennel-huntsman, Jack Greenway, his pack succeeded in killing, during the 1904–5 season, eighteen hinds and two stags in the Cloutsham districts.

Oxenholme Staghounds

See Lunesdale and Oxenholme Staghounds

James Parker's Staghounds

County in which hunt operated: Essex
Period of hunt's existence: c.1847

History: Little is known of this small pack, which was maintained privately by James Parker for hunting deer in Essex during one of the periods in which the activities of the Essex Staghounds were temporarily suspended.

Pendle Forest Harriers

About the beginning of the twentieth century the Pendle Forest Harriers had occasional days after some carted stags which had been supplied by Mr Peebles, who was resident in the district. In 1906 Lord Ribblesdale formed a pack of buckhounds (q.v.) to hunt in the same area.

E Morton Pleydell's Roebuck Hounds

County in which hunt operated: Dorset
Period of hunt's existence: 1815–29
Kennels: Hounds kept at Manor House, Milborne St Andrew
Pack: About eighteen couple – a mixture of small foxhounds and large harriers
Master: Edmund Morton Pleydell, 1815–29

History: This pack started to hunt roe in 1815, but during the next three years it hunted both roe and hare. From 1818, until the pack was disposed of in 1829, it hunted roe only. Mr E Morton Pleydell lived at Whatcombe House.

Quantock Staghounds

County in which hunt operates: Somerset
Period of hunt's existence: 1901–7, 1917 and still extant
Kennels: Bagborough, Taunton

Over Stowey, Bridgewater (prior to 1917)
Pack: twenty-five couple
Masters:
1901–7 E A V Stanley (hunt disbanded 1907–17)
1917–31 Colonel (later Sir) Dennis Boles
1931–54 Mrs E M Wimbush.
1954–9 Sir Jeremy Boles
1959–60 A committee: Acting Master, G Woodhouse
1960–62 L H W Preston
1962–9 G P Roffe-Sylvester
1969–76 Mrs W R Thrower
1976–8 Mrs W R Thrower and W Robins
1978–80 W Robins

History: Owing to the abundance of deer in the Quantock range, the Devon and Somerset Staghounds found themselves incapable of hunting adequately the whole of their territory. Accordingly, Mr E A V Stanley of Quantock Lodge established, in 1901, a pack to hunt this particular part of Somerset, and did so with considerable success, particularly during the 1904–5 season when seventy-four deer were accounted for. In 1907 Mr Stanley gave up the pack and it was not re-started until 1917 when Colonel (later Sir) Dennis Boles, the Master of the West Somerset Foxhounds, kept the pack going at his own expense until 1931, when Mrs Wimbush took over the mastership.

The Quantock Staghounds hunt twice a week, the subscription (1979–80) being £100 for a family or £80 for one horse, with a £10 cap per day for autumn stag and £12 per day for spring stag hunting. For hinds the cap is £6 per day. For those who follow the hunt by car, the season ticket for owners of Landrovers is £25, whilst for cars, £5. Occasionally this pack is invited to hunt some of the outlying districts of the Devon and Somerset country.

The best centres for hunting are Bridgwater, Taunton and Williton.

Queen's Hounds

See Royal Buckhounds

Radclyffe's Roe Deer Hounds

County in which hunt operated: Dorset
*Period of hunt's existence: c.*1856–?
Master: C J Radclyffe

History: A pack of hounds was kept at Hyde Park, Wareham, for hunting roe deer in Dorset during the second half of the last century by C J Radclyffe and his father, but how long it remained in existence is not known. During the two seasons of 1856 and 1857 this pack is recorded to have killed nearly forty roe.

Ranston Bloodhounds

County in which hunt operated: Dorset
Period of hunt's existence: 1871–80
Kennels: Irwerne Minster, Dorset

Pack: About sixteen couple of bloodhound/foxhound cross, the hounds being black and tan, and standing 27 to 28 in. (68–71 cm) high at the shoulder.
Master: Lord Wolverton

History: The formation of the pack was a draft of eight couple of foxhound/bloodhound cross which had been bred by Captain Roden of Kells. Co. Meath, he himself having gone to Mr Jennings of Yorkshire and Mr Cowen of Blaydon Burns, near Newcastle, for the blood. The bloodhound stock used by Captain Roden was said to be direct descendant of the old black St Huberts with all their distinguishing marks.

By 1875 Lord Wolverton had increased the pack to sixteen and half couple, with which he hunted red deer in Dorset. The Ranston pack was probably the last bloodhounds used for stag hunting in England.

The pack was given the title of the Ranston Bloodhounds because while a new mansion at Iwerne Minster was being built, Lord Wolverton rented neighbouring Ranston from the owner, Sir Edward Baker.

In 1880 Lord Wolverton sold the pack to Lord Carrington (q.v.) who retained them for only about a year.

Ribblesdale Buckhounds

Counties in which hunt operated: Lancashire and West Riding of Yorkshire
Period of hunt's existence: 1906–19
Kennels: Originally at Bolton-by-Bowland but subsequently moved to Ellenthorpe, Gisburn
Pack: About twenty to twenty-five couple, principally Kerry beagles
Masters:
1906–11 Lord Ribblesdale and Peter Ormrod
1911–14 Lord Ribblesdale and A L Ormrod
1914–19 Lord Ribblesdale

History: This pack, which had been formed in 1906 by Lord Ribblesdale of Gisburn Park, near Clitheroe, with Peter Ormrod as Joint Master, had been built up by the latter who had crossed a Kerry beagle bitch with a foxhound dog, the majority of which had been obtained from the Belvoir Hunt. The reverse cross, between a Kerry dog and a foxhound bitch, never gave such satisfactory results. Doghounds stood about 25 inches (63–64 cm), the bitches being some three inches (7–8 cm) smaller. The music of this pack was said to be 'quite unique in tone' with the depth of the bloodhound 'and the additional sharpness of the foxhound'.

The Ribblesdale Buckhounds hunted the country which lay between such towns as Preston, Clitheroe and Garstang in Lancashire, and Settle and Skipton in Yorkshire. Both black fallow deer and Japanese sika deer, some of which were obtained from Peter Ormrod's estate at Wyresdale Park, Scorton, near Garstang, were turned out and in a very short time there were sufficient deer in the area to hunt two days a week.

Duke of Richmond's Staghounds

County in which hunt operated: Sussex and elsewhere
Period of hunt's existence: c. 1738–50

History: According to Christy the second Duke of Richmond and Gordon, of Goodwood House, Sussex, 'who succeeded his father in 1738 and died in 1750, built the first known private kennels and established a private pack of hounds in the village of Charlton, and not only did he hunt the fox but he appears to have also had a pack of Staghounds, all run at his own expense for the sport of himself and friends'.[48]

Riley-Smith's Staghounds

County in which hunt operated: West Suffolk
Period of hunt's existence: 1900–4*
Kennels: Nether Hall initially, but in 1902 hounds were moved to Barton Hall, Bury St Edmunds. At this date the pack was nineteen couple of hounds.
Deer paddock: Nether Hall, Bury St Edmunds initially, but moved to Barton Hall in 1902. Twenty-five deer were kept at the latter place.
Master: F Riley-Smith (*see also page 223*)

History: This pack was originally formed in 1864 by Sir (then Mr) E Walter Greene. After being temporarily suspended for nineteen years from 1870 to 1889, it was re-established by Sir Walter, who hunted the pack for a further eleven years before handing over the hounds and deer to Mr F Riley-Smith in 1900. The best centre for hunting was Bury St Edmunds.

Ripley and Knaphill Harriers

The Ripley and Knaphill Harriers used to hunt roe in Swinley Forest, near Windsor *c.*1899, but it is not certain how long this practice continued.

Roscommon Staghounds

County in which hunt operated: Co. Roscommon
Period of hunt's existence: 1874–1903
Kennels: South Park, Castlerea
Pack: fifteen and a half couple of hounds
Deer paddock: South Park, Castlerea. Fifteen deer were kept in the paddock.
Masters:
1874–90 Major Balfe
1890–1 Lord De Freyne
1891–2 Major Balfe
1892–3 Mr Talbot
1893–1900 Major Balfe
1900–1 Committee, with a Field Master
1901–3 George Jackson

History: The Roscommon Staghounds were established in 1874 by Major Balfe, who held the mastership until 1900, with the exception of the season 1890–1 (Lord De Freyne) and 1892–3 (Mr Talbot).

The country consisted almost wholly of pasture – no foxhound packs operated in the same area. The best centres were Roscommon, Castlerea and Boyle.

---

* In 1904 Mr Riley-Smith was relieved by Mr Eugene Wells, under whose name the pack then became known.

The hounds were the property of the Master who received a subscription of £600. A cap was taken.

Owing to agitation during the 1902–3 season, stag hunting was suspended, although during that period it seems that O W O'Grady Young, of Castlerea – the Honorary Secretary of the hunt – worked a small pack of draghounds in the Castlerea portion of the country.[8]

Lord Rothschild's Staghounds

County in which hunt mainly operated: Buckinghamshire
Period of hunt's existence: 1839–*c.*1918
Kennels: Originally at Mentmore, but moved to Ascot since *c.*1874.
Pack: About thirty couple of hounds, consisting of a high percentage of Belvoir strain. Doghounds stood about 24 to 24½ in. (61 to 62 cm). The bitches were invariably mated with staghounds, and never to foxhound.[48]
Deer paddock: Ascott, near Leighton Buzzard
Masters:
1839–74 Baron Meyer de Rothschild
1874–? Lord Rothschild and Leopold de Rothschild
1884–? Sir N de Rothschild
1899–1906 Lord Rothschild
1906–15 Lord Rothschild and Leopold de Rothschild
1915–17 Leopold de Rothschild
1917–18 Major Evelyn de Rothschild and Captain Anthony de Rothschild

History: This pack was established in 1839 (also given as 1844[30]) by Baron Meyer de Rothschild and throughout its existence it was maintained by a member of the Rothschild family.

Reg. Reynolds was the last huntsman of this pack.

In 1912 the country in the Vale of Aylesbury was described as 'a ditch and brook country, almost entirely sound old pasture. No wire worth mention, a committee of farmers attend to the removal of what exists, if necessary'.[10]

Hunting took place on Monday and Thursday, the best centres being Aylesbury, Leighton Buzzard and Winlow. The Whaddon Chase Foxhounds shared the same country.

Royal Buckhounds

Counties in which hunt operated: Berkshire and Buckinghamshire
Period of hunt's existence: *c.* 1703–1901
(Prior to this date the pack consisted of two branches – the Household or Privy Pack, which had been in existence since about 1528, and the Hereditary or Manorial Pack, which dated back to the fourteenth century.)
Kennels: Royal Kennels, Ascot, Berkshire
Pack: About forty couple of hounds
Deer paddock: Swinley, near Ascot, in which about twenty-five deer were kept
Masters: (since 1703) J P Hore gives a complete list of Masters from the reign of King Edward III to the reign of Queen Victoria, arranged in three groups:

(i) The Hereditary, or Manorial Pack, 1362–1707
(ii) The Household, or Privy Pack, 1528–1702
(iii) The United Pack, 1703–1895

For details of the Masters of the Hereditary or Manorial Pack, and of the Household or Privy Pack, see Hore, pages 389–90.[113]

1703–5 Sir Charles Shuckburg
1705–11 Walter, Viscount Chetwynd
1711–12 Sir William Wyndham
1712–15 George, Earl of Cardigan
1727–32 Colonel Francis Negus
1733–6 Charles, Earl of Tankerville
1737–44 Ralph Jenison
1744–46 Earl of Halifax
1746–57 Ralph Jenison
1757–82 (?) Viscount Bateman
*c.*1782 Earl of Jersey
*c.*1783 Viscount Hichingbroke, Earl of Sandwich
*c.*1806 Earl of Albemarle
*c.*1807 Marquis Cornwallis
*c.*1823 Lord Maryborough, Earl of Mornington
*c.*1830 Viscount Anson, Earl of Lichfield
*c.*1834 Earl of Chesterfield
*c.*1836 Earl of Errol
*c.*1841 Lord Kinnaird
*c.*1842 Earl of Rosslyn
*c.*1847 Earl of Granville
*c.*1849 Earl of Bessborough
*c.*1853 Earl of Rosslyn
*c.*1854 Earl of Bessborough
*c.*1859 Earl of Sandwich
*c.*1860 Earl of Bessborough
*c.*1867 Lord Colville of Culross
*c.*1869 Earl of Cork
*c.*1875 Earl of Hardwick
*c.*1881 Earl of Cork
*c.*1885 Marquis of Waterford
*c.*1886 Lord Suffield
*c.*1887 Earl of Coventry
*c.*1892 Lord Ribblesdale
*c.*1898 Earl of Coventry

History: Prior to the beginning of the eighteenth century there were two branches of the Buckhounds – the Hereditary or Manorial Pack being one, and the Household or Privy Pack being the other. In about 1703 these two branches merged to become the United Pack. For the full story of the Royal Buckhounds reference should be made to Hore's *The History of the Royal Buckhounds*[113] and also to Lord Ribblesdale's *The Queen's Hounds.*[160] Neither of these authorities, however, was able to record the sad end of the Royal Buckhounds, for this did not come about until 1901. Following increasing criticism of the cruelty of this form of sport in the press, King

Edward VII, on his accession to the throne, decided to disband it. As a result, His Majesty personally visited the newly appointed huntsman Frank Goodall, and handed him a cheque for £1000 as a solatium for early and unexpected dismissal.[50]

About 1823 the pack, owing to in-breeding, had sunk to pretty low levels and was sold to a Colonel Thornton who took it to France and disposed of it there. The pack was replaced with hounds from the Charlton Hunt, which were presented to the King by the Duke of Richmond.

On the disbandment of the Royal Buckhounds in 1901, the Berkshire and Buckinghamshire Farmer Harriers were converted into staghounds (q.v.) and hunted approximately the same country as the Royal Establishment.

Prior to about 1890 the Royal Buckhounds hunted an expanse of pasture known as the Harrow Country, but due to agitation from the farmers of the district, the Earl of Coventry, who was then Master, discontinued hunting in this hay country and devoted more time to hunting in Windsor Forest. In its later years among the most favoured meets of the Royal Buckhounds were those held at Uxbridge, Hillingden, Hayes, Beaconsfield, Brick Bridge and Ricking's Park.[80]

Rushmore Buckhounds

About the end of the eighteenth century Lord Rivers kept a pack of buckhounds with which he hunted the fallow buck in Cranborne Chase, Wiltshire.

Savernake Staghounds

Counties in which hunt operated: Wiltshire and Berkshire
Period of hunt's existence: c. 1898 and re-started in 1956–68
Kennels: Savernake Home Farm, Marlborough. Formerly at Durley, Savernake (1899)
Pack: At the end of the last century, about thirty to thirty-five couple, but when the hunt was re-started in 1956 only about fourteen couple were kept.
Masters:
Prior to 1898 E C Dawkins, Hooper Deacon, G W E Baring
1899–1900 J L Phipps
1956–68 Lady Rosemary Brudenell Bruce

History: This pack was re-started in 1956 but after only twelve years was finally disbanded in 1968. Previously hounds had been kept by the sixth Marquess of Ailsbury for hunting outlying deer around Savernake Forest. Meets took place twice weekly. Records of previous family packs go back many centuries.

During its twelve-year existence after the war, this private pack met on one day (Wednesday) in the week, there being no subscription or cap. In 1899, however, days of meting were 'uncertain'.[7]

South Coast Staghounds

County in which hunt mainly operated: Sussex
Period of hunt's existence: 1889–*c.* 1902 (deer hunted only from 1897)

Kennels: The Elms, Bedhampton, near Havant. In 1900 the kennels were moved to Hope Cottage, Patching, near Worthing.
Pack: About fifteen couple of hounds (21 in. (33 cm) foxhound bitches)
Deer paddock: Chidham, near Emsworth. Six red deer hinds usually kept in the paddock.
Master: 1889–1902 H G Kay

History: Mr H G Kay established a pack of harriers in 1889 and hunted a very wide extent of country from Cosham to Shoreham; in 1897 he changed from hare to deer.[7] Much of the country in Sussex was formerly hunted by the Goodwood Foxhounds. During the existence of the South Coast Staghounds part of their country was shared with the Hambledon Foxhounds.

By 1901 deer were being hunted on Fridays and hares on Tuesdays – the latter in the country between Ford and Shoreham, and the deer between Arundel and Chichester, which was the country over which the Goodwood Foxhounds originally operated.

The South Coast was a subscription pack with a minimum subscription of £5 and a 10s. (50 pence) cap. Meets took place one day a week, the best centres being Portsmouth, Havant and Chichester.

South Westmeath Staghounds

County in which hunt operated: Co. Westmeath
Period of hunt's existence: 1889–*c.* 1907
Kennels: Ballykiernan, Athlone
Pack: Twenty to twenty-five couple of hounds (23 in. (58–59 cm) harriers and foxhounds)
Deer paddock: Hall Moate. Ten deer normally kept.
Masters:
1889–92 H B Adderley
1892–5 R Hudson
1895–7 Lord Castlemaine
1897–9 The Hon. R A Handcock
1899–1907 Edward Wakefield

History: The South Westmeath Staghounds were established in 1889 to hunt the southern part of Co. Westmeath. Their country consisted of about three-quarters pasture, the remainder being made up of woodland, moorland and a little plough, with Moate being the best centre. The Westmeath Foxhounds hunted over part of it.

The pack, which hunted twice a week, was the property of a committee, the minimum subscription being three guineas a year. A 2s. 6d. ($12\frac{1}{2}$ pence) cap was taken.

Lee Steere's Staghounds

Counties in which hunt operated: Surrey and Sussex
Period of hunt's existence: *c.* 1840–65
Kennels: Crawley, Sussex
Master: H Lee Steere

History: About 1840 Mr H Lee Steere of Hale House, Ockley, who had previously hunted a pack of harriers which followed both hare and fox, started a pack of staghounds, and for about the next twenty-five years, hunted the carted deer in parts of Surrey and Sussex. Mr Lee Steere kept about twelve deer for hunting in his paddocks.

When the pack was given up in 1865 no-one seems to have taken over either the hounds or the deer, but within two years another pack of staghounds was hunting the carted deer in this part of England – Mr W Farnell Watson's Staghounds (q.v.).

The Lee Steere family were also associated with the Warnham Staghounds which were formed out of Mr Farnell Watson's Staghounds, H Lee Steere being Master 1889–90 and H C Lee Steere 1890–1917.

Sturt's Staghounds

The Norwich Hunt, which was supported by the Norwich Sportsmen's Society, under Mr Sturt, was sometimes referred to as Sturt's Staghounds. It operated in Norfolk *c.*1793, but no details are available.

Lord Suffield's Staghounds

County in which hunt operated: East Norfolk
*Period of hunt's existence: c.*1836

History: Little is known of this pack which was formed by the fourth Lord Suffield and seems to have had a very short existence.

About sixteen years later, however, the fifth Lord Suffield formed the Gunton Staghounds (q.v.) in 1854, but this pack seems to have flourished only for about two or three years.

Suffolk Staghounds

County in which hunt operated: Suffolk
*Period of hunt's existence: c.*1883

History: Little information is available, except an entry in an old *Hunting Directory* to the effect that Charles Chaston was Master of the Suffolk Staghounds in 1883. Charles Chaston was also Master of the Norfolk and Suffolk Staghounds, as well the Waveney Harriers, so doubtless it referred to the former pack.

Surrey Staghounds

Counties in which hunt operated: Surrey, Kent and Sussex
*Period of hunt's existence: c.*1851 to 1915
*Kennels: c.*1870, Smitham Bottom, Coulsdon
*c.*1893, Horleylands, Horley
Pack: Generally, about twenty-five to twenty-six couple of hounds, but in 1912 the pack numbered fifty-two couple. They were described as having rather weighty shoulders, a tendency to throatiness and had length in body. They averaged as a pack about 23 in. (58–59 cm) full as against the 25 or $25\frac{1}{2}$ in. (64 to 65 cm) of former years.[27]
Deer paddock: Originally in Carshalton Park, but transferred to Holtye in Kent about 1908.
Masters: Early in the nineteenth century to 1851, a committee, with John

Shaw acting as Field Master.*

1851–69 Arthur Heathcote
1869–78 Mosse Robinson
1878–94 Tom Nickalls
1894–1901 Fred Gregory
1901–15 Captain McTaggart

History: During the early part of the last century the 14th Earl of Derby started a pack of staghounds (q.v.) with kennels at The Oaks, Woodmansterne, and with almost limitless country over which to hunt, stretching from London in the north, practically to the sea at Brighton in the south. When Lord Derby gave up his hounds in about 1851 the pack then assumed the name of the Surrey Staghounds.

According to Charles Armstrong[50] some parts of the country over which the hunt operated were 'not exactly adapted for superior hunting of any kind, whilst, in other parts one might imagine himself riding over lovely Northamptonshire'. Their country, however, covered parts of three counties – Surrey, Sussex and Kent, and consisted of about one half pasture, a third plough and the remainder wood and moorland.

The Surrey Staghounds were a subscription pack, the minimum subscription in 1898 being twenty-five guineas for one day per week, with a full subscription possible by arrangement. A cap of one sovereign was taken – the Master had no guarantee.[7] Twelve years later the subscription was twenty-five guineas for a season, with a £1 cap.[10]

Meets took place on three days a week, Tuesday, Thursday and Saturday, Redhill being the best centre.

By 1910 the country, owing to the increase in building, was gradually becoming more cramped, with the open country getting further from London. The best part was then in the Godstone Valley, Edenbridge and Bolney districts. Hunting was suspended during the First World War and was not resumed at the end of hostilities.

The deer: The deer were originally kept at Carshalton Park which, at the end of the last century, was the home of John F W B Taylor. In this 140-acre park the number of red deer seems to have varied from about fifty in 1907 to about one hundred hinds, calves and haviers in 1899, one half of which were running deer.[7] There were also some fallow deer, about forty in number, but these were not hunted. These fallow were the descendants of the original deer in the park which was enclosed in about 1746. The red deer were probably introduced about the time of the establishment of the Surrey Staghounds just prior to the middle of the last century, but no mention is made by Shirley of their presence there in 1867.[174]

During the last few years of its existence, the Surrey Staghounds kept their deer at Holyte in Kent.

Surrey Farmers' Staghounds

See West Surrey Staghounds.

---

* The last surviving member of this committee was John Shaw, who was born in 1803 and died in 1900. John Shaw has often been described as the 'Father of the Surrey Hunt'.[50]

Sussex Staghounds

County in which hunt operated: Sussex
Period of hunt's existence: c.1930–31
Kennels: Astley House, Lewes
Pack: Twenty-two couple
Master: T Walls

History: These hounds hunted over portions of Sussex which were previously hunted over by the Warnham Staghounds and the Surrey Staghounds. Unfortunately the Master, Tom Walls, sustained a serious fall, and after but a brief existence the hunt was given up.

The best centres were Lewes, Hassocks and Haywards Heath; meets were on Tuesdays and Saturdays.

The subscription was fifteen guineas (twenty-five guineas for a married couple) and a cap of two guineas.

Templemore Staghounds

Counties in which hunt operated: Co. Tipperary, Co. Leix and Co. Offaly
Period of hunt's existence: c. 1879–1908
Kennels: (prior to 1903) Lloydsboro, Templemore
1903–78 Brittas, Thirles
Pack: About twenty couple of hounds
Deer paddock: Prior to 1903 at Lloydsboro, Templemore
1903–8 Brittas, Thirles
About twelve red deer were kept
Masters:
1879–85 CD Webb
1885–92 G Jackson
1892–4 Captain Birch
1894–6 HJ Butler
1896–1900 Captain Lloyd
1900–1 George Jackson
1901–3 A committee
1903–8 F Knox

History: The Templemore Staghounds were established in 1879, by CD Webb, when Sir John Carden gave up his pack of harriers, and for the next six years Mr Webb hunted hares, or a fox if one was found. Then in 1886 Mr Jackson started to hunt deer and fox alternately, and this practice continued until 1896 when Captain Lloyd converted the pack to staghounds.

The Templemore country covered some 672 square miles and extended into the counties of Tipperary, King's (Co. Offaly) and Queen's (Co. Leix). It consisted almost wholly of pasture with very little plough, wood or moorland. Two packs of foxhounds also operated in the same area – namely the Earl of Huntingdon's and the Tipperary Foxhounds.

The Templemore was a subscription pack, and apparently met on Tuesdays and Fridays in counties Leix and Offaly, and once a month on Monday, Thursday and Saturday, in Co. Tipperary.[7]

Earl of Thanet's Staghounds

Little information is known about these staghounds except that at the beginning of the last century the Earl's pack hunted a stag that had been turned out of Whinfield Park as far as Red Kirks, near Annan in Scotland, before returning to Whinfield Park – a circular distance estimated at over eighty miles. But this long hunt proved fatal to both stag and the only two hounds that had kept up with it, for after leaping the park wall, the stag fell dead from exhaustion, as did also the two hounds following, shortly before reaching the wall.

Tilney Staghounds

County in which hunt operated: Essex
Period of hunt's existence: c.1760
Master: Earl Tilney

History: The original pack of the Essex Staghounds (q.v.) is supposed to have been kept at Tilney House by Earl Tilney and to have been known as the Tilney Staghounds. The Earl died in 1784, but some little time before that the pack had been disposed of to some sporting residents of the district.

Tiverton Staghounds

County in which hunt operates: Devon
Period of hunt's existence: 1896 and still extant
Kennels: Formerly at Alswear, South Molton, but subsequently moved to Leigh Barton, Loxbear, near Tiverton. Recently Mouseberry Farm, Worlington (near Witheridge) has been purchased and permanent kennels installed for the pack.
Pack: About fifteen couple. At the beginning of the century the pack consisted of about twenty-five couple.
Masters:
1896–1911 Sir J J H Heathcoat-Amory
1911–15 Captain H H Heathcoat-Amory
1915–19 C Slader
1919–34 J Yandle
1934–5 P Yandle
1935–46 P and A Yandle
1946–51 F J Ellicott
1951–7 T Pennington
1957–8 T Pennington and K Webber
1958–68 A H P Besley and A L Hosegood
1968–9 A H P Besley and Mrs A H P Besley
1969–78 Committee: Acting Masters, S C Gillbard and T R S Venner
1978–80 Committee: Acting Masters, J Lucas and T R S Venner

History: This pack, formerly referred to as Sir John Amory's Staghounds, was established in 1896 as an offshoot of the Devon and Somerset Staghounds in order to hunt the deer which were increasing and causing damage in the Stoodleigh Court district, Tiverton.

Most of the country lay south of the Barnstaple to Taunton railway but in 1897 some country north of the railway line was also included.

Prior to the formation of the Quantock Staghounds by Mr E A V Stanley in 1901, the Tiverton Staghounds used to visit the Quantock Hills and on average killed about three deer each season in that area.

About half of the country is moorland, the remainder plough, woodland and pasture. The Tiverton and Dulverton Foxhounds hunt part of the country.

In 1979–80 the annual family subscription was £40, whilst a combined mounted and car follower subscription was £30 plus VAT. The cap was £7 on stag hunting days, £5 for hind hunting, both inclusive of V.A.T.

The best centres for this hunt are: Tiverton, Dulverton, Witheridge, Bampton and Chulmleigh. Meets usually take place on Wednesdays and Saturdays for hind hunting, whilst for stags there will probably be three days a fortnight, on Monday, Saturday and Wednesday.

Union Hunt

Counties in which hunt operated: South Norfolk and north Suffolk
Period of hunt's existence: c.1827

History: Little is known about the activities of this hunt which was primarily a harrier pack but, apparently, hunted the occasional deer. One such occasion was on 17 March 1827 when hounds hunted a deer near Hempnault presented for the occasion by Alexander Adair. This pack subsequently became known as the Henham Harriers.[98]

H Villebois' Staghounds

County in which hunt operated: West Suffolk
Period of hunt's existence: c.1837–41
Master: H Villebois

History: Mr H Villebois commenced hunting with a pack of harriers in 1827 but ten years later it seems that the carted deer was their more usual quarry.

The exact date Mr H Villebois gave up his pack is not known, but it was probably about 1841 or 1842, for about that time he disposed of some, if not all, of his deer to Captain J Anstruther Thomson for the 13th Light Dragoon Staghounds[98] (q.v.).

John Walter's Deer Hounds

During the eighteenth century John Walters of Stevenstone had a pack of hounds with which he hunted the deer around Torrington and Hatherleigh in Devon.

Ward Hounds

In about 1830 two foxhound packs – the Dubber and the Hollywood – amalgamated and became known as the Ward. For a time the Ward hunted bagged foxes, but when Mr Peter Alley of Newpark became Master, the pack changed to hunting first fallow, and then red deer. About 1854 the Garrison Staghounds amalgamated with the Ward Hounds and the combined pack became known as the Ward Union.

Ward Union Staghounds

Counties in which hunt operates: Co. Dublin and Co. Meath
Period of hunt's existence: (Under present name) Since about 1854 and still extant
Kennels: Since 1864, Ashbourne, Co. Meath
Hounds: Varied between thirty-five couple in 1898 to about twenty-one in 1950
Deer paddocks: At the end of the last century the deer, about forty-three in number, which had more than doubled themselves by 1912, were being kept at Howth Castle Park, which was formerly the home of J Gaisford St Lawrence, but most of the park has now been built over and no deer remain. For a number of years the deer were then kept at Ratoath Manor, Co. Meath, during the winter months and at Slane Castle, Navan, during the summer. This practice was abandoned, however, after the First World War, and for the next forty years the deer were kept at Slane Castle which belonged to the Marquis of Conyngham.

In 1960 the deer were removed to the kennels at Ashbourne where a ten-acre (4 hectare) wired-in enclosure has been erected.
Masters: Masters of the Ward Union since its amalgamation in 1854:
1854–63 Peter Alley
1863–4 Charles Alley
1864–6 Captain Montgomery
1866–83 Leonard Morrogh
1883–90 E C Wellesley
1890–1919 P Maynard
1919–25 T L Moore
1925–39 Justice Wylie
1939–48 A L Moore
1948–9 A L Moore and G V Malcolmson
1949–50 A L Moore
1950–59 G V Malcolmson
1959–62 G V Malcolmson and E Craigie
1962–6 Eric Craigie and S W N Collen
1966–7 Eric Craigie, S W N Collen and Raymond A Keogh
1967–9 Raymond A Keogh and T F Roe
1969–70 Raymond A Keogh
1970–73 Raymond A Keogh, J R Craigie and T C Mangan
1973–5 Raymond A Keogh, J R Craigie, T C Mangan and Denis Coakley
1975–9 Raymond A Keogh, J Roy Craigie, Denis Coakley and F J Duffy

History: The pack takes its name from Ward, a hamlet and river in Finglas Parish, Dublin, and a roadside hotel, The Union.[29] In 1828 there were two packs hunting the present Ward Union country – the Dubber and Hollywood. It would appear that under the mastership of Mr Gerard of the Bay, these two packs amalgamated in 1830 and became known as the Ward Hounds.[7] In about 1834 the Ward Hounds were hunted by Captain J Stanley who, in turn, handed the pack over in 1836 to Peter Alley of New Park. Prior to 1836 the Ward Hounds had hunted bagged foxes, but under Mr Alley's mastership the hunt changed first to fallow deer, and later to red deer.

In about 1840 Lord Howth brought Mr Broadley's Staghounds over from Leamington and hunted them with a subscription until, in 1848, the pack was sold to the Dublin Garrison and for the next few years was known as the Garrison Hounds. Following the outbreak of war in the Crimea, the pack was amalgamated about 1854 with the Ward Hounds and the name of the Ward Union Hunt first came into existence.

The Ward Union country, which is shared with the Meath Foxhounds, lies in Co. Dublin and Co. Meath and sometimes part of Co. Kildare, the best centre being Dublin. Formerly the country was nearly all grass but since the Second World War there has been a considerable increase in the amount under tillage.

Present subscriptions (1978–9 season) are £50 for farmers and £100 for all others, as compared to £15 and £25 respectively about twelve years ago. The cap is £3 per day, with visitors paying £15 per day. Prior to the First World War there were three meets per week, but nowadays hounds are hunted twice weekly.

The deer: In 1948 there were eighty red deer and thirty fallow deer in Slane Castle Park (about 350 acres – 140 hectares). Included among the former were fifteen haviers which were used for hunting (carted deer). Stags are generally castrated as yearlings and up to three years old.

In 1940, and again in 1964, some hinds were obtained from the Co. Down Staghounds, who keep their deer at Montalto, Ballynahinch. Before the Second World War, a few deer were obtained from Warnham Park, Sussex, which park has also supplied fourteen stags and thirteen hinds since 1954, the last consignment, consisting of two stags and four hinds, being received in 1974.

About 1960, owing to quarrying in part of Slane Park which resulted in the park walls being damaged and many deer escaping, it was decided to remove the remnants of the herd to a new wired-in enclosure of about ten acres (4 hectares), which had been erected at the Kennels at Ashbourne.

Warnham Staghounds

Counties in which hunt operated: Surrey and Sussex
Period of hunt's existence: (under name of Warnham Staghounds) 1882–1917*
Kennels: Ockley, near Dorking
Pack: Twenty-two couple of hounds, size about 23 in. (58–59 cm) high
Deer paddock: Warnham Court, near Horsham, Sussex. About twenty-two deer were kept in the enclosure.
Masters:
1882–9 A Labouchere
1889–90 H Lee Steere
1890–1917 H C Lee Steere

History: Prior to 1882 a private pack of staghounds had operated in Surrey and Sussex since about 1840 – first under the mastership of H Lee Steere (q.v.) *c.*1840–65, and then under Farnell Watson Sr 1867–79 and W Farnell Watson, Jr, 1880–2 (*see next entry*).

When Mr Farnell Watson relinquished the mastership of his private pack he presented the hounds to a small committee who appointed Mr A

* No hunting during the war, and the hunt was not re-started afterwards.

Labouchere as Master and for the first time the pack, which was now a subscription pack, became known as the Warnham Staghounds.

The Surrey Union, Crawley and Horsham and Lord Leconfield's packs hunted over portions of the Warnham Staghound country. The minimum subscription was £25 with a £1 cap.

Farnell Watson's Staghounds

Counties in which hunt operated: Surrey and Sussex
Period of hunt's existence: 1867–82
Kennels: Henfield
Masters:
1867–79 W Farnell Watson, Sr
1880–82 W Farnell Watson, Jr

History: Since about 1840 Mr H Lee Steere had been hunting a pack of staghounds in Sussex, the quarry being the carted deer, but this was disposed of in 1865. Shortly after Mr Steere had given up his pack, Mr Farnell Watson of Henfield, who had previously had his own pack of harriers, used these same hounds, together with a gift of six couple of the Brookside Harriers which had formerly belonged to Mr Lee Steere, to hunt the deer. Mr Farnell Watson obtained his initial stock of deer from Mr Lucas of Warnham Court, near Horsham and from Sir Clifford Constable in Yorkshire.

Mr Farnell Watson died in November 1879 and was succeeded in the mastership by his son – also called W Farnell Watson – who did not recommence hunting until 1880. Two years later Mr W Farnell Watson handed over the pack to a small committee, who appointed Mr A Labouchere as Master and from that date the pack became known as the Warnham Staghounds (*see previous entry*).

Waveney Staghounds

The Norfolk and Suffolk Staghounds (q.v.), under the mastership of Mr Charles Chaston in about 1873, were sometimes referred to by this name.

T L Wellesley's Staghounds

County in which hunt operated: Essex
Period of hunt's existence: c.1810
Master: T Long Wellesley

History: This was a private pack owned and hunted by Mr Tilney Long Wellesley, which was kennelled at Wanstead House. But the extravagance of Mr Wellesley's menage was too lavish to last. He kept forty or fifty horses, arrayed his hunt servants in Lincoln green and spent his money so freely that it was not long before he had to flee from his creditors by escaping, in an open boat, down the Thames one dark night. His wife died from worry, the Court of Chancery deprived him of the custody of his children, and for the remainder of his life he lived on the bounty of his great soldier-uncle, the 'Iron Duke'.[27]

Eugene Wells' Staghounds

County in which hunt operated: West Suffolk
Period of hunt's existence (under title of Eugene Wells' Staghounds) 1904–6

Kennels: Buxhall Vale, Stowmarket
Pack: Twenty couple of hounds
Deer paddocks:
Nether Hall, Bury St Edmunds
Buxhall Vale, Stowmarket (1905–6)
Fifteen deer were kept
Master: Eugene Wells

History: This pack was formed by Sir (then Mr) E Walter Greene in 1864 who, apart from a period of nineteen years (1870–89) when stag hunting was suspended, hunted hounds until relinquishing the mastership in 1900 in favour of Mr F Riley-Smith. Mr Eugene Wells took over the mastership from Mr Riley-Smith in 1904 but hunted the pack only for about three seasons before handing over to Mr WP Burton in 1906.

This was a private pack with no subscription or cap.

West Suffolk Staghounds

County in which hunt operated: West Suffolk
Period of hunt's existence: (under name of West Suffolk Staghounds) 1911–21
Kennels: Gedding Hall, Bury St Edmunds
Pack: About twenty couple of hounds
Deer paddocks: Nether Hall, Bury St Edmunds
Masters: (since pack became known as West Suffolk Staghounds):*
1911–14 WP Burton and P Middleditch
1914–15 P Middleditch and Miss Partridge
1915–21 P Middleditch

History: This pack was originally formed by Sir (then Mr) E Walter Greene in 1864, when it was known as Mr Greene's Staghounds. Then, for about the next twenty-eight years, apart from a period of about nineteen years (1870–89) when the pack was temporarily suspended, this private pack changed its name with each mastership until, in 1911, it became known as the West Suffolk Staghounds under the joint mastership of Messrs WP Burton and P Middleditch. Prior to that date, since 1906 it had been known as Mr WP Burton's Staghounds.

About twenty deer were kept at Nether Hall by kind permission of Sir Walter Greene, the owner.

The country hunted over was practically the same as that of the Suffolk Foxhounds.

West Surrey Staghounds

County in which hunt operated: West Surrey
Period of hunt's existence: c.1885–1907

* Previous masters, under whose name the pack took its title, had been:
1864–70 E Walter Greene (later Sir)
1889–1900 Sir Walter Greene (the first date is also given as 1891[7])
1900–4 F Riley-Smith
1904–6 Eugene Wells
1906–11 WP Burton.

Kennels:
*c.*1880 Motspur Park, Old Malden
*c.*1886 Acre Hill, Chessington
*c.*1898 Woodlands Park, Leatherhead
*c.*1900 Chessington
Pack: Twenty couple of hounds
Deer paddock:
*c.*1898 Woodlands Park, Leatherhead
*c.*1900 Chessington (twenty deer)
Masters:
*c.*1885 Squire Blake
1888–91 Sir David Evans
1892–4 WJ Twigg
1894–5 A committee
1895–6 EH d'Avigdor
1896–9 A committee, with MD Rucker as Master
1899–1903 AJ Curnick
1903–7 EW Robinson

History: The origin of this pack of staghounds was the Morden Harriers during the mastership of Squire Blake, with kennels at Motspur Park, Old Malden. Some years prior to being transformed into staghounds, they hunted deer once a week, which were kept near the kennels.[27]

In 1886 the pack hunted stag regularly under the name of the Surrey Farmers' Staghounds, and the kennels were removed to Acre Hill, Chessington. The hunt assumed the title of the West Surrey Staghounds in 1894, and continued for another thirteen years before the hounds were sold and the establishment given up in 1907. During these years the kennels were moved twice, once to Woodlands Park about 1898 and then to Chessington in 1900.

The hunt kept about twenty to thirty deer in their paddock.

The minimum subscription was fifteen guineas, a cap being taken.

Westacre Staghounds

County in which hunt operated: West Norfolk
*Period of hunt's existence: c.*1821–9
Kennels: Swaffham
Pack: Black coloured hounds which originally came from Jamaica, with a strong strain of bloodhound.
Deer paddock: Swaffham Heath
Master: The Rev. Robert Hamond

History: A notice, advertising the sale of the pack, appeared at the first Newmarket meeting on 22 April 1829

Greswolde Williams' Staghounds

Early in the century a pack of hounds belonging to Mr Greswolde Williams was hunting the carted deer in the Malverns, but no other information is available concerning the activities of this private pack.

Lord Wolverton's Bloodhounds

See Ranston Bloodhounds.

Yeatman's Harriers

Mr yeatman, of Stockhouse, hunted both roe and hares with the same pack of hounds in Dorset during the last century.

Glossary of Ancient & Modern Terms used in connection with Deer & their Habitat

'There was a peculiar kind of Language invented by Sportsmen of the Middle Ages,' wrote the Reverend W B David, 'which it was necessary for them to be acquainted with.'

The following is a list of some of these ancient and modern terms. The language of sport has a considerable vocabulary, but in the main only those terms which are connected with deer, their pursuit and their habitat, have been included. It will be noticed that some ancient terms, such as antler, royal, etc., are not given the same interpretation today, whilst others, such as brocket and espeyard (used to denote the age of a deer) have not been used consistently among the various authorities.

In the compilation of this Glossary the following authorities – arranged in order of date – have been consulted.

EDWARD, Second Duke of York, *The Master of Game* (*c.*1410)
DAME JULIANA BERNERS, *The Boke of St Albans* (1486)
G. TURBERVILLE, *The Noble Art of Venerie or Hunting* (1576)
NICHOLAS COX, *The Gentleman's Recreation* (1721) 6th edn
W. OSBALDISTON, *The British Sportsman* (1792)
JOSEPH STRUTT, *The Sport and Pastimes of the People of England* (1801)
REV. W B DANIEL, *Rural Sports* (1801)
H J PYE, *The Sportsman's Dictionary* (1807)
JOHN SOBIESKI and CHARLES EDWARD STUART, *Lays of the Deer Forest*, Vol. II (1848)
J E HARTING, *Essays on Sport and Natural History* (1883)
LT.-COL. H H CREALOCK, *Deer-stalking in the Highlands of Scotland* (1892)
'SNAFFLE', *The Roedeer* (1904)
REV. W H P GRESWELL, *The Forests and Deer Parks of the County of Somerset* (1905)
LT.-COL. J R HARVEY, *Deer Hunting in Norfolk* (1910)
ERIC PARKER, *Game Pie* (1925)
J B THOMAS, *Hounds and Hunting through the Ages* (1934)
C E HARE, *The Language of Field Sports* (1949) revised edn
THE BADMINTON DIARY (1962)
G KENNETH WHITEHEAD, *Deer Stalking in Scotland* (1964)
G KENNETH WHITEHEAD, *The Deer of Great Britain and Ireland* (1964)
F J TAYLOR PAGE (Editor), *Field Guide to British Deer* (1971), 2nd edn
DONALD and NORMA CHAPMAN, *Fallow Deer* (1975)

Glossary

*Note: Terms in **bold italics** are in modern use.*

A

Abaiters A head that is going back – see **abate**
Abate Going back – i.e. a deer's head that has lost points, or is losing size due to old age
Abatures Places where deer have lain and pressed down the herbage
Aber 'Making the aber' – i.e. disembowelling. Modern term ***gralloch***
Account Hunted game is said to be accounted for when killed
Advancer Upper forward tine (tray) on fallow buck head
Affeted Proportioned, in relation to a deer's head
Agist Literally a bed or resting place, thus signifying a place to take in and feed the cattle of strangers in the forest
Agistment Signifies the herbage of lands or woods, or money received for same
Agistor One of the officials of a royal forest that takes beasts to dispasture within the forest. This post is still retained in the New Forest
Alaunts Ferocious breed of hound used for both hunting and as a war dog
All on When every hound in the pack is present, the whipper-in reports to the huntsman '*All on*'
Anal tush see ***tush*** (***anal***)
Anointing post Tree on which an area of trunk is oily and worn smooth by deer depositing scent
Antler Deer carry ***antlers*** – not horns. Antlers are normally carried only by the male deer, but in the case of the reindeer and caribou it is usual for the females to have them also. In two species – the water-deer and musk deer – neither sex ever bears antlers
Antler The brow tine – the first branch of a male deer's **attire**, was formerly called the **antler**
Assart Plucking up those woods that are thickets, by the roots, in order to convert the land into arable pasture
Assemble Deer assemble for the **rut**
At bay see ***bay***
At force see **hunting at force**
At lodge Deer resting is said to be **at lodge**
Attachment The Court of Attachment, or the **Woodmote** Court, is one of the three Courts of the Forest
Attire The **head** or **antlers** of a deer
Advancer see **advancer**

B

Bachelor group Herd of male deer
Back-antler Rear tine of fallow buck head
Backer see **bater**
Back-tine see **back-antler**
Bailiwick District
Bald-faced White blaze down face of deer
Baldrick Sling for hunting horn

Bare-buck Five-year-old fallow buck

Bark Typical sound made by a roe deer and muntjac. Red deer also bark on occasions

Basal snag Spiked tine at base of deer's antlers

Bate see ***going back***

Bater Stag with head having gone back to two or four points, i.e. a ***switch*** type of head

Battue Deer drive

Bay The second point of a deer's antlers – also spelt **beas**, **bez**, **biz-antler**. On moose antlers, the indentation behind the brow palmation

Bay The cry of a hound

Bay, at Stag nearing the end of a hunt, stands **at bay** to face the hounds

Beadle Officer of a royal forest

Beam Main stem of antlers

Beam The circumference of the **antler** – generally measured between the **bay** and **tray** tines – or if the former is absent, between the **brow** and **tray** tines at the thinnest circumference, is often referred to as the **beam**

Beam, lower Circumference of red deer antler between bay and tray tines at the thinnest place

Beam, upper Circumference of red deer antler at thinnest place above tray tine

Beamed-head Head of a stag in its seventh year was often described as **beamed** or **branched**

Beamed-frontlet Head of matured stag

Beas Manwood[132] refers to the **brow** tine as **beas**. See ***bay*** also

Beat An area of a forest under the jurisdiction of a forester

Beat A drive for deer or other game sometimes referred to as **beat**

Beaters Men used to drive game to hunters

Beat-up Hunted deer walking, trotting or even swimming up-stream

Beating-up Replacement of failure and losses in a plantation (Forestry term)

Beauty points Additional points awarded to a trophy for colour, pearling, etc., when measured under the C.I.C. formula

Bed Where a deer lies down is said to be his **bed** or his **harbour**

Bedded A roe was said to be **bedded**, whereas a stag is ***harboured*** and a fallow buck **lodged**

Bedel An officer of the forest whose duty was to warn all the Courts of the Forest and make all Proclamations, etc.

Beds A roe, retiring to rest, **beds**

Bed-up see **bed**

Bell (Belleth) The sound made by a red deer stag during the rut, also **belling**. Modern term ***roar***

Belloweth The roe deer, in ancient terminology, **belloweth**. **Bellowing** has also been used to describe the sound made by the red deer stag during rutting time – see also **bell**

Berner Man in charge of hounds – could be either huntsman or kennelman

Beue, beuy see **beve**

Beve Collective term for six or more roe deer – variously spelt **beue**, **beuy**, **bevy** or **bey**

Bevy see **beve**
Bevy grease The fat of a roe deer
Bey Collective term for roe deer – see also **beve**
Bey Alternative spelling for **bay** tine – see ***bay***
Bez palm Second point of caribou antler
Biche Female red deer in her third year – also **bise**
Bise see **biche**
Biz-antler Ancient spelling for bay tine – see ***Bay***
Black-antler The rear tine of a fallow buck's antler, occasionally referred to as such – see also **back-antler**
Black stag One that has been rolling in a peat hag or bog
Blanche Term for heading back game
Blanches Tricks of a hunted deer
Blaze Mark or gash on tree for guidance in a wood. See also **blemishes**. Could also describe white face of deer – see ***bald-faced***
Blemish Hounds returning to point where they first took up the hunt
Blemishes Marks – Often **blazes** or gashes on a tree, for guidance in a wood
Blench The ruse of a hunted stag to push up another deer to take its place
Blinks Broken boughs for marking in which direction a deer has run
Block An area in a forest, often delineated by ***rides***
Blooding deer Refers to young male deer that was hunted in order to introduce young hounds to buck hunting
Blooding hounds Giving hounds the paunch or gralloch of dead deer to devour
Blue hind Hind that has not bred the previous season – see also ***yeld***
Bokeying Rut of the roe deer
Boone and Crockett Club Organization formed by Theodore Roosevelt to foster the ideals of conservation and sportsmanship in big game hunting with a rifle
Boss Coronet or base of antler. Also wide base of buffalo or musk ox horns
Bossets The small knobs of a ***knobber*** stag's head
Boundary Forests must be bounded by **marks** and **meers**. Modern term for boundary of a Scottish deer forest is ***march***
Bow-bearer A junior officer of the forest whose task was to make Inquisition of any trespass done
Brace Group name for two fallow bucks – see also **leash**
Brace Two greyhounds – see also **couple**, **leash**
Brace Description of a pair of game birds
Brach Used to refer to bitch hounds
Braches Scenting hounds, taken in couples by the berners – also spelt **raches**, **ratches**
Braggard Pregnant hind or doe
Branche, branched The head of a stag was described as **branched** in its seventh year
Branches The points or tines of a stag's antlers, sometimes referred to as **branches**

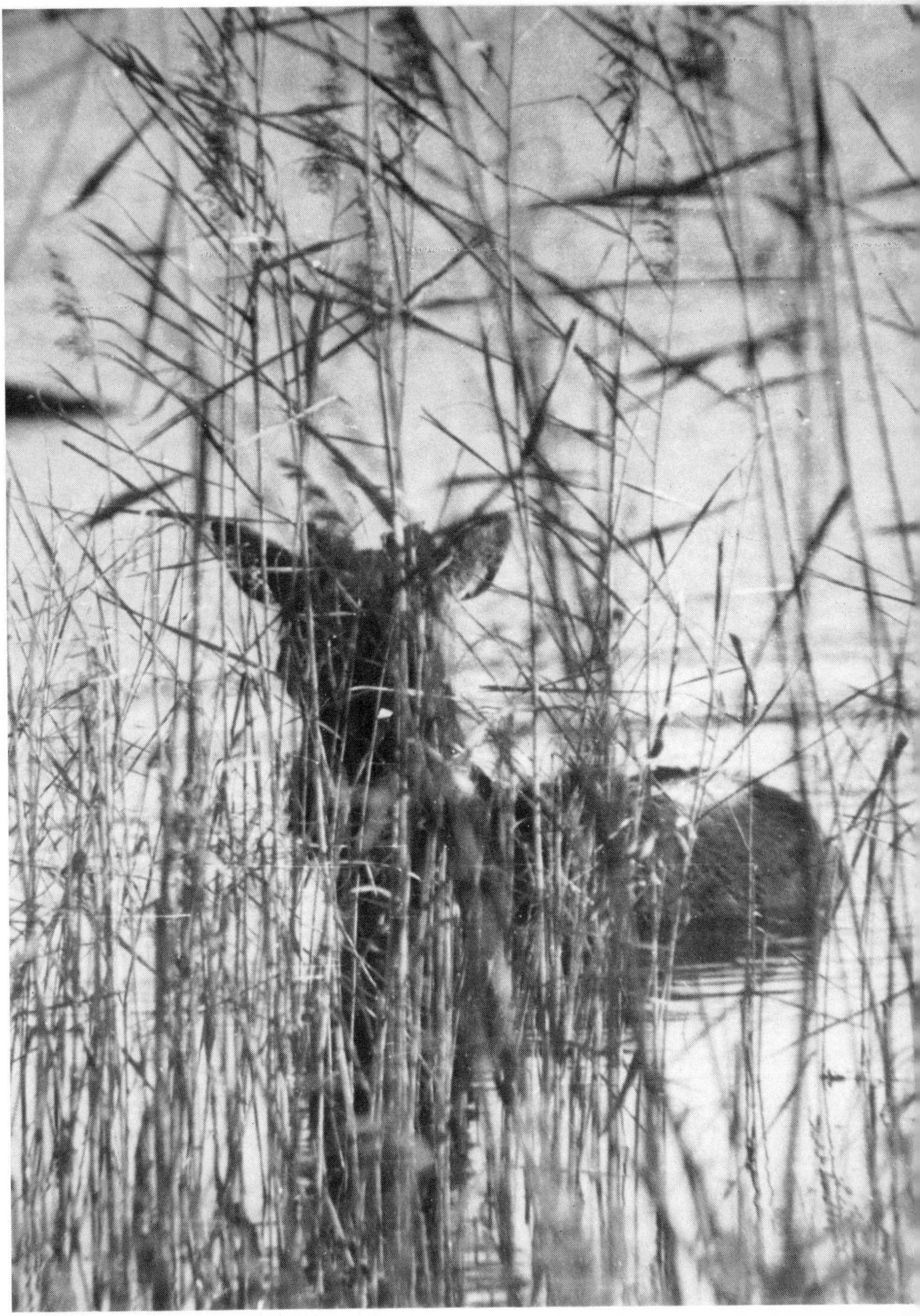

40 At the end of a hunt the stag frequently stands at bay in water

41 Rod and noose used by the Co. Down Hunt for taking deer in water

42 Close-up of the noose

41 Rod and noose used by the Co. Down Hunt for taking deer in water

42 Close-up of the noose

40 At the end of a hunt the stag frequently stands at bay in water

43 Stag being taken by boat; Co. Down Staghounds

44 Fallow buck

45 New Forest Buckhounds; returning to the kennels after a day's hunting

46 Hounds in full cry

47 *Left* Roe buck in August

48 *Above* Sika deer stag

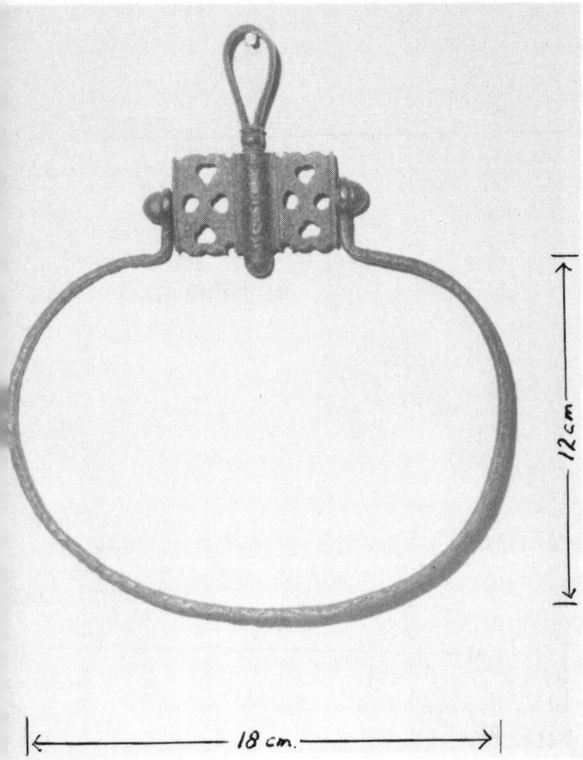

49 *Top left* Dog gauge used in the Forest of Blackburn to decide whether a dog should be 'lawed' or not

50 & 51 Man-traps were formerly used to deter poachers from entering the forests, but their use was prohibited in 1827. The usual type of man-trap (*above*) had large spikes set at intervals along the jaws; the other photograph (*top right*) shows the so-called humane trap with plain jaws

Brashing Removal of the lower branches of a plantation at the end of the thicket stage

Braunch The brow point of a fallow buck's head

Break A wide **ride** separating a forest into blocks

Break-out A hunted deer, when leaving a covert, is said to **break-out**

Break-up To cut up a deer – see also **brittle, undo**

Breaking herd A hunted deer, on quitting the herd, and running on its own

Breaking-up The death of a stag; see also ***take***

Breeding-season Period when young are born, as distinct from ***rutting*** season, which is over an extended period

Brisket Lower portion of a deer's chest – see also **essay**

Brittle see **break-up**

Broacher Male red deer in its second year. See also **spitter**

Broaches First head of a Red deer stag – occasionally used to denote ***tines***, or ***points*** – also spelt **broches**

Brocard Male roe deer of third year and upwards. Occasionally used for red deer also

Broaches First head of a red deer stag – occasionally used to denote

Brock, brocke Male red deer in its third year

Brocket Male red deer in its second year – occasionally used for third year as well. Also spelt **broket**

Brocket's sister Second year hind. See also **hearse**

Broket see ***brocket***

Broomed Description of horn – generally sheep or goat – that has had the end worn away

Brow The lower or first point on the antler

Browse Except when a deer eats grass it is said to ***browse***. See also ***feed***

Browse line The levels up to which the branches have been eaten by deer

Brush Penis of buck referring to tuft of hairs at end. See also **pensel**

***Buck*, bucke** Correct name for male roe or fallow deer. In old parlance, the word **buck** referred to a male fallow deer of six years of age. Should also be used for male of muntjac and Chinese water-deer. In the New Forest **buck** describes a male fallow deer with a nice palmed antler

Buck of the first head Fallow deer buck in its fifth year

Buckstall Toil or trap in which to take or capture deer

Bull Correct term for male wapiti, moose, elk, caribou or reindeer

Bullocke Second year male red deer – see also ***knobber***

Bulloke see **bullocke**

Bunch A mob of deer – West Country term

Bunches The velvet covered knobs of the growing antler

Bur, burr The rough edged perimeter of the coronet

Burnished A stag's antlers when hard are said to be **burnished**. Also used to describe condition of ***beam***

Burnishing Rubbing the antlers after the velvet has been removed

Butcher-weight Weight of a carcase without head, feet, skin and all internal organs, etc.

Button First signs of growth of new antlers

Button-head Small antlers produced by roebuck during first year

C

Cabache Cut off stag's head near the antler – also spelt **caboche**
Cabar-crom A stag with one point growing down and backwards
Cabers see ***switch*** head
Caber schloch, **Caber slach**, **Caber slash**, **Caber slat** – variations in spelling of **cabers** – see ***switch***
Cablish Brushwood
Caboche see **cabache**
Calf Correct name for young red deer. Also used for sika deer. In ancient terminology **calf** generally referred to a female deer in its first year
Call Horn sounded to encourage hounds – see also **recheat**
Calling Attracting deer – generally roe – to the sportsman during the rut by imitating the call of another deer. In roe stalking, the doe; in stag stalking, either sex
Campestres Beasts of the chase, so called because they haunt the plains and fields more than the forests
Canopy Continuous cover formed by the crowns of forest trees
Cap Money collected from the ***field*** at a meet
Cape Headskin of deer
Carted deer A park deer that is used for hunting with hounds, the intention being to catch it (***take***) alive so that it can be returned to the enclosure for hunting on future occasions
Cast When male deer discard their antlers they are said to ***cast*** – see also **mew** and ***shed***
Cast The action taken by the huntsman in directing his hounds to regain the scent which has been temporarily lost
Cast off Releasing a hound or hounds for the hunt
Casting his chaule Means, literally, 'hanging his head' – the action of a hunted stag when tired
Catch-up Catching-up deer for removal to a new area
Central point Sometimes used to describe the ***tray*** tine
Centiorari Writ from a higher court for records to be released of a case that has been tried in a lower court
Chace see **chase**
Chacechiens The slippers
Challenge During the rut a stag, when roaring, is said to ***challenge*** a 'rival' stag
Challenge When hounds, being cast off, find the scent and begin to cry, they are said to ***challenge***
Change When hounds quit a scent for a new one
Charchion A whip
Chase Privileged place for deer, etc. described as 'being of a Middle Nature betwixt a Forest and a Park'. A **chase** was formerly used for hunting by subjects of the monarch, as distinct from a royal chase – also spelt **chace**
Check Hounds are said to **check** when scent is temporarily lost
Chief warden Officer of the forest
Chiminage Toll levied for passage through a forest

Chop To kill soon after being found – generally refers to hare hunting
C.I.C. Conseil International de la Chasse
Claw Deer's cloven foot – see ***slot***
Clean When the velvet has dried up and been discarded from the antlers, they are said to be ***clean***
Clean After removal of the stomach and entrails, etc. the weight of the deer is said to be ***clean*** weight. Generally speaking ***clean*** weight should include heart and liver (as both are edible) but may be without
Cleaves*, cleeves** The toes of a deer. ***Cleave is one half of a cloven foot
Cloven feet The feet of deer and other ruminants
Coat Name generally used to describe a deer's skin
Coddes Testicles of a hart
Cold Faint scent of an animal, which may be several minutes to few hours old
Come-to-horns To decoy deer by rattling horns (antlers) – an American expression
Comely Description of a 'fair doe'
Common Unenclosed waste land, belonging to a community
Common grazing Unenclosed land over which a local community has grazing rights
Compartment Subdivision of a forest used for management purposes and usually about 25–30 acres (10–12 hectares)
Coney In old parlance, generally indicated a rabbit of greater age than one year
Conservation The action necessary to protect deer and their habitat from exploitation
Contre Hunting a 'heel trail' was said to run **contre**
Cookie Antlers without brow, bay or tray tines but with forked tops. Crealock refers to a **cookie** as a stag with forked top and brow tines[58]
Cool stag Fresh deer for coursing, as opposed to the driven or hunted animal
Coppice A crop springing from the root stocks of the previous one (hardwood only)
Core area That part of an animal's home range which is used frequently
Coronel see ***coronet***
Coronet The base of the antler adjoining the pedicle
Corrie Hollow in mountains affording shelter for deer
Cotying Droppings of a fallow deer – see also **croties, fewmets**
Couched Resting deer
Counterfeit An abnormal head
Couple Act of coition between animals – see also ***cover***
Couple Correct term for two or more (even numbered) hounds, i.e. ten couple indicating twenty hounds
Couple and half Correct term for three or more (uneven numbered) hounds, i.e. ten and half couple indicating twenty-one hounds
Cover Act of coition between two animals – see also **couple**
Cover Undergrowth or foliage etc. giving deer shelter or concealment
Cover Ancient term for a hart that is harbouring
Covereth Stag going to a covert to harbour
Covert Described as those 'woods which are thickets and full of trees touching one another, and signifies a covering or hiding place for the **deer**'

Cow Correct name for female of wapiti, moose, elk, caribou and reindeer

Creep Worn place under wire or fence where deer have passed

Croches Top points of a stag's antlers. Modern term ***crown*** if the three points form a **cup**

Crockets Points at top of antlers

Crokes Stomach of red deer

Cromagach (Gaelic meaning crooked). Derivation of ***cromie***

Cromie Stunted goat-like heads principally produced by some stags on Jura

Cross, to Dislodge roe deer by hounds

Croties, crotties Droppings of fallow or roe deer. See also **cotying**

Crouched Description of the head of a stag of six or more years of age

Crown see ***cup***

Crowned Ancient term for the first head of a deer

Crowned-head Head bearing not more than three or four tines, the **croches** or top tines being placed aloft, all of one height

Crowned tops According to Osbaldiston the first head of a deer[152]

Cry The sound of hounds – see also ***tongue***

Cryptorchid Condition in which the testis is in the abdomen rather than in the scrotum

Cull Killing surplus or unwanted deer

Cup The three uppermost points of a stag's antler, if in form of a ***cup*** or ***crown***, is so described

Curée Ceremony of giving hounds their ***reward*** – **curée** eventually became ***quarry***

Currachd an righ (Gaelic) In English means, literally, 'The King's Cap', which is the second compartment of the stomach

D

Da, daa, dae Ancient spelling of ***doe***

Dagger point Royal or fourth tine

Dags The spike antlers of a young red deer in its second year

Dai, dais Ancient spelling of ***doe***

Dartines Name sometimes applied to brow and bay tines on wapiti (American)

Deafforest Signifies discharge from being a forest and therefore free and exempt from forest laws

Deer Name for all members of the *Cervidae*, both male and female. In North America the term **deer** generally refers to whitetail and mule deer only

Deer-feld Ancient description of a deer-park

Deer-fold Alternative spelling for above

Deer forest An open area or estate, inhabited by deer. Unnecessary for it to contain trees, generally being a forest in name only

Deer hayes (hays) Large nets in which to catch deer

Deer lays Large net for catching deer

Deer leap Raised ramp outside a park deer fence by which deer can gain entry into the park – see also **salteries** or **saltatoria**

Defouleth Footsteps showing that the deer has recently re-entered water

Delayed implantation Delay in the growth of the foetus within the body of the female roe deer until several months after fertilization

Dental pad The hard pad of tissue at the front of the upper jaw of ruminants against which incisors of the lower jaw bite

Der . . . Names of places beginning with **der** signify that wild beasts formerly herded there

Descendeth A hunted deer entering a pool

Dew claws Vestiges of additional toes set above the cleaves

Discovereth Stag leaving covert 'discovereth itself'

Disforest Cut down trees of forest

Dislodge Rouse a fallow buck

Doe Correct name for female roe or fallow deer. Also for muntjac and Chinese water-deer. In ancient terminology **doe** generally referred to a female fallow deer in its third year

Dog-killers Name sometimes applied to brow and bay tine on wapiti antlers (American)

Done After the kill the deer is **done**, i.e. disembowelled

Doo Ancient spelling of ***doe***

Doppel-kopf Antlers with double coronets (German)

Dose Reward given to hounds after hunt – see also ***reward***

Double, double-back When a hunted animal turns back on its course

Double brows Sometimes used to describe antlers with brow and bay tines

Double head Condition in which a buck carries both the current and previous year's antlers – known in Germany as **doppel-kopf**

Double royal Twenty points

Doubling A hunted deer turning in its tracks – also running to and fro. See also **treasons**

Doubling the horn Succession of lively notes blown on a hunting horn

Drift A mob of deer – West Country term, but not now used

Drive, driving The practice of driving deer to waiting guns – see also ***moving***

Droppings The excrement of deer – see also **cotying**, **croties**, **fewmets**, **fumes**

E

Easter count Traditional practice in eastern U.S.A. to count the points on both sides of an antlered trophy – see ***western count***

Echelle Term sometimes used in Ardennes district to denote a ***hochstand***. Also ***perche***

Ectoparasite Parasite living on the outside of an animal

Emboss To emboss or track a deer in a wood or thicket

Embossed Hunted deer foaming at the mouth – also used to describe a tired stag – see also **imbosh**

Emprimed A stag or hart forsaking the herd

Encorne The act of turning a dead stag's antlers downwards with the throat uppermost preparatory to cutting off the head, i.e. decapitation

Endoparasite Parasite living inside an animal

Enlarge Releasing the carted deer prior to a hunt

Entire Male animal that has not been castrated

Entries Places in thickets where deer have passed

Entry Old term for branches broken by a deer's head – see also ***rack***

Eres of roebuck Target, or white rump patch
Ergots Dew-claws of a deer
Espeyard Third year male red deer. Occasionally used for fourth year as well
Esquire Small stag accompanying a warrantable, or big stag. Often called the big stag's ***fag***
Essay The breast or brisket of a deer
Establishment The stage at which a forest crop is accepted as fully grown
Estovers Boughs, etc., allowed for making a hedge in a wood
Expeditating of dogs Cutting-off three claws of the forefeet of dogs to prevent them chasing deer – see also **lawing**, **hambling**, **hocksynewing**, **hoxing**
Eyre Circuit Court

F

Faeces Droppings or excrement
Fag Small stag in company with an old beast – see also **esquire**
Fair-doe Correct description of a good doe. For a good stag, buck or hind the word **great** is used
Fair-roe buck Male roe in its fifth year
Faked spread Mounted trophies in which the taxidermist has used loose antlers or those on a split skull to produce a greater spread than the natural one
Fat-buck season Time of year when bucks are in prime condition
Fat season Literally **grease time** or buck hunting season
Fawn Correct term for young of fallow deer (either sex) during its first year. Also indicates young of muntjac and Chinese water-deer
Feather A hound **feathers** when he waves his stern before being certain of the scent to give tongue
Feaut Track of a beast, whether by scent, footprint, slot or blood
Fee deer Perquisite of a free deer out of the forest. See **ranger**
Feed When a deer eats in a cornfield or on grass, it is said to ***feed*** – see also ***browse***
Fence month Month during which there used to be complete protection of deer, i.e. 9 June to 9 July when female deer are having their young
Feut see **feaut**
Fewmets Droppings of deer – occasionally spelt **fewnets**
Fewmishing see **fewmets**
Fewterer Ancient name for **slipper**
Field Mounted followers of a pack of hounds
Fighter point Sometimes used for ***brow*** tine
Final crop The best trees of a plantation, selected to grow on to maturity
Find Rousing a stag or roe deer – see also ***found***
First antler The brow tine
Flag Tail of deer (American term)
Flaming head Beam ending in two points both growing upwards, i.e. forked
Flay Skinning a deer – more generally a red deer – see **flean**
Flean Skinning a red deer – see **flay**

Flehmen A behaviour reflex sometimes exhibited by males, usually after savouring the female's urine. It consists of raising the head, curling back the upper lips and dropping the lower lip

Foil Sometimes used to describe an animal that has turned back on its own tracks

Foil Footprints of deer that is scarcely visible on grass. Originally used for tracks of roe deer – also **foin**

Foiled Term applied to ground much traversed by hounds, horses, cattle, sheep etc.

Foiled down Hunted deer swimming downstream

Foin Track of deer – see also **foil**

Folies see **tryst**

Followers Young animals following a matured female

Following Term sometimes applied to ghillie who is carrying the rifle and 'following' the stalking party

Folly see **rascal**

Folly Fine imposed for killing a young stag or buck

Foot-geld An amercement (fine) for not expeditating dogs in the forest

Forest Anciently described as 'a certain Territory of woody grounds and fruitful pastures, privileged for wild Beasts and Fowls of Forest, Chase and Warren to rest and abide in, in the safe Protection of the King, for his princely delight and pleasure'.[132] See also ***deer forest***

Forest law Laws, as distinct from **common law**, which provided for control and management of royal forests

Forest service Formerly when a bishop went on a great hunt, the tenants in those parts were bound to set up for him a field-house or tabernacle with a chapel, and furnish him with dogs, horses and provisions, etc.

Forestalling Artificial means of trapping wild deer; or preventing their return to the forest

'Forester' Local name for a wild deer on Brandon, Somerset

Forester Formerly an officer 'sworn to preserve Vert and Venison in the Forest and attend upon the wild beasts within his Bailiwick'

Fork The two points on the extremity of the antler in form of a fork

Forked heads Heads having double **croches**

Forlange Sound on a horn to denote that the stag was far ahead

Found When hounds rouse the stag he has been ***found***

Foyles Tracks of deer

Franchise Privilege or exceptional right granted to a person

Frank-chase A liberty of **free-chase** by which all persons that have lands within the compass thereof, are prohibited to cut down trees without view of the forester

Fray A deer rubbing its antlers against a tree

Fraying The process of discarding the velvet from the antlers by rubbing against a tree or bush, etc.

Fraying-post Post or tree against which a deer rubs its antlers

Fraying-stock Same as above

Free-chase see **frank-chase**

Free warren A franchise or place granted by royal grant, for keeping beasts and fowls such as hares, conies, etc.

Fresh Opposite to ***cold*** when referring to tracks
Fresh found A deer is **fresh found** when, during a hunt, it lies down and is, as it were, raised for a second, subsequent time
Fues Droppings of a red deer – see also **fumes**, **fumet**
Fues According to Greswell, the feet of a hart[90]
Full-cry Describes hounds running hard and true after their deer
Full-headed buck Fallow buck of greater age than six years
Full stag see ***entire***
Fumes Droppings of a red deer – see also **fues**, **fumet**
Fumet Droppings of a red deer – see also **fues**, **fumes**
Fur-antler see **sur-antler** (***bay*** tine)
Furch (Gaelic) Two haunches of venison that have not yet been divided
Furnished When antler growth is complete, the stag is said to be **furnished**
Furniture Head or antlers of a deer – see also **attire**
Furrows Rough channels in beam of antler
Fur-royal see **sur-royal**

G

Gait Deer step, or motion
Gallery Path worn by deer in close cover
Galloper Two, three or four-year-old stag
Game Edible birds and animals that are objects of the chase
Game-keeper Person who has the care of keeping and preserving the game. In former days his authority was limited
Garron Highland pony used on a deer forest for bringing in the deer – see also **girn**
Gaze, at Deer stand ***at gaze*** when they stop to look
Gazelle Male roe deer in its second year – occasionally used for female in second year also – see also **girl**
Geld Castrate
Gelt-buck Castrated five-year-old buck
Gentleman The rifle- or sportsman often referred to as the ***gentleman*** by the Scottish stalker
Gestation Period between mating (**rut**) and birth of the young deer
Ghillie An assistant who accompanies the stalker and 'rifle' when stalking
Girl, girle Roe deer in its second year – see also **gazelle**
Girn Pony used for bringing in deer – see also ***garron***
Girt The size of a stag
Gives tongue A hound **gives tongue** when hunting
Glandage The season of turning hogs into the woods during **mast-time**
Glass Telescope used in deerstalking, often referred to as the **glass**
Glassing Sometimes used to describe **spying** the ground with a telescope
Glitters Impressions on the surface of the antler
Glùnachan (Gaelic) Knee caps made from deer skin which, on rough ground, were worn with the kilt by the old Highland deerstalker in order to protect the knees while crawling
Gnat Small mechanized vehicle used to bring in deer, and in a number of forests has replaced the pony
Going-back Antlers of deer that have deteriorated through age or disease
Good nose A tufter, or indeed any hound, must have a ***good nose*** for

picking up the scent of a deer in cover or elsewhere
Gorget White throat patch in roe
Grace time see **grease time**
Gralloch Removing the stomach and entrails etc., from a deer
Grandeln Tushes or canine teeth in red deer (German)
Grass Term used in stalking for killing a deer
Grease A fat hart or buck was said to be in **grease**. The fat of a roe deer was called **heavy grease**
Grease-time Season when stags and bucks are fattest and fit for killing, i.e. autumn
Great buck Male fallow deer of at least six years of age. Should describe a buck with a wide palm and a number of points (New Forest Buckhounds)
Great head Same as ***great buck*** above
Great herd Denotes a herd of sixty to eighty beasts
Great soar Male red deer in its fifth year – see also **stag** and **great stag**
Great stag Male red deer in its fifth year – see also **great soar**
Gres Ancient term for buck
Grete beuy Twelve roe deer in a group were said to be a **grete beuy**
Grete herde see **great herd**
***Groan*, groaneth** Sounds of a fallow buck at rut – see also **troat**
Ground flora The lower layer of plants growing on floor of forest
Growth rings The concentric layers sometimes visible in sections of a pedicle
Gutters Rough channels in beam of antlers
Gutting a deer see ***gralloch***
Gyrle Roe under two years of age – sometimes referred to as a yearling roebuck

H

Ha-ha Sunken fence bounding park
Hallow Ceremony of giving hounds their **reward**; also called **querry** or Quarré
Hambling Cutting the knees of large dogs to prevent them chasing deer – see also **expeditating**, **hocksynewing**, **hoxing** and **lawing**
Harbour Stag retiring to rest is said to **harbour**. A stag going to harbour is sometimes said to 'take his hold' or **covereth**
'Harbour, goes to' Stag, having left the herd, goes to a covert on its own.
Harbourer The member of the hunt whose job it is to find a suitable (warrantable) stag for hunting
Hardel Term used for binding the four legs of a roe deer together – head between forelegs – for carrying home. Also used for tying couples of hounds together ready for slipping
Harem A number of female deer acquired by a stag or buck during the rut
Harns Exmoor farmers often refer to stags' antlers as **'harns'** i.e. horns
Harrier Old term for huntsman
***Hart*, hert** Male red deer of six years or more. The term **hart** is still, occasionally used on the Atholl Forest instead of the more usual term **stag**. *The Badminton Diary* (1962) suggests that **hart** denotes a 10-pointer

Hart hounds Hounds used to drive the deer up to huntsmen at a battue
Hart of ten Warrantable stag, i.e. one of ten points and large enough to hunt. In ancient venery, a stag in its sixth year
Hart of the first head Stag in its sixth year
Hart of the second head Stag in its seventh year
Hart of twelve A 12-pointer, but not necessarily a ***royal***
Hart resigned A stag whose head will not improve further
Hart royal In former times this denoted a hart hunted by the king or queen. Today it would refer to a 12-pointer with three points atop in the form of a cup or crown, and all his 'rights'
Hart royal proclaimed In former times this denoted a stag that had been hunted by the king and escaped
Hautboy A form of **vert** that provides food and browse for the game
***Havier*, hevier** A castrated deer
Hays Nets for taking rabbits and hares – see **toils** for deer nets
Head The head and antlers of a stag or buck frequently referred to as **head**
Heading back see **blanche**
Hearde see **herd**
Hearse Female red deer in its second year – see also **brocket's sister**. *Also spelt* **hearst**, **herse**, **hert**, **hyrsel**
Hearst see **hearse**
Hearts Two-year-old red deer hind (*The Badminton Library*)
Heat, in Time of rut
Heavier see ***havier***
Heavy grease Fat of a roe deer
Heavy stag Stag above four years old
Heel Hounds run 'heel' when they go in the reverse direction taken by the quarry
Heel trail Doubling back – see **contre**
Heerde see ***herd***
Heimuse see **hemuse**
Heinuse see **hemuse**
Held The pack used to be **held** coupled while tufting was in progress. Now the pack is always confined to a building or vehicle
Hemule Male roe deer in third year
Hemuse, heimuse, heinuse Roe deer, more generally in its third year – occasionally may refer to one in its fourth year
Herbivorous Descriptive of animals, such as deer, which eat plants etc.
***Herd*, herde, herdys** The correct term for group of deer. Twenty was said to be the smallest number 'which maketh a herd of any deer, except the roe, which is six' – see also **littell**, **mydyll** and **grete herde**
Herd with rascal and folly Warrantable stag when accompanied by other smaller stags
Herdlenge The dressing of the roe deer
Herse Second year hind
Hert see **herd** – sometimes referred to as **hearse** – see above
Hevier see ***havier***
Hide Skin of deer
Hide Small place of concealment for waiting hunter

High grease of deer Very fat deer
High forest A plantation continued in growth to mature stag after thinning
High seat Elevated stag, generally in a tree, from which to wait for deer passing for feeding etc.
Hill*, the** When proceeding to stalk deer, the sportsman is often said to have gone to the ***hill
Hind Correct term for female red deer – also sika deer. HJ Pye calls a roebuck in its first year, a hind[159]
Hinde, hynde In ancient terminology referred to a female red deer in third year
Hinde calf Stag calf in its first year (Nicolas Cox)[57]
Hit off the line A hound or pack is said to **hit off the line** when it finds scent and starts hunting
Hochsitz German for ***high seat*** – see above
Hochstand Same as ***hochsitz*** – see above
Hochsynewing see **hambling**
Hog dressed Weight of a carcase without head, feet and all internal organs, but with skin on
Hold hard Stopping hounds from following an unwarrantable deer
Hollering (**halloa**) A loud, high cry given when a deer is viewed
Home range The area where an animal spends most of its time
Hoop-headed 'A stag whose horns are curved upwards, and between which the space narrows towards the points.' (CP Collyns)[52]
Horn Frequently, yet incorrectly, used to describe the ***antlers***
Horn geld A tax within the bounds of the forest for all manner of horned beasts
Hound a stag Cast hounds at a stag
Hoxing see **hambling**
Humble Name sometimes given to ***hummel***
Humbles see **numbles**
Hummel Male red deer that never grows any antlers – see also ***nott***
Hunt Pursuit of wild animals
Hunt counter Hunting by the heel or track, rather than scent
Hunting The chase of a wild animal, particularly in its natural haunts. In the United States of America all forms of shooting are described as **hunting**
Hunting at force Hunting by scent with a pack of hounds, as distinct from coursing or shooting deer
Hurdle To skin and cut up a roe deer
Hynde Ancient spelling of ***hind***
Hyrsel see **hearse**

I

Imbosh Foam at the mouth of a distressed or hunted deer – see also **embossed**
Imperial Although 14-pointers are frequently referred to as **imperials,** there seems to be no justification for it
Imprime Term used sometimes for unharbouring the hart
Imprint Impression of slot mark

Inclosure see **park**
Infraorbital gland see **suborbital gland**
Inside span Measurement at widest place between main beams
Interdigital gland Scent gland between the cleaves of a foot
Intergrade Hybrid animal resulting from the cross of two distinct species

J

Jinnock Two-year-old hind
'John McNab' To kill a stag, grouse and salmon in one day
Jumps Places where deer jump over fences instead of passing under them
Justice-seat or eyre of the forest is a Court of Record, which assesses fines for offenders that have been presented at the Court of Attachment

K

Keel Outer edge of horn – generally sheep – close to which the tape is laid when measuring length
Keeper of the forest An officer who is the principal officer of the forest, and responsible for all the deer therein
Kennel of hounds In ancient phraseology it was more correct to say Kennel of Hounds – Pack being reserved for beagles
Kid Young roe deer of either sex in its first year – see also **gyrle**
***Kill*, the** The end of a successful hunt
***Knobber*, knobbler** Second year male red deer
Knobbler Small antlers of male red deer in its second year, i.e. a **brocket**
Knobs Large **pearling** on a stag's antlers
Knott see ***nott***

L

Labelles Neck skin of a stag's head which has been severed from the body
Laid in, *laid on* While the tufters may be 'laid-on' the line of a deer, this expression is more often used in the sense that the 'pack was laid-on'
Lair Occasionally used for impression left where a stag has lain
Launde Special area in forest reserved exclusively for deer
Law The period of time given to a deer that has been uncarted, before the hounds are laid on
Lawing see **expeditating**
Lawn A level plain in a park or between two woods – see also **launde**
Lay on see ***laid on***
Layer see **lair**
Layr A deer's haunt
Leash Three greyhounds make a **leash** – see also **couple**
Leash Group name for two fallow deer – see also **brace**
Leash Name for the lead by which a greyhound is led – ancient word **liam**
Leasing Practice of dispensing rough justice on the spot for offences such as arriving late at a meet, holloring at a wrong deer, etc.
Length The **length** of an antler is from the base of the coronet, along the outside edge to tip of longest tine on top
Let slip Releasing a greyhound
Liam see **leash**

Lift A huntsman **lifts** hounds when he takes them to where he believes they will 'hit off the line'.

Lifters Name sometimes applied to brow and bay tines on wapiti (American)

Ligging Lair of deer

Line Route taken by hunted animal

Littel (Little) herde Twenty deer generally referred to as a **little herde** – (likewise **small herd**)

Lodge Fallow buck retiring to rest is said to **lodge**

Lodging Correct name for harbouring a fallow buck

Lop-eared Ears set in pendulous fashion

Jumpy jaw Swollen lump on jaw caused by bacterial infection

Lymer Hound similar to a bloodhound, led by a strap or line (Liam)

Lymerer In former days the lymerer with his hound (**lymer**) in **leash** on the day prior to the hunt, searched for a deer to hunt, i.e. the work now done by the ***harbourer***

Lyome String by which a hound is led – see also **liam**

M

Mainprise Signifies the taking of a man into 'friendly custody', i.e. he has more freedom than one on **bail**

Make the rascal void Eliminate the smaller deer prior to hunting a larger stag

Male deer Used to describe a yearling stag that has not yet developed antlers

March Scottish expression for denoting an estate boundary

Mark Boundary of a forest

Mast Fruit of wild trees such as oak, beech, etc.

Mast-time Season when the **mast** is ripe

Master buck Buck holding a rutting territory

Meer Boundary mark

Meet Correct term for the meeting of hounds and men for a day's hunting

Melanistic Dark pelage in a deer of normal lighter colour

Menée Sound to be blown on the hunting horn to denote a male deer

Menil A colour variety of fallow deer that is spotted in both summer and winter

Metacarpal Cannon bone of the fore leg

Metatarsal Cannon bone of the hind leg

Meuse Track through a fence – see also ***rack***

Mew To discard the velvet from antlers – also used for casting antlers; also used to describe hawks moulting

Mewing Sound made by fallow deer during submissive behaviour, and also by young fawns – also **peeping**

Middle herd (mydyll herde) Denotes a herd of about forty deer (except **roe**)

Midel One of the three relays of hounds used for hunting in former times

Misprint Step irregularly – failure to register footprints

Mixed woodland Wood that contains both deciduous and coniferous trees

Mob Term used sometimes for ***herd*** of deer

Monarch Sometimes used (but erroneously in my opinion) to denote a

14-pointer – see also **imperial**
Monorchid Stag with only one testicle
Monyplies The third bag in the stomach
Moot Blast on a hunting horn – two were blown after the deer had been unharboured, four at the death
Mort Blast on the horn to denote the end of a hunt – see also **prise**
Moss The velvet on an antler
Moving deer The practice of gently 'moving deer' rather than driving by force – to waiting sportsmen. Deer can be moved by giving them one's 'wind' or scent
Mowse The ***burr*** of an antler
Mule Ancient term for the ***burr*** of an antler
Murderer A deer with switch type antlers which are lethal weapons against another deer
Murrain Ancient term for almost any disease affecting ruminants
Mute Ancient term for a pack of hounds
Mute Describes hounds that do not throw their tongue when on the line of a deer
Mutes Droppings (more especially of birds)
Mydyll bevy Ten roe deer in a group were said to be a **mydyll bevy**
Mydyll herde see **middle herd**

N

Natural regeneration The self-seeding of forest trees in contrast to sowing or planting
Near-antler Left antler
Nether vert Description of undergrowth – see also **vert**
Nocturnal Describes an animal which is active during the hours of darkness
Non-typical An antlered trophy that does not conform to the typical pattern of the species
Nott West Country term for a male red deer that never produces antlers – occasionally spelt **knott** – see also ***hummel***
Nowte A ***hummel*** or ***nott*** stag has occasionally been referred to as a **nowte**[176]
Numbles Originally the liver, kidney and entrails of a deer (the word later became **umbles**, then **humbles**, hence **humble-pie**)
Nusance of the forest 'Whatsoever tends to the Hurt or Destruction of the Forest or of the Vert or Venison, the source is a nusance of the forest'[132]

O

Oestrus The season when the female is receptive or 'on heat'
Off-antler The right antler
Offer Small point sufficiently long to hang something on it
'*Old stag*' Adult stag
Ollanaich Brow-point (Gaelic)
Open Hound is said to **open** when he throws his tongue
Os False toe, or dew claw of hart and hind
Oscorbin The gristle from the brisket of the deer was, in ancient times, following a kill, the reward left for the ravens

Ossification Conversion to bone
Outside curve Measurement of an antler along the outside curve, from base to extremity
Over vert Description for high wood – see **vert**

P

Pace Speed of movement as measured by the length of step or stride. Also slot or track of deer
Pack Correct name for a number of hounds collected together for hunting, except the tufters
Paddock A small park or enclosure in which to keep deer
Paegened Original name for **verderer** – one of the chief officials of the forest
Paint A New Forest term for a blood-trail left by a deer which has been shot
Pair General term – act of coition between animals
Pair Two animals of same breed but of different sex
Palm The palmated top of a fallow buck's antlers
Palmed Descriptive of a fallow buck's antlers
Palmed-head If croches grow in form of a man's hand, it is called a **palmed head**
Parcel Collective term for a number of hinds together
Parfitières The most reliable hounds
Park A place specially enclosed for beasts of venery
Parker 'One that hath the Custody or Keeping of a Park'
Pass The normal point at which a deer will cross an obstacle, or over the shoulder of a hill
Pattern The arrangement of footprints in the trail, varying with gait
Pearling see **pearls**
Pearls The roughness of the beam and burr
Peck-order Social behaviour between animals of different age groups
Pedage Money given for passing through a forest
Pedal gland see ***interdigital gland***
Pedicle The bone from which the antler grows
Peeping see **mewing**
Pelage Hair of animals
Pensel Penis of buck – also **brush**
Perambulation To establish the boundaries of a piece of land
Perche Term used in Ardennes to denote a ***hochstand***
Perfect Note on horn sounded when hounds are hunting on right lines
Perruque Malformed antler growth, caused by an injury to the testicles, resulting in extreme cases, to part of the forehead being covered by a mass of antler, frequently in velvet. See also **wig antler**
Piece Sandwiches taken to the hill (out deerstalking) often referred to as the ***piece***
Pies Ancient term of French origin, referring to a footprint of a deer
Pillar The bone from which the antler grows – i.e. ***pedicle***
Piner A deer that is ill-nourished
Pins Deer hairs indicating that a deer has been hit by bullet
Piste Tread or track made by a horse

Poca-bhuide (Gaelic) Literally meaning the 'yellow bag' – the first compartment of the stomach. Also spelt **poch-bhui**

Point Often used to denote **tine** – i.e. brow, bay, tray, etc.

Point Distance over which a deer or fox takes hounds during a hunt

Pole crop A plantation in the early stages of thinning

Pollarding A New Forest term for the casting of antlers

Poll-buiridh (Gaelic) Wallowing pool

Polled Male deer without antlers – see ***hummel***

Polygamous A male animal – such as a red deer stag or fallow buck, etc., which usually has more than one female during the rut

Pomeled Spotted, as in young deer

Pope and Young Club Organization founded in U.S.A. to encourage bowhunters to maintain a tradition of qualitative hunting and good sportsmanship

Preorbital gland see **suborbital gland**

Prick, pricks First head of a fallow buck

Prickers Whippers-in

Pricket Male fallow deer in second year. A few ancient writers used **pricket** to denote a male red deer in its third year. In the New Forest it describes a yearling fallow buck showing small spike antlers

Pricket's sister Female fallow deer in its second year

Pride of grease Deer in fattest time of year

Prise Four blasts blown on hunting horn to denote end of hunt – see also **mort**

Proclaimed see **royal hart proclaimed**

Proffereth The moment a hunted deer is about to enter water to 'soil'

Pronking The stiff-legged gait often displayed by a fallow deer bounding off on all four feet

Proto-forester The one whom the ancient kings used to make Chief of Windsor Forest to hear Cause of Death or Maim, or of slaughter of the king's deer in the forest

Pulled down The moment a hunted deer is caught (taken) by hounds

Purlieu Originally all the ground adjacent to a royal forest which, during the reign of Henry II, Richard I and John, was added to the forests, but subsequently disafforested by the *Charta de Foresta*

Purlieu-men Those who had grounds in the **purlieu** of the forest, and if duly qualified according to law, may hunt in their own land

Q

Qualification Qualification to hunt or own a hound, etc., i.e. unless a layman had forty shillings per annum, he could not have a dog, net, etc., to destroy deer

Quarry Derived from the word **curee**. 'The hounds' reward was called the *Quyrreye* (quarry) because eaten on the hide (sur le quir). It is, therefore, technically incorrect to refer to the wild animals in the course of being hunted as the "quarry".' (Hare)[94]

Quat A deer is said to '**go quat**' when it lies during the course of a hunt

Querry see **hallow**

Questing Seeking a hunted stag

R

Ra, raa Ancient spelling of ***roe***

Raches see **braches**

Rack Usual term in North America for a deer's antlers

Rack Path cut through a young plantation to facilitate access

Rack Branches broken by a deer's entry – see also **entry**

Rae Ancient spelling of ***roe***

Rags see **tatters**

Rai Ancient spelling of ***roe***

Ramhundt Small dog formerly permitted in forest without being lawed

Ranger Formerly a forest official appointed by King's Letters Patent with a yearly fee of £20 or £30, and a fee deer, both red and fallow, out of the forest

Rape of the forest Trespass committed in forest by violence

Rascal, rascall In hunting parlance, until a stag is six years of age, and warrantable, he is said to be **rascal** or **folly**

Raches see **braches**

Rating Ticking off hound for **running riot**

Rattling Hunting by **rattling** two antlers together – an American expression. Method used for hunting white-tailed deer

Ray Ancient spelling of ***roe***

Reafforested Reafforestation of any forest which has been disafforested

Real Tine on stag's antler

Rear Rouse up a deer

Receiver 'Who-so-ever receiveth within the Forest any Malefactor either in hunting, or killing, knowing him to be such, or any of the King's venison, is to be treated as a Trespasser'[132]

Rechasing Driving back the deer into the forest from which they had strayed

Recheat Sound on horn calling hounds back, if following wrong line

Reclaim Signified to make tame

Recover Hounds 'recover' the line of a hunted deer even though it may be miles away

Redress a stag Put a stag off his changes

Reeve Stags 'in their raging desire or Lust have a peculiar noise, which the *French* called *Reeve*'[57]

Regard Look into all matters connected with the forest

Regarder Officer of the king's forest, to look into (**regard**) all matters connected with the forest, including **vert** and **venison**

Register To place the hind foot in the slot made by the fore-foot

Reid deer Ancient spelling of ***red deer***

Relays Two or three couple of hounds, held by **berners**, for uncoupling at the appropriate time

Rennying-hounds Ancient term for pack of **braches** or scenting hounds

Replevin Any park within the bounds of any forest, which is not enclosed according to Assize of the Forest, can be seized by the king

Reproductive cycle The annual cycle of changes that occur in the reproductive organs

Reproffereth Hunted deer about to re-enter water for the second time
Resigned A 'hart resigned' is one whose antlers will not improve further
***Reward*, rewarde** see **hallow**
Rhinarium The area of naked skin on the nose
Riall Ancient spelling of ***royal***
Ride A wide track or break separating a forest into blocks
Ridges Rough edge between **gutters** on a deer's antlers
Riding forester His duty was to lead the king whilst hunting
'*Rifle, the*' Name by which the sportsman, whilst stalking deer, is often referred to
Rig Colloquial term for **cryptorchid**
Rights Perquisites given to various people – and hound – after the hunt
Rights An antler with brows, bays and trays is said to have its **rights**
Ring, see ***roe ring***
Ring-run The circling runs of a roe – see also **treasons**
Ring-walk Describes the route of the lymerer or **harbourer** round the covert when checking for a stag
Riot see **running riot**
Roar The sound of a red deer stag during the ***rut***
Roar, the Descriptive name sometimes applied to the ***rutting season*** – and in particular in New Zealand
Rocking chair A large set of antlers – an American expression
Roddel Group term for deer (after the German)
Roe-baiting Hunting of one buck by one hunter, accompanied by a dog
Roebuck of the first head Roebuck in fourth year – also simply **roebuck** (in fourth year)
Roe ring The circle or ring – often in the form of a figure eight – made by a roebuck chasing a doe during the rut
Rogue Name applied to a deer causing persistent damage to crops or forestry
Roller A deer which, after being shot, falls down a steep place, thus making the venison useless
Roo Ancient spelling of ***roe***
Rosette Alternative name for ***coronet***
Rounding Trimming the points of a hound's ears to prevent them being torn and give a uniform appearance
Rouse, roused Disturbing the harboured or lodged deer – generally done by the ***tufters***
Royal A 12-point stag's head, with all its ***rights***, and 3 points on top in the form of a cup which should be 'large enough and deep enough to hold a glass of wine' is known as a **royal**

Occasionally in the past, it would appear that a 10-pointer was also known as a **royal**, whilst a **double-royal** denoted 20 points and a **triple royal** 30 points. The **royal** was also referred to as 'the fifth point of a deer's horn' (J Sobieski Stuart).[178] In the United States the **royal** wapiti head has 7 symmetrical points on each beam.

Royal antler In former times the ***tray*** tine was called the **royal antler**
Royal forest A tract of land, not necessarily woodland, formerly used by the king for hunting. Such land was subject to forest law
Roual hart A hart that was hunted by the king

Royal hart proclaimed A **royal hart** that has escaped being taken
Royal point Normal fourth point on antler of wapiti
Rubbing Damage caused to trees by deer
Rubbish Animals which should be culled
Rubs Places where deer have rubbed the velvet off their antlers
Ruminant An animal, such as a deer or domestic cattle, which chews the cud
Run A stag that has been long at the rut and has lost condition, is said to be **run**
Run The line of pursuit of a hunted animal
Run to herd Hunted deer joining up with a herd of deer
Running hounds Hounds of chase as distinct from the **tufters**
Running riot Staghounds following any other animal than deer
Running time (season) Rutting period (American)
Running to and fro see **doubling**
Ruse see **blenche**
Rut Mating season of deer
Rutting season Mating season of deer
Ryding time Mating season of deer

S

Saddle a stag To load it on to a pony's back for removal to larder
Saddle-up Describes deer carcase loaded up on to a pony
Saint Hubert Club Named after the patron Saint of Hunting. St Hubert Clubs exist both in Great Britain and many countries abroad. Its objects are to create fraternity among sportsmen, whether they hunt, shoot or fish
Saltatoria Deer leap to enable wild deer to jump into a park, but once inside they cannot escape
Saltatorium see **saltatoria**
Sanctuary Originally referred to that part of deer territory containing the lair. Now used to denote that portion of a deer forest that is normally left undisturbed as a ***sanctuary*** for the deer
Sarbote Ancient term meaning to become footsore
Say see **take say**
Scalp Portion of ***cape*** nearest to antler
Scantilon Lymerer measuring the slot of a deer with a twig
Scanty-head Stag with small antlers
Scent Smell of game
Scent-gland Area of skin producing odoriferous compounds
Scoring The marks made by a deer's antlers on the bark of trees
Scrape A patch of ground scraped with the feet of a deer – often prior to resting
Screaming scent Exceptionally strong scent for hounds
Sear-wood Dead boughs cut off trees in a forest
Season, in The period of heat or oestrus in female deer
Seek and find Term used for rousing roe deer
Selective shooting Killing any deer which is old, diseased or injured, or whose removal from the herd is desirable
Sengill see ***single***
Separation day Day of shedding antlers

Set-up A deer is said to be **set up** by hounds
Sets the covert Describes the work of the ***harbourer*** whilst checking a covert for a stag
Sewed see **sued**
Sewel see **sewelling**
Sewelling Coloured rags etc. tied to a cord in order to scare the deer. Sometimes used during a deer drive to prevent the deer moving in an unwanted direction
Sexual dimorphism Difference in form between the sexes
Shed The more modern term for casting or mewing of antlers
Shelts A pony that is used to carry a deer carcase
Shikar club Formed in 1908, the aims of the Shikar Club are to develop the social side of sport by bringing together at an annual dinner, sportsmen whose primary interests are both hunting and preserving the larger game animals of the world
Shootable stag A beast of suitable age and type to be killed
Shoulder point A tray tine on a stag's antlers. (Still used on Wyvis Forest.)
Shovel-head Head of an old fallow buck
Shrinkage Normal decrease in size of trophy as it dries out. Trophies, therefore, cannot be officially measured until after a *waiting period* of sixty days
Sibling Young deer
Signs The tokens by which to judge the size and age of a deer
Silvesters Ancient name given to beasts of the forest, because they haunt the woods more than the plains
Single Tail of a deer
Singleth Denotes a hunted deer separated from the herd
Sink Description of a hunted stag, when tired, lying down and putting his nose close to the ground to prevent the scent flying
Sinking himself Hunted stag lying down in water
Sitting-up Waiting in a hide or up in a high-seat for deer to appear
Sitz-platz A term which is often – but erroneously – used to describe a ***hochsitz*** or ***hochstand***
Skinned Skinning roe deer – see **flean**
Slain 'Of a hart and all manner of deer, they say they are slain'
Slipped, slipping Releasing a hound to track or run a wounded deer to bay
Slipper Men who lead greyhounds prior to slipping – see **fewterer**
Slot Track or footprint of a deer. Although now more commonly used for all species of deer, originally referred to the track of red deer. See also **foil** and **view**
Slot Deer's cloven foot
Slotting Tracing the footprints of a deer – usually done by ***harbourers***
Small herd see **littel herde**
Snag Small point on a deer's antler – see ***offer***
Snet Fat of all kinds of deer
Snowcat Mechanized vehicle used on some forests to replace the pony
Snow-shovel Name sometimes given to brow point of caribou antler
Snow trac Mechanized vehicle used on some forests to replace the pony

Snow tric Small mechanized vehicle used on some forests to replace the pony

Soar Fourth year male fallow deer. Some ancient writers use it for fourth year male red deer as well. Also spelt **soare**, **sore** and **sour**

Soil Deer taking to water – but more commonly applied when a stag uses a muddy soiling pit or wallow

Soppe, soppers Herd of deer

Sore see **soar**. In New Forest **sore** describes a buck with small points protruding from a small or narrow palm

Sorel, sorrel Third year male fallow deer. In the New Forest **sorel** describes a buck with a small head of three tines, but without palm

'*Sort him out*' An expression sometimes used in Scotland for ***gralloching*** a stag

Soule Stag being on its own

Spade Deer of three years old

Spaid see **spayad**

Span Generally refers to the widest inside span between the antler beams, as distinct from ***spread***

Spavid see **spayad**

Spay To kill a deer with a knife

Spay To castrate, or remove the ovaries of a female animal – occasionally spelt **splay** in former times

Spayad, also spelt **spayard, spaid, spavad, spayart** Third year male red deer

Spayed Killed with a knife a stag at bay – generally referred to as a stag in velvet; other stags were generally killed with an arrow

Spayed Describes a bitch hound that has had the ovaries removed to prevent breeding

Speak Sound of a hound

Spears The third year head of a stag

Special vert Fruit-bearing trees and shrubs – see **vert**

Speculum The area on the rump around the tail of a deer

Spellers The top points of a fallow buck's antlers

Spent A hunted deer, when tiring, is ***spent***

Spike-buck Buck with spiked antlers without any tine or branches

Spillers see ***spellers***

Spines Name sometimes given to pearling on roebuck's antlers

Spire Third-year male red deer – see **spires**

Spires The 'uprights' on the first head of a male red deer were sometimes referred to as **spires**. A true ***switch*** head, without brow tines, is also sometimes referred to as a **spire**

Spitter Second-year male deer – see **broacher**

Splay The spread of the ***slot***, due to opening of the cleaves

Splay see ***spay***

Spoon-head Head of young fallow buck

Spoor Comprehensive term used for track of all wild animals

Sport-head A deformed head – generally of a roebuck

Spread Maximum over-all spread of antlers – see ***span***

Spurs The points of a roebuck's head

Spy Searching for deer – generally with telescope or binoculars

Squire Young stag accompanying an old stag, often referred to as such – see also ***fag***

Stable Name given to a stand from which to shoot deer when driven, principally in a park

Stables Huntsmen and kennelmen with hounds in leash that were stationed at allotted points round a forest during the chase, were called **stables**

Stable-stand Place where **stables** were set

Staff-herding Employment of a person to follow cattle in the forest

Stag Male red deer in its fifth year. In carted deer hunting the deer, irrespective of sex, is referred to as the ***stag***

Stag of ten Stag with antlers bearing ten points

Staggard Male red deer in its fourth year

Staggart see **staggard**

Staggers A disease in which a deer loses control of its hind quarters – similar to sway-back in sheep

Staggie Four or five-year-old stag

Stained Describes scent that has been spoilt by passage of cattle, sheep, horses etc.

Stalk, stalking Correct term for quiet approach of deer, particularly in the open, in order to get within shot

Stalker Correct name for the professional 'keeper' on a deer forest

Stalkers Ancient name for a salmon net

Stand Territory of a rutting fallow buck

Stand Fixed position from which to hunt

Stand at gaze To stand watching

Step The interval between one hoof print and the next

Stern The tail of a hound

Steward Judicial officer of the forest

Still-hunting The (very) slow pursuit of a deer in woodland. Occasionally refers to hunting from a ***stand***

Stinking flight The roebuck and doe were included among the animals of **stinking flight** – i.e. left a strong scent

Stride The interval between successive impressions of the same foot

Stripping Removing the bark from trees with the teeth

Stroke Term used for 'blow the horn'

Stynt Hound relay that is unable to pick up the line of the deer

Sub-orbital gland Scent gland situated near corner of eye

Sued The harbourer **sued** with the **lymer** hound for a hart or buck – also spelt **sewed**

Suet Fat of red and fallow deer – see also **tallow**

Summed, summing Describes the number of points on a deer's head

Sur-antler The bay tine of a stag's head

Sur-antler royal Alternative for **royal antler** or ***tray***

Surcharger One who has Common in a forest but puts more cattle in to depasture than he has a right to do

Surcleaves see **dew claws**

Sur-royal The point above the **royal antler** or ***tray***. In Norman times it seems that the third tine – ***tray*** – was also referred to as the **sur-royal**

Suture line Line of demarcation between adjacent bones on the skull

Swainmote A Court that was held prior to the Justice Seat
Sway The deviation of footprints from the median line
Switch Head consisting of four points (beam and brow points only) or just two points (beam only)

T

Tailed Hounds are said to have **tailed** when on line of deer
Tainchel Ancient deer drive – also spelt **tinchel**
Take Successful conclusion to a deer hunt, whether the deer is killed or not, as in carted deer hunting
Take his hold Stag going to covert
Take-off A deer's skin was **taken-off**
Take say To draw the edge of a knife along the middle of the belly to discover how fat the deer was
Take soil When a hunted deer takes to water it is said to **take soil**
Taking assaye see **take say**
Tallow Fat of red or fallow deer
Talon Heel of deer
Tappish Description of a hunted deer skulking
Tappy 'To **tappy**' is an old hunting term for lying hidden
Target The white rump patch of a roe deer in winter
Tatters When the velvet hangs from the stag's antlers it is said to be in ***tatters***
Teasers, teazers Hounds let loose at beginning of hunt to separate the warrantable stag from other deer. Also used to tease forth the hart to be shot
***Tegg*, teg** Female fallow deer in her second year
Tenderlings Velvet from off the top points
Territory An area regarded by a deer as its own property. Such an area is generally marked off by deer rubbing its antlers or various glands of its body against rocks, bushes, etc.
Thicket A stage of growth between the closing of the canopy and the first thinning
Thinnings Selective removal of inferior timber from a plantation
Thrashing The activity which describes a buck flaying bushes or small trees with its antlers
Throw-his-tongue Description of sound of hound whilst hunting – see also **speak**
Thrust-out-of-their-buttons Process of starting to grow a new head (antlers)
Tinchel see **tainchel**
Tinckell Term used for scouts or men in ancient deer drives
Tine Each point or branch on an antler
Tithes A forest paid no **tithes** whilst in the hands of the king, but if in the hands of a subject, tithes were paid or the forest was disafforested
Toady stag A big stag's **fag** – see also **squire**
Toils Park nets of great strength and length used for catching-up deer alive – see also **hays**
Tongue Voice of hound when hunting. A hound 'gives tongue' or 'throws his tongue'

Tops The uppermost points of a deer's antlers
Tourn Ancient term for rut of roe deer
Towrus A roebuck eager for the rut, is said to go to his **towrus**
Toyle see **toils**
Trace Original term for track of deer
Track The footprints of deer – more correctly ***slot*** marks
Trail The sequence of footprints and other marks denoting the passage of deer
Trajoining When a roe crosses and doubles back, it is called **trajoining**
Tray The third point or tine on the antlers of a stag. Also spelt trey, trez
Treasons The **ring-runs** and **doublings** of a roe deer
Tress Extra front tine on antlers of **staggard**, i.e. male red deer in its fourth year
Trey, trez Alternative spellings for ***tray***
Trip Flock of goats
Trip Ancient term for deer in flight
Trippeth Deer in flight
Triple royal In ancient terminology denoted a 30-point stag
Troaches see **troachings**
Troachings The small branches on the top of a deer's head, also spelt **troches**
Troat The sound of a rutting fallow buck – also ***groan***
Troches see **troachings**
Trophy The head or antlers of a male deer
Truewind A wind that keeps steady without changing direction
Tryst, tryste Position taken up by the ancient hunters whilst waiting for the game to be driven to them. Also called **folies**. **Killing at the tryste** signified a small deer drive whereas **tainchel** signified a large one
Tuft To **tuft** is to hunt
Tufters Name of hounds used to rouse the harboured stag
Tufting Describes the method of rousing a harboured stag by means of three or four couple of steady hounds known as ***tufters***
Tundra Treeless land covered for the most part with lichens, moss and similar plants in summer, but in winter is generally covered in snow
Tush Canine tooth in upper jaw of red deer, and some other species. Fallow and roe deer do not normally have **tushes**. Also **tusk** and **grandeln**
Tush **(anal)** Tuft of white hair – which emerges from the lower edge of the white rump patch (target) of a roe doe in winter coat
Tusk see **tush** (canine tooth)
Typical head An antlered trophy whose general pattern conforms to that normally produced by the species

U

Umbles see **numbles**
Underplanting The introduction of a new crop under the partial canopy of an older one
Undo To cut open a deer – modern term ***gralloch*** – used also for dressing a deer

Uneven head In Europe, antlers bearing an uneven number of points i.e. 9, 11, or 13 etc. are generally referred to as uneven 10-pointer, uneven 12-pointer or uneven 14-pointer, etc.
Unharbour Putting to flight a stag that had been harboured
Unleashed When the pack is **unleashed**, the tufters are taken back to kennels
Uprear Finding hart or buck with lymer hound
Uprights The first head of a stag. Also used if main beam ends in a single point[58]
Use West Country term to denote that a deer has been using a field

V
Vauntchasse Relay of hounds
Vauntellery The casting off of a relay of hounds before those already hunting, come up
Vauntlay Last relay of hounds released when stag becomes tired
Vaut At rutting time, a hart or buck was said to 'make their **vaut**'
Veel Male red deer calf
Velteres Small dogs permitted in forest without being 'lawed'
Velvet Skin covering of antlers during development
Velvet-head Description of deer's antlers during growth – see ***velvet***
***Venison,* venaison** Correct term for deer meat
Venison deer Fallow deer sometimes referred to by this name
Verderer Judicial officer of the king's forest
Vert 'Anything that beareth green leaf – more especially thick coverts – which may give cover and feed to the deer. It is of three sorts, **over-vert**, which is Great Woods and trees; **nether-vert** which is all manner of under-wood, bushes, thorn, etc., and **special-vert** which may be either if it bears fruit'[132]
View Old term for footprints of fallow deer but often used for track of any deer on soft ground
View-approval It was necessary to get the **view** of the forester before any trees could be cut down in a **frank chase**
Vivary Signified a place in land or water where living things are kept – i.e. may signify a park or warren, etc.
Voice The vocal sound of the male deer – generally during the rut
Voyes Ancient term of French origin for footprint or **view** of a deer

W
Waiting period A period of sixty days drying out time that must elapse after a trophy is shot before it can be measured officially
Walkers Forest officers appointed to walk about a certain space of ground committed to their care
Walking In Texas (U.S.A.) the word ***walking*** is more commonly used than ***stalking***
Wallow The place where a deer takes a mud bath
Wanlass, winlass Deer driven to a stand for the nobility to shoot was called 'driving the wanlass'
Warden of the forest The Chief Warden of a forest is an officer of great authority and next to the Chief Justice in Eyre. He is not a judicial officer
Ware haunch Rating of foxhounds for 'running riot' after deer

Warrantable A stag must be five or six years old before it is said to be 'warrantable' for hunting, i.e. it should have 10 points consisting of its 'rights' and two a-top

Warren A franchise or liberty by grant of the king, or by prescription, for the preservation of beasts and fowls of warren, i.e. hares and conies, etc.

Waste Signifies a spoil and destruction in the covert and pastures of the forest

Waster An ailing deer

Weep Sound of hunting horn occasionally referred to as **weep**

Well-affeted Description of a well proportioned head

Well-opened Description of a wide spreading head

Western-count Traditional practice in western parts of U.S.A. when points on only one side of an antlered trophy are taken into account. See ***eastern count***

Whickering Sound made by fallow does during the rut

Whistling Sound made by sika deer of both sexes

White hart silver A heavy fine laid upon T de la Lynde, a Dorsetshire baron for having killed a white hart that had given good sport to Henry III (probably that had been *proclaimed*) and was continued to be paid annually until the latter part of the sixteenth century

White stag Description of a stag that is not ***run***, i.e. not been rutting

Wig-antler An alternative name for ***perruque*** antlers

Wiles Traps or engines that deer are taken with

Wilson A name sometimes given erroneously to a 14-pointer

Winlass see **wanlass**

Winter-heyning A season when all agistment was prohibited, for the purpose of reserving the food for the deer

Wood-geld Gathering or cutting of wood within the forest for which there is no payment

Woodmote Former name for the Court of Attachments

Woodward Officer of the forest whose charge is to look after the woods and vert there

Y

Yard Place where deer can find food in winter

Yearling Either sex, one-year-old

Yeld Describes a hind that has not had a calf the previous summer – not necessarily barren. See also ***blue hind***

Yell see **yeld** – from **yell**, scot-dry, without milk

Yellow bag see ***poca-buidhe***

Yeoman berners at horse Kennelmen

Bibliography

The following are the most important books and literature dealing with the hunting and stalking of deer in Britain, as well as legislation through the centuries. A more complete list of literature dealing with deer in Britain will be found in the Bibliographies to my two books, *The Deerstalking Grounds of Great Britain and Ireland,* and *Deer in Great Britain and Ireland.*

A

1 ALDIN, Cecil (1935) *Exmoor, The Riding Playground of England.* London; H F & G Witherby.

2 AMATEUR SPORTSMAN (1804) *Sporting Anecdotes.* London; Albion Press.

3 ANON (1901) *About the Surrey Staghounds.* London; Vinton & Co. Ltd.

4 APSLEY, Lady (1948) *Bridleways through History.* London; Hutchinson & Co.

5 ARBUTHNOTT, Lord (11 April 1974) *Venison Sale Safeguard. The Field.*

B

6 BAILLIE-GROHMANN, W A & F (ed.) (1909) *The Master of Game.* London; Chatto & Windus (*see 69*).

7 BAILY'S HUNTING DIRECTORY (1898–9) London; Vinton & Co. Ltd.

8 BAILY'S HUNTING DIRECTORY (1902–3) London; Vinton & Co. Ltd.

9 BAILY'S HUNTING DIRECTORY (1904–5) London; Vinton & Co. Ltd.

10 BAILY'S HUNTING DIRECTORY (1912–13) London; Vinton & Co. Ltd.

11 BAILY'S HUNTING DIRECTORY (1920–21) London; Vinton & Co. Ltd.

12 BAILY'S HUNTING DIRECTORY (1926–7) London; Vinton & Co. Ltd.

13 BAILY'S HUNTING DIRECTORY (1950–51) London; Vinton & Co. Ltd.

14 BEAUFORT, Duke of and MOWBRAY, Morris (1885) *Hunting.* The Badminton Library, London; Longmans, Green & Co.

15 BELL, E Weston (1892) *The Scottish Deerhound.* Edinburgh; David Douglas.

16 BELL, John (1839) *A Copious and Practical Treatise on the Game Laws.* London; William Crofts.

17 BERNERS, Dame Juliana (1486) *The Book of Saint Albans.* London; Elliot Stock.

18 BIRKETT, Lady (1924) *Hunting Lays and Hunting Ways.* London; John Lane. The Bodley Head Ltd.

19 BLOME, R (1686) *The Gentlemen's Recreation.* S Roycroft.

20 BOWEN, Muriel (1954) *Irish Hunting.* Tralee; The Kerryman Ltd.

21 BRANDER, Michael (1964) *The Hunting Instinct.* Edinburgh & London; Oliver & Boyd.

22 BRANDER, Michael (1968) *A Dictionary of Sporting Terms.* London; Adam & Charles Black.

23 BRANDER, Michael (1971) *Hunting and Shooting*. London; Weidenfeld & Nicolson.
24 BRINDLEY, 'Jim' (1923) *Reminiscences and Rhymes of the Ward Union Hunt*. Dublin; Brindley & Son.
25 BRITISH FIELD SPORTS SOCIETY (1947) *The Game & Hunting Laws at a Glance*. London; British Field Sports Society.
26 BRITISH HUNTS & HUNTSMEN (1910) *The North-east and Western Midlands of England & Wales*. London; The Biographical Press.
27 BRITISH HUNTS & HUNTSMEN (1909) *England South-east, East and East Midlands*. London; The Biographical Press.
28 BRITISH HUNTS & HUNTSMEN (1908) *England, South West*. London; The Biographical Press.
29 BRITISH HUNTS & HUNTSMEN (1911) *England, North, Scotland and Ireland*. London; The Biographical Press.
30 BRITISH SPORTS & SPORTSMEN (1912) *Hunting*. London; British Sports & Sportsmen.
31 BROWN, W J (12 September 1963) *A Guide to the Deer Act. The Field*.
32 BRUSEWITZ, Gunnar (1969) *Hunting*. London; George Allen & Unwin Ltd.
33 BUCHAN, John (1936) (14th edn) *John McNab*. London; Hodder & Stoughton Ltd.
34 BUCHAN-HEPBURN, Sir John (1945) *The Time of Life*. London; Robert Hale Ltd.
35 BUDGETT, H M (1933) *Hunting by Scent*. London; Eyre & Spottiswoode
36 BUND, J W Willis (1897) *Oke's Game Laws*. (4th edn) London; Butterworth & Co.
37 BUTLER, A J (1930) *Sport in Classic Times*. London; Ernest Benn Ltd.
38 BUXTON, Aubrey (1955) *The King in His Country*. London; Longmans, Green & Co.
39 BUXTON, E N (1884) *Epping Forest*. London; Edward Stanford.

C

40 CARLETON, John W (1842) *The Sporting Sketch Book*. London; How & Parsons.
41 CARTER-PLATTS, W (July 1910) *The Ribblesdale Buckhounds – A 'Made' Hunt*. Extract from Fry's.
42 CECIL (1854) *Records of the Chase*. London; Longman, Brown, Green & Longmans.
43 CHAFIN, William (1818) *Anecdotes of Cranbourn Chase*. London; J Nichols, Son & Bentley.
44 CHALMERS, Patrick R (1935) *Deerstalking*, London; Philip Allan.
45 CHALMERS, Patrick R (1936) *The History of Hunting*. The Lonsdale Library, Vol.XXIII. London; Seeley Service & Co. Ltd.
46 CHAPMAN, Donald & Norma (1975) *Fallow Deer*. Lavenham, Terence Dalton Ltd.
47 CHETWYND, Sir George (1824) *An Epitome of the Game Laws from the Twenty-Fourth Edition of Dr Burn's Justice of the Peace*.London; A Strahan.
48 CHRISTY, Theodore (N.D.) *Random Recollections of an Essex Sportsman*. Colchester; Benham & Co. Ltd.
49 CLARKSON, Ewan (1972) *The Running of the Deer*. London; Hutchinson.

50 COATEN, A W (1909) *British Hunting.* London; Sampson Low, Marston & Co. Ltd.

51 COCKAINE, Sir Thomas (1591) *A Short Treatise of Hunting.* Shakespeare Assoc. Facsimiles No.5 (1932) London; Humphrey Milford, Oxford University Press.

52 COLLYNS, Charles Park (1902) *Notes on the Chase of the Wild Red Deer.* London; Lawrence & Bullen, Ltd.

53 COOK, Donald (8 November 1969) *Most Manly of Beasts. The Shooting Times & Country Magazine.*

54 COOK, Donald (6 June 1970) *Dr Collyns & The Red Deer of Exmoor. The Shooting Times & Country Magazine.*

55 COOK, Donald (21 November 1970) *Harbourer to the Devon & Somerset. The Shooting Times & Country Magazine.*

56 COX, J Charles (1905) *The Royal Forests of England.* London; Methuen & Co.

57 COX, Nicholas (1721) *The Gentleman's Recreation.* (6th edn.) London; J Wilcox & others.

58 CREALOCK, Lieut.-Gen. H H (1892) *Deer-stalking in the Highlands of Scotland.* London; Longmans, Green & Co.

59 CROPPER, C J (1902) *The Oxenholme Hunt.* Kendal; Atkinson & Pollitt.

60 CUMING, E D (1909) *British Sport Past and Present.* London; Hodder & Stoughton.

61 CUPPLES, George (1894) *Scotch Deer-Hounds and Their Masters.* Edinburgh and London; William Blackwood & Sons.

D

62 DANIEL, Rev. W B (1801) *Rural Sports* (2 vols). London; Bunny & Gold.

63 DAY, J Wentworth (1935) *King George V as a Sportsman.* London; Cassell & Co. Ltd.

64 DAY, J Wentworth (1938) *The Dog in Sport.* London, George G Harrop & Co. Ltd.

65 DEACON, Edward E (1831) *A Practical Treatise on the Game Laws.* London; Saunders & Benning.

66 DE CHARTRES, The Duc (1870) *About the Surrey Staghounds.* London; Vinton & Co. Ltd.

67 'DRIFTER' (1941) *Packs They Used to Follow.* Series of articles in *Horse & Hound.*

68 DRYDEN, H (1844) *The Art of Hunting or Three Hunting MSS.* Northampton; William Mark.

E

69 EDWARD, Duke of York (*c.*1410) *The Master of Game.* Edited by WM. A & F Baillie-Grohman (1909) London; Chatto & Windus.

70 EDWARDS, Lionel and WALLACE H Frank (1927) *Hunting & Stalking the Deer.* London; Longmans, Green & Co. Ltd.

71 EVERED, Philip (1902) *Stag-hunting with the Devon and Somerset 1887–1901. An Account of the Chase of the Wild Red Deer on Exmoor.* London; Chatto & Windus.

72 EVERITT, Nicholas (1910) *Shots from a Lawyer's Gun.* (5th edn) London; Everett & Co.

F

73 FISHER, Arthur O (1930) *Exmoor and Other Days*. London; Constable & Co. Ltd.

74 FISHER, WR (1887) *The Forest of Essex*. London; Butterworths.

75 FORBES, Alexander R (1905) *Gaelic Names of Beasts (Mammalia), Birds, Fishes, Insects, Reptiles, etc.* Edinburgh; Oliver & Boyd.

76 FORTESCUE, Earl (N.D.) *Records of the North Devon Staghounds. (1812–1818)*. Printed for Private circulation.

77 FORTESCUE, Hon. John (1887) *Records of Staghunting on Exmoor*. London; Chapman & Hall, Ltd.

78 FORTESQUE, Hon. John (1925) *The Story of a Red Deer*, London; MacMillan & Co. Ltd.

79 FRASER, Sir Hugh (1923) *Amid the High Hills*. London: A & C Black, Ltd.

G

80 GÊLERT (1849) *A Guide to the Foxhounds & Staghounds of England to which are added the Otter-hounds and Harriers of Several Counties*. London; Whittaker & Co.

81 'A GENTLEMAN OF THE MIDDLE-TEMPLE' (1766) *A New Treatise on the Laws for Preservation of the Game*. London; H.M. Law Printers.

82 GOLDSMITH, Walter & Co. (1930–31) *The Hunting Diary*. London; The Proprietors, Walter Goldsmith & Co.

83 GOSLING, R (1726) *The Statutes at Large, Made for the Preservation of the Game*. London; H.M. Printers & The Assigns of Edward Sayer, Esq.

84 GOSS, Fred (1931) *Memories of a Stag Harbourer*. London; HF & G Witherby.

85 GRAVES, Lord (N.D.) A Letter in *Records of the North Devon Staghounds, 1812–1818*. Printed for private circulation; *see* Fortescue, Earl.

86 GRAVES, Lord (1814) *A Letter addressed to Lord Ebrington, relating to the Stag Hunting Establishment*. Exeter, Trewman & Son.

87 GREAVES, Ralph (*c.*1950) *A Short History of the Ward Union Staghounds*. Dublin; Reid-Hamilton (Ireland).

88 GREAVES, Ralph (*c.*1951 and *c.*1956) *The Norwich Staghounds*. London; Reid-Hamilton Publishers Ltd.

89 GREAVES, Ralph (*c.*1958) *Hunting in Norfolk and Suffolk*. London; Field Sports Publication.

90 GRESWELL, Rev. WHP (1905) *The Forests & Deer Parks of the County of Somerset*. Taunton, Barnicott & Pearce, Athenaeum Press.

H

91 HALL, Herbert Byng (1848) *Highland Sports and Quarters*. London; George Routledge & Co.

92 HALL, Herbert Byng (1849) *Exmoor – or the Footsteps of St Hubert in the West*. London; Thomas Cautley Newby.

93 HAMILTON, Archibald (1907) *The Red Deer of Exmoor*. London; Horace Cox.

94 HARE, CE (1949) *The Language of Field Sports*. Revised edition. London; Country Life Ltd.

95 HAREWOOD, Harry (1835) *A Dictionary of Sports*. London; Thomas Tegg & Son.

96 HART-DAVIS, Duff (1978) *Monarchs of the Glen.* London; Jonathan Cape.
97 HARTING, J E (1883) *Essays on Sports and Natural History.* London; Horace Cox, 'The Field'.
98 HARVEY, Lt.-Col. J R (1910) *Deer Hunting in Norfolk.* Norwich; The 'Norwich Mercury' Co. Ltd.
99 HELPS, Arthur (1861) (edited by) *Leaves from the Journal of our Life in the Highlands from 1848 to 1861.* London; Smith, Elder & Co. (*see* 192).
100 HENDY, E W (1946) *Wild Exmoor through the Year.* London; Eyre & Spottiswoode.
101 HER MAJESTY'S STATIONERY OFFICE PUBLICATIONS (1832) *Game (Scotland) Act* 2 & 3, Wm.4.c.68. London; H.M. Stationery Office.
102 HER MAJESTY'S STATIONERY OFFICE PUBLICATIONS (1913) *Ground Game (Inclusion of Deer) (Scotland) Bill.* London; H.M. Stationery Office.
103 HER MAJESTY'S STATIONERY OFFICE PUBLICATIONS (1951) *Report of the Committee on Cruelty to Wild Animals.* (Cmd.8266) London; H.M. Stationery Office.
104 HER MAJESTY'S STATIONERY OFFICE PUBLICATIONS (1959) *Deer (Scotland) Act* 1959. C.40. London. H.M. Stationery Office.
105 HER MAJESTY'S STATIONERY OFFICE PUBLICATIONS (1963) *Deer Act* 1963. C.36. London; H.M. Stationery Office.
106 HER MAJESTY'S STATIONERY OFFICE PUBLICATIONS (1966) *Animals – Deer – The Deer (Close Seasons) Scotland Order* 1966. No.56. London; H.M. Stationery Office.
107 HER MAJESTY'S STATIONERY OFFICE PUBLICATIONS (1967) *Deer (Amendment) (Scotland) Act* 1967. C.37. London; H.M. Stationery Office.
108 HER MAJESTY'S STATIONERY OFFICE PUBLICATIONS (1968) *Sale of Venison (Scotland) Act* 1968. C.38. London; H.M. Stationery Office.
109 HEWETT, H P (1963) *The Fairest Hunting.* London; J A Allen & Co.
110 HEWETT, H P (*c.*1970) *Staghunting.* Pamphlet for Young Sportsmen. No.7. London; British Field Sports Society, publication No.99.
111 HIEOVER, Harry (1853) *Sporting Facts and Sporting Fancies.* London; Thomas Cautley Newby.
112 HOOD, Thomas (1830) *The Epping Hunt.* London; Charles Tilt.
113 HORE, J P (1895) *The History of the Royal Buckhounds.* Newmarket; J P Hore.

I

114 IRVINE, Alexander Forbes (1856) *Treatise on the Game Laws of Scotland containing the Principal Statutes and Forms.* (2nd edn) Edinburgh; T & T Clark.

J

115 JAMES, David & WILSON STEPHENS, (edited by) (1960) *In Praise of Hunting.* London; Hollis & Carter.
116 JEFFRIES, Richard (1894) *Red Deer.* (3rd edn) London; Longmans, Green & Co.
117 JOHNSON, T B (1830) *The Hunting Directory.* London; Sherwood, Gilbert & Piper.
118 JOHNSON, T B (1848) *The Sportsman's Cyclopaedia.* London; Henry G Bohn.

L

119 LAMPSON, S M (12 September 1957) *Hound of the Scottish Kings. Country Life.*

120 LASCELLES, Hon. Gerald (1915) *Thirty-five Years in the New Forest.* London; Edward Arnold.

121 LEWIS, James (10 October 1968) *The Age-old Art of the Harbourer on Exmoor. The Field.*

122 LEWIS, James (7 November 1968) *The New Forest Buckhounds out until Dusk. The Field.*

123 LEWIS, James (13 February 1969) *Hind Hunting: The Devon and Somerset. The Field.*

124 LEWIS, James (28 February 1970) *Hind Hunting with the Devon and Somerset. Shooting Times and Country Magazine.*

125 'LEX' (1933) *Sports and the Courts.* London; Herbert Jenkins Ltd.

126 LLOYD, Jack Ilvester (1973) *Hounds of Britain.* London; Adam & Charles Black.

127 LOCKE, John (1849) *The Game Laws.* (3rd edn) London; Shaw & Sons.

128 LOOKER, Samuel J (1922) *The Chase.* London; Daniel O'Connor.

M

129 MACDERMOT, E T (1936) *The Devon and Somerset Staghounds (1907–1936).* London; Collins.

130 MACKENZIE, Osgood Hanbury (1922 *A Hundred years in the Highlands.* London; Edward Arnold.

131 MACNALLY, L (6 February 1964) *Deer Coursing in the Highlands. The Shooting Times and Country Magazine.*

132 MANWOOD, John (1665) *A Treatise of the Laws of the Forest.* (3rd edn) London; Company of Stationers.

133 MARSHALL, H J (1948) *Exmoor, Sporting and Otherwise.* London; Eyre & Spottiswoode.

134 MARTIN, E W (1959) *The Case Against Hunting.* London; Dennis Dobson.

135 MCCONNOCHIE, Alexander I (1923) *The Deer and Deer Forest of Scotland. Historical, Descriptive, Sporting.* London; H F & G Witherby.

136 MERSEY-THOMPSON, Col. R F (1907) *A Hunting Catechism.* London; Edward Arnold.

137 MILES, Henry D (N.D.) *British Field Sports.* London; William Mackenzie.

138 MILLAIS, J G (1897) *British Deer and Their Horns.* London; Henry Sotheran & Co.

139 MILLER, Thomas (N.D.) *Sports and Pastimes of Merry England.* London; Darton & Co.

140 MOORE, Daphne (5–11 June 1975) *Fate of the Royal Buckhounds. The Shooting Times and Country Magazine.*

141 MOORE, Patrick (1965) (edited by) *Against Hunting.* London; Victor Gollancz, Ltd.

142 MORGAN, W A (edited by) (1899) *The 'House' on Sport.* (Vol. 2) London; Gale & Polden, Ltd.

143 MORRIS, M O'Connor (1878) *Hibernia Venatica.* London; Chapman & Hall.

144 MORRIS, M O'Connor (1900) *Hibernia Hippica.* London; Harrison & Sons.

N

145 NELSON, William (1751) *The Laws Concerning Game.* (4th edn) London; Henry Lintot.

146 NESS, John William (1818) *A Treatise on the Game Laws of Scotland; with an Appendix, containing the Principal Statutes and Leading Cases, on the Subject.* Edinburgh; Michael Anderson and John Thomson & Co.

147 NEVILL, Ralph (1910) *Sporting Days and Sporting Ways.* London; Duckworth & Co.

148 NEVILLE, Hugh (1879) *The Game Laws of England for Gamekeepers.* London; Davis & Sons.

149 NEVILLE, Hugh (1884) *The Game Laws of England.* London; John Van Voorst.

150 NIMROD, Tom Oakleigh and others (1844). *The Illustrated Book of Rural Sports.* (2 vols) London; Henry G Bohn.

151 NOYES, Frank (5 March 1970) *Deerhunting thanks to the Farmers. The Field.*

O

152 OSBALDISTON, William (1792) *The British Sportsman.* London; J Stead.

P

153 PAGE, F J Taylor (1971) (edited by) *Field Guide to British Deer.* (2nd edn) Oxford & Edinburgh; Blackwell Scientific Publications.

154 PARKER, Eric (1925) (compiled by) *Game Pie.* London; Philip Allan & Co.

155 PERCEVAL, P J S (1909) *London's Forest, Its History, Tradition and Romance.* London; J M Dent & Co.

156 PORTER, Alexander (1907) *The Gamekeeper Manual* (3rd edn). Edinburgh; David Douglas.

157 PORTLAND, Duke of (1933) *Fifty Years and More of Sport in Scotland.* London; Faber & Faber, Ltd.

158 PRIOR, Richard (1965) *Living with Deer.* London; Andre Deutsch, Ltd.

159 PYE, Henry James (1807) *The Sportsman's Dictionary.* (5th edn). London; John Stockdale.

R

160 RIBBLESDALE, Lord (1897) *The Queen's Hounds and Staghunting Recollections.* London; Longmans, Green & Co.

161 RITCHIE, James (1920) *The Influence of Man on Animal life in Scotland.* Cambridge; University Press.

162 ROSS, John (edited by) (1925) *The Book of the Red Deer.* London; Simpkin, Marshall, Hamilton, Kent & Co. Ltd.

163 ROW, Charles (1928) *A Practical Guide to the Game Laws.* (2nd edn) London; Longmans, Green & Co. Ltd.

164 RUSSELL, Dan (8 September 1973) *The Farley Stag. The Shooting Times and Country Magazine.*

165 RUSSELL, Joanna (11 July 1968) *The Dogs that Shakespeare Knew. The Field.*

S

166 'SABRETACHE' (1948) *Monarchy and the Chase.* London; Eyre & Spottiswoode.

167 ST JOHN, Charles (1878) *Sketches of the Wild Sports and Natural History of the Highlands*. London; John Murray.
168 SANDYS-WINSCH, Godfrey (1973) *Gun Law in England and Wales*. (2nd edn). London; Shaw & Sons, Ltd.
169 SCARTH-DIXON, William (1912) *Hunting in the Olden Days*. London; Constable & Co. Ltd.
170 SCARTH-DIXON, William (1923) *The Lunesdale and Oxenholme Staghounds, Sedburgh and Lunesdale Foxhounds, and the Vale of Lune Harriers*. London; The Hunts Association.
171 SCARTH-DIXON, William (N.D.) *Devon and Somerset Staghounds*. London; The Hunts Association.
172 SCROPE, William (1839) *The Art of Deer Stalking*. London; John Murray.
173 SHACKLE, Major E W (1936) *Hunting the Carted Deer*. Contribution to *Deer, Hare & Otter Hunting*. (Lonsdale Library). Vol.XXII. London; Seeley Service & Co. Ltd.
174 SHIRLEY, E (1867) *Some Account of English Deer Parks*. London; John Murray.
175 SMITH, W M'Combie (1904) *The Romance of Poaching in the Highlands of Scotland*. Stirling; Eneas Mackay.
176 'SNAFFLE' (1904) *The Roedeer*. London; E M Harwar.
177 SNELL, F J (1903) *A Book of Exmoor*. London; Methuen & Co.
178 SOBIESKI, John & STUART, Charles Edward (1848) *Lays of the Deer Forest*. (2 vols) London; William Blackwood & Sons and Charles Dolman.
179 SOMERVILLE, Wm (1896) *The Chase*. London; George Redway.
180 STONEHENGE (1875) *British Rural Sports*. (12th edn). London; Frederick Warne & Co.
181 STRINGER, Arthur (1780) *The Experienced Huntsman*. Dublin; L Flin.
182 STRUTT, Joseph (1801) *The Sports and Pastimes of the People of England*. (New edition, enlarged and corrected by J C Cox, 1903). London; Methuen & Co.
183 SUFFOLK AND BERKSHIRE, Earl of, Hedley Peek and F G Aflalo (1897) (edited by), *The Encyclopedia of Sport*. (2 vols) London; Lawrence & Bullen, Ltd.

T

184 TAPLIN, William (1803) *The Sporting Dictionary and Rural Repository of General Information upon every subject appertaining to The Sports of the Field*. (2 vols) London; Vernor & Hood, Longman & Rees, J Scatcherd, J Walker & J Harris.
185 TENNET, Horace Kent (1924) *Vert and Venison*. Privately printed.
186 THOMAS, Joseph B (1934) *Hounds and Hunting Through the Ages*. London; Williams & Norgate, Ltd.
187 THURSBY, Sir George (1936) *Deer Hunting in the New Forest*. Contribution to the Lonsdale Library, vol. XXII, *Deer, Hare and Otter Hunting*. London; Seeley Service & Co Ltd.
188 TURBERVILLE, George (1576) *Noble Arte of Venerie or Hunting*. Reprint (1908) from the Bodleian copy. London; Clarendon Press.
189 TURNER, G J (1901) *Select Pleas of the Forest*. London; Bernard Quaritch for Selden Society.

U

190 UNDERHILL, George F (1897) *Hunting and Practical Hints for Hunting Men*. London; Bliss, Sands & Co.

191 UNDERHILL, George F (1903) *The Master of Hounds*. London; Grant Richards.

V

192 VICTORIA, QUEEN (1868) edited by Arthur Phelps *Leaves from the Journal of Our Life in the Highlands* (from 1848 to 1861). London; Smith Elder & Co.

193 VOWLES, Alfred (1920) *Stag-hunting on Exmoor*. Taunton; Barnicott & Pearce, The Wessex Press.

194 VOWLES, Alfred (1936) *Wild Deer of Exmoor*. Minehead & Williton: Cox, Sons & Co. Ltd.

W

195 WALLACE, H F (1913) *British Deer Heads*. London; Country Life Ltd.

196 WALLACE, H F & EDWARDS, L (1927) *Hunting and Stalking the Deer*. London; Longmans, Green & Co. Ltd.

197 WARRY, G Taylor (1896) *The Game Laws of England, with an appendix of the Statutes Relating to Game*. London; Stevens & Sons.

198 WATSON, Alfred E T (1903) *English Sport*. London; Macmillan & Co. Ltd.

199 WATSON, Alfred E T (1911) *King Edward VII as a Sportsman*. London; Longmans, Green & Co.

200 WELFORD, Richard Griffiths (1846) *The Influence of the Game Laws*. London; R Groombridge & Sons and J Gadsby.

201 WESTON, W J (1953) *Law and the Countryman*. London; Rupert Hart-Davis.

202 WESTON, W J (1 September 1955) *Damage by Deer and Dog*. *Country Life*.

203 WHITAKER, J (1892) *A Descriptive List of the Deer-Parks & Paddocks of England*. London; Ballantyne, Hanson & Co.

204 WHITEHEAD, G Kenneth (1950) *Deer and Their Management in the Deer Parks of Great Britain and Ireland*. London; Country Life, Ltd.

205 WHITEHEAD, G Kenneth (7 April 1950) *A Close Season for Deer*. *Country Life*.

206 WHITEHEAD, G Kenneth (8 September 1951) *A Law to Protect Deer*, *The Field*.

207 WHITEHEAD, G Kenneth (14 March 1952) *Deer Need a Close Season*. *Country Life*.

208 WHITEHEAD, G Kenneth (9 December 1954) *Why no Close Season for Deer? Country Life*.

209 WHITEHEAD, G Kenneth (1960) *The Deerstalking Grounds of Great Britain and Ireland*. London; Hollis & Carter.

210 WHITEHEAD, G Kenneth (24 August 1961) *The Phantom Stag*. *Country Life*.

211 WHITEHEAD, G Kenneth (15 September 1961) *Deer and the Law*. *The Shooting Times and Country Magazine*.

212 WHITEHEAD, G Kenneth (1 March 1963) *The Deer (England & Wales) Bill*. *The Shooting Times and Country Magazine*.

213 WHITEHEAD, G Kenneth (26 March 1964) *Shortcomings of the Deer Acts*. *Country Life*.

214 WHITEHEAD, G Kenneth (1964) *The Deer of Great Britain and Ireland.* London; Routledge & Kegan Paul.

215 WHITEHEAD, G Kenneth (1964) *Deer Stalking in Scotland.* London; Percival Marshall & Co.

216 WHITEHEAD, G Kenneth (17 March 1966) *'Odd Man Out' – The Implication of the new Deer (Close Seasons) (Scotland) Order 1966.* The *Shooting Times & Country Magazine.*

217 WHITEHEAD, G Kenneth (19 May 1966) *When Red Deer seek Low Ground. The Shooting Times and Country Magazine.*

218 WHITEHEAD, G Kenneth (31 January 1970) *Venison Control. The Shooting Times and Country Magazine.*

219 WHITEHEAD, G Kenneth (14 August 1971) *Time for a Close Season. The Shooting Times and Country Magazine.*

220 WHITEHEAD, G Kenneth (30 May 1974) *The Law for a Poacher. The Field.*

221 WHITEHEAD, G Kenneth (16 May 1974) *Tagging of Venison. The Field.*

222 WHYTE-MELVILLE, G J (1875) *Katerfelto – A Story of Exmoor.* London; Chapman & Hall.

223 WHYTE-MELVILLE, G J (1878) *Riding Recollections.* London; Chapman & Hall.

224 WIGGIN, Col W W (1936) *Stag Hunting on Exmoor.* Contribution to the Lonsdale Library, Vol.XXII, *Deer, Hare & Otter Hunting.* London; Seeley, Service & Co. Ltd.

225 WILLIAMSON, Henry (1931) *The Wild Red Deer of Exmoor.* London; Faber & Faber, Ltd.

226 WILLIAMSON, Henry (1933) *The Old Stag and Other Hunting Stories.* London and New York; G P Putnam's Sons.

227 WINANS, Walter (1908) *The Sporting Rifle.* London & New York; G P Putnam's Sons.

228 'WOODMAN' (1962) *Notes on the Game Laws of England and Wales.* London; Herbert Jenkins.

229 'WOODMAN' (14 September 1962) *The Law & Deer. The Shooting Times & Country Magazine.*

230 'WOODMAN' (11 September 1971) *Deer and the Law. The Shooting Times and Country Magazine.*

231 WOOLRYCH, Humphrey W (1858) *The Game Laws, including the Law as to Deer and other Wild Animals.* London; V & R Stevens and G S Norton; H Sweet and W Maxwell.

232 WYMER, Norman (1949) *Sport in England.* London; George G Harrap & Co. Ltd.

General Index

Numbers in *italics* indicate description of pack

Index of Places, Forests, Parks and Districts etc.

Index of People